THINKING THE UNTHINKABLE

Meanings of the Holocaust

Edited by
Roger S. Gottlieb

PAULIST PRESS
New York/Mahwah

Library of Congress Cataloging-in-Publication Data

Thinking the unthinkable: meanings of the Holocaust/edited by Roger
  S. Gottlieb.
      p.   cm.
    Includes bibliographical references.
    ISBN 0-8091-3172-2
    1. Holocaust, Jewish (1939–1945)   2. Holocaust, Jewish
  (1939–1945)—Causes.   3. Holocaust (Jewish theology)   4. Holocaust,
  Jewish (1939–1945)—Influence.   I. Gottlieb, Roger S.
  D804.3.T49   1990
  940.53′18—dc20   90-33601
                                                                       CIP

Published by Paulist Press
997 Macarthur Boulevard
Mahwah, New Jersey 07430

Printed and bound in the
United States of America

CONTENTS

ACKNOWLEDGEMENTS

Excerpt from "Why? Towards a Theory of the Holocaust," from THE DIALECTICS OF DISASTER: A PREFACE TO HOPE by Ronald Aronson. Reprinted by permission of Verso.

Excerpt from "Religion and the Origins of the Death Camps: A Psychoanalytic Interpretation," reprinted with permission of Macmillan Publishing Company from AFTER AUSCHWITZ by Richard Rubenstein. Copyright © 1966 by Richard Rubenstein.

Excerpt from "Adolf Hitler's Childhood: From Hidden to Manifest Horror," from FOR YOUR OWN GOOD by Alice Miller. Translation copyright © 1983 by Alice Miller. Reprinted by permission of Farrar, Straus and Giroux, Inc.

"Us and Them," from THE SURVIVOR: AN ANATOMY OF LIFE IN THE DEATH CAMPS by Terence Des Pres. Copyright © 1976 by Oxford University Press, Inc. Reprinted by permission.

"The Right Way to Act: Indicting the Victims," from ECHOES FROM THE HOLOCAUST by Abigail Rosenthal. Copyright © 1988 by Temple University. Reprinted by permission of Temple University Press.

"The Anti-Semite," from ANTI-SEMITE AND JEW by Jean-Paul Sartre. Copyright © 1948 and renewed 1976 by Schocken Books, published by Pantheon Books, a Division of Random House, Inc.

"Doubling: The Faustian Bargain," from THE NAZI DOCTORS: MEDICAL KILLING AND THE PSYCHOLOGY OF GENOCIDE by Robert Jay Lifton. Copyright © 1986 by Robert Jay Lifton. Reprinted by permission of Basic Books, Inc., Publishers.

"The Death of My Father" and "Yom Kippur," from LEGENDS OF OUR TIME by Elie Wiesel. Copyright © 1968 by Elie Wiesel. Reprinted by permission of Henry Holt and Company, Inc.

"Authenticity of Being," from WITH GOD IN HELL: JUDAISM IN THE GHETTOS AND DEATHCAMPS by Eliezer Berkovits. Reprinted by permis-

"The Memory of the Offense," from THE DROWNED AND THE SAVED by Primo Levi. Copyright © 1986 by Giulios Einaudi editore s.p.a. Torino translation copyright © 1988 by Simon and Schuster, Inc. Reprinted by permission of Summit Books.

"Remembrance and Resistance," reprinted by permission of SOCIAL THEORY AND PRACTICE (Volume 14, Number 1, Spring 1988).

TO JACOB AND AIDLA GREENSPAN, WHO SURVIVED THE HOLOCAUST,
AND TO THEIR DAUGHTER, MIRIAM GREENSPAN
*Their enduring example of courage and love inspired me
to seek the meanings of the Holocaust in my own life.*

AND TO ALL THE SURVIVORS
In gratitude for the lessons you continue to teach us all.

APPRECIATIONS

My wife, Miriam Greenspan, has been instrumental in helping me think and feel about the Holocaust. Without her influence, this book would never have been created. Her detailed and valuable criticisms—and at times her direct and heartfelt way of putting things—have shaped all of my contributions here.

Richard Schmitt and Jerry Samet gave me helpful comments on the Introduction.

As in the past, the secretarial staff of the Department of Humanities, Worcester Polytechnic Institute—Margaret Brodmerkle, Penny Rock, and Lisa Johnson—were extremely helpful in many ways.

"IN EVERY GENERATION, WE ARE OBLIGED

TO REGARD OURSELVES AS THOUGH

WE HAD ACTUALLY GONE OUT FROM EGYPT."
from the Passover *Haggadah*

Roger S. Gottlieb

INTRODUCTION

I. THINKING THE UNTHINKABLE

The purpose of this book is to serve our need to make meanings out of the Holocaust: to determine its impact on our personal lives, our society, and our future as human beings. The guiding thread of these essays is a shared belief that the Holocaust possesses terribly important meanings for us, meanings which may shape or alter our beliefs about human nature, morality, politics, and spiritual life.

Several serious and enduring questions are explored here: What were the central causes of the Holocaust and how do our explanations of it affect our understanding of social life (Part I)? What do we know about the murderers and the martyrs that can help us understand the magnitude of evil, the depth of suffering, and the stunning capacity to survive (Part II)? How does the Holocaust challenge conventional religious teaching and change our spiritual life (Part III)? How widespread is German guilt for the atrocities? Did the Jews go "like lambs to the slaughter"—or was Jewish resistance much greater than most people think (Part IV)? How can we grapple with our emotional responses to the event, authentically remember it, and do justice to survivors (Part V)?

When discussions of the meanings of the Holocaust occur, they often reflect one or another partial point of view. This book offers a wide variety of political, ethical, and spiritual perspectives, by authors of very different beliefs and backgrounds. Their contributions demonstrate that facing the Holocaust requires both understanding everything in a new way *and* using our most cherished intellectual and moral resources from the past. For example, Elie Wiesel challenges the possibility of traditional Jewish observance in concentration camps, while Eliezer Berkovits claims that Jews facing the gas chambers maintained their identity most fully when they lived their faith to the end, staying

1

"With God in Hell." Ronald Aronson, seeking causes of the event, uses a neo-Marxist framework to link Germany's economy, politics, and social psychology. Yet Richard Schmitt asserts that Marxism—purporting to be a total theory of history—cannot comprehend this event. Similar problems arise when we seek to assess guilt and responsibility for the Holocaust, when we try to define what sorts of acts constituted Jewish resistance, and when we focus on the consciousness of the victims and the executioners. In all these cases we find a tension between the uniqueness of the Holocaust and our need to understand it in familiar ways.

As difficult as it is, finding the meanings of the Holocaust is an essential task. If we do not seek its meanings we cannot begin to understand how it occurred or how to integrate it into our moral, political, and spiritual visions. At the same time, no political theory, spiritual perspective, or ethical discussion can capture the full reality of this event. There will always be a painful gap between theoretical *explanation* and human *understanding*. We cannot master the Holocaust with our thinking, we can only deepen ourselves in our relation to it. Even if all our intellectual questions were answered, we would still cry: "But how can this be?" Nevertheless, if we are to find meanings as well as sorrow and despair, to alter our lives as well as mourn the victims, we must try to *think* this unthinkable event.

II. SOME TASKS FOR THOUGHT AND MEMORY

But *how* shall we think? How can we avoid trivializing it, seeking to master it by stretching some familiar theory to fit its unique contours or using our understanding for partisan purposes? How can we be true to the past while living ethically in the present?

These are not easy tasks. We may be transfixed by the brutal facts and by our emotional and political responses to them. Looking directly at the record can provoke such overwhelming responses that thinking —theorizing, arguing, comparing, questioning, challenging and changing what we believe—may seem utterly beside the point. The emotions it arouses in us are so powerful that we may become quite literally speechless and thoughtless.

We also may not want to trivialize the Holocaust with pat explanations and familiar theories. We may be afraid that rational discussion will diminish our appropriate feelings of grief and rage. If we are intellectuals by training or profession, we may be hesitant to feed the Holocaust into the endless academic mill of books, papers, and journals.

These temptations to thoughtlessness can be appreciated and transcended. If the Holocaust is not reflected upon, we will become a slave to its images and our immediate responses to them. The Holocaust will not affect our theories and our actions, but remain encapsulated like a forsaken shrine that we remember and do not use—or use without awareness.

Yet not all acts of bringing the past to consciousness are really acts of *authentic* thought—that is, ways which do justice both to the specific reality of the Holocaust and to our tasks as people who face moral responsibilities in the present.

Consider first a familiar form of thinking about and remembering. We make a list of things to do over the weekend: go to the store, clean the attic, wash the floor, phone grandma. Writing down each potential act on paper both locates and limits it. Once written, we know the tasks as things which can be handled—and then easily forgotten. In fact, we only make the list in order to forget what we have just remembered. In this remembering-in-order-to-forget, this thinking-in-order-not-to-think, we show our mastery over and our essential unconcern with that which we remember.

When we remember the Holocaust in this way we act as if the Holocaust can have no impact on our "subjectivity." By subjectivity I mean that dimension of our identity which confronts problems that are both crucially important and necessarily without definitive solution.[1] We cannot be done with these problems because part of their solution is our continuing response to them. To be truly subjective, we will struggle with them all of our lives. For instance, we should never be satisfied with pat, comfortable, or habitual answers to questions about what it means to love, to face death, or to pray. These issues call forth our subjectivity. If we treat them as easily settled, subject to objective solutions or conventional rules, we will be trivializing them and ourselves.

The Holocaust poses many subjective problems for us. For instance, how will it affect our understanding of morality when we learn that many Jews had to choose between saving the life of a sister or a wife, a father or a son, one child or another? How can we understand the long-standing debate about whether Jews were oriented to resistance or passivity when we find that resisters had to face the Nazi policy of collective reprisal, a policy which meant that many Jews would be starved, tortured or murdered as punishment for one person's resistance? Under what conditions (as Simon Wiesenthal asked in "The Sunflower") should we forgive one of the killers? These moral dilemmas demand a continual searching rather than any quick or simple answer. Such an understanding requires that we "think ourselves" *out* of our everyday existence and *into* the Holocaust. Conventional forms of moral reasoning and ethical principles may well be inadequate to this task, for they did not originate in a genocidal universe. If we try to make the Holocaust fit our familiar categories, if we presume that we ourselves need not change in order to remember it authentically, we will inevitably distort it.

Although we may have to suspend our conventional forms of understanding, it will not do to encapsulate the Holocaust in a sterile shroud of mystery, regarding it as a permanently inexplicable and horrible enigma. This approach to the Holocaust is, paradoxically, another form of trivialization. Though there can never be a final truth about the Holocaust which will set our minds "at rest," there must be "truths for us" which will guide us in inner reflection and outer action. The Holocaust must not remain fundamentally alien, like a shrine or an idol. If this occurs, then we cannot find meaning in it. And that which has no meaning cannot connect to our personal identities and social relations. This would be a terrible loss.

Finally, our memory of the Holocaust should avoid obsession. Here the event is remembered but everything else, including the self, is forgotten. We immerse ourselves in images of death. The gas chambers and barbed wire, burnt buildings and burning bodies seem at times to be more real than our own lives. Our daily existence becomes an echo of a Holocaust which never ends.

Obsession may be a necessary stage in coming-to-grips with the Holocaust, both for those who are personally close to the event and those who approach from social and historical distance. It is clearly preferable to various forms of denial or avoidance, and to remembering only in order to forget.

Yet obsession is inauthentic nevertheless, because it attempts to blot out the self who is the subject, the agent, of the act of remembering. We cannot have a relation to the Holocaust if we dissolve ourselves in it, if our own reality—which is necessarily a reality of living after the Holocaust—is negated by acts of imagination in which we seek to become the past. If only the Holocaust is real—which is what remembrance-as-obsession suggests—then neither our present nor our future is important. Our need to act as moral agents is frozen by the spectre of the past and the relevance of the Holocaust is diminished.

For a morally authentic memory, the full reality of the Holocaust is remembered as a problematic and continuing event in our own lives.

Our duties to survivors, the best way to teach its lessons to our children, the ways in which we may prevent its recurrence or reappearance in new form—these are the tasks which our remembrance of the Holocaust can best serve.

All who would find meanings in the Holocaust face these tasks of authentic thought. However, the Holocaust is not only a universal event, but one with particular victims and executioners. While not all the victims were Jews, all the Jews were victims. And while not all Christians were murderers (many were heroes and martyrs) all the murderers were Christian—in that broad sense of belonging to the dominant religious culture of Europe. This fact imposes different tasks of thought and memory—and different barriers to that authenticity—on Jews and Christians.

Jews and Authentic Memory

In recent years Jews have put a great deal of energy into remembering the Holocaust. We have produced scholarly works, oral histories, and fictional settings. From the Israeli government to the Jewish political lobby in this country, from Holocaust museums in Israel to the annual remembrance observances which fill synagogues throughout the world, Jews remember.

These acts of memory did not come easily. For the first dozen or so years following the Holocaust very few wanted to think about it. Many of the survivors were crippled by shame and fear and did not want to speak. Many other Jews (and Christians) did not want to listen. Meanwhile, the fledgling state of Israel defined itself in absolute opposition to victimhood.

These particular fears and obstacles have been overcome. We have made the world and ourselves aware of what happened. And the injunction "never forget" has been taken into the very heart of modern Jewish culture.

But in these acts of continuing memory there lurk some dangerous temptations, seductive patterns of thought and feeling which threaten to distort our relation to both past and present.

What are these temptations?

First is the temptation of the *arrogance of pain*. When we succumb to this temptation we act as if the suffering we have endured as a people is in and of itself a mark of virtue. Using our past suffering to define our present values, we inevitably focus deeply on victimization. No people, we tell ourselves and others, has had such a history of pain. No group has ever been so persecuted. The Holocaust is a unique, genocidal event, incomparable to other massacres of other people. Since our troubles cannot be calculated in conventional human terms they set us apart, now and forever. They make us special, unique, chosen. They make us better and more deserving.

I will not address here either the uniqueness of the Holocaust or the history of Jewish persecution. There is no question that we have suffered greatly at the hands of non-Jews, and that in the staggering scope of its terror and dehumanization, and the role played by administrative and technological resources, the Holocaust is unique in many ways.

But even if the Holocaust *is* unique, we can still wonder to conclude from that fact. Are the virtues Jews manifest in the present more virtuous because we have suffered more? Does the non-Jewish world owe Jews something special? Can the past suffering guarantee Jewish virtue now?

The arrogance of pain is a temptation because it seeks to substitute a past reality for the demands of subjectivity, communication, and morality in the present. If Jewish history makes us special in some way it is in the same way that any group's history makes it special: it confers on the group a set of problems it has to face. If Jews cling to past suffering as a proof of our present morality, we abdicate our responsibility to forge our moral, religious, cultural, and political identity on its own terms. By defining myself solely in terms of my past tragedy, I inadvertently grant the Nazis a victory that they cannot win without my complicity.

Does the non-Jewish world have an obligation to Jews because of the Holocaust? Yes and no. It should take responsibility for what it did and what it failed to do, and to seek the roots of its behavior in its culture, religion, and politics. And it owes Jews a hearing: to listen to the Jewish perspective on the Holocaust in particular and anti-semitism in general. The heirs of the perpetrators have an investment in not seeing things as clearly as the heirs of the victims. In all cases of oppression, people need to listen longest and hardest—and with the greatest openness of heart and mind—to the victims.

But the non-Jewish world owes this debt to Jews *not* because Jewish history makes Jews special, but because, as moral human beings, non-Jews have to destroy their capacity for genocide or be destroyed by it. It is a task which all non-Jews face if they are to maintain a moral identity, not a special gift which I am owed because my people suffered in the past. As a Jew I do not need anything special *because* of the Holocaust, merely what I deserve as a human being with a particular history. Further, even if the Holocaust had never happened, anti-semitism is *still* an intolerable evil. Even if the death camps had never been, Israeli Jews deserve a safe and secure homeland.

The arrogance of pain may be partly motivated by the unconscious hope that convincing Gentiles of the uniqueness of the Holocaust will end violent anti-semitism. As understandable as this hope is, it is misplaced. Guilt is not a very good motivator, at least not for very long. It turns too quickly and too frequently to resentment. Moreover, majorities do not treat minorities humanely because they see those minorities as different, special, or chosen. Rather, it is only when a sense of commonality, of shared humanity *despite* differences, emerges that oppressed groups can begin to hope for a margin of safety.

The arrogance of pain also tends to ignore the fact that the Holocaust—both as past event and as prophecy of future possibilities—did not happen only to Jews. Five million others—homosexuals, mental patients, leftists, gypsies, prisoners of war—were victims as well. There has been enough murder—both then and since—for us to renounce the social or emotional isolation of the special victim. And with the threat of nuclear war and ecological destruction it is daily possible that, as Elie Wiesel put it, "the whole world will become Jewish."

Along with the arrogance of pain, it is important for Jews to resist the *temptations of despair and guilt*. These especially haunt the hearts of those who have themselves been intimately connected with the Holocaust: survivors, children of survivors, and those of us who feel that every Jew, regardless of personal history, is, in a sense, a survivor and a child of survivors.

The Holocaust can color Jewish spirits with a hopeless grayness of death and despair. As we educate ourselves and our children about the Holocaust, we will inevitably experience powerful feelings of sadness, depression, and rage. We also may compare our lives to the victims, and wonder how we would have responded in their place.

While these feelings are genuine, we must struggle not to be dominated by them. It does not really make sense to evaluate our lives in terms of a standard of genocide. The dead are ill served if we live in depression, misery, or fear, succumbing to despair and guilt which are not fully ours. If there is one truth about those who perished or survived, it is that they were living their own lives, undefined by examples from history or the imitation of the past. As they woke out of the illusion that this was simply another pogrom or expulsion, they came to a reality which could be understood only on its own terms—or not at all. An authentic memory of them, therefore, requires that we live in *our* present, not seek to recreate or escape the heroism or suffering of others.

As a middle-class Jew in the United States I have my own resources and face my own problems, not those of the Warsaw Ghetto uprising. The Israeli people face the Arab nations and the Palestine Liberation Organization, not Hitler and the Nazis. Today's prejudice is the anti-semitism of *this* world, not of 1941. I cannot authentically remember my past if I impose it on my present.

Similarly, I offer little real honor to the six million if I use their suffering as an excuse for not delighting in Jewish identity—an identity whose grace, richness, and joy should not be obscured by the Holocaust. While our adult fears and guilts may reflect a serious attempt to com-memorate that which needs to be remembered, what can we be commu-nicating to our children if we make Jewish identity synonymous with victimhood?

Christians and Authentic Memory

After the Holocaust, Jews are necessarily tempted by the arrogance of pain, an arrogance which in part implies that both then and now the Holocaust is something which only happened—and only could happen —to Jews. Christians need to guard against the converse temptation: an *arrogance of universality* which suggests that the Holocaust is in essence a *human* problem, containing profound enigmas about our human capac-ity for evil, the presence or absence of God in modern times, the nature of guilt and forgiveness, of meaning and meaninglessness. Christians, that is, must guard against the temptation to forget the one fact about the Holocaust which Christians must never forget: that it was first and foremost an event in which Christians attempted to destroy the Jewish people.[2] While there are symbolic meanings which may derive from this enormous crime, the crime itself should not be primarily thought of as a symbolic occasion for a universalizing eloquence which ignores the bit-ter, particular truths.

Self-proclaimed Christians both participated in and passively ac-cepted the Holocaust. For Christians who take their religious identity seriously, this is a terrible burden. It is not a burden of direct guilt, for before long all those who took part in the event will be dead. Rather, it is a burden of individual and collective self-examination. Those who would delight in the truly prophetic accomplishments of Christian faith and community must seek to understand this greatest of Christian failures. To do so they need to ask: What in Christian culture supported or allowed this event to happen? How can serious Christians distinguish between authentic Christian faith and institutions and those which par-ticipate in or tacitly ignore genocide? Which elements of genocidal Christianity have manifested themselves *since* 1945—for example, in support of various nations' foreign policies, toleration of the creation of nuclear stockpiles, passivity before threats to the natural environment?

If there is to be lasting reconciliation after atrocity, Christians have to face these questions—both in the solitude of the individual heart and in the most public of forums.

At the risk of presumption, I would ask serious Christians to consider a particular dimension of Christianity in this regard. I wonder if there is a Christian tendency to externalize the reality of sin—to remove it from its proper place as a temptation in the human heart and locate it in an alien Other. Once sin is externalized, Christians find it easy to dehumanize an entire group by identifying them with that Otherness. When Christian voices confidently assert that sin is located in abortion clinics or secular humanism, in homosexuals or atheists, they create a mentality in which sin is seen to be always somewhere else. In a world in which all dimensions of social life are so permeated by violence, Christians need to fashion a concept of sin which is both critical of human failings and non-violent, both transforming of the self and respectful of difference. Until such a concept becomes normative for Christians, the religious roots of anti-semitism will remain alive. Perhaps it is necessary to recover or reemphasize that element of Christianity which is rooted in individual and communal struggle to forge a lifelong imitation of Christ. In this struggle, one's own sincerity and faith are always in question, and thus one has considerably less energy to expend condemning non-Christians.

The second major temptation for Christians is, ironically, a negation of universality. Instead of forgetting that the Holocaust essentially happened to Jews, Christians may be tempted by a *comforting distance*, and think of the Holocaust as something which happened forever and only to someone else.

We all may feel a secret, guilty thrill of gratitude and relief when we find out that someone else's child is ill, or someone else's husband was struck down by a drunk driver. Only partly thought, and perhaps accompanied by feelings of compassion or guilt, we say to ourselves: "Better them than us . . ." There is, I believe, a certain fascination with the Holocaust just on this ground: that because it happened to the Jews, *it cannot happen to us*. The endless fascination with pictures of the death camps, the ritual-like incantation of the magic number "six million"— these and similar practices provide a kind of superstitious guarantee: if it happened to them, we are safe.

The comfort of distance walls off the Jewish experience, and allows the onlooker to examine it from a place of illusory safety. It provides a false reassurance that the Jewish fate cannot befall Christians. Of course

Christians are not likely to be murdered for the crime of Christianity in Europe. But they might be murdered for other reasons: our collective madnesses in this century have made genocide a universal possibility.

Christians therefore need to realize not only that the Holocaust happened to Jews and not to some anonymous victim called "mankind," but also that in a certain sense they too could *become Jewish*. The terrible human vulnerability of our times springs from the fact that modern states combine immense technological power with emotional pathology. With this fact in mind, Christians can join Jews in their moral urgency never to forget the Holocaust.

III. THE HOLOCAUST AND HUMAN UNDERSTANDING

As we seek to open our hearts to the Holocaust's truths, so we also need to integrate it into our theoretical understanding of the human condition. What good will it do us, after all, if we feel deeply about the Holocaust, but ignore it when we try to make some intellectual sense of life? Our attempt to fully comprehend the world and the human condition will be inadequate if we avoid or deny the darkest moments of human history.

By way of a contribution to the task of integrating the study of the Holocaust into larger theories, I will now discuss how it can affect our understanding of human nature, rationality, and social justice. The following discussion is clearly not a finished argument. It does, however, indicate how the Holocaust may transform what we think—and how we act. Our beliefs about human nature, rationality, and social justice are not merely of academic interest, confined to the armchair or the classroom. They shape the way governments act, how we organize our schools, churches, and charities, and what we tell our children about good and evil.

Human Nature

Most people in the world simply did not believe that the Holocaust was possible. Even Zionist Jews, who denied the possibility of ending anti-semitism within the Diaspora, found it hard to believe eyewitness accounts of the extermination camps. Virtually everyone saw the present in terms of the past: as yet another pogrom or expulsion. According to historian Lucy Davidowicz: "That period [of annihilation] struck Jews like a cataclysm of unparalleled proportions, a natural disaster without historical precedent or rational meaning. . . ." Raul Hilberg concurs:

Locked within their ghettos, under strict surveillance and unrefined terror . . . the Jews . . . tried to assess the possible authenticity of the reports [of extermination camps] in the light of experience and logic. The horror of an enterprise that could deliberately destroy human beings who were innocent of any wrongdoing was inconceivable. The senselessness of the undertaking further determined the acceptance of the information. . . . These evaluations were for the most part shared by all levels of Jewish leadership and by the masses as well. The information about the death camps was rejected all over Europe, not only by the Jews.[3]

This global denial helps show how fundamentally different the Holocaust was from anything which had gone before. Of course the world had seen both mass murders and attempts to destroy an entire group. But there are two other characteristics of the Holocaust which distinguished it from anything people had ever witnessed.

First, the perpetrators intended to destroy an entire community— as an end in itself and to a great extent without reference to other, ulterior goals. Of course various sectors of German society did benefit from the political use of Jews as scapegoats and the economic values of expropriated Jewish property and Jewish slave labor. But genocide was no real "use" to anyone. There is, in fact, evidence that in the latter part of the war pursuing the Final Solution was at odds with Germany's military goals.[4]

Second, this pursuit of mass murder was neither a temporary aberration nor a crazed outburst. The Nazi machine was calm, orderly, and "scientific." Detailed records were kept of a carefully conceptualized process in which human death became an industry. The entire process was conceived of and directed by Germany's "best" administrative, political, and scientific minds.

The unique characteristics of the Holocaust challenge our theories of human nature. These are theories that seek to explain human behavior in the most general way possible. If they are successful, they will tell us, in the broadest terms, why both individual psychology and society as a whole are what they are.

Biological theories of human nature claim that people act the way they do because they are motivated by physiologically based, instinctual "drives."[5] These unchangeable drives, some theories claim, include a basic aggression which causes individual and collective violence. Though morally objectionable, such behavior is inevitable because it stems from permanent, biological, forces. If we repress aggression we will cause psychological imbalances and the violent behavior will return anew. Thus for biological theories of human nature which posit aggression as a dominant human impulse, the Holocaust is simply another example of the violence endemic to the human animal.

Yet many of the people who planned and executed the Final Solution did not seem to do so out of aggression or hostility. They may have disliked or been contemptuous of Jews, but these feelings were far exceeded by their behavior. Moreover, for many Germans, Jews were not enemies to be annihilated (whatever official propaganda stated), but objects to be treated "according to orders," about whom one had no more aggressive feeling than one had toward building roads or generating electricity. All these were "things" which the Nazi machine was called on to organize and dispose of.

This aspect of the Holocaust is described in Hannah Arendt's account of Adolph Eichmann (see also Richard Schmitt's essay on objectivity and Robert Lifton's on "doubling"). It appears that Eichmann—who ordered mass deportations to death camps—was motivated more by devotion to duty than aggression.[6] He took no joy in the destruction of the Jews and felt guilty for once striking a Jewish leader. His "happiness" resided in his ability to carry out his duty, to look good in the eyes of his superiors, to obey orders from higher sources effectively and thus fulfill his social role. Comparable attitudes are found in Himmler's praise of the S.S. for resisting the temptation to spare their particular "favorite Jews"—that is, for resisting their own personal wishes. "To have carried this out and . . . to have kept our integrity . . . this is an unwritten . . . page of glory. . . ."[7] Similarly, historian Raul Hilberg describes complex bureaucratic decisions whose goal was to distinguish "political" from "personal" killings. These decisions legitimized only the legal, orderly killing of Jews, and prohibited rash violence by "unauthorized" individuals.[8]

Were these instances of surface orderliness and self-control sublimations of aggression? Was "duty" a mask for hate? Perhaps. But the only evidence for this claim is the actions themselves, and we can just as easily see what the Nazis did as an example of people acting out social roles as of biologically-based aggression. Brutality toward the Jews may have been caused as much by the desire to be a "good German" as by some primitive urge to kill. Further, much of the Nazis' financial support—and thus their capacity to affect public opinion—derived from the self-conscious desire of Germany's ruling group to manipulate public opinion. This dimension of Hitler's rise depended on cool strategy, not blind rage. The motivation here was not the lust for violence, but the calm pursuit of continued power by an economic and political elite.

With these two points we begin to see that explanations of the Holocaust should center on social roles and social structure, not biology.

Also, if a theory puts too much emphasis on biologically caused aggression, it will have little to say about the heroism, self-sacrifice, and love shown by the victims. Yet these actions need explaining as much as those of the murderers. In the face of the fact that we find love alongside violence, biological theories typically assert that our drive for aggression coexists with a drive for cooperation or affection. Human life becomes a battleground between aggressive and cooperative drives, between love and death. But then this theory of human nature will not be much help in explaining why particular actions occurred. What, after all, will determine which drive will triumph? To explain the outcome in particular cases, we will again be forced to turn away from biological motivations, and toward the psychological and social forces which operate in a particular personal and historical context.

Liberalism and Marxism are two *socially-oriented theories* which have offered pictures of how human development as a whole can be understood. Like theories focusing on instinctual aggression, they too are challenged by the Holocaust.

Liberalism claims that human history necessarily tends toward the development of rationality, order, progress, and democracy.[9] As history unfolds, the growth of scientifically acquired knowledge will lead society to be increasingly dedicated to individual fulfillment and social justice, since both of these accord with the rational pursuit of self-interest by individuals. The more human beings are awakened to the nature of their interests and the rational fulfillment of those interests, the more society as a whole will reflect the values of rationality and justice. Rationality is inherent in human beings, and progress toward increased rationality is the basic movement of history.

Liberalism is challenged—perhaps defeated—by the eruption of German Fascism after the emergence of German democracy, by the rise of a brutal mysticism in one of the most "civilized" and "rational" of modern nations, by the substitution of pseudoscience for rational thought (for instance theories of racial superiority and the rewriting of history to make the Jews the source of Germany's post-World War I problems), and by the creation of a machine for mass murder in the first country to have introduced social welfare legislation.

Liberalism is baffled by regressions, since they are caused by rejections of reason. These rejections contradict its cheerful expectation that human reason will steadily develop in history. Without a faith in the "natural" human attraction to Reason and its accomplishments, the classical Liberal theory of history cannot be maintained. The Holocaust thus reduces Liberalism to a political ideology and a set of moral values. While other events, from the First World War to the nuclear threat, add to the stress on Liberalism, the Holocaust is the most dramatic and crushing challenge to its hopes.

Marxist theory claims that history is determined by the development of productive forces and by the struggle of the economically and politically oppressed workers against the rich and powerful owners. In each historical period the interaction of class struggle and technological development causes fundamental social changes, eventually transforming the entire society. This pattern leads in the general direction of both greater technical power and greater political freedom. The decisive point of this process is the transition from capitalism to socialism. Socialism becomes possible because capitalism develops forces of production adequate to guarantee each human being a comfortable life "beyond scarcity." Capitalism will be overthrown when the working class recognizes that social resources will be used for its benefit only when they are collectively controlled. This recognition will create a revolutionary working class, as an inevitably unstable capitalist economy produces ever larger social crises.

This picture—found in the writings of Marx and many of his followers[10]—is contradicted by the complete triumph of Nazism over the German left. Fascism won in a highly industrialized nation that had a long history of working class political activity. Yet in the face of a social and economic crisis, the majority of the population turned to the Nazis. Two large Marxist-oriented parties—the Social-Democrats and the Communists—could neither win over the majority of the population nor effectively resist.

Marxist theory does remain essential to any explanation of the social factors which led to Hitler's rise to power. More persuasively than other social theories, it can show the relation between Germany's drive for territorial expansion and the needs of its large corporations, how the ideas of Nazism helped unify a country divided by class conflict—and defeat the anti-capitalist perspective of a sizable portion of the working class—and how the worship of Hitler fit in with the necessary expansion of state power which accompanies the transition from competitive to monopoly capitalism.[11] That is, Marxist theory can show the development of Nazism to be partly the outcome of comprehensible motives held by human beings not completely unlike ourselves.

But Marxism's continued success as a theoretical tool for analyzing social life now coexists with its failure as a theory of history and human nature as a whole. In traditional Marxism's vision of history, there is no room for the possibility that the socialist project might ultimately fail.

The basic historical confidence of traditional Marxism is thus shattered by Nazism's defeat of the left, especially since that defeat occurred in a country which should have been ripe for revolution.[12] Of course a traditional Marxist could reply that this or that factor obstructed a working class victory, and that "next time" those factors will be overcome. Yet the scope of the Nazi madness was so vast that we can hardly trust to guarantees that the "next time" will not take a similarly terrible form.

In refuting the fundamentally optimistic theories of Liberalism and Marxism, the Holocaust poses a fundamental barrier to any confident expectations about the human future. With this confidence gone our personal lives are irrevocably altered. We can still try to be moral human beings, but can no longer expect that acting rightly will create a better world for us, our children, or that abstraction "the human race."

The Holocaust and Rationality

What is it to be a rational human being? What can reason tell us about right and wrong? These questions are brought into stark relief by the Holocaust.

At one time "reason" referred to our capacity to discover and know the highest, most appropriate goals and values for human beings. Since the seventeenth century, however, this concept has come under attack. And in the last century an antagonistic position—call it "positivism"—has emerged.[13] For positivism, there can be no truly rational justification of our basic values and highest goals. Only science and technology are truly rational, for only they provide experimentally tested knowledge and efficient, successful tools. Values and norms, "oughts" and "shoulds," good and bad—these notions have no place in science or technology and are the mere product of our non-rational desires, interests, and choices.

The Holocaust (along with such other typically modern events as the creation of nuclear weapons) points to the essential absurdity of positivism. Positivism gauges the rationality of the Nazis' actions independently of any evaluation of the goal to which those actions were directed. But if goals cannot be rationally justified, then there is no reason why efficient Nazis cannot be considered "rational." The only "irrationality" of the Nazi enterprise, on this view, would be inconsistencies or inefficiencies. And, for positivism, we have no justified, rational way to assert that the Nazis were wrong in what they did.

These conclusions do not logically refute positivism. An adherent of that position could reply: "We simply can't say in any final sense what is right or wrong, rational or irrational. Science tells me what the world is like and technology helps me get what I want. They do not speak of these other matters at all. Of course I am as repelled by the Nazis as you are. I too find them bizarre and hideous. But, in the end, these are just our particular feelings about the matter. We cannot really 'know' that they are evil or crazy, just that we don't like them. I know how to prove things scientifically and how to make machines work, but how do you 'prove' that someone is morally wrong? And if someone is not seeing little green men or claiming to be Napoleon, how can you prove that he's crazy just because he wants to do things you don't like?"

My reply to the positivist is that attempting to murder an entire human community is itself conclusive evidence of an insane degree of irrationality, and such a goal is absolutely wrong. If ways of justifying beliefs drawn from science and technology cannot support these claims, then we need to find other ways to support what we believe. Perhaps, as many recent feminist theorists have suggested, we should not be looking for supposedly objective and absolute principles when we think about these matters, but should instead draw from the culturally female form of moral reasoning based in empathy and compassion.[14] Surely any act of true empathy directed toward the Holocaust will tell us that it was terribly wrong, and that we can be as sure of this as we are of any theorem from physics. We will also realize that there is something extremely irrational about directing one's energies toward any murder, let alone the murder of an entire community. What is insane is to convince ourselves that our deepest feelings of connection, mutual recognition, love, and care are somehow less "true" than what we can learn in a laboratory. In losing the truth of these feelings we are in fact more likely to end up perpetuating or accepting genocide, or even the global ecological destruction we currently face.

Of course it is not easy to call a socially shared goal wrong and insane, and the Holocaust *was* perpetrated or tacitly ignored by an entire nation, not just a handful of evil madmen. Yet in a century which has given us the Holocaust, the nuclear arms race, and threats to the basic conditions of our survival as a species, understanding "social madness" is of crucial, life-saving importance. This is not the madness of a single individual who is somehow "out of touch" with the social consensus. Rather, it occurs when an entire mass of people support each other in beliefs and actions that are fundamentally opposed to human values and to life itself. A positivist rationality cannot diagnose such madness. What is needed, rather, is that we teach our hearts and souls to feel the life and pain of other people—and of nature itself—as our own. Such a teaching is rational in the deepest sense of the word—that is, it promotes life, human community, and a future for our children and the planet as a whole. It is this sense of rationality that events such as the Holocaust can teach us to preserve.

I realize that we cannot simply substitute the burning passion of immediate feeling for the cold deliberations of positivist calculation. For too many people flames of passion lead to hate, not love, destruction, not healing. Thus the shattering of the positivist sense of rationality creates a crucial moral task: to create a form of rational feeling, thinking, and knowing that will integrate the intelligence of science and technology with the wisdom of love and compassion. This terribly important task will require first that we transcend the social roles which divide feeling and calculation, nurturance and intelligence, care and technology. That is, we must find some new way to be men and women which promotes human wholeness rather than alienation, power, and submission. Nazism, after all, raised the ideology of masculinity to previously untried heights of folly. Its worship of the "great father," consignment of women to social submissiveness, and celebration of brutality expressed pervasive male fantasies in state power. An understanding of the Holocaust developed along these lines could have enormous significance both for understanding the past and saving the future.

Social Justice and Historical Tragedy

As the precipitating event in the formation of the state of Israel, the Holocaust contributed to the creation of an "historical tragedy," a morally perplexing conflict in which injustice can only be redressed at the cost of further injustice.

Without the rise of Nazism there would not have been sufficient Jewish immigration to Palestine to create even a potentially independent Jewish community there. Without the Holocaust, the world would have been even less sympathetic in its support of the formation of a Jewish state against the will of more than half the population of Palestine (that is, the Arab citizens) and of all the surrounding countries. The Holocaust won over the vast majority of world Jewry to the Zionist enterprise. In short, the social and emotional impetus for the creation of a Jewish homeland after the devastation of European Jewry cannot be overstated.

The Holocaust thus served as motive and justification for the formation of Israel. Yet this formation caused—and, some will claim, required—the creation of a stateless mass of Palestinian Arabs. The satisfaction of the claims of justice of the Jews resulted in a great injustice done to Palestinians.[15]

What are we to make of this painful conflict? Contemporary

theories of justice will not be much help. These theories typically argue for principles that guarantee a just treatment of all members of the community. Contemporary social contract theorist John Rawls, for example, claims to describe social rules that will necessarily be just for everyone. Unfairness is allowed only when it benefits the group as a whole or makes the least advantaged persons better off. He does not consider situations in which a group must accept an injustice from which other people benefit. Similarly, Marx sought a "universal class" the redress of whose wrongs would result in the ending of all forms of oppression. Such "universalism" is irrelevant to contexts in which we create a new injustice to redress an old wrong.

Other philosophers have talked about what it is like to face unavoidable moral conflict.[16] However, these authors focus on individual decisions, not the fate of communities in history. Equally important, they describe dilemmas from the point of view of a particular agent forced to choose between conflicting obligations—that is, forced to fulfill one obligation at the expense of another. The Israeli-Palestinian conflict, however, is defined by the struggle of two adversaries, two "moral agents," *each* of whose claims can be satisfied only if the other's are frustrated. Compromise is extremely difficult, seemingly impossible: historically, satisfaction of the minimal demands of each group excluded satisfaction of those of the other. The Zionist movement sought at the very least a bi-national state in which Jews would have equal rights and power with Palestinians. The Palestinians sought national independence in their homeland with the Jews as no more than a national minority. Until very recently the leading adversaries (the Palestine Liberation Organization and the Israeli government) continued to take positions which made compromise impossible.

This perplexing conflict is shaped by the long history of European anti-semitism and the immediate impact of the Holocaust. Actions by imperialist powers and the Arab governments are also significant. When we situate an injustice in such a broad historical context, achieving the kind of abstract justice described in most ethical theory is impossible. No one is clearly "right," no one clearly wrong. Who is there to punish? How can we reward the victims with what they truly deserve, when that would only create another round of tragedy and victimization?

The perplexing relation between the Holocaust and the Middle East conflict is all the more striking because some might claim that by establishing Israel the Jews have achieved some measure of "recompense" for genocide. Now it is highly doubtful—if not offensive—to talk of "recompense" here. But even if one could support this claim, it would still leave a crucial question unresolved: How can Palestinian Arabs be made to pay a moral debt which Europeans owe to Jews?

When injustices are so much the product of complicated and long-term historical factors, conventional moral theory is stymied. The Israeli-Palestinian conflict may be the most extreme example of this, but it is not the only one. Moral problems of the justice of Affirmative Action, for instance, reflect the difficulty we have in understanding how to redress the history of injustice done by whites to blacks and men to women.

The moral perspective which will solve these dilemmas has yet to be created. I believe, however, it must take two things into account. First, our moral confusion over issues such as the Israeli-Palestinian conflict or Affirmative Action derives partly from our habit of thinking about morality from the point of view of individual agents. Yet groups as well as individuals take part in moral relationships, and we act morally not just as single persons, but as members of communities. This becomes clear when we remember that what is distinctive about genocide is that it is not the murder of a large number of individuals, but the attempt to destroy an entire people.

Second, we have to build our sense of morality around the realization that the world is, in certain essential respects, morally imperfect. Ethical theory can no longer presuppose that a complete accomplishment of moral values is possible. In a post-Holocaust age moral theory must consider that at times we can meet the needs of one group only at the cost of hurting another. Such tragic choices are not exceptions, but essential parts, of moral life. This awareness is yet another sobering meaning of the Holocaust.

Conclusion

I will conclude by suggesting some more hopeful tasks for our capacity to think about, remember, and forge meanings for the Holocaust. I believe that it is possible—strange as it may sound—to find comfort as well as anguish here. We can do so not as an evasion or denial, but as an opening to the Holocaust's full reality. Our reflections may include a focus on the victims' courage and love as much as on the barbarism of the killers, and we can find some measure of peace and hope in remembering the acts of resistance and humanity which we now know were performed by both Jews and Gentiles. We can also support each other as we struggle for authentic acts of memory and meaningful understanding.

A full remembrance of the Holocaust may lead us to embrace that saving grace which is the human capacity to love—a capacity which survived not only after the Holocaust but in it. Our collective memory of this survival is perhaps our greatest treasure in facing the pain, fear, and despair which our search for meanings of the Holocaust will inevitably produce.

NOTES

1. The concept is best developed by Søren Kierkegaard, *Concluding Unscientific Postscript* (Princeton: Princeton University Press, 1968), pp. 125–62.

2. Comparable problems arise when people forget that German Fascism was significantly shaped by the interests of the German economic and political ruling class, or that it was structured by a rigidly sexist ideology.

3. Davidowicz, *The War Against the Jews* (New York: Bantam, 1975), p. 466. Raul Hilberg, *The Destruction of the European Jews* (New York: Harper, 1961), pp. 474–75.

4. For the conflict between military objectives and the Final Solution, see Davidowicz, pp. 191–97. For a financial cost-accounting which indicates the strain the Final Solution placed on the German economy, see Hilberg, pp. 644–46.

5. For example, theories of Friedrich Nietzsche, Sigmund Freud, Konrad Lorenz, and Robert Ardrey. The discussion which follows is not meant to suggest that the Holocaust provides a unique problem for these theories. Other modern events do so as well. I believe, however, that the particular details of the Holocaust make it perhaps the most difficult historical event for these theories.

6. *Eichmann in Jerusalem* (New York: Penguin, 1963).

7. Davidowicz, p. 200.

8. Hilberg, pp. 646–49.

9. This traditional use of the term has little in common with the contemporary meaning which identifies Liberalism with high government spending and social permissiveness. For classic Liberalism, see the works of John Stuart Mill and James Mill. For an opponent's summing up of Liberalism as a theory of history, see Dostoyevsky's *Notes From Underground*.

10. See, for instance: Karl Marx and Friedrich Engels, *The Communist Manifesto;* Rosa Luxenburg, "Social Reform or Revolution" in Rosa

Monthly Review, 1971); and the 1891 *Erfurt Program* of the German Social Democratic Party, the most influential party of the Second International, described in Carl F. Schorske, *German Social Democracy* (New York: John Wiley, 1955), pp. 5–7.

11. Rudolf Hilferding, *Das Finanzkapital* (Vienna: Wiener, 1910); V.I. Lenin, *Imperialism the Highest of Capitalism* in *Collected Works*, Vol. xix (London: Lawrence and Wishart, 1942); Rosa Luxemburg, *The Accumulation of Capital* (London: Routledge, 1951). Of course a Marxist analysis of these issues, while necessary, is hardly sufficient. Any Marxist explanation needs to be accompanied by accounts of the history of anti-semitism, the role of gender, and the effects of mass psychology.

12. There has developed a tradition of western Marxism, which is marked in part by the degree of importance it accords to non-economic social relations and processes, and by its refusal to commit itself to a theory of history. Some of this work is a direct response to the rise of Nazism. See Roger S. Gottlieb, *History and Subjectivity: The Transformation of Marxist Theory* (Philadelphia: Temple University Press, 1987), and *An Anthology of Western Marxism: From Lukacs and Gramsci to Socialist-Feminism*, edited by Roger S. Gottlieb (New York: Oxford University Press, 1989).

13. The sources of positivism range from David Hume's denial of the logical relations between "ought" and "is" to Karl Popper's claim that rationalism in science and social life can only be founded on a species of "faith" or personal decision.

14. See Carol Gilligan, *In a Different Voice* (Cambridge: Harvard University Press, 1982), and Nel Noddings, *Caring: A Feminine Approach to Ethics* (Berkeley: University of California Press, 1986). A detailed analysis of Nazism from a feminist perspective remains to be written; that is, one which shows the ways in which Nazism was an extreme outbreak of cultural masculinity.

15. For surveys of the history involved, see Walter Laqueur, *A History of Zionism* (NH: Schocken, 1976); Maxime Rodinson, *Israel: Colonial-Settler State?* (New York: Monad, 1973).

16. In particular, the works of Søren Kierkegaard and Jean-Paul Sartre come to mind.

Part I
WHY DID IT HAPPEN?

If we are to try to make meanings out of the Holocaust, our first and perhaps most desperate thought must be: "How could it happen?" In these first selections four authors struggle with this question and show the necessity of using fundamentally different perspectives to help shed light on this terrible darkness. Ronald Aronson seeks to link the particular pathology of the Nazi leadership with the collective psychology, sociology, and economic structure of German society as a whole. Richard Rubenstein finds the origins of the death camps in the German response to the "mythic structure of Christianity," and appeals to unconscious motivations of immense power and scope. Richard Schmitt suggests that an attitude of detachment, of "murderous objectivity," both enabled educated people to carry out the Final Solution and keeps contemporary theoreticians from understanding it. Finally, Alice Miller's troubling essay points to a root of the Holocaust in Hitler's own early childhood suffering.

Ronald Aronson

WHY? TOWARDS A THEORY
OF THE HOLOCAUST

WHO IS RESPONSIBLE?

How far can we now generalize beyond Hitler, his circle, and the SS troops involved—beyond even the Nazi movement and its supporters —in attributing the Final Solution to German *society* or *Germany*? It is true that no matter how hard we look beyond Hitler we never see more than a relative handful of key actors. But this tells us more about our century's machinery of destruction than about the man Hitler and the German nation-state. Those who could win control over the machinery and organize society around it, needed in the end only a relative handful of obedient servants to operate it. Hitler, we may say, got all the cooperation that was needed.

If genocide can be performed by strikingly few, it is no less striking how many accomplices it requires. Hundreds of thousands were asked only for their complicity, and gave it. Whether or not they desired to exterminate the Jews, they certainly acted, in the only ways that mattered, to bring that end about. Similarly, those who had voted Nazi, whatever reasons they might give, had acted in the ways available to *them* to bring to power a movement incorporating violence, obedience, antisemitism, militarism, and unreason. The two and a half million who joined the Nazis by 1935 more directly endorsed and participated in the movement. All those who became agents and beneficiaries of the antisemitic policies must also be numbered among the accomplices, as must those who knew what was being done to the Jews after 1941 but acquiesced. Even more directly connected are the hundreds of thousands who, though neither directing the Final Solution nor guarding the camps, provided the machinery through which it took place: those disposing of the victims' property, taking inventories of their gold teeth, manufacturing and shipping gas, performing the voluminous paperwork, directing and profiting from the starving labourers. In the end

25

millions acted and assented: those who knew it was happening but let it continue, as well as those who aided and abetted it more directly. They all bear a share of the responsibility for the murder of six million Jews.

Certainly the average German—let us say, the SPD voter who withdrew after 1933 and kept to himself—is no more responsible for the Final Solution than the average American was responsible for the laying waste of Vietnam. Certainly no more, but also no less. Not only all those who participated in one or another phase of the preparation for genocide, or in the Final Solution itself, but also all those who knowingly accepted without opposition their society's actions thereby made those actions *their own*. The Nazis did not demand active involvement; having reduced the population to passivity they needed only complicity. Already in some sense *theirs* in historical origin—just as the technological hubris that destroyed Vietnam is a part of American national identity—the Final Solution further came to belong to tens of millions in Germany and elsewhere by virtue of their silent acquiescence.

To be sure, Nazi Germany was ruled by terror, and opposition meant grave consequences. The concentration camp system had originated as a way of detaining opponents of the regime. There were many who inwardly opposed what was done to the Jews, but went along because they felt they had to.[1] On this level Milgram's experiment is illuminating. The military, for example, was whipped into subservience to Hitler's policy, and many of the millions of military and civilian accomplices must have been decent people who hated Nazism but saw no alternative to obedience to their society's rulers. Nazi Germany, after all, was a society whose policy from the beginning was deliberately and systematically to transform its citizens into passive agents.[2]

One of the most remarkable facts about the Nazi extermination of Jews is that it proceeded virtually without incident or opposition among Germans. Opportunities were certainly available to resist, sabotage, or at least undermine, the Final Solution.[3] It was more than terror, or merely obedience, that caused the exterminations to be carried out so efficiently and be accepted so silently by the citizens of the Third Reich. After all, it was open resistance (culminating in Cardinal Galen's famous sermon), which led the Nazis to abandon their euthanasia programme.

Similarly, even under 'totalitarian' rule most of Germany's seventy million faithful sullenly let die the Nazi pagan 'Faith Movement'. Yet the many and complex steps preparing for and carrying out the Final Solution were taken virtually without incident.[4] Certainly, opposition to the other Nazi projects had developed in peacetime, and they threatened 'Aryans' themselves; while the extermination programme was secret, took place in wartime, and involved 'non-Aryans'. But the overwhelming mood towards the relatively few outcast and then departing Jews seemed to be, if not outright hostility then at least indifference to their fate.[5]

After all, was the Final Solution not rooted in a millennial Christian history of antisemitism, given new focus by recent German history? Did not the Nazis take power on a programme of antisemitism, behind a leader obsessed by it and who gave frequent warning of his intentions? And hadn't the militaristic racists defeated their opponents politically by 1933? And did not their new order proceed, as promised, to organize itself psychologically, socially, economically and culturally for war and expansion and against the Jews? From the start did it not carry out persecution, disenfranchisement, expropriation, and pogrom, and was not this accepted by millions of Germans? And was there not available in the SS—those claiming after all to be the best, the purest Germans in a racial state—a cadre willing to destroy the Jews? And did not this operation proceed with staggering efficiency? Taken together these by-now rhetorical questions point towards another: was not the extermination of the Jews as much an outgrowth of German history and society as the Nazis themselves? If we would understand *why* the Jews were exterminated these reflections point us not towards Hitler's psyche alone, but towards the social soil in which such evil became ascendant.

THE HERITAGE OF DEFEAT

What radical social pathology led to and was expressed in the radical extermination programme? The secret which accompanied Germany into the years of inflation and depression was its history of defeat—not only widely resented defeat at the hands of the Allies in the First World War but that of the peasants three hundred years earlier, that of the bourgeoisie in the nineteenth century, and that of the proletariat after the war.

If one step in this history was the peasants' defeat by the aristocrats in the sixteenth century, another was the later aristocratic reaction to modernization. They squeezed the peasants harder rather than leading a drive for genuine modernization of the kind which, in the case of England, broke the peasantry as a social force and drew the aristocracy and bourgeoisie close together. By 1848 the constellation of forces had become such that no bourgeois–democratic revolution was possible: the latter knew defeat in advance. Paraphrasing Marx, Barrington Moore sketches the resulting bourgeoisie: 'a commercial and industrial class which is too weak and dependent to take power and rule in its own right and which therefore throws itself into the arms of the landed aristocracy and the loyal bureaucracy, exchanging the right to rule for the right to make money.'[6] They were too few, too timid, and too weak; the aristocracy was too strong and, soon, would become the only effective safeguard against the rising proletariat.

To say that the bourgeoisie never triumphed in Germany is to say far more than meets the eye. Moore helps us to see how a mad political outlook had already developed in the late nineteenth century and could become a mass phenomenon in the twentieth because, in 1848, the then-rational one had been defeated. The lower middle class developed the furious will and strength to run amok because, a century earlier, their regressive hopes had not been liquidated by an ascending bourgeoisie. No matter how brutally, he argues, the American, French, and British bourgeoisie contributed to gradualism and democracy by successfully making society over in *their* image. Certainly, they did this to serve their own interest; but they functioned simultaneously as a modernizing, progressive force which, for a time, led and furthered humanity's struggle for freedom and dignity. Their revolution against the feudal world could become 'everyone's' only because it was a *relatively* humanizing, civilizing, and democratizing struggle. The country of the Final Solution was one in which industrialization, the fundamental economic advance, took place without the parallel human, political, social, and cultural advance embodied in constitutional government, an effective parliament, revocation of aristocratic privileges and the victory of new ideas of human dignity and political equality. A decisive revolutionary rupture with the past in the service of the present and future never happened in Germany, even though it industrialized virtually overnight.[7]

ANTISEMITISM AND VÖLKISCH THOUGHT

The key to German society's 'illness', to its 'distorted social development' was the defeat of the social forces that might have brought progress in human terms—a more democratic government, a more equal society, a more humane and rationalistic outlook—to accompany breakneck technological and economic progress. On the ideological level this defeat left open space for regressive and anti-rational outlooks to assume a legitimacy and currency unthinkable where successful revolutions had assured the hegemony of values such as reason, equality and progress. At the same time the irresolution and lack of congruence between and within the social, legal, political, economic and educational realms generated tensions which promoted ever more virulent strains of such thought. Regressive outlooks are present in any industrializing society, but in Germany the irrationalist and antisemitic protest against modernity was strong and widespread enough to be a contender for ideological dominance.

We must understand what this means—that prejudice became paranoia. People who hated the coming of the modern world believed what they said when they blamed it on the Jews as the people of the city, of the political and cultural vanguard, of internationalism and commerce.[8] And they were taken seriously, as age-old Christian antisemitism became absorbed and reshaped into this new current of protest.

In 1880 200,000 students signed a petition calling for the exclusion of Jews from government service, public and professional life in Germany. As George L. Mosse points out, antisemitism, antimodernism and *völkisch* (i.e. romantic folkish) thought—generally united in a single outlook—became 'commonplace bourgeois notions' in the late nineteenth century.[9] Espoused by respected thinkers and academicians like the historian Treitschke, this current did more than develop claims to scientific, moral and political legitimacy: 'The fact is that schools dominated by the *völkisch* ideology were so numerous as to constitute the centre rather than the fringe of German education.'[10]

How secure were the Bismarckian reforms, including emancipation of the Jews, in a climate in which the antisemitic *völkisch* outlook 'had permeated much of the nation' even before Hitler came on the scene?[11] Reforms were not won as the fruit of popular struggles, but imposed from above.[12] Not achieved through a real defeat of prebourgeois social forces, they rested therefore on shaky soil. This climate of uncertainty, concealed beneath the spectacular rise of German industrial capitalism and of the German socialist movement, is remarkably symbolized in a passage from a letter written in 1917 by Walter Rathenau, then director of General Electric Company, to Mrs. von Hindenburg: 'Although myself and my ancestors have served our country as best as we could, I am, as you would presumably know, as a Jew a second-class citizen.'[13]

THE MOMENT OF TRUTH

Nevertheless, it seemed for some time that Germany was the world's most modern and potentially most revolutionary society. It seemed also —among Jews—that assimilation and not antisemitism was the real 'Jewish problem' in Germany.[14] But the real weakness of its progressive forces was revealed. Less in the stampede to war in 1914—which was, after all, universal—than in the defeated revolution and deadlock following the collapse of the Hohenzollern monarchy and discrediting of the feudal aristocracy. The heritage of defeat here reappears in an especially vicious form: the betrayal of a class by its own party leaders.

1918 was the most propitious moment yet for a decisive victory of 'modernity' in Germany. The military was demoralized by the allied victory and the workers had declared a republic. Even if not a socialist republic, a liberal democracy was in the offing which might forever sweep away the pre-bourgeois forces from German life. To achieve this the Social Democratic government would, in Moore's words 'have had to get to work at once to take control of the armed forces, the administrative bureaucracy, and the judiciary, remoulding them as instruments loyal to the Republic. It would have had to adopt an economic policy that included a degree of government control over certain areas of heavy industry, with some concessions to the workers over conditions on the shop floor. In doing all that, the government would have had to be willing to forestall the National Assembly by taking a series of essentially irreversible decisions necessary as the foundation for a liberal and democratic version of capitalism.'[15]

The social basis for this vigorous policy existed in the militant and active revolutionary movement, organized into workers' councils. But the Social Democratic leaders did not seek to change the 'wrong, outdated, anachronistic distribution of power'[16] among the classes of German society. Sebastian Haffner concludes that Fritz Ebert, the SPD leader 'did not want a republic, he wanted to save the monarchy.'[17] Hating the revolution 'like sin,' Ebert sought to share power with the bourgeoisie and the aristocracy. His and the SPD's main animus became directed not against the old order, but against the repeated risings of workers.[18] In the end, during the revolutionary wave, the SPD not only failed to push for a liberal democratic programme but accepted, rehabilitated and made common cause with the old bureaucracy and aristocracy against the workers themselves.

No wonder that while administering the state apparatus, even at the height of a wave of popularity which gave them eleven million votes in 1919, the SPD made no effort to gain real control of it. Why? Perhaps Moore's description of the bourgeoisie of 1848 can be slightly altered and so made apposite for the SPD of 1918 and after: the party which represented the majority of the working class was too weak and dependent to take power and rule in its own right and therefore threw itself into the arms of the bourgeoisie, the discredited landed aristocracy and the bureaucracy. It exchanged the right to rule and to reshape Germany for the right to further workers' interests under a revived old order.

One can scarcely exaggerate the effect of this failed revolution on subsequent events. Germany was in a constitutional crisis of the deepest sort; yet the one force which could have decisively swept aside pre-bourgeois social classes, institutions and ideology had been defeated. More than defeated: betrayed by its own leaders in collusion with the old order, the working class was now split into two parties. It was in the anomalous position of being formally 'in power' while its leaders continued to call on volunteer soldiers—the *Freikorps*—to put down workers' risings. On the other hand, of course, the old aristocracy and bureaucracy hated the 'Marxist' republic which had been manipulated into negotiating a humiliating peace, while the army remained intact and undefeated. In as much as the *Freikorps* led to the Nazi stormtroopers, the nonrevolutionary SPD republic was saved by those who would soon become its own gravediggers.

If the parties of the working class did not exercise real power after the war, the old order was historically played out, unable now to unite Germany even under a military dictatorship. At the same time, national-ism was intensified by a humiliating and economically draining peace, and by French occupation of the Ruhr. The peace was both too severe and not severe enough,[19] because it humiliated the old order yet allowed the retention of its minions intact—especially the bureaucracy and mili-tary. For all its limits, socialism had had a corrosive effect on the old Germany by bringing the masses to the centre of the historical stage, so that in the Republic the old nationalist and aristocratic parties had become irrelevant. The army remained perhaps the most significant force to be reckoned with under Weimar, yet it too was no longer able to rule. Not strong enough to assume hegemony in the nineteenth century, the bourgeoisie was now structurally even less able to take leadership in a society where socialism was already on the agenda. The worsening political stalemate of the Weimar republic thus reflected a social crisis in which no traditional class was capable of asserting hegemony either by itself or in coalition. One could scarcely imagine a more welcoming soil for the *völkisch*, anti-modern, irrationalist outlook to be turned into a mass-based political party.

THE LOWER MIDDLE CLASS AND NATIONAL SOCIALISM

The party that emerged owed its origin, nature and phenomenal growth to many things: defeat, failed revolution and constitutional crisis, the deep penetration of the antisemitic and *völkisch* outlook, and the postwar economic crises. In the postwar peace settlement Germany had lost 13 per cent of its prewar territory, 10 per cent of its people, 15 per cent of its arable land, 75 per cent of its iron ore deposits, 44 per cent of its pig iron capacity, 38 per cent of its steel and 26 per cent of its coal capacity. Inflation, tied to the punitive reparations Germany had to pay the Allies, exploded the life savings of many of the hard working and thrifty between 1919 and 1923. After a period of stability the Depression struck, bringing unemployment rates of over 30 per cent by 1932. The Nazis had dropped from 6.5 per cent of the vote in May 1924 to 3.0 per cent that December, and then to 2.6 per cent in 1928. But in the 1930 elections Nazi support skyrocketed to 18.3 per cent, giving them the second largest delegation to the Reichstag.

Barrington Moore confirms that the NSDAP was indeed largely the party of the lower middle class—the 'little men,' including teachers, small merchants, white-collar employees and officials, farmers and self-employed craftsmen.[20] Who were these people? The first thing that leaps to the eye, in the studies by Theodore Abel in the 1930s, and Milton Mayer in the 1950s, is that most of their subjects appear quite ordinary and conventional. 'There is little to be found in them,' says Peter Merkl of Abel's respondents, 'that seems sinister or ominous. And yet the consequences of their common foibles, errors, and delusions cost an estimated fifty million human lives and untold destruction and misery.'[21]

If there is a direct line of mad rage from *Mein Kampf* through the Nazi movement's tactics and actual behaviour in power to the Final Solution, it is not immediately evident in these people. They are overly sentimental, ardent nationalists respectful of hard work and honesty, authoritarian and antisemitic. As Barrington Moore describes the respondents in Abel's study, their values are those of early competitive capitalism, they are 'petty bourgeois rather than bourgeois . . . with a strong overlay of both bureaucratic and even feudal features.'[22] They are people we can understand and sympathize with, rather than savages from the political gutter.

Hitler himself was patently one of these 'little men.' His jerkiness, exaggerated gestures and insecurity were those of one who lacks the grace and self-confidence learned through operating the levers that reproduce society. His writing reads like that of an autodidact lacking training, culture and polish. He was filled with resentment towards his betters, and indeed towards the whole world. He lacked faith in the future and longed to have been born 'earlier.'

Certainly idealizing the past or one's childhood does not prefigure evil to come, even if it does show desire to withdraw from a traumatic present. The same is true of intense nationalism. But the Nazis absorbed these attitudes into *National Socialism,* which is a definite leap beyond the more ordinary kinds of irrationality. In its deep structure it is a contradiction in terms. The worker who tells his story in Abel's account shows the irreconcilable pressure of idealized family and fatherland on the one side, and his experience and identification as a worker on the other. We can see his 'synthesis' of reactionary sentiment and class struggle in his acceptance of National Socialism. Its inherent inauthenticity was his authentic resolution. Abel's other essays show people living under similar enormous pressures, tensions, blockages and contradictions who chose to 'resolve' their situation by leaping beyond it, either towards the chimera of National Socialism, by faith in the absolute leader, or by fixating upon 'the Jew' supposedly 'polluting' their blood or defiling their race.[23]

As an outlook, National Socialism represents a fantastic joining of two irreconcilables. Nationalism united all classes, socialism sprang from class struggle; nationalism needed a foreign enemy, socialism claimed to be internationalist; nationalism deeply respected existing authority, socialism sought (in people's minds at least) to overthrow it. As a mass movement, Nazism was deeply marked by social-democratic aspirations and the workers' struggles against class society. This philosophy of the 'little man' who wants to leave society as it is begins by articulating enormous resentment against wealth and privilege, only to end by effacing this resentment in the larger community of the fatherland.[24] Its inherent illogic is such that it can be held together as outlook and movement only by three recourses: to an absolute leader, who will mystically cement together the otherwise irreconcilable by force of personality; to aggressive national expansion, as the only way of creating the material means for a 'socialism' providing economic benefits for the workers and poor without disturbing existing economic structures too much; and to virulent antisemitism, as the main defining pole of a Germanic fantasy-community for which class boundaries were irrelevant.[25] As an outlook National Socialism was not only articulated without style or grace, as Neumann pointed out,[26] but it was also contradictory, illogical, and founded on a systematic distortion of reality. Because Nazism *could not be* rational it aggressively promoted the rejection of reason itself, and based itself instead on regression.

Regression was one of the strongest currents of Nazism: its explicit goal was to return to the past. In fact, the movement coalesced around a virulent hatred for modernity. According to Nazi ideology the alienated, depersonalized, faceless twentieth-century world was to be reversed in the pure *Völkisch* state. Medieval virtues, especially of physical prowess, would be given a central place. The peasant, the tiller of the soil rooted in nature, would be honoured once more, and craftsmanship would become socially important again. Irrationalism and obedience to the leader were to replace Enlightenment notions of reason and political democracy. Women would be returned to their role of home-maker, mother and helpmeet for the Aryan warrior.

The very notion of the *Volk*, so central to Nazism, was a deliberate regression from what was seen as the cosmopolitanism and internationalism of the modern world. The Jews were hated primarily as bearers of modernity: an international people, an urban people, adept in the ways of modern capitalism and often proponents of socialism as well. Elemental values common to liberal democracy and socialism—such as equality, civil rights and liberties, the dignity of all people, the importance of rational deliberation and democratic decision-making, rule by law—were violently rejected by Nazi ideology and practice.[27] On the very first page of *Mein Kampf* Hitler introduced a key reversal of both bourgeois and socialist dreams for international peace and respect between nations; through conquest the German *Volk* would increase their daily bread, using swords as ploughshares. Against the panoply of slowly developed civilized values was asserted a brutal vision of Aryan domination: survival of the fittest, subservience to authority, and 'blood purity.'

These analyses take Nazi ideology seriously. We have learned that antisemitism, as the pivot of this ideology, must be taken equally seriously. These key strands of Nazism perpetuated the rejection of modernity and rationalism found in nineteenth-century romantic thought, but they gave it a new active and violent mass character. What was also new in Nazism was its political specificity—it blamed Versailles and the Jews for the actual suffering of Germans in the late 1920s and early 1930s, it physically attacked Jews, broke up meetings, engaged in violent demonstrations, street fighting and political assassinations. And, as its ideology and actions gathered support, it sought political power. The 'little man' gave Nazism the dynamism, force, and organizational strength to impose its will upon a Germany in crisis, with decisive assistance from the military and large capital. For all other classes it was not the right time: they were either timid, without a popular base, defeated, or obsolescent. The 'little man' alone sought and acquired power.

THE 'LITTLE MAN' IN POWER

He did it in a characteristic way, however: by surrendering all power to Adolf Hitler, by abandoning the heart of his social and economic programme, by compromising with his betters and projecting his impotent rage away from *this* situation. Nazism was a 'socialism' which, in power, would not attack the capitalists, which deeply respected authority, and buried class struggle in aggressive expansion and hatred of the Jews. The point is that the profoundly unrevolutionary yet highly explosive character of this 'fools' socialism' reflected the fundamentally impotent structural position of the lower middle class. The years after 1933 verify that the Nazi project—to guarantee the social status of the *Mittelstand* and protect it against both the working class and capital was, as Kühnl has said, 'objectively illusory.' The 'little man's' energies were 'directed towards the restoration of a past historical situation and social structure which has long been superseded by the development of the productive forces.'[28]

In other words, economically and technologically Germany's problems and needs had become those of an advanced capitalist society. Their inherent distance from the real levers of effective social power is expressed in the fact that, by themselves, the social forces of Nazism were incapable of grasping the last rung on the ladder to political power. Without *Reichswehr* and bourgeois acceptance the Nazis would have remained forever suspended between a hopeless putschism on the one hand and their one third of the vote on the other. The fact that Hitler was invited into office by Hindenburg in 1933 is more than symbolic: other classes, in other societies, have had the means and the will to take power *against* their national bourgeoisies and/or military forces. By contrast the very unrevolutionary thrust of 'revolutionary' Nazism suggests, among other things, that its leading group, even if it produced a Hitler and entered the halls of power, could never be genuinely dominant.

Why? The nature of the lower middle class was to depend structurally on large capital—socially, economically and ideologically. Its desires to turn back the clock remained purely subjective. Having no authentic —that is to say, independent and potentially realizable—long-term political, social or economic interests of its own, it was indeed as incapable of actual rule as it was of seizing power on its own.

But after all, did not the Nazis take power in one way or another, bringing tens of thousands of their own into leading positions, and did not Hitler utterly dominate Germany—including, finally, the military, the bureaucracy and the bourgeoisie? We can see this process unfold in Allen's account of Thalberg between 1930 and 1935, and it explains why Mosse uses *revolution* without inverted commas to refer to the Nazi takeover and its aftermath.[29] Indeed, did they not worship power, and exercise it—to promote German recovery, to create a totalitarian society, to expand by the threat of war, to conquer Europe with the most powerful war machine ever developed, and ultimately to assume the power of life and death over whole peoples?

But these were products of an all-powerful *impotence*. The Nazis were structurally incapable of doing the one thing that really mattered to their social class: undoing history. The paradox is vividly demonstrated in the Nazi treatment of department stores, a process that must have puzzled so many of Hitler's loyal supporters.

No capitalist institution had been as prominently attacked along the Nazis' road to power as the largely Jewish-owned department stores—this was in keeping with the necessarily superficial 'anti-capitalism' of a class which would attack its larger, more modern and efficient competitors—especially if they were Jews—but not the very market and property system of which it hoped to remain a respected part. After 30 January 1933, many of the anticipated steps were taken against department stores. Exceptionally high taxes were levied on turnover. Jewish stores were boycotted. Permanent limits were placed on chain and department store expansion. Department stores were excluded from handling certain profitable government and party business, and were boycotted repeatedly by various party groups. The failure rate of their apprentices before local examining boards rose appreciably, and the press and the mails discriminated against their advertising.

But, as the policy of a fundamental non-revolutionary government, these could only be temporary or half measures, taken ambivalently. Rapid economic recovery within the existing order, a vital need of the Nazi regime, depended on encouraging the most efficient—in this case, the largest, most highly developed—economic forms. Corporate capitalist realities undercut petty-bourgeois dreams as the banks, industry and government officials all saw the necessity of keeping the department stores healthy. Already in July 1933, the Reich Minister of Economics decreed for example that two large Jewish chains, which now had huge government investments, could not be allowed to go under. By 1936 turnover at the large stores had risen back to 86 per cent of that of 1932. By 1938 the threats had been removed, if not the formal restrictions. A 1935 official Party statement criticized the inadequacies of small shops, emphasizing that retail outlets where working people could buy cheaply did not deserve discrimination if maintaining the standard of living was the most important economic objective. Thus did the Nazi 'revolution' capitulate to the priorities of modern capitalist society, which it had no serious intention of dismantling.[30]

The vicissitudes of Nazi policy towards department stores reflect the fact that a non-socialist movement of 'little men,' even if it held state power, could develop no sensible alternative to furthering the interests of monopoly capitalism.[31] As Poulantzas has argued, this was indeed a secret of fascism: it accelerates the consolidation and stabilization of the economic supremacy of big finance capital over the other dominant class and class fractions. But this is by no means to be interpreted as meaning that fascism represents the economic interests of big capital "exclusively." Fascism, rather, operates in the economic sense, as a factor *neutralizing* the contradictions among those classes and factions, while regulating development to ensure the exclusive domination of the big capital.'[32] This 'exclusive domination' did not give large capitalists a free hand—rather, they had to submit to what Neumann called a 'command economy' in which Hitler's priorities ruled to such an extent that some authors have ridiculed the idea that capitalism was favoured under the Nazis. But to argue the point of whether (Nazi) politics or (bourgeois) economics was in command during the Third Reich is to miss the forest for the trees: a society need not be commanded by big capital to serve the latter's fundamental interests. Even if the logic of his course led him there, serving the interests of big capital was not the main mission of Adolf Hitler.[33] Driven repeatedly into the arms of the bourgeoisie, Nazism continued to dream of going backwards to a more hospitable time but was carried forward by deeper currents than it could ever comprehend. The inevitable 'compromise' between Nazism's original base and military and economic realities was brutally announced on 30 June 1934, on 'The Night of Long Knives' which destroyed the Nazi 'Left.' For all the talk of revolution during the Nazi era and by historians since, basic property relations were not even questioned, the corporate sector became ever more the lynchpin of the economy, and the German capitalism that rose from the ashes after 1945 had stunning continuity with that of Weimar and the Third Reich.

Economically speaking, fascism's hidden historical role may have been to create an alliance between monopoly capital and the 'little men,' but this was accomplished only by intensifying the contradictions between them to the disadvantage of the latter.[34] For Adolf Hitler's social class, the Third Reich was a disaster. The Germany of 1939, as David Schoenbaum summarizes its results, confounded all expectations: 'Objective social reality, the measurable statistical consequences of National Socialism, was the very opposite of what Hitler had presumably promised and what the majority of his followers had expected him to fulfill. In 1939, the cities were larger, not smaller; the concentration of capital greater than before; the rural population reduced, not increased; women not at the fireside but in the office and the factory; the inequality of income and property distribution more, not less conspicuous; industry's share of the gross national product up and agriculture's down, while industrial labour had it relatively good and small business increasingly bad.[35] In the command economy all of this took place deliberately:

wages and prices were controlled, large farms and estates were encouraged, migration from country to town and town to city was permitted, women were encouraged to work.[36] In other words, while railing against the modern world, Hitler, like all fascists, was a great modernizer.[37]

IMPOTENCE IN POWER

My point is not that fascism served the bourgeoisie, which it did, after all, only by commanding it and by plunging Germany into total war. Nor is it that the 'little man' was swindled during the Third Reich, which he was. But, above all, as Bloch said of the peasant, the petty bourgeois was 'situated in an older place.'[38] The 'swindle' confirmed that as a class, the petty bourgeoisie had no programme. That is, no programme which could be put into effect in the Germany of the 1930s. Its rabid desire to turn back the clock represented a fundamental historical impotence, and thus could only be 'achieved' symbolically through a mad break with that reality.

Impotent? As I have emphasized, one of the most striking characteristics of Nazism was Hitler's power lust. The worship of the Führer already promoted in *Mein Kampf* was central to the conversion of so many to Nazism, and was built into the movement's ethos and electoral appeal. In power, Hitler took every step possible to achieve absolute power. The German state attained unparalleled domination over the Western world. How do these undeniable facts square with my emphasis on the *impotence* of the social class upon which the movement was built?

In the most basic social sense, the Nazi obsession with power only confirmed their *lack* of it. This points us towards the terrible fracture in German society in which the class which sought and then held political power was unable to dispose over the prevailing technical-economic complex to achieve any socially meaningful goal.

The nature of Nazi power is the decisive consideration. Certainly any sophisticated discussion of Nazism has to acknowledge the relative autonomy of the political from the economic apparatus, and recognize that at this decisive moment in history power in one realm did not automatically translate to power in the other.[39] A key but generally unposed question about power is the congruence of an aspiring social force with society's actual level of development.

As Bloch said: 'Not all people exist in the same now.'[40] Those who clamoured for a return to the past rejected, and ultimately took a kind of suicidal vengeance on, the twentieth-century world. They were, in

Bloch's term, a 'non-synchronous remainder' living a 'non-synchronous contradiction.' The primary problem was not that the German lower middle class turned to Nazism in droves but that it *existed in the first place* as a particularly regressive social constellation retaining political and ideological legitimacy in the fatal conjuncture of the 1920s and 1930s. Bloch speaks of 'synchronous contradictions' in which the 'impeded future' contained in the Now can be set free by a social class whose being is synchronous with the possibilities of this 'impeded technical benefaction.'[41] No political force, try as it may, can reshape a society *against* its actual historical possibilities. If it can indeed cripple or destroy the society, there is no wishing away the realities of an attained level of historical development. Even the ruler of Germany's totalitarian state was impotent to achieve the illusory aims of his class in the face of its fundamental historical weakness—in the face of the inappropriateness of its goals to the prevailing economic-technical complex and its possibilities. In that society, only a genuinely alternative movement in power could have avoided the economic fate of Nazism, its ultimate acquiescence to the structural limits imposed by German capitalism even as it commanded it. Genuine power is socially effective power, the ability to shape society in accord with its actual possibilities, to move confidently towards the future, to be congruent by orientation and disposition with the demands of *this* society. The Nazis lacked all of these. The ascendancy of this class was the most sinister reflection of a situation in which no other social class was sufficiently strong or sufficiently hegemonic to rule, and the movement able to grab state power was based (in Fritz Stern's words) on a 'wild leap from political reality.'[42]

We have seen that the 'wild leap' had already been taken from the very beginning of Nazism in *Mein Kampf;* indeed it received its shape long before, in the middle of the nineteenth century. If the projection of all of Germany's problems onto the Jews was already built into Nazism this testifies to the incongruence of the 'little men' with the advanced capitalist world. This meant that forces rooted more authentically in that world, like monopoly capital, were bound to triumph when it was a question of hard economic realities, such as ending the depression or preparing for war.

Nevertheless, this virulent outlook had already achieved a certain autonomy from its social sources, was a 'normal' current of German life, and could be reshaped into a legitimate political programme. Their despair about the present, the impossible project of revising history, the redemption of the *Volk*, the turn to unreason, and the fixation on the Jews as the cause of all evil—each step of this wild leap constituted part of the appeal of Nazism. The other part was its determination to *do something* about all of this. Once the Nazis were in power, this determination would meet the limits of reality.

THE FINAL SOLUTION

From the beginning the Nazi *enragés* represented the impossibility of reshaping the twentieth century to the tastes and needs of the *Mittelstand;* they stood for the urge to retreat from a world they hated, and the impossibility of that retreat. They also represented the mad and evil visions of victory which grew out of this feverish, yet sterile soil. After 1933 the Nazis possessed the political power—and military and technological means—with which to try to carry out this retreat imagined as a victory.

Retreat imagined as a victory: this is after all, the meaning of the torchlight parades, the burning of books, the creation of a specifically 'Aryan' culture, the great rallies and celebrations. But none of this could pacify either the pain which had driven the lower middle class onto the political stage—which must only have intensified as their actual social and economic situation worsened—or the antisemitic rage which was its insane product. Given the inevitability of its failure on every other level, Nazism could succeed *only* by addressing and solving 'the Jewish problem.'

This is why the logic of Nazism leads to the Final Solution. It seems clear that no one, even Adolf Hitler, fully and consciously grasped that this is where the rupture with reality by his impotent class would lead. In their first years of power, writes Schleunes, the Nazis 'stumbled' towards a solution. Each step was an improvisation, a response to specific pressures and situations, and each step led to a further impasse. 'They were certain only that a solution was necessary. This commitment carried the Nazi system along the twisted road to Auschwitz.'[43]

The extermination of six million Jews, successfully eliminating Jews from most of Central and Eastern Europe, was the Nazis' one great victory. The Final Solution reflects impotence in power. In radically fulfilling the dream of *völkisch* antisemitism it was the act of those who, having no effective power to shape the social world, still disposed over the political and military might to try to destroy the force allegedly at the source of its evils. This logic, inherent in Nazism from its origin, was finally stated by Hitler in 1939 and put into action by him in 1941 or 1942.[44] As Germany's defeat in the war became at first possible, then likely, then inevitable, the extermination apparatus only intensified its mission. As the prospect of real victory faded, their mad project to save civilization from the Jewish demon only accelerated. By exterminating the people who incarnated it, evil could still be destroyed. Only in this barbaric way could the 'little man' become the master race.

UNFIT FOR THE MODERN WORLD OR PART OF IT?

In conclusion, what is the source of the impotent and mad rage that led to the Holocaust? Much about Nazism seems to dispute my analyses of it as a lower middle class phenomenon. From the beginning the party proclaimed itself beyond class conflict, seeking to harmonize proletarian and bourgeois in the Aryan state. However deluded, its primary object was the well-being of all Germans, irrespective of class. Moreover, it called itself not only the 'National Socialist' but the 'German Workers' Party.' And in fact, by 1935 over a quarter of its membership were industrial workers—the largest number (662,000) of any occupational category in the 2.5 million member party.[45] This leads us to the root question: was Nazism the response of a 'backward' class resisting integration into the modern world,[46] or did it rather reflect a rage towards that world by those already accustomed and acculturated to it? Was the real root of the problem that Germany, industrializing later than Britain, developed unevenly, its older social layers put into exaggerated tension with its newer ones until an explosion was reached?

For Bloch the central characteristic of Nazism was that it emerged from 'non-synchronous' people—remnants of earlier social forms who persisted into a present for which they were unfit. 'If misery only afflicted synchronous people, even though of different positions, origins, and consciousness, it could not make them march in such different directions, especially so far backwards. They would not have such difficulty "understanding" the Communist language which is quite completely synchronous and precisely oriented to the most advanced economy. Synchronous people could not permit themselves to be so largely brutalized and romanticized, in spite of their mediate position, which keeps them economically stupid, in spite of all the semblance that it has a place there.'[47]

Or is the root of Nazism exactly the opposite, the *successful* progress of the modern world? In *Dialectic of Enlightenment*, Max Horkheimer and Theodor Adorno emphasized that self-denial and renunciation were inherent in the Western programme of the domination of nature, a project not limited to bourgeois society but whose literary record was at least as old as the *Odyssey*. Fascism, and indeed antisemitism, are seen as one pole of the dialectic of Western civilization itself. As domination progressed, so did the mad revolt of brutalized nature, culminating in the antisemitism of twentieth-century totalitarianism—rooted precisely in its most 'synchronous' people.

Its result was not liberation but barbarism: 'the rebellion of suppressed nature against domination, directly useful to domination.'[48] The Frankfurt thinkers saw this barbarism as dialectically linked to the progress of civilization. This is what Herbert Marcuse meant by saying that totalitarian violence 'came from the structure of existing society.'[49] For Marcuse, Adorno and Horkheimer, intensified domination and renunciation make such explosions inevitable. Did Auschwitz express the barbarity chosen by those unwilling or unable to join the modern world, as I have suggested with Bloch, or is its secret the explosion of the repressed side of our long journey away from barbarism and towards civilization? In fact, Auschwitz surely reflects *both:* a consummately civilized barbarism. If they broke through barriers to behaviour long equated with being civilized itself, the Nazis did so under the full weight of domination and renunciation, possible only in advanced civilization, using the technical and organizational sophistication available only in that civilization. The 'return' to the most brutally primitive levels of behaviour was a product of the present using the tools of the present.

In other words, we must turn to modernity itself, as well as the lower middle class rebellion against it, to explain the Holocaust. Or rather, not to 'modernity' as such, but to the fact that after the workers' defeat in 1918 no alternative remained to its most oppressive forms. Defeat was the universal formative experience in Germany. Demoralized, without a way forward, many workers felt such defeat no less than the lower middle class. The ideological and political amalgam they accepted was rooted in a despair which they could see as their own, containing much truth about the destructive side of the modern world. Truth, that is, perceived from the sad position of being unable to create a more humane modern world. If workers moved towards Nazism it was because defeat had made them responsive to the rage of the lower middle class.

Rather than confusing our class analysis, this fact completes it. As during any social crisis, as with any movement, the dominant party was not wholly of a single class. Others joined it for their own reasons, lending their own weight to the movement while accepting its central thrust. In this tragic situation, the impotent rage of the 'little man' without a way forward became generalized beyond the class in which it originated and to whose situation it gave focus. In the years of crisis after the war, more and more Germans became despairing, turned therefore into 'little men,' and found their way to the Nazi revolt. Their mixture of fantasy and reality, of impotence and power, of regression and modernity pointed towards total war and extermination of the Jews as its natural outcome.

NOTES

1. Peter Phillips places great emphasis on the system of terror and conditioning. See *The Tragedy of Nazi Germany*, New York, 1969, ch. 4.

2. This is well described in William Sheridan Allen's account of the first months of Nazism in power in Thälberg. See *The Nazi Seizure of Power: The Experience of a Single German Town 1930–1935*, Chicago 1965, Part Two.

3. See Höhne, *The Order of the Death's Head*, New York, 1970, pp. 370–3, 397–400.

4. See Ibid., pp. 394–6.

5. See Richard Grunberger, *The 12-Year Reich: A Social History of Nazi Germany 1933–1945*, New York 1971, pp. 460–6.

6. J. Barrington Moore Jr., *The Social Origins of Dictatorship and Democracy: Lord and Peasant in the Making of the Modern World*, Boston 1966, p. 437.

7. Ibid., pp. 413–508.

8. In addition to George L. Mosse's writings cited above, see his *Germans and Jews: The Right, the Left, and the Search for a 'Third Force' in pre-Nazi Germany*, New York 1970, ch. 2 and 3.

9. Mosse, *The Crisis of German Ideology*, New York, 1964, p. 151.

10. Ibid., p. 154.

11. Ibid., p. 301.

12. Moore, *Social Origins*, p. 291.

13. Quoted in Ralf Dahrendorf, *Society and Democracy in Germany*, Garden City 1969, p. 67.

14. Karl A. Schleunes, *The Twisted Road to Auschwitz*, Urbana, 1970, ch. 1.

15. Barrington Moore, *Injustice*, White Plains, 1978, p. 329.

16. Sebastian Haffner, *Failure of a Revolution: Germany 1918–19*, London 1973, p. 14.

17. Ibid., p. 77. See also pp. 81–2.

18. For the prehistory of this fratricide see Carl E. Schorske, *German Social Democracy 1905–1917: The Development of the Great Schism*, Cambridge, Mass. 1955, Part V.

19. Henry Pachter, *Modern Germany*, Boulder, 1978, p. 104.

20. Moore, *Injustice,* pp. 398–411; see Kühnl, 'Problems of a Theory of German Fascism,' pp. 28–31.

21. Peter Merkl, *Political Violence under the Swastika,* Princeton, 1975, p. x.

22. Moore, *Injustice,* pp. 412–13.

23. Theodore Abel, *Why Hitler Came into Power,* New York 1938.

24. Nolte, *The Three Faces of Fascism,* pp. 312–23.

25. Nazi ideology is studied by Jäckel as well as by Horst von Maltitz, *The Evolution of Hitler's Germany* (New York 1973). Although they have both rightly insisted on the theoreticians of 'opportunism') and on the internal coherence of the Nazi world view, both stop short of doing for the Nazi period what Mosse does for the pre-Nazi-period—namely, of showing the internal logic of völkisch thought.

26. Franz Neumann, *Behemoth,* New York, 1944, p. 37.

27. *Mein Kampf,* pp. 442–51.

28. Moore, *Injustice,* p. 32.

29. See for example, *The Crisis of German Ideology,* New York, 1974, ch. 17, and *Nazism,* New Brunswick, 1978, pp. 120–22.

30. See David Schoenbaum, *Hitler's Social Revolution: Class and Status in Nazi Germany 1933–39,* Garden City 1967, pp. 132–43.

31. Poulantzas, *Fascism and Dictatorship,* London, 1974, pp. 237–64.

32. Ibid., p. 98.

33. For a discussion of recent Marxist thinking on this question see Anson Rabinbach, 'Toward a Marxist Theory of Fascism and National Socialism', *New German Critique,* no. 11, Spring 1977, p. 138.

34. Poulantzas, pp. 71–113.

35. Schoenbaum, *Hitler's Social Revolution,* p. 285.

36. See Karl Hardach, *The Political Economy of Germany in the Twentieth Century,* Berkeley 1980, pp. 64–9.

37. George Lichtheim, *The Concept of Ideology and Other Essays,* New York 1967, p. 227.

38. Ernst Bloch, 'Nonsynchronism and the Obligation to its Dialectics', *New German Critique,* no. 11, p. 35.

39. See Anson Rabinbach, 'Poulantzas and the Problem of Fascism,' *New German Critique,* 8, Spring 1976, pp. 137–8.

40. Ernst Bloch, *On Karl Marx,* New York, 1981, p. 22.

41. Ibid., p. 35.

42. Fritz Stern, *The Politics of Cultural Despair: A Study in the Rise of the Germanic Ideology,* Garden City 1965, p. 361.

43. Schleunes, p. viii.

44. See Yehuda Bauer, 'Genocide', *Annals of the American Association of Political and Social Science,* July 1980, pp. 41–2.

45. Moore, *Injustice*, pp. 403–9.

46. Barrington Moore's works form perhaps the most sophisticated argument for this position. In addition to *Injustice* see *Social Origins*, where the democracy and gradualism of liberal capitalist society are compared with fascism and Communism.

47. Bloch, p. 28.

48. Max Horkheimer and Theodor W. Adorno, *Dialectic of Enlightenment*, New York 1982, p. 185.

49. Herbert Marcuse, Foreword to *Negations: Essays in Critical Theory*, Boston 1968, p. xii.

Richard C. Rubenstein

RELIGION AND THE ORIGINS OF THE DEATH CAMPS: A PSYCHOANALYTIC INTERPRETATION

The Eichmann Trial is now a part of history. In fate and in substance, the killer has been reunited with his victims. The dreary rehearsal of the facts was perhaps important, but the trial always pointed beyond itself to the question of *why* Eichmann and thousands of others, often men of exceptional ability and education, were compelled to elect their grue-some careers as executioners. Once the defendant's legal sanity was established, psychological considerations were precluded by the nature of the judicial process. Nevertheless, the question of why the events took place remains of far greater consequence than the legal question of the guilt of the participants. Though the Germans initiated the extermina-tion machine, they were by no means without the active support and sympathy of many of the people whom they had overwhelmed. To achieve a catharsis of insight into the origins of the death camps is by no means a solely German necessity.

Men will be trying to understand why it happened for centuries. No two explanations will entirely coincide. No single attempt at explana-tion, including this one, will be entirely adequate. There are, however, some aspects of the death camps concerning which we are now quite certain. Common-sense explanations simply don't explain. None of the ordinary hypotheses of lawlessness, lust, the desire for personal gain, utility, or even simple hatred is really plausible. In order to understand the Nazis, we are forced beyond the ordinary canons of common sense. Nazi motivations largely defied normal expectations or predictions.

Considerations of usefulness did not deter the Nazis. Had their primary interest been to win the war, they never would have made the death camps such a central concern. They would have utilized, rather than alienated, every available talent, Jewish or gentile. Toward the end of the war, the dazed and defeated Germans were promised that Ger-man science would produce a secret weapon capable of turning the tide. Not infrequently an atomic weapon was hinted at. Ironically one of the

46

most important sources of talent available to Germany's enemies in creating nuclear weapons was German-trained scientists who fled their native land when anti-Semitism left them no alternative. The sheer need for a compliant labor force in wartime should have dictated an entirely different approach, not only to the Jews but to the subject nations as well. Had final victory really been the Nazi aim, their whole conduct of the war would have been different. The history of the period suggests that, for the diehard Nazis as opposed to the average German, the war was not a means to victory. It was an end in itself wherein the Nazis permitted themselves behavioral freedoms impossible in peacetime. The Nazis often seemed far more intent upon achieving irrational victories over defenseless Jews and Gypsies than a real victory over their military opponents. They won the war that really counted for them, the war against the Jews. Eichmann's alleged statement that, though all else fail, he would go to his grave content in the knowledge that he had helped to kill over five million Jews is very much to the point.

In dealing with a movement guided by so great an element of mystique and ritual, it is impossible to avoid the question of religious origins. Although the Nazis have been called pagans, they were never genuine pagans like the ancient Greeks. They were satanic anti-Christians, saying no to much that Christianity affirmed and saying yes to much that was absolutely forbidden in Christianity. There is a striking parallel between the diehard Nazi and the priest who celebrated the Black Mass in medieval witchcraft. The satanic priest was never an atheist or a pagan. His problem was that he believed too much. He celebrated the Black Mass, not because of lack of belief, but because he hated God and wanted to invert normal religious standards. Had he really been an unbeliever, he would not have been so dependent upon religion to determine the character of his rebellion.[1] He would in all probability have found better and more constructive ways to occupy his time. The Nazis were religious rebels rather than genuine unbelievers.

In one area the Nazis took Christianity very seriously. They did not invent a new villain. They took over the two-thousand-year-old Christian tradition of the Jew as villain. Nor did the Nazis create a new hatred. Folk hatred of the Jews is at least as old as Christianity. The Nazis intensified what they found. They created very little *de novo*. Nevertheless, in their intensification of the old hatreds, the Nazis added a new and radical element which had never been present in Christianity. They transformed a theological conflict, normally limited in its overt destructiveness by religious and moral considerations, into a biological struggle in which only one conclusion was thinkable—the total extermination of every living Jew. Where Christianity usually rested content in seeking to convince the Jews of the error of their ways and to seek error's remedy in conversion, Nazism had no interest in regarding the Jews as anything but objects to be exterminated. Nothing the Jews could do by way of confession, submission, surrender, betrayal, or apostasy could have altered their destined roles in the Nazi system.

The roots of the death camps must be sought in the mythic structure of Christianity. This assertion must not be regarded as an imputation of guilt against Christianity for the death camps. The Nazis were rebels *against* Christianity. The religious rebel is far more demonic than the simple pagan or the genuine atheist. Myths concerning the demonological role of the Jews have been operative in Christianity for centuries without creating so dire an entailment. In addition to the religious background, the peculiar ambivalence of an influential part of the German literary and intellectual community toward Christianity in the nineteenth and twentieth centuries, as well as the response of the German people to defeat after World War I, were necessary preconditions before the Nazis could utilize the religious myths with such explosive force.

The oldest origins of the death camps may be seen in the extremely complicated relationships of ancient Judaism and primitive Christianity. The rival faiths have never been entirely distinct and independent religious movements. The Church has always regarded herself as the fulfillment and the true successor of the Synagogue. This is very apparent in the writings of St. Paul, the apostle who first carried the message of Christianity beyond the confines of the Jewish community. For Paul, only a Christian was a true Israelite. The Jews who rejected the Christ, though Israelites by birth, could not be considered Israelites after the spirit. In making his point, Paul delighted in drawing a parallel between the rivalry of Christian and Jew in his day and the ancient rivalry between Ishmael and Isaac. In Abraham's times, not all who were of the patriarch's *flesh* became children of his promise. Paul drew the conclusion that only those who had faith in the Christ, as Abraham had faith in the Lord, would truly belong to the community of God's elect. Faith in the Christ, not membership after the flesh, was for Paul the *conditio sine qua non* of participation in the New Israel.[2] Paul never doubted that the Church was the fulfillment of the old Jewish community, because he was convinced that the revelation incarnate in the Christ was the fruition of the revelation originally given to Moses. From its inception, Christianity considered itself the successor of Judaism rather than an entirely different religion.

The conception of the Church as the true Israel necessarily involved a very negative evaluation of the old Israel. This is not yet explicit in Paul. He regarded the "unbelief" of the Jews as part of the divine plan whereby the gentiles were first to be brought to the Lord, and he was convinced that ultimately the Jews would accept the Christ. He felt a real sense of kinship with those whom he regarded as erring brethren.

Within a hundred years, the split had become bitter and irrevocable. The Jews had fought two wars against the Romans in C.E. 66–70 and 132–135. As a result of the first war, the Jerusalem Temple, the center of Jewish religious life, was destroyed. The young Church took this as a double sign. It was seen as confirmation of Paul's contention that those who lived in the Christ were dead to Jewish Law, a great part of which required the destroyed Temple for its observance. It was also taken as proof of God's punishment of the Jews for their rejection of the Christ and complicity in his death.

During the Second Roman War (132–135), a significant part of the Jewish community, including Rabbi Akiba, regarded Simeon Bar Kochba, the leader of the revolt, as Israel's true Messiah. The Christians, many of whom were still of Jewish extraction, naturally interpreted this as a compounding of Jewish vice. Not only had the Jews rejected Christ, the true Messiah, but they had gone astray after a false pretender. When the Romans defeated the Jews and inflicted their devastatingly cruel revenge upon the losers, the Christians took the event as further proof of God's rejection of Israel and the truth of Christianity.

The development of the bitter religious antagonisms is plainly visible in the writings of Justin Martyr, a Palestinian Christian apologist who flourished about one hundred years after Paul. Paul's mild doctrine of the Old and New Israel was altered by Justin into an extreme contrast between the Church as the New Israel and the Synagogue as the despised and rejected of the Lord. There is a remainder of compassion in Paul which is absent from Justin. In Justin's writings an old Jewish idea—God's punishment of sinful Israel—has been combined with a new sin, the murder of the Christ. This murder was soon regarded as the murder of God. As we shall see, the Christian conception of the Jew as deicide is a significant component of the religious origins of the death camps.

In his *Dialogue With Tryphon,* Justin frequently expresses the conviction that Jewish disaster is nothing more than what the Jews deserve. A frequently quoted passage indicates how violent these feelings have become. Referring to circumcision, Justin declared:

> [It] was given for a sign . . . that you alone suffer what you now justly suffer; and that your land may be desolate, and your cities burned with fire; and that strangers may eat your fruit in your presence, and not one of you may go up to Jerusalem.[3]

This was the reaction of one of the earliest and most important Christian theologians concerning the fate of the Jews after their defeat in the Judaeo-Roman war of 132–135. Justin understood that Judaism and Christianity are religions of history and that a principal validation of their claims must be the evidence of history. Few such evidences are as enthusiastically set forth in Justin as the historical fact of Jewish defeat by the Romans. For both Justin and his rabbinic opponents, the war is more than a military contest. The Romans are the retributive instruments of the Lord against a sinful Israel. They play the same role in Justin's interpretation of history as did the Babylonians in the prophetic interpretation.

Sigmund Freud has suggested in *Moses and Monotheism* that envy of the Jew as the chosen of the Lord is an important component in anti-Semitism. This envy would seem to be exemplified in the Church's claim to be the true Israel. In effect, Justin claims that the Christians rather than the Jews are now the well-beloved of the Father. The Jews made an extraordinary claim about themselves—that they were in a special and decisive way God's chosen people. Instead of ridiculing the claim, a very significant segment of the non-Jewish world took it seriously. Lacking power of their own, the Jews compensated by magically claiming a pre-eminent portion of divine concern. To their ultimate disaster, the claim was met with neither scorn nor ridicule. Once accepted, as it was in a paradoxical way by Christianity, it aroused envy and the desire to displace the favored child.

Though the Jews were hated before Christianity, especially in Hellenistic Egypt, the special and frequently pathological character of the hatred for them under Christianity must be seen as in part related to one of the oldest conflicts between Jew and Christian, that of who had the right truly to be reckoned as the elect of the Lord. By insisting that it was the New Israel, the Church made the claim that only its adherents were truly Jews before the Lord. Those who prized this status were necessarily threatened by the real Jews, who challenged the claim simply by their continued existence. Apart from anything the Jews said or did to appease their more powerful rivals, the very existence of the Jews was a threat to the New Israel. This was underscored by greater Jewish familiarity with the world which had given birth to Jesus and their continued rejection of him. Even when the manifest dialogue between Jew and Christian was cordial, Christians could surmise that Jews regarded the Christ-tradition as an embellished fantasy on the career of another Jew. Soren Kierkegaard has commented that the faith of a Christian dwells over a sea of doubt seventy thousand fathoms deep. He has also suggested some of the hideous pain which such doubt can render. Through no one's fault, the unspoken denial of Jesus by the Jews was frequently the occasion of much pain and potential loss of personal moorings in the believing Christian.

In the concentration camps Jews were murdered, not for what they did, but for what they were. No possible alteration of Jewish behavior could have prevented this fatality; the crime was simply to be a Jew. Jewish existence and the tenacity of Jewish survival were in and of themselves an affront to the claims of the Church. Faced with this survival, the Church usually interpreted Jewish existence as did Justin —that is, as filled with deserved sorrow, thus establishing the greatest possible credulity for the Christian claim to being the true Israel.

In the nineteenth and twentieth centuries, the Church's claim to being the New Israel was better understood by Christianity's Teutonic enemies than Jews or Christians. Resentment against Christianity and its enforced displacement of the Teutonic gods has been a significant motif in German life and letters since the Napoleonic wars. This resentment had important roots in the peculiar historical and geographical situation of the Germans. One root can be found in the old tension between the Teutonic north and the Latin south, from which Catholic Christianity originated. Charlemagne's forced conversion of the Saxons and Luther's break with Rome were in part manifestations of this tension. Modern German nationalism was first aroused during the War of Liberation against the French, 1806–1813. Many of the German writers of the day interpreted their war against the French as a continuation of the age-old struggle of Teuton against Latin. Christianity was regarded as the product and imposition of a foreign Latin culture. It was resented in influential German circles. Nazism was an outgrowth of this aspect of German cultural history. Few themes are as vulgarly persistent in the stenographic reports of Hitler's wartime "table talk" as his hatred and contempt for Christianity.

Few German philosophers have been as influential as Hegel. Though by no means an anti-Semite in the twentieth-century sense, he gave one section of his *Early Theological Writings* the title, "Is Judea Then the Fatherland of the Teutons?" Hegel complains that Christianity has emptied Valhalla of its gods and forced the German people to accept Jewish gods and fables in place of their own.[4] This observation presupposes the Hegelian concept of *Volksreligion,* in which the religion, mythology, and social organization of an ethnic community (*Volk*) are regarded as a single organic unity. When any element in the constitution of the *Volk* is displaced or discarded, the unity of the whole is broken. Such a breach in *Volk*-unity occurred when the indigenous Teutonic gods were displaced by the foreign gods and myths of the Jews. For

Hegel, the gods of a people are an objectification of the inner nature of that people. By rejecting their ancestral gods, the Germans were in the deepest sense rejecting themselves. Hegel did not carry his own logic to its ultimate conclusion in action. He was, however, followed by others such as Erich Ludendorff and Alfred Rosenberg who were more prepared than he to enter that realm. They concluded that German alienation and self-estrangement could be terminated only by an end to the Jewish gods of Christianity.

This hankering for the simplicities of an indigenous *Volk*-community was to become part of the reaction against the distressing complexities of an evolving modern technopolitan culture, with its confusing mixture of morals, faiths, and peoples. The yearning figured very largely in Nazi ideology. It received one of its simplest formulations in the watchword of Hitler's Reich, *"Ein Volk! Ein Reich! Ein Führer!"* In such a community there could be no room for the disturbing dissonances of the Jews or even of Jewish Christianity.

There is a double irony in the claim of the Church that it is the New Israel. It was inconvenient for the Teutonists to uproot the powerful Christian Church. They did vent their anger on the infinitely weaker Jews, thus providing themselves with a cheap victory for Teutonism. It would have been infinitely more difficult for the Nazis to uproot the hold of Christianity on the German people. That, however, was their ultimate intent. The ancient Jewish-Christian quarrel over the true Israel led to the utilization of the original Israel as a surrogate victim for the presumed sins of the New Israel in effecting the alienation of the German people from their native traditions. There were times when the Nazis had a clearer image of what and why they were fighting than either Jews or Christians.

While this helps to explain the origins of the conflict, it does not explain the murderous hatred felt by the anti-Semite for the Jew or why only extermination was regarded as the "final solution." This can in part be accounted for by the accusation against the Jews that they are the deicides, the murderers of God. The Christian religion, alone among the religions of the world, begins with a murder—the murder of God. Since then, it has used the cross, the instrument of execution, as its decisive symbol. In Christian thought the Jews play a twofold role: they provide *both* the incarnate Deity *and* His murderers. The assertions that the Christian Church is the true Israel and that the Jews are the rejected ones are of a piece. Without the alleged special relationship between Israel and God, with its implied magic potency, the Jews could never have provided either God or His murderers. Furthermore, the very envy implicit in the assertion that the Christians are now the elect of God was bolstered by the accusation that those formerly chosen (the Jews) exhibited deicidal hostility, thereby compelling the Father to seek a new and truly beloved child.

The seemingly contradictory complex of claims and accusations is not at all unlike the dynamics of sibling rivalry. Even the accusation "You have murdered or wanted to murder the Father" has this element. In Christian theology, Jesus as the Christ is God, the Son of God. The violence done to His person is, however, equally a violence against God the Father.

The accusation that a rival has sought to do away with the Father is a mode of displacing one's own feelings of guilt for similar unconscious hostility. The anti-Semite could thus envy the Jew as the beloved of the Father and, at the same time, regard him as the despised rival who wanted to murder the Father. The entire system exaggerated the importance of the Jews out of all realistic proportions. They were not seen merely as the defeated and impotent people they were, lacking a normal political life of their own; instead, the very marginality of their existence elicited mythic interpretations. Those who were homeless (*heimatlos*) became uncanny (*unheimlich*), the decisive actors in the drama of God and the devil, sin and innocence, salvation and eternal damnation. They were regarded as possessing a terrible magic potency, both as the people in whose midst God-in-the-flesh had been born and as His murderers. This helps to explain the irrational delusion, so persistently held, that the Jews must be destroyed lest they destroy the non-Jewish world.[5]

The terrible significance of the accusation of deicide cannot be overstressed. At the extremely important vulgar level, the cry of "Christ-killer" has, more often than not, accompanied the instigation of anti-Semitic violence. One of the most searing scenes in André Schwartz-Bart's *The Last of the Just* is the one in which the little German children anticipate the development of Nazism by almost murdering little Ernie Levy as a Christ-killer. In our own times, the deicide theme has been examined by Freud, Dostoevsky, Sartre, and others who have understood that the murder and/or displacement of God is mankind's most demonic fantasy.

According to Freud, civilization and religion began with a "primal crime" in which the father of the original human horde was cannibalistically murdered by his sons, in order to gain sexual possession of his females. The father proved more potent dead than alive. His son-murderers experienced intense regret at their terrible deed and tried consciously to suppress its memory. The unconscious memory of the deed continued to agonize the sons and their progeny, thereby causing the murdered father to be imagined as the Heavenly Father. For Freud, the supreme object of human worship is none other than the first object of human criminality. Freud maintained that a great deal that is irrational and opaque in the ritual and myth of both Christianity and Judaism can be traced back to mankind's unconscious memory of its earliest parricide and to the contradictory feelings of guilt and promethean self-assertion which the criminal deed engendered. In the sacrificial death of the Christ, Freud saw a "return of the repressed." Mankind was compelled to repeat, at least symbolically, its original crime against God, while attempting to atone for the continuing feelings of guilt which that unconscious memory sustained.

We will never know whether Freud's aetiological myth is historically correct. It is psychologically illuminating that Christianity depicts itself as commencing its independent career with such a crime. Freud also believed that the cannibalistic aspects of the primal crime are repeated in the Mass, which he regards as both a symbolic repetition of and a ritual catharsis for the original crime.

Freud's myth of the origins of religion is less important in terms of what it tells about human history than in what it suggests about the agonies and conflicts which continue to beset mankind.[6] Adult maturity is bought at a terrible price. Control of one's deepest instincts is the precondition for all men of their continuing participation in the social order. This is brought about with neither ease nor good will. Every society hangs precariously over the precipice of mankind's conflicting feelings concerning its instinctual life. There is something in all men which would destroy the slender fabric of personal and social control that makes civilization possible. If Freud's myth of original parricide tells us little about human origins, the myth intuits a great deal concerning the awesome ambivalence men feel toward those who symbolize authority and civilization. *The murder of God is an immensely potent symbol of man's primal desire to do away with his impediments to instinctual gratification.*

Very frequently Christians object to the assertion that they are taught that the Jews are the Christ-killers. They claim that they are taught that *all* men are responsible through their sins for the death of the Christ. This is the way in which the subject is dealt with in many church schools today. The attempt to share the blame is of doubtful efficacy. Though all men may have been responsible from the religious point of view, the actual deed was committed by a specific group of men. The New Testament is explicit as to who these men were. It is equally explicit with regard to the continuing involvement of their descendants in the affair. Pontius Pilate does not make the ultimate decision. He offers the Jews the opportunity to choose Jesus or Barabbas for release from the death penalty. The Jews chose Barabbas. Pilate insists that he finds no fault with Jesus. He washes his hands of the affair and permits the execution. The onus of guilt is clearly upon the Jews. In Matthew they reply to Pilate's protestations of innocence: "His blood be upon us and on our children" (Matthew 27:25). The murder of God is thus depicted as a continuing source of guilt of the Jewish posterity.

The explosive significance of the crucifixion story as the myth of the death of God is well illuminated by Ivan Karamazov's reputed remark in Dostoevski's *The Brothers Karamazov*: "*If God does not exist, all things are permitted.*" In both Judaism and Christianity, all moral restraints are ultimately derivative of God's lordship over the created world. The wish to murder God is the terminal mythic expression of mankind's ineradicable temptation to moral anarchy. A world without God would be a world with no impediment to the gratification of desire, no matter how perverse or socially harmful. The perversity of the human heart finds its ultimate expression in the myth of the murder of God.

The death camps are one possibility in a world devoid of God. As Hannah Arendt has suggested,[7] the realm of the impossible ceases to exist in such a world; the limitations of reality become a parenthesis to be overthrown. By the same token, the desire for a world without limitation is a regressive hankering for the unrestrained gratification of the anarchic desires of childhood. There is an awesome fatality in Hitler's description of himself at the beginning of *Mein Kampf* as a *Müttersohnchen*, a little mother's boy. Though Hitler claimed that he outgrew this stage, many who knew him closely were convinced that he never did. In his hatred of his father, in his contempt for the limitation of moral as well as military reality, in his irrational intuitionism, in his utter failure to achieve an adult sexual relationship with a woman,[8] and in his final suicidal mania for himself and his country, the *Müttersohnchen* remained triumphant.

Leon Poliakov has suggested that the Nazi movement and its culminating expression, the death camp, were part of an anti-value explosion of the German people.[9] This is consistent with the idea of deicide. One wishes to murder God in order to be all that there is to be, all that one can be, and above all to do all that one wishes to do. The death camp was the place where the morally impossible finally became the commonplace and even the trivial for the Nazis; their desire was impeded only by the boredom of gratification.

The accusation that a people is deicidal implies that they are utterly beyond law. This may seem a strange accusation to make against the Jews, a people who were the creators of so vast a system of religious law. This seeming paradox did not escape Justin Martyr's attention. Unwit-

tingly this basically decent philosopher helped to create the demonological interpretation of the Jews which was to result in so much
bloodshed throughout the centuries. Justin maintained that only the
excessive moral weakness of the Jews made it necessary for them to be
placed under the discipline of the law. He interprets their outward
personal and moral conformity as the fruit of a terrible inner lawlessness. In a sense, Justin was an excellent intuitive psychologist. Socially
compliant behavior is achieved through an inner struggle against regressive anarchic tendencies. Unfortunately Justin turned his intuition
of what is a universal conflict into evidence of a special Jewish proclivity
toward evil. This contrasted, according to Justin, with those who experience the freedom of the Christ; they need none of the legal constraints
of the Jews. Only the enormity of the temptations of the deicidal people
make the special restrictions and inhibitions of the Law necessary.

A universal tendency toward moral anarchy was thus identified and
displaced onto the Jews. During the Middle Ages, the identification of
the Jew as the moral anarchist was intensified by his further identification with the Devil and the Anti-Christ. These identifications were already implicit in the crucifixion story and the rivalry between the two
religious communities. The identification with the Devil is explicit in the
Fourth Gospel, in which Jesus is depicted as saying to those who reject
his mission:

> If God were your Father, you would love me, for I proceeded
> and came forth from God; I came not of my own accord, but he
> sent me. . . . You are of your father the devil, and your will is to
> do your father's desires. He was a murderer from the begin-
> ning, and has nothing to do with the truth, because there is no
> truth in him. . . . But because I tell the truth, you do not be-
> lieve me. (John 8:42–45)

In medieval Europe, the only people who openly and successfully resisted Christianity were the Jews. The Germans tried and failed. Since
the Jews were the one people resident in Europe who had seen the
Christ and beheld His passion, their stubborn refusal to acknowledge
Him was ascribed to the supernatural power of their satanic master. The
only other group which continuously resisted Christianity were the
members of the satanic witch cult. The Jews were depicted as openly
worshipping the blackest of masters, whereas his non-Jewish devotees
were depicted as at least having the decency to pay their homage in
secrecy.[10]

The identification of the Jew with the Anti-Christ was implicit in the earliest Jewish rejection of the Christ. In medieval popular mythology, the final return and triumph of the Christ would be preceded by a battle waged between the forces of the Christ and those of the Anti-Christ. As the Christ was the son of God, born of a Jewish virgin, the Anti-Christ would be born of the union of a Jewish whore and the Devil. He would be raised in Galilee and trained by sorcerers and witches in the black arts. At the age of thirty he was to announce himself to the Jews in Jerusalem as their Messiah. His actual mission would last only three and a half years, the duration of Jesus' ministry. During this time he would unite all previous heresies, utilize the blackest of arts, and raise up a huge army to do his evil work. In some versions of the tradition, the army of the Anti-Christ is to battle against the legions of the Christ in a final armageddon in which Christ will ultimately be victorious. This was tied in with the myth of the ten lost tribes of Israel who were regarded as dwelling in prosperity somewhere in Asia in vast numbers. At the summons of the Anti-Christ, they would form a formidable host challenging the Lordship of the Christ over Christian Europe.[11] This is a medieval anticipation of the myth of "Jewish" Bolshevik hordes which the Nazis used so effectively. It was supported by the realistic dangers which stemmed from invasions and threats of invasions which Europe faced from the Huns, Turks, Mongols, and Arabs. Fear of the Anti-Christ's legions was a reflex of the folk anti-Semitism of European culture. The aggressive intentions of the anti-Semites elicited retaliatory anxieties which were embodied in the Anti-Christ myths.

It is interesting to note in passing that the identification of the Devil with the Jews has survived even Hitler in the German theater. In the recording of Goethe's *Faust*, Part I, presented by the Düsseldorf Schauspielhaus and recently released by the Deutsche Grammophon Gesellschaft, Gustof Gründgens plays Mephisto with distinctly Yiddish overtones. Gründgens popularized this interpretation of the Devil under the Nazis and has not seen fit to alter his Yiddish Mephisto nor apparently has anyone strongly objected in spite of the terrible history of our times.

The Anti-Christ was a sort of polar opposite of the Christ. As the Devil's Messiah, he represented a demonic reversal of the value system normative in Christian Europe. Unfortunately the Jewish response was hardly ever relevant. Faced with the Christ-killer accusation, Jews usually took the accusation seriously at the *manifest* level and protested their innocence. Seldom if ever did they understand that the accusation was an attempt by the accuser to deny his own lawless temptations by ascribing them to the Jews. The Jewish protestation of innocence only made matters worse. One of the worst aspects of the two-thousand-year-old Judaeo-Christian encounter has been their mutual incapacity to understand what was vital to the other. There was apparently no way in which Jew and Christian could simply acknowledge the problem of overcoming inner lawlessness to be a universal one. Each side could only bolster its own uncertain conviction of virtue by blackening the other. This dreary procedure has yet to be terminated.

No motive other than indecent willfulness and dedication to the demonic was permitted to explain the continued Jewish rejection of Christianity. Trachtenberg points out that the Jews were regarded as knowing the truth about the Christ but deliberately rejecting it. They were more often regarded by the Church as *heretics* than as *infidels*. No imagined crime was too heinous to be ascribed to them. As they had been guilty of the crucifixion, they were regarded as symbolically repeating the crime by the sacrificial murder of Christian victims especially at Passover time.

The blood libel accusation has persisted down to our own times. It was utilized by the Nazis. In the light of what we know of the sacrificial mode of religious life, the continued utilization of the ritual murder accusation against the Jews is by no means inexplicable. Religious sacrifice had its origins partially in the ritual murder of a human victim. The purpose of the offering was to assure the continued well-being and prosperity of the community through the death of the victim. Vicarious atonement figures very largely in such practices. There seems to be something in most of us which, when we are sufficiently threatened, sees safety in the death of another. "Let him die instead of me" is an age-old cry of mankind.[12]

From a psychoanalytic point of view, the doctrine that the death of the Christ atones vicariously for the sins of mankind is an example of the *return of the repressed*. In Biblical Judaism, atonement was effectuated by the scapegoat offering on the Day of Atonement. The animal's character as a surrogate for an original human victim now seems indisputable. At some time in the past, the community or communities which had preceded Israel offered human victims to effectuate atonement and cleansing. When John the Baptist greets Jesus upon seeing him at the River Jordan, he is depicted as saying: "Behold the Lamb of God who taketh away the sins of the world" (John 1:29). John is depicted as reidentifying the intended human victim with the animal surrogate. The circle was thus completed. Once again the death of a divine-human victim brought forgiveness and security. The promise Christianity offers to its believers is that this once and for all human sacrifice has the power to save mankind from its sins. Many of the dynamic elements of ritual murder are present.

There are, however, significant differences between the ritual aspects of the crucifixion and other sacrificial deaths. In pagan ritual murder, the community accepts its own guilt for participating in the sacred violence. No outsider is blamed for the deed, which is regarded as a sad and bloody necessity. The community must choose between two unpleasant alternatives: a limited act of violence in which one dies for all, or the very real danger that all will succumb as a result of the false mercy of omitting the sacrifice. Faced with these alternatives, the pagan accepted his own guilt and reluctantly committed the bloody deed.

In Christianity, the victim is no longer a pre-eminent member of the community but the incarnate Deity. Furthermore, the Church did not have to accept the guilt of the deed. The guilt was ascribed to the Jews. Little attention, however, has been paid to the fact that the death of Jesus was a once and forever act. Insofar as the need for a scapegoat remained an urgent psychic necessity, as it was in times of stress, the memory of the one sacrifice was insufficient to satisfy the hunger for a victim. There is real irony in the age-old anti-Semitic accusation that the Jew practices ritual murder. The radical anti-Semite lives in a world which remains endangered as long as it is uncleansed of Jewry. For the anti-Semite, there is only one solution, the extermination of the Jew. This is ritual murder, made infinitely less painful by the Christ-killer accusation. The sins and the guilts which beset his existence demand the death of the Jew. The Nazi "final solution" represented one vast explosion of all of the repressed forces which in paganism had been channeled into the controlled and regulated slaughter of one victim at a time. When the anti-Semite accuses the Jew of ritual murder, he accuses him of the very crime which he himself intends to commit. What he fails to comprehend is the inherent gratuity of the whole process. The death of the victim never solves real problems. The only thing the death of six million Jews may have taught some Germans was that they had only themselves to blame for their own predicament. There were no longer any Jews available upon whom to hang the onus of defeat.

As I have suggested, though Nazism has been attacked as pagan, the movement was never really pagan. Such accusations do an injustice to paganism. Nazism was an inverted and demonic transformation of Jewish and Christian values, combined with a Romantic hankering after a paganism it never understood. It needed the Judaeo-Christian *yes* to assert the Nazi *no*. The Greeks were pagan. For them the decisive misdeed was *hubris*, the taking upon oneself of more than one's allotted portion in the nature of things. *Hubris*, man's rebellion against his limits, was always a limited self-aggrandizement. It was exhibited in the folly of Oedipus, seeking to avoid a fate which came closer with every step he took to escape it; it was also manifest in the desire of Clytemnestra, whose adulterous passion irretrievably furthered the fated destruction of the house of Atreus. *Hubris* never signified complete and total lawlessness, such as is implied in the notion of *deicide*. It was followed, as night follows day, by inevitable *nemesis*, which righted the wrong and restored nature's disturbed equilibrium. Good and evil were rooted in the very nature of the cosmos itself. Evil was in a sense unnatural; inevitably the fates would overtake its perpetrators. All things were measured out, and even the gods could not trespass their assigned limits.[13]

Nazism is the product of a negative reaction to the Judaeo-Christian world. As much as the nineteenth- and twentieth-century Teutonists wanted to rid themselves of Christianity, they were far more influenced by it than they imagined. In the end, the Nazis were able to *negate* Christianity and its values while using the Christian myth of Jewish villainy to their own purposes. They were never able to restore a genuine paganism. Perhaps Goethe foresaw the ironies of a German attempt to restore paganism when in *Faust*, Part II, he made the union of Faust, the German, and the Greek Helen of Troy result in the birth of Euphorion. Euphorion very quickly evaporates into nothingness. Nazism is Judaeo-Christian heresy, not paganism. It presupposes, though it overturns, both its *mythos* and its *ethos*.

The difference between the Judaeo-Christian conception of *sin* and the Greek conception of *hubris* is of decisive importance. In the Judaeo-Christian universe, good and evil are not rooted in the nature of things. The natural and the moral worlds are regarded as entirely dependent upon the omnipotent will of the Creator. He who created the natural world also created good and evil. *Sin,* in both Judaism and Christianity, is rebellion against the will of the Creator. Righteousness is conformity with that will. Furthermore, as Kierkegaard has suggested in *Fear and Trembling,* the particularities of God's will are not subject to man's critical scrutiny, no matter how opaque or puzzling they may seem. We are to conform because of the ultimate authority of the Source, regardless of whether we understand why we comply.

Only in the Judaeo-Christian conception of a divinely created cosmos does deicide make sense as an anti-value explosion. It did not make sense in paganism, for the pagan believed that even the gods were governed by law and necessity. There could be no comparable deicidal myths in paganism, because riddance of the gods could not effectuate a riddance from the norms to which even the pagan gods were said to be subject. There are in paganism myths of the death of the gods. There are dying gods aplenty, but no pagan could ever say as Ivan Karamazov is reported to have said: "If God does not exist, all things are permitted."[14]

Only in Biblical religion was the motive for deicide meaningful, for only in Biblical religion were all norms derivative of a God who transcended them. *Murdering God makes sense only when all values derive from Him.* In such a system the deicidal act is an assertion of the will to total moral and religious license. This is the real meaning of the Christ-killer accusation which has been repeated *ad nauseam* for almost two thousand years. Though there were other social and economic conditions which were necessary before the theological antecedents of anti-Semitism could be turned into the death camps of our times, only the terrible accusation, known and taught to every Christian in earliest childhood, that the Jews are the killers of the Christ can account for the depth and persistence of this supreme hatred.

In a sense, the death camps were the terminal expression of Christian anti-Semitism. Furthermore, enough "I like Eich" comments have been passed or inscribed on toilet walls since the Eichmann trial to indicate that the enterprise still strikes dark admiration in a great many people. Without Christianity, the Jews could never have become the central victims. Nevertheless, it would be a vast oversimplification to suggest that Christianity was responsible for the camps. Christianity provided an indispensable ingredient, the demonological interpretation of the Jews, but only anti-Christian heretics could use this material as did the Nazis. Psychologically speaking, one of the purposes of the deicide accusation against the Jew was to enable Christians to lead a decent life. The myth of Jewish guilt was an important element in the Christian moral universe. Unconsciously intuiting mankind's most demonic temptation, the murder of God and subsequent moral anarchy, the Christian often sought to ward off the temptation by projecting it on his stereotype of the Jew. This projection was realistically supported by the fact that the Jews were heir to similar moral struggles within their own natures. There was a kernel of truth to the accusation that the Jews wanted to kill God or had done so symbolically, insofar as all men are possessed of the same yearning for infantile omnipotence. Nevertheless, the crucifixion tradition sought to avoid murder and violence. It represented a very human attempt to come to terms with some terribly dark inner forces. Normally the system of Christian religious restraints worked. Though the average Christian seldom looked upon the Jew with the kindliest of vision, he was under no compulsion to extirpate the deicide in himself by the actual murder of the Jew.

The darker aspects of the myth came to the fore, united with the Teuton's resentment of Jewish Christianity, when the delicate balance of civilization was upset in Germany by the real or fantasied catastrophes which followed upon defeat in World War I. The shock of national defeat and the inability of the German people realistically to accept the fact that they had brought their predicament upon themselves were important ingredients in the witches' brew from which the death camps were ultimately spawned. Reality, symbolized by the defeated German political community and its external relations, became increasingly unacceptable. During the inflation of 1923, more than the currency was spurious. Increasingly the German method of dealing with this unacceptable reality was marked by regressive modes of action.

The very selection of Adolf Hitler by the German people and the demonic fascination he exerted upon them cannot be divorced from the radical rejection of normality and its restraints which took place under Nazism. Hitler was the man from nowhere, possessed of an all-consuming infantile fury, with nothing to lose. He offered the Germans the simplest and most infantile method of dealing with their real and imaginary enemies—extermination. His multiform abnormalities increased his fascination in a culture which was in despair over the political and social complexities of modern civilization. The relations between a leader and his community are in any event emotionally overdetermined, but never so completely as in the mysterious affair between Hitler and the Germans. He elicited from them something demonic, atavistic, and insane. The man, the people, and the hour were made for one another.

NOTES

1. I am indebted for this insight to Jean Paul Sartre's *Baudelaire*, H. Martin Turnell (Norfolk, Conn.: New Directions Books, 1950), pp. 71 f.

2. Paul's fateful discussion of the place of Israel in the Christian dispensation is to be found in Romans 9–11.

3. Justin Martyr, *Dialogue With Tryphon*, tr. A.L. Williams (London: SPCK, 1930), II, 107.

4. G.W.F. Hegel, *Early Theological Writings*, tr. T.M. Knox and Richard Kroner (Chicago: University of Chicago Press, 1948), pp. 145 ff. For a contemporary discussion of the importance of the conflict between Teuton and Latin for the growth of German anti-Semitism, cf. Erik H. Erikson, *Childhood and Society* (New York: W.W. Norton, 1963) pp. 347 ff.

5. The parallel between the Jew and the witches of the Middle Ages is important. Bruno Bettelheim has suggested that an irrational fear of the Jew's capacity to do great harm provided the SS with the inner justification necessary to do their work in the camps. Cf. Bettelheim, *The*

Informed Heart (Glencoe, Ill.: The Free Press, 1960). Cf. Norman Cohn, "The Myth of Jewish World-Conspiracy," *Commentary*, June 1966.

6. Cf. my article, "Psychoanalysis and the Origins of Judaism," *The Reconstructionist*, December 2, 1960.

7. In *The Origins of Totalitarianism* (New York: Harcourt Brace, 1951).

8. Cf. Ernst "Putzi" Hanfstängel, *Hitler: The Missing Years* (London: Eyre and Spottiswoode, 1957).

9. Cf. his *Harvest of Hate* (Syracuse: Syracuse University Press, 1954).

10. Joshua Trachtenberg has gathered an impressive catalogue of such identifications of the Jew with the demonic in his book, *The Devil and the Jews* (New Haven: Yale University Press, 1943).

11. Cf. Trachtenberg, *op. cit.*

12. Cf. James George Frazer, *The New Golden Bough*, ed. Theodore H. Gaster (New York: Criterion Books, 1959).

13. Cf. Martin P. Nilsson, *Greek Piety* (London: Oxford University Press, 1948).

14. This analysis has some affinities with Albert Camus's comments on Christianity in his essay "Helen's Exile" in *The Myth of Sisyphus*, tr. Justin O'Brien (New York: Vintage Books, 1955), pp. 134 ff. I am deeply indebted to Camus for many of my insights.

Richard Schmitt

MURDEROUS OBJECTIVITY:
REFLECTIONS ON MARXISM
AND THE HOLOCAUST

As I begin to write about the Holocaust[1] I am filled with a deep sense of shame—shame at surviving when my friends did not because they were Jews while I, in the language of the Nazis, am a *Mischling*—a half-breed. I am ashamed to be thinking abstractly about the events which for the participants meant horror and death. But the victims of the Holocaust have been dead for forty-five years or more. Their life and death and their experiences are beyond our reach. The question for us is not what effect our words will have on them—we know the sad answer to that. The questions for us are about origins, causes and the prevention of future Holocausts.

While the world builds Holocaust memorials, and the Holocaust literature continues to grow, and authors declare over and over again that the world has been totally changed by Auschwitz, the sad reality is that mass brutality is as much on the agenda as it was in the 1930s and 1940s. The undoubted uniqueness of the Holocaust has been used to distance ourselves from it, to isolate it as a unique event that has no connection with who we are and what we do. That distancing has allowed us to go about our business as usual, exterminating whole populations in Vietnam, in Cambodia, in Afghanistan, watching others die in the Sahel, and standing by while massive oppression is visited on the people of South Africa, of Chile, of Argentina.

The Holocaust did not make the world new. It merely reiterated that the world needs to change—a lesson stated equally forcefully by Hiroshima and Nagasaki and the arms race that followed the slaughter of World War II. But that lesson has not yet been learned. It seems clear that the evil that made it possible for Germans and their allies to practice mass killings has not been eradicated. In thinking about the Holocaust, we need to think about ourselves.

I want to raise a question that has troubled many: What are the sources of the distancing that enabled men and women, who did not seem much more wicked than most of us, to stand by calmly as others suffered sharply and died ignominiously. What allowed ordinary German citizens to look away when their Jewish neighbors were harassed, persecuted and finally taken away. What allowed an army of German bureaucrats to orchestrate the mass murder of Jews, Gypsies, homosexuals,[2] Jehovah's Witnesses, of forcibly recruited workers from all over Europe by turning the human tragedy into a technical bureaucratic problem? It is important to understand from the beginning that that question applies not only to Germans (or Poles or Ukrainians); it applies to everyone. Jean Amery described the situation of German and Austrian Jews in the 1930s in these terms:

> there was no way out. . . . All of Germany—but what am I saying—the whole world nodded its head in approval of the undertaking. . . . One must remember: when after World War II streams of refugees poured out of the various communist ruled lands into the West, the countries of the proclaimed free world outdid one another in their willingness to grant asylum and aid, although among the emigrants there was only a handful whose lives would have been directly threatened in their homeland. But even when it long since should have been clear to any discerning person what awaited us in the German Reich, no one wanted to have us. (Amery, 1981:87)

This question about distancing applies to everyone. *It applies to us.* In thinking about some of the conditions that made the Holocaust possible, we are thinking about what it is about us that makes us tolerate and even support continued wars, mass deaths and migrations all over the globe.

I will talk about distancing in connection with Marxism. There are several reasons for that.

The Holocaust teaches us that the world has to change. Anyone who believes that change is urgently needed turns to Marx for help. He is the preeminent theorist of social change. While most social theorists praise the world as it is, or suggest minor changes, Marx was always the spokesman of the radicals, and it is clear that nothing short of radical change will prevent World War III, the ultimate Holocaust. It is important to see that Marxism as a reasonably coherent outlook is not very helpful in our search for an understanding of how the world has to change even though certain Marxian themes cannot be overlooked when we think about the Holocaust. It is even more important to see that Marxism, particularly in its 'scientific' incarnations, is an example of the distancing from others that is one of the sources of the horror of the Holocaust.

I have more personal reasons for beginning this reflection about the Holocaust with Marx. While I survived, and was fortunate to be able to come to the United States and to get an essentially free education, I noticed very soon that not everyone in this country is as fortunate as I. Color, and class, and gender keep significant portions of our population poor and poorly educated. Only Marxists have been seriously trying to understand the fact that the richest country in the world is beset by poverty, ignorance and unhappiness. What is more, within limits, Marxist explanations are persuasive. But German Fascism and the Holocaust serve to set the limits to Marxian explanations of our experiences.

I. MARXISM AND THE HOLOCAUST

Among the sources of Marxism are a keen theoretical interest in the workings of capitalism—Marx is one of the inventors of the science of economics—and deep outrage over the plight of workers in the first half of the nineteenth century. Child labor, twelve, fourteen and sixteen hour working days, a total lack of health and safety measures in work places, deplorable wages and living conditions—all were the rule rather than the exception.

From these sources flows Marx's theory. It begins with his economic analysis that shows that capitalists make money because they pay the worker only a portion of the net income due to the worker's activity. One can calculate how much a worker adds to the total net income of a firm and then show that the worker's wages are only a portion of that additional income. The rest goes toward the capitalists' profits. As a consequence, the relation between worker and capitalist is from the very beginning conflictual. The worker wants to increase his or her share of the product; the capitalist wants to reduce the workers' share.

This economic analysis provides the foundation for Marx's politics: the working class, constantly struggling against the capitalists whose profits are pretty directly dependent on low wages for the working class, will organize itself to gain control over the production process. But since capitalism consists essentially of capitals which are privately owned and competing against each other, a system where workers, as a group, control the production process could be instituted only if capitalism were first abolished. The organizations of workers whose original aims are to improve their lot under capitalism will soon understand that capitalism, as a system, is the real enemy and will work to substitute their own collective control over production for the control by the private capitalists.

Marxist theory, therefore, focuses on the formation of classes in the society, and on the conflicts between classes that bring about fundamental change. Class differences and class struggles are regarded as basic. All the other divisions in societies, such as religious, ethnic, or gender divisions, tend to be understood in Marxist theory as derivative from class divisions.

Only a small portion of the continuing outpouring of writings about Marxism is devoted to the question of what sort of explanation Marxist theory can produce for the rise and triumph of Fascism in Germany. I am aware of very few attempts of Marxists to explain the Holocaust. It is easy to understand that silence. Marxist explanations of Fascism are not adequate. Marxism has nothing of use to say about the extermination of gays, of Jews, Gypsies, and many others.

These are some of the essential ingredients in German Fascism and in the Holocaust which do not find adequate treatment in Marxist theory.

Nationalism. The extermination of the Jews and other less valuable races was to serve the purification of the German nation. Germans felt threatened *as* Germans; their national identity, always fragile, was seriously imperiled after the defeat in World War I. Lifton has suggested that similar nationalist motives were involved in the Turkish massacre of the Armenians in 1915. (Lifton, 1986)

But Marxist theory does not recognize nationalism as a separate historical force. Marx deals with the whole issue by declaring that "The working man has no country." The later theories of nationality that originated in the Soviet Union and were designed to illuminate the actual nationalities' problems experienced in that country recognized a right of national self-determination but did not recognize the right of one nation to destroy another. But that is what German nationalism has meant, and not only German nationalism. The mass slaughter of World War II, and the wars since then, have again and again been made palatable by appeals to national interest. Marxism is not equipped to take that appeal seriously. It cannot explain why reasonable people accept national self-interest as a sufficient justification for the death of large numbers of one's compatriots and citizens of other nations. Without taking that seriously, German Fascism and the Holocaust are unintelligible.

Racism. The Holocaust as well as, for instance, the policy of Vietnamization—letting Asians fight Asians in a war that was considered to the advantage of us Americans—presupposes the notion that white skinned people are more valuable than all others, and that the life of white skinned people may be preserved at the expense of the life of those others, whether they be Jews or Vietnamese. While Marx and Engels were well aware of the phenomenon of racism and understood it concretely, their theory does not shed any light on it in theoretical terms. (Schmitt, 1988)

Progress. Marx and Engels shared the nineteenth century belief that history moves in a positive direction. In spite of the massive suffering of large numbers of people, which Marx recorded eloquently in *Capital,* they thought that humanity was moving toward a social order of greater material well-being, and greater freedom and self-determination for all human beings. The struggles of classes, the struggles over imperialism, would in the end yield a society of great justice and human dignity. I agree with Ron Aronson that we must moderate that hope at the end of the twentieth century, the century of unprecedented mass slaughters, of which the Holocaust was only one example. (Aronson, 1988)

Human Rationality. Finally, Marx and Engels assumed that human beings are, on the whole, rational in a perfectly straightforward sense: they choose the best means to accomplish their ends. Thus Marx is at pains to show that the suffering of the British workers in the early parts of the nineteenth century made some sense in that it supported the consolidation of the economic and, hence, the political power of the rising capitalist class. We can understand what motivates the capitalist who works children ten or twelve hours a day under utterly unhealthy conditions, and we can predict what sorts of social changes will alter the ends of human beings so that the exploitation of one class by another ceases to be rational. Once we abolish capitalism with its private owner-ship of means of production and the tooth and nail competition between capitalists, exploitation makes no more sense and hence will disappear.

In the perspective of the Holocaust, that sense of rationality, still very popular among social scientists, must be rejected. The doctors in Auschwitz were rational in that sense when they debated, as a purely 'technical' question, whether children should be separated from their mothers on the way to the gas chambers. (Lifton, 1986:175) But there is something deeply the matter with a notion of rationality that can conceal from itself its utter inhumanity and discuss mass murder, whether in Auschwitz or in the factories of early capitalism, as a problem of a purely instrumental nature. I shall return to that point below.

With this I have come to my central question. Marx shares with the majority of Western intellectuals a certain conception of rationality and objectivity, of the detachment required by responsible intellectuals. The Holocaust teaches us how evil that intellectual stance can be. It also teaches us that it may well be the death of all of us.

Marxism is not equipped to provide an adequate account of the Holocaust.[3] Some aspects of it can, however, only be understood if we draw on insights derived from Marx. I will point to some of these in what follows.

II. DISTANCING: SOME EXAMPLES

Primo Levi, a trained chemist, was an inmate in Auschwitz who survived. He got work in the synthetic rubber plant, the 'Buna', after being interviewed by a Dr. Pannwitz. Here is his description of that interview:

> Pannwitz is tall, thin, blond: he has eyes, hair and nose as all Germans ought to have them. . . . I, Haeftling 174517, stand in his office . . . and I feel that I would leave a dirty stain whatever I touched.

> When he had finished writing, he raised his eyes and looked at me. From that day I have thought about Dr. Pannwitz many times and in many ways. I have asked myself how he really functioned as a man. . . . Because that look was not one between two men . . . [it] . . . came as if across the glass window of an aquarium between two things that live in different worlds . . .

> One felt in that moment, in an immediate manner, what we all thought and said of Germans. The brain which governed those blue eyes and those manicured hands said: 'This something in front of me belongs to a species which it is obviously opportune to suppress. In this particular case, one has to first make sure that it does not contain some utilizable element.' And in my head, like seeds in an empty pumpkin: 'Blue eyes and fair hair are essentially wicked. No communication possible. I am a specialist in mine chemistry. I am a specialist in organic syntheses. I am a specialist. . . .' (Levi, 1961:96/7)

Here is a memo, written by a German functionary about alterations in the vehicles used to gas Jews in Chelmno:

> Since December 1941, ninety-seven thousand have been pro-cessed (*verarbeitet* in German) by the three vehicles in service, with no major incidents. In the light of observations made so far, the following technical changes are needed:
>
> 1. The vans' normal load is usually nine per square yard. In Saurer vehicles, which are very spacious, maximum use of space is impossible, not because of any possible overload, but because loading to full capacity would affect the vehicles' sta-bility. So reduction of the load space seems necessary. It must absolutely be reduced by one yard, instead of trying to solve the problem as hitherto, by reducing the number of pieces loaded. Besides this extends the operating time, as the empty void must be filled with carbon monoxide. On the other hand, if the load space is reduced, and the vehicle is packed solid, the operating time can be considerably shortened. . . .
>
> 2. The lighting must be better protected than now. The lamps must be enclosed in a steel grid to prevent their being dam-aged. Lights could be eliminated, since they are apparently never used. However, it has been observed that when the doors are shut, the load always presses hard against them [against the doors] as soon as darkness sets in. This is because the load naturally rushes towards the light when darkness sets in, which makes closing the doors difficult. Also because of the alarming nature of darkness, screaming always occurs when the doors are closed. It would therefore be useful to light the lamp be-fore and during the first moment of operation.
>
> 3. For easy cleaning of the vehicle there must be a sealed drain in the middle of the floor. The drainage hole's cover, eight to twelve inches in diameter, would be equipped with a slanting trap, so that fluid liquids can drain off during the operation. During cleaning, the drain can be used to evacuate large pieces of dirt. . . . (Lanzmann, 1985:103/4)

Note the complete absence of human beings from that memo. Only ghostly "pieces" and a disembodied "load." Reality breaks through for a moment in the screams of Jews being locked into a dark truck as the carbon monoxide begins to blow into the compartment.

Notice also the dispassionate tone of the memo. Does its author have any feelings? Not toward Jews, obviously. Neither does Dr. Pannwitz toward the emaciated, hollow-eyed Primo Levi. Mass murder could become a technical problem only by withdrawing all emotions from the experience of the murderers. One withdraws to one's professional self. Even Primo Levi must do that. He reminds himself that "I am a specialist in mine chemistry. I am a specialist in organic syntheses. I am a specialist . . ." to push back his rage, his fear, his despair and proceeds to "pass" the examination to which Dr. Pannwitz subjects him, complete with a discussion of a well-known English chemistry textbook of which Pannwitz shows him a copy.

Distancing is an essential prerequisite for mass extermination. "The Auschwitz self depended upon radically diminished feeling, upon one's not experiencing psychologically what one was doing." (Lifton, 1986: 442) Lifton interviewed a number of the doctors who had run the exterminations at Auschwitz. One of them, a Dr. B, was asked how it would be were he to meet Mengele again, who had by then disappeared to South America. B said "And there would result—as I know him—completely emotionless talk. Talk without emotions. Emotions, they remained at Auschwitz, for all of us." (Lifton, 1986:325)

This distance was achieved by a number of techniques. To begin with, the victims were rendered as subhuman as possible as quickly as possible. "The *Lager*," Primo Levi writes, "was a great machine to reduce us to beasts." (Levi, 1961:36) Then the process of killing needed to be depersonalized. The original mass slaughter in open mass graves turned out to be insupportable even for Nazis. According to Hoess the Kommandant of Auschwitz, "Many members of the *Einsatzkommandos* [the soldiers who originally shot large numbers of Jews in Russia and Poland], unable to endure wading through blood any longer, had committed suicide. Some had even gone mad. . . . Himmler is said to have become ill while watching mass shooting, after which he ordered 'more humane' killing." (Lifton, 1986:159) The Berlin bureaucrats tried very hard to remain at a distance from the actual killing. They "preferred not to know too many details about the camps." (Lifton, 1986:198) It is this distancing that we need to understand if we are to understand something about the Holocaust and are to understand what we can do to prevent more mass slaughter.

III. DISTANCING IN EVERYDAY LIFE

The phenomenon of distancing throws light on the unwillingness of so many, both in Germany and around the world, to respond to the plight of the Jews during the 1930s and 1940s. There are many situations where a person witnesses the experiences of others but does not respond:[4] in the middle of the night, the family next door is taken away to a concentration camp, the Jewish community paper in your community reports steadily about atrocities committed against Jews in Europe (Blumenthal, 1985:99), people in a Polish village see daily the column of starving, ragged Jewish prisoners being marched to and from work but do not react (Lanzmann, 1985). There are adults, in New Orleans in the early 1970s, who, day after day, yell racial slurs and hateful threats at six year old black children for going to a white school. (Coles, 1986:22) In cases like that, we want to ask why they did not respond to the suffering they saw before their very own eyes? That question is not only about why they did not act—in many situations that was too dangerous. But we want to ask: How could they not *feel* the suffering they witnessed?

One distances oneself from others by preventing oneself from responding to the other's pain. As long as you are moved by the plight of others, you cannot distance yourself from them. So you must put a gulf between your self and your own feelings. This happens in different ways. I can be so angry, or so frightened, or so obsessed by the need to accumulate more possessions, that there is no room for any feelings for you. Wholly overwhelmed by feelings pertaining to me, I am not able to respond to you and your experiences. My feelings for myself put a distance between you and me.

The alternative is to suppress my feelings for you, or to suppress all my feelings. If I do not want to resonate with your experiences, I must suppress the emotions they evoke in me. Everyone left one's emotions at Auschwitz, Dr. B, said, and that means that those in charge not only suppressed all feelings of sympathy, but equally all feelings of hatred. Mass murder was possible if one suppressed all feelings of guilt and terror. Himmler said in an address to S.S. officers:

> Most of you know what it means to see a hundred corpses lying together, five hundred, or a thousand. To have gone through this and yet, apart from a few exceptions—examples of human weakness—*to have remained decent,* this has made us hard. (Plant, 1986:75; my italics)

Whatever feelings Himmler may have had about the Final Solution, they were buried deep down so that he could consider himself and his fellow officers to be "decent" human beings. To be decent was to be "hard," that is, not to feel anything. To distance oneself from others, one has to dissociate oneself from one's own emotions.

Such dissociation from one's emotions is widely practiced; we cannot get along without it. I cannot write about the Holocaust without dissociating myself to some extent from the feelings of horror and grief its images continue to evoke in me. Bruno Bettelheim survived Dachau and Buchenwald by distancing himself to a certain extent from the suffering of his fellow prisoners. (Bettelheim, 1960) In remembering the victims, we must dissociate ourselves, to some extent, from our grief and shame, so that we can celebrate their resistance and learn from their dreadful death. (Gottlieb, 1988) Putting a distance between oneself and one's feelings, and between oneself and others, is not peculiar to mass murderers; it is something that everyone does. It is often essential to do so.

The examples discussed so far were of two different kinds. Sometimes one dissociates oneself from a particular feeling. In other situations one distances oneself globally by dissociating oneself, more or less, from all feelings. This global dissociation is very common everywhere, not only among Nazis.

IV. GLOBAL DISSOCIATING

I began this discussion of dissociating with the observation by one of the camp doctors from Auschwitz that "Emotions—they remained at Auschwitz." We have seen some particularly grim examples of that complete dissociation from one's own emotions. Here dissociating from others and oneself is no longer a defense against particular, painful emotions or a defense against a particularly stressful experience. Here all emotions are repressed. One no longer dissociates oneself from this emotion or that, but from emotions altogether.

A number of explanatory hypotheses for this global dissociation from one's own emotions have been formulated.

Many writers have noticed the way in which the death camps were like factories, carefully organized to 'process (*verarbeiten*),' as the Nazis said, human beings. Hence there has been a tendency to ascribe the dissociating to modern technology. Thus Steven Katz points out that the Holocaust required the cooperation of large numbers of persons who worked on the railroads, ran the industries that built plants near the camps, crafted and enforced the relevant legal apparatus, used their

medical skills for mass murder, or just looked the other way when persons were deported or gangs of prisoners passed in the road:

> The substantive impact of technology on the murderers . . . [is]
> the anesthetizing properties of modern technology . . . [it] . . .
> redefines the landscape of the technocrats' reality in terms not
> improperly described, using Buber's vocabulary, as I-IT. In
> this landscape the concern is with others as "thing" not per-
> sons, with an impersonal and utilitarian calculus that measures
> (and sometimes murders!) rather than relates and cares. (Katz,
> 1988:265–268)

But perhaps the Nazis' industrial techniques and metaphors should not
be taken at face value, but rather be understood as one more technique
of distancing, of concealing the reality of the extermination camps behind the screen of ordinary industrial activity. The industrial methods of
mass-extermination have also been described as the extreme case of the
rationalization of the use of labor:

> . . . the final step in the rationalization of labor relations was
> taken in World War II by the great German business corpora-
> tions that invested huge sums in the construction of factories at
> the death camps for the express purpose of utilizing the avail-
> able and infinitely replenishable pool of death-camp slave
> labor. The employers' responsibility for the maintenance of the
> work force was reduced to an absolute minimum. . . . (Ruben-
> stein, 1978:40)

and

> I.G. Farben's decision to locate at Auschwitz was based upon
> the very same criteria by which contemporary multinational
> corporations relocate their plants in utter indifference to the
> social consequences of such moves: wherever possible costs,
> especially labor costs must be minimized and profits maxi-
> mized. (Rubenstein, 1978:58)

Here the dissociation from feelings and other human beings is directly
blamed on capitalism and its particular form of instrumental rationality.
Capitalists were only too eager to profit from the availability of unusually cheap labor in the German extermination camps. (Arendt, 1965)

Here the Marxian analysis of capitalism is essential in order to understand this.

Other explanations of the Holocaust attribute global dissociating to political liberalism:

> Liberalism does not inspire courage because it is hard pressed
> to offer an account of the good that, in the end, is not
> anchored in the tastes and preferences of individuals. . . .
> (Thomas, 1988:108)

According to liberal political theory, we are all separate individuals, each out to improve his or her life. For each, the decisive consideration is his or her own interests, however the individual may define them. In such a world there is little incentive for showing moral courage on behalf of others. The needs of others are, ultimately, their concern just as mine are for me to meet. Thus liberalism encourages a narrowly self-regarding ethic which will not spur persons on to be heroic in the effort to help others. The good liberal is not likely to respond to the distress of others where that response may be at all costly. Liberalism requires global dissociating from one's feelings.[5] This analysis of the moral consequences of liberalism owes a good deal to Marx's comments about the moral ambiguities of capitalism and its politics.

There are other explanations: global dissociating is the logical outcome of Judeo-Christian beliefs (Rubenstein, 1978:28) or of the rationalization that eventuates in modern bureaucracy (Rubenstein, 1978:22). All of these explanations are striking. One cannot reject them out of hand as obviously false.

But it is legitimate to ask in each case whether the institution we have chosen as the cause is not rather itself just one more symptom of another underlying condition. Is capitalism the underlying cause and technology the symptom or vice versa? What is the relation of political liberalism to capitalism? Marx has one answer to that question. Liberalism has a very different answer. Nor are these the only two answers available. Each of these attempted explanations tells us something important about the Holocaust, but does not provide us with an understanding of its real causes.

More importantly, with these causal explanations we are letting ourselves off too easy. If we blame the bureaucracy, those of us who are not bureaucrats can rest easy that past and future mass murders are not our responsibility. The same is true if we blame the Holocaust on capitalism while being good anti-capitalists, or anti-liberals, or humanists rather than engineers ourselves. What is more, once we have found the institution which we are going to blame, we need look no further for other ways in which in a society like ours, dissociating from feeling, from self and other, is constantly demanded and constantly practiced by *each and every one of us.*

Global distancing is practiced very widely in our society today. It is practiced in many different situations, by many different people, because it is demanded by the dominant conception of what it means to be a rational, mature adult. Here is a partial list of these beliefs and practices, which perpetuate dissociation from one's emotions:

1. A familiar notion of rationality is the conception of a person who acts rationally, who calculates carefully what is best to do in the light of the available information and whose action is the result of that careful calculation. This sort of rationality, sometimes called "instrumental rationality," concerns the adaptation of means to ends, in the light of the available information, and the conformity of actions to the choices of means. (A person might choose the proper ends but still act irrationally by neglecting to follow his or her own choices.)

The Nazi doctors at Auschwitz who debated as a "technical question" whether or not to separate children from their mothers on the way to the gas chambers exemplify this sort of rationality. Only means, not ends, are subject to rational discussion. Hence it is as rational to select the right means for a truly evil as for a noble end. Taking the term "rational" in that instrumental sense of the term does not "prevent us from speaking of suicide, homicide or genocide as rational behavior." (Elster, 1983:15) This sort of rationality is not only widely practiced but it is recommended to us by the most respected contemporary philosophers. (Rawls, 1971:143)

2. The dominant concept of professionalism is a clear application of this conception of rationality. Bettelheim speaks of the pride in their professional competence that Nazi doctors and some inmate doctors used in order to conceal from themselves and others that they were murderers. Dr. Mengele would deliver a baby with perfect care and sterile technique only to send mother and baby to the gas chamber half an hour later. (Bettelheim, 1960:261/2)

Contemporary discussions of professionalism show that the professionalism of a Dr. Mengele is not, in principle, different from that recommended in current texts on professional ethics.

> Professionals confine themselves to providing means to their
> clients' ends and proposing solutions to their self-defined

problems. Parsons calls this "specificity of function." The authority of the professional is based on technical competence,
rather than status, wisdom, or moral character . . . To put this
in general terms, the professional renders disinterested and
impartial service to whomever fortune puts in his hands. . . .
(Kultgen, 1988:73–74)

The parallel between this conception of the professional with his particular form of instrumental rationality forcefully recalls Arendt's comment about the *Sachlichkeit*—being "disinterested and impartial"—es-
teemed by Eichmann and the S.S.:

This 'objective' attitude—talking about concentration camps
in terms of 'administration' and about extermination camps in
terms of economy[6]—was typical of the S.S. mentality, and
something Eichmann, at the trial, was still very proud of. By its
objectivity (*Sachlichkeit*), the S.S. dissociated itself from such
'emotional' types as Streicher, 'the unrealistic fool' . . .[7]
(Arendt, 1965:69)

3. The work of professionals is "grounded in science or quasi-sci-
entific theory. . . ." These theories guide the work of professionals,
much of whose work concerns the lives and well-being of other human
beings. The relevant theories are about or have a direct bearing on
human beings, whether we are talking about the theory of education, of
individual or group functioning, of revolution, as in the case of Marx, or
of nuclear deterrence, as in the case of defense strategists.

Such theories, in the ambience of objectivity and rationality that
prevails in our society just as much as in Nazi Germany, tend to be
technical, and abstract. Consistency is of central importance. Above all
these theories are intended to be objective and that means, once again,
dispassionate, withdrawn from emotion.

Much of their [viz. the defense experts'] claim to legitimacy,
then, is a claim to objectivity born of technical expertise and to
the disciplined purging of emotional valences that might
threaten their objectivity. (Cohen, 1987:717)

But to the extent that they are 'objective' in that sense, these theories are
also withdrawn from their subject, from the warm and pulsating, rarely
consistent, never transparent reality of human beings.

Building theories of that sort is often defended by the complexity of the subject. Human reality is immensely complex. A reasonable procedure is therefore to build oversimplified models in the beginning, and then add more and more features in the attempt to approximate reality. This is how Paul Sweezy defends Marx's procedure in the three volumes of *Capital*. (Sweezy, 1942) One cannot quarrel with that defense, but, as I shall argue below, in the current atmosphere of global distancing expected of professionals, the model never comes any closer to the human reality because we are, from the beginning, prevented from encountering that person in the only way one can, by feeling for, with, and about them.

4. The professional bureaucrat, today a very common species both in government and in business, where they are called 'managers' or 'executives,' illustrates the same detachment:

> When fully developed, bureaucracy also stands, in a specific sense, under the principle of *sine ira ac studio* (without anger or taking sides). Its specific nature, which is welcomed by capitalism, develops the more perfectly the more the bureaucracy is 'dehumanized', the more completely it succeeds in eliminating from official business love, hate, and all purely personal, irrational, and emotional elements which escape calculation. This is the specific nature of bureaucracy and it is appraised as its special virtue. (Weber, 1958:215/6)

It would be difficult to get a clearer statement of the ways in which bureaucracy is committed to global dissociating. At the same time, Weber's claim of the close connection between bureaucratic management and capitalism is clearly very plausible. We see here that although Marxism, as I argued in section I, cannot explain the Holocaust completely to us, we cannot understand it without drawing on the conception and critique of capitalism that we owe to Marx.

5. This bureaucrat may administer a massive effort at helping famine victims. Or he may be an Eichmann competently transporting huge numbers of Jews to their death. However prevalent, the underlying concept and practice of instrumental rationality is deficient.

At least some philosophers have understood this and sought a conception of rationality that could apply to the choice of ends. But there, too, the presupposition dominated that thinking and feeling are distinct processes and that feelings disturb thinking and must therefore be controlled. There is a traditional conception of the rational person as one who thinks carefully before acting, who is not swayed by emotion but rather surveys facts carefully and applies principles and rules that he or she has previously chosen as his or her own. The basic assumption is that one can either be the victim of one's emotions—in that case one is not rational—or that one may be rational by "being in control over the processes whereby one's desires are formed." (Elster, 1983:21) Being 'emotional' is tantamount to being irrational. Emotions must be controlled; preferably one must control the process by which they are formed.

One is reminded of Himmler's statement that while the S.S. had witnessed mass slaughter, they had remained "decent" and "hard." Not swayed by emotions, even in the face of nameless suffering, they retained their moral integrity by being proof against emotions.

This conception has a long history. In Kant's ethics, written at the end of the eighteenth century, being a moral person meant that one followed rational principles, and principles were rational if they were adopted for purely intellectual reasons and remote from feelings and desires. The fundamental assumption here is, of course, that thinking and feeling are distinct psychological processes which are, moreover, in conflict. A person is rational if his thinking, his cool, unemotional thinking, has the upper hand; if emotions sway thinking, a person is irrational. (Lloyd, 1984:68)

6. Closely allied to this portrait of the rational person is the concept of autonomy: the autonomous person is not swayed by others, by collective pressures or demands but only by what he or she has decided for himself or herself to be correct. But deciding for oneself is, once again, to be aloof from one's emotions. The autonomous man

> is not overly dependent on others and not swamped by his own passions. . . . He has, one may say, procedural independence, self-control and competence. (Haworth, 1986:1)

The central notion of the autonomous person is, once again, the rational agent we met earlier, the person who steps back from his or her desires, and examines them cooly and detachedly, who acts toward himself or herself as a bureaucrat surveys his or her client, calmly and unemotionally.

7. At the very center of this entire conception of persons is a very specific notion of objectivity.

Knowledge, of course, does require objectivity. When Neo-Nazis and other anti-semites claim that the Holocaust never happened, we are not going to be satisfied to say that 'for me' the Holocaust occurred, while, perhaps, for you it did not. Six million Jews were killed agonizingly by the Nazis. That is true. It is true objectively, i.e. for everyone.

When we seek knowledge, be it in science or in everyday life, we seek knowledge that is, in that sense, objective, that is true for all relevant persons. It is widely believed that to strive for objectivity or, as we also say, "to be objective," one must dissociate oneself from one's emotions about the matter under investigation:

> In order to understand the Holocaust, it is necessary to adopt a mental attitude that excludes all feelings of sympathy or hostility towards both the victims and the perpetrators. (Rubenstein, 1978:2)

Here, once again, in the descriptions of how one can best search for objective knowledge, the underlying assumption is that feelings disturb the inquiry and that we must dissociate ourselves from them. In this way, the doctors that researched the most efficacious and 'humane' methods for killing excluded "all feelings of sympathy or hostility towards . . . the victims."

Global dissociating from feelings pervades our culture. It is recommended for seeking means to achieve one's ends, as well as in the reflections about the most desirable ends. It is recommended as the proper attitude for the professional as well as the administrator, be that in government or in private business. It is, finally, recommended for the scholar, as well as for the person who is trying to ascertain the facts in some everyday matter. But these activities: discovering what the world is like, ranging from checking the refrigerator to see what there is to eat, to discovering the cure for AIDS, or the origin of the galaxies in the primeval void; deciding on courses of action, ranging from making a menu, to planning measures to protect the ozone layer; administering, ranging from getting the children off to school or to bed, to running a university, or a multinational corporation or a large country—in all of these activities, which cover pretty much most of what we do from early morning to late at night, we are urged to put our feelings aside, to practice global dissociating in order to be more rational, more autonomous, more objective.

It is not hard to see that the complete separation from feelings that chills the heart when we read about it in accounts of Auschwitz is not foreign to us. We may be different in degree, but we are not different in kind. In that respect, the Holocaust is not unique: we withdraw from our own feelings and thus from others, steadily and continually.

V. GLOBAL DISSOCIATING IS THE ROAD
TO MASS MURDER

Defining objectivity in terms of global dissociating has become in-
defensible. If the preceding is not sufficient to make that clear, let me
add one more observation: This kind of objectivity involves tremendous
self-deception. Claudia Koonz raises the question of how guards and
commandants managed not to become either happy sadists or utterly
depressed. They

> imposed on themselves a fake reality, telling themselves that
> the fake world they had created matched their inner selves.
> They relegated 'obeying orders' to their public responsibilities,
> and created a private fantasy within which they deceived them-
> selves into thinking that they were not so bad after all. (Koonz,
> 1987:413)

One form of this splitting of the person was to separate their masculine
public life, where they did not feel, from their private life of family, of
love of children, where they did feel. The horrible reality was hidden
behind saccharine fantasies of traditional patriarchal family life, of subservient wives who knew nothing of their husbands' 'work' but were
fulfilled by nurturing their beautiful, blond children bearing Germanic
names. But being in love with a fantasy picture is only compounding the
self-deception. These men were dissociated from their feelings, but they
did not see their situation accurately. They did not see what they were
doing. They did not see their private life with any degree of accuracy
either, because they were acting out a conventional charade.

Carol Cohen provides a contemporary example of the same kind of
self-deception. She observes the sexual as well as sexist metaphors that
defense planners use. There are clearly hidden agendas in the arguments that these experts conduct with one another about weapons of
mass destruction. But being globally dissociated from their emotions,
they are unaware of those male agendas, about the size and potency of
one's weapon. These hidden agendas cannot begin to be addressed
unless it becomes legitimate, indeed obligatory, to go behind the surface
of the techno-jargon and ask what emotions lie beneath the pretense of
rationality.

None of this is to be construed as an argument against the constant
striving to be objective. It is clear that wishful thinking is no substitute
for a careful investigation of facts or meticulous sifting of evidence. Nor
is angry thinking or fearful thinking to be trusted without careful scrutiny. Emotions do distort our view of the world.

At the same time, emotions connect us to the world and to the humans that make up our common world. Auschwitz, Hiroshima and the earth after World War III are worlds created by the dissociation from emotions. Our emotions, for ourselves, and those we love, and all those whose pain we can only too easily feel if we only have the fortitude to do so, can clearly tell us that these are not the creations of rational men, but of fiends—fiends no less for the fact that most of us, in less spectacular ways, objectify other human beings—as doctors, teachers, therapists, lawyers or social workers. Yes, we want to be, we *must* be objective, but the objectivity achieved by global dissociating is appropriate only on the surface of Mars or in the cold, dark reaches of outer space.

Objectivity is essential; as *presently understood* it is lethal. Feminist thinkers of the Second Wave have understood this for a number of years. A great deal of very important work is being done in clarifying alternative ways of understanding thought and the demand for objectivity. We can continue to strive for a reliable understanding of the world while emphatically rejecting the accepted definitions of objectivity and rationality. (Code, 1988) (Miller, 1986) (Noddings, 1984) (Ruddick, 1983) (Seller, 1988)

VI. MARXISM AND THE HOLOCAUST

That brings us back to Marx. Marx's theories are clearly in the messianic tradition that Christianity inherited from Judaism. The world as we know it is full of suffering and injustice. But sometime in the future the world will be transformed and, as the Sermon on the Mount has it, "the meek shall inherit the earth." But Marx, unlike Jesus, is not a religious prophet; his messianism is secular and humanist. It is human beings themselves who will create a better world and specifically "the meek" or, in Marx's language, "the proletariat."

Since Marx, as a secular humanist, could not claim divine inspiration for his predictions, he needed to provide evidence for his predictions. Such evidence takes the form of a complex theory of the workings of society, as we know it, as well as a theory of social change. With both of those theories in hand, Marx felt confident that capitalism would collapse, brought to the brink of ruin by its own internal tensions, aggravated by an ever more rebellious and powerful working class.

Marx's theory is necessarily abstract; it omits a lot of concrete detail. There is no problem about that. But we do need to ask whether what is omitted is what should have been omitted and what is included is

what should have been included. Does Marx's theory give us an accurate, albeit much oversimplified, version of the world as we know it?

Marx's theory predicts that the majority in all countries will take
control over their lives and take power so that they can run the economy
and politics themselves and employ available resources for the benefit of
all instead of for the benefit of a minority class of capitalists. For that
prediction to be plausible, the majority of human beings must not only
be leading troubled lives—which they do—but they must perceive their
lives in the terms in which Marxist theory describes them: economic
exploitation, and domination in the workplace and, hence, in politics,
must be high on their list of complaints. These complaints must take
precedence over worries about the power and prestige of their nation,
over worries about threats from other races or ethnic groups, over
worries about changes in their society that threaten their traditional
values—such as changes in the family, in the role of fathers in relation to
their children, or husbands in relation to their wives.

There is good reason to think that, in fact, most human beings
perceive their problems in rather different terms. Hence women have
distanced themselves from orthodox Marxist analyses of the oppression
of women; black people subscribe to Marxism, if at all, only with serious
reservations. (Robinson, 1983) The oppression of women has taken
precedence over class oppression for many women. Racial oppression
has taken precedence over class oppression for many blacks. Besides, as
we saw much earlier, neither nationalism nor ethnic or racial fears or
hostilities are adequately understood by Marxism. National honor and
prestige, it turns out, is much more important to many workers than the
advancement of their class.

Marx was aware of racism, sexism and nationalism. But he missed
the full depth of those conditions and hence the intensity of passion with
which racism or sexism or national dishonor is resented. The reasons for
that error are clear: Marx was a scientist. He strove for objective knowledge of social mechanisms, and that meant that he strove for a detached
and dispassionate understanding of social structure and change. Rationality, he believed along with everybody else, is distinct and opposed to
emotions. Like most other scholars, Marx denied that thinking is en-
meshed in emotion. What workers *felt* about their lives was therefore
part of the irrational baggage that they had to free themselves from,
perhaps with the help of Marxist intellectuals, just as those intellectuals
themselves had freed themselves from the baggage of emotion. Accordingly he did not understand that if one is to grasp the outlook of others,
it is not sufficient to observe their situation and to draw one's conclusions from that. One must not only *talk* to those others but one must be

open to the emotional stance these others take, listening carefully to how the world presents itself to them instead of merely reconstructing what one thinks should be their thinking about their lives. One cannot, as a white person, begin to understand what racism means to its victims unless one makes an effort to feel the pain and anger it causes. General talk about sexism is not sufficient for genuine understanding. Men need to allow themselves to feel the rage and frustration women feel. In order to appreciate the force of national chauvinism among workers, one must open oneself to their fears and resentments. A purely intellectual appreciation of the pleasures and pains of others does not provide an understanding of the importance that others' values have for them. One therefore also is in no position to predict what others will feel and do.

Marx's use of the standard conception of objectivity concealed from him the complexity of human goals and self-understandings. He thought that if his rational theory was correct, he could predict what people would do. He failed to notice that one must test the applicability of one's rational theory by entering into the ways in which others see their world, by entering into their emotions.

Marx is, of course, not alone in this. Most undertakings to make life better for particular groups of persons are devised by professionals armed with a theory. Whether that theory applies to the persons whose lives it is designed to improve is usually not asked because social science today is as hostile to emotion as Marx's theory was, and thus the perceptions of the supposed beneficiaries of various theories remain hidden and unexplored.

But in seeking false objectivity, they close themselves off against their own emotions as well as those of beneficiaries as much as of victims—and, often, it is not clear that the supposed beneficiaries do not end up being victims—and thus perpetuate the practices which, at their worst, favor mass murder. Marxism is not able to help us understand the Holocaust because it shares the dominant, but mistaken, conceptions of objectivity that were in part to blame for it.

VII. CONCLUSION

The literature about the Holocaust continues to grow. The bulk of it points fingers. It blames German nationalism, German anti-semitism, the failure of the German Churches, of the Pope. (O'Brien, 1989) While the Germans, their Churches and the Pope undoubtedly deserve that blame, the function of finger pointing is, of course, always to deflect attention from the person who points. But no one is innocent of the Holocaust; everyone participates in maintaining the hard-hearted objectivity, the self-deceived concept and practice of rationality that eventuated not only in the Holocaust but also in the Russian mass murders of the 1920s and 1930s, or in Vietnam or Cambodia. For we live and participate in a world which believes, mistakenly, that it is rational to defend oneself against one's feelings and thus to be inured against the pain of others. In that world, the suffering we witness or know about does not move us to act. That objectivity makes us into guilty bystanders to past and future holocausts. It may well be the death of us all.

NOTES

1. I have written this paper for my children, Addie and Eli, in the hope that when they grow up, they will regard its lesson as self-evident. Lucy Candib is, as always, the joint author.

2. While the total number of German homosexuals that fell victim to the Nazis is very small compared to the huge numbers of people who died, the complete silence about this part of the Nazi purification of the non-existent Aryan race in the Holocaust literature is quite startling. (Plant, 1986)

3. These shortcomings of Marxist theories, among others, have given rise to a large literature of rethinking and revision of Marxist theory. (Anderson, 1976) (Gottlieb, 1987)

4. To be sure some failures to respond are not due to distancing. Some people are distant in time, or geographically, or culturally. We are therefore unable to enter into their experiences.

5. It is, however, very important to remember that the Nazis were violent anti-liberals themselves, despising the liberals' insistence that the individuals have a right to refuse to subordinate their good to that of the whole. The entire theory that Jews, gypsies, communists, etc. etc. must be sacrificed for the good of the German Volk would not have made much headway among people who were devoted liberals. That is saying a great deal in favor of liberalism.

6. The extermination camps were administered by the *Wirtschafts-Verwaltungshauptamt* the 'Main Administrative Office for Economic Affairs.'

7. Streicher, an impassioned anti-semite, was the editor of *Der Stuermer*, the weekly newspaper given over entirely to strident anti-semitic propaganda.

REFERENCES

Amery, J. (1981), *At the Mind's Limits: Contemplations by a Survivor on Auschwitz and Its Realities* (Bloomington: Indiana University Press).

Anderson, R. (1976), *Considerations of Western Marxism* (London: Verso).

Arendt, H. (1965), *Eichmann in Jerusalem* (New York: Viking).

Aronson, R. (1988), "The Holocaust and Human Progress," in A. Rosenberg and G. Myers, eds., *Echoes from the Holocaust: Philosophical Reflections on a Dark Time* (Philadelphia: Temple University Press) 223–242.

Bettelheim, B. (1960), *The Informed Heart* (New York: Free Press).

Blumenthal, D.R., ed. (1985), *Emory Studies on the Holocaust* (Atlanta: Witness to the Holocaust Project).

Code, L. (1988), "Experience, Knowledge and Responsibility," in M. Griffiths and M. Whitford, eds., *Feminist Perspectives in Philosophy* (Bloomington: Indiana University Press) 187–204.

Cohen, C. (1987), "Sex and Death in the Rational World of the Defense Intellectuals" *Signs* 12: 687–718.

Coles, R. (1986), *The Moral Life of Children* (Boston: Houghton Mifflin).

Elster, J. (1983), *Sour Grapes* (Cambridge: Cambridge University Press).

Gottlieb, R. (1987), *History and Subjectivity* (Philadelphia: Temple University Press).

Gottlieb, R. (1988), "Remembrance and Resistance: Philosophical and Personal Reflections on the Holocaust" *Social Theory and Practice* 14: 25–40.

Haworth, L. (1986), *Autonomy: An Essay in Philosophical Psychology and Ethics* (New Haven: Yale University Press).

Katz, S. (1988), "Technology and Genocide: Technology as a 'Form of Life,' " in A. Rosenberg and G. Myers, eds., *Echoes from the Holocaust: Philosophical Reflections on a Dark Time* (Philadelphia: Temple University Press) 262–291.

Koonz, C. (1987), *Mothers in the Fatherland: Women, the Family and Nazi Politics* (New York: St. Martin's).

Kultgen, J. (1988), *Ethics and Professionalism* (Philadelphia: University of Pennsylvania Press).

Lanzmann, C. (1985), *Shoa* (New York: Pantheon Books).

Levi, P. (1961), *Survival in Auschwitz* (New York: Collier Books).

Lifton, R.J. (1986), *The Nazi Doctors: Medical Killing and the Psychology of Genocide* (New York: Basic Books).

Lloyd, G. (1984), *The Man of Reason: 'Male' and 'Female' in Western Philosophy* (Minneapolis: University of Minnesota Press).

Miller, J.B. (1986), "What Do We Mean By Relationships?" *Work in Progress* 22: 1–23.

Noddings, N. (1984), *Caring: A Feminist Approach to Ethics and Moral Education* (Berkeley: University of California Press).

O'Brien, C.C. (1989), "A Last Chance to Save the Jews?" *New York Review of Books* 36: 27–31.

Plant, R. (1986), *Pink Triangle* (New York: Henry Holt).

Rawls, J. (1971), *A Theory of Justice* (Cambridge: Harvard University Press).

Robinson, C. (1983), *Black Marxism: The Making of the Black Radical Tradition* (London: Zed Books).

Rubenstein, R. (1978), *The Cunning of History* (New York: Harper and Row).

Ruddick, S. (1983), "Maternal Thinking," in J. Trebilcot, ed., *Mothering* (Totowa, N.J.: Rowman and Allanheld) 213–230.

Schmitt, R. (1988), "A New Hypothesis about the Relations of Race, Class and Gender," *Social Theory and Practice*, Fall 1988.

Seller, A. (1988), "Realism versus Relativism: Toward a Politically Adequate Epistemology," in M. Griffiths and M. Whitford, eds., *Feminist Perspectives in Philosophy* (Bloomington: Indiana University Press) 169–186.

Sweezy, P. (1942), *The Theory of Capitalist Development* (New York: Monthly Review).

Thomas, L. (1988), "Liberalism and the Holocaust: An Essay on Trust and the Black Jewish Relationship," in A. Rosenberg and G. Myers, eds., *Echoes from the Holocaust: Philosophical Reflections from a Dark Time* (Philadelphia: Temple University Press) 105–117.

Weber, M. (1958), *From Max Weber: Essays in Sociology* (New York: Oxford University Press).

Alice Miller

ADOLF HITLER'S CHILDHOOD: FROM HIDDEN TO MANIFEST HORROR

My pedagogy is hard. What is weak must be hammered away. In my fortresses of the Teutonic Order a young generation will grow up before which the world will tremble. I want the young to be violent, domineering, undismayed, cruel. The young must be all these things. They must be able to bear pain. There must be nothing weak or gentle about them. The free, splendid beast of prey must once again flash from their eyes. I want my young people strong and beautiful. That way I can create something new.

ADOLF HITLER

INTRODUCTION

My desire to learn more about Adolf Hitler's childhood did not emerge until I began to write this book, and it took me quite by surprise. The immediate occasion was the realization that my belief, based upon my experience as an analyst, that human destructiveness is a reactive (and not an innate) phenomenon either would be confirmed by the case of Adolf Hitler or—if Erich Fromm and others are right—would have to be completely revised. This question was important enough for me to try to answer, although I was very skeptical at first that I would be able to summon up empathy for this human being, whom I consider the worst criminal I have ever known of. Empathy, i.e., in this case the attempt to identify with the perspective of the child himself and not to judge him through adult eyes, is my sole heuristic tool, and without it, the whole investigation would be pointless. I was relieved to discover that for the purposes of my study I was successful in keeping this tool intact and was able to regard Hitler as a human being.

To do this, I had to free myself from thinking of "what is human" in traditional and idealizing terms based on splitting off and projecting evil; I had to realize that human being and "beast" do not exclude each other (cf. the Erich Fromm quotation on page 177). Animals do not suffer from the tragic compulsion of having to avenge, decades later, traumata experienced at an early age—as was the case, for example, with Frederick the Great, who was driven to become a great conqueror after the terrible humiliation he suffered as a child. In any event, I am not familiar enough with an animal's unconscious or its degree of awareness of its past to make any statements on the subject. So far, it is only in the human realm that I have discovered extreme bestiality; only there can I trace it and search for its motives. And I cannot renounce this search unless I am willing to be made into an instrument of cruelty, i.e., its unsuspecting (and thus guiltless yet blind) perpetrator and propagator.

If we turn our backs on something because it is difficult to understand and indignantly refer to it as "inhuman," we will never be able to learn anything about its nature. The risk will then be greater, when we next encounter it, of once again aiding and abetting it by our innocence and naïveté.

Over the past thirty-five years, countless works dealing with the life of Adolf Hitler have appeared. No doubt, I heard more than once that Hitler was beaten by his father, and even read it several years ago in a monograph by Helm Stierlin without being particularly struck by the fact. Since I have become sensitive, however, to the demeaning treatment children are sometimes subjected to in the first years of life, this information has taken on much greater importance for me. I asked myself what the childhood of this person had been like, a person who was possessed by hatred all his life and for whom it became so easy to involve other people in his hatred. As a result of reading *Schwarze Pädagogik* and of the feelings it awakened in me, I was suddenly able to imagine and feel what it must have been like for a child growing up in the Hitler household. What had previously been a black-and-white film was now in color, and it gradually merged to such an extent with my own experiences of World War II that it ceased being a film and turned into real life. This was not only a life that had been lived at a certain time and place in the past but one whose consequences and whose likelihood of being repeated I believe concern us all here and now as well. For the hope that by means of rational agreements it might be possible in the long run to prevent nuclear annihilation of the human race is at bottom a form of irrational wishful thinking and contradicts all our experience. As recently as the Third Reich, not to mention countless times before that, we have seen that reason constitutes only a small part of the human being, and not the dominant part, at that. All it took was a Führer's madness and several million well-raised Germans to extinguish the lives of countless innocent human beings in the space of a few short years. If we do not do everything we can to understand the roots of this hatred, even the most elaborate strategic agreements will not save us. The stockpiling of nuclear weapons is only a symbol of bottled-up feelings of hatred and of the accompanying inability to perceive and articulate genuine human needs.

The example of Hitler's childhood allows us to study the genesis of a hatred whose consequences caused the suffering of millions. The nature of this destructive hatred has long been familiar to psychoanalysts, but psychoanalysis will be of little help as long as it interprets this hatred as an expression of the death instinct. The followers of Melanie Klein, who in spite of their very accurate description of infantile hatred still define it as innate (instinctual) and not reactive, are no exception. Heinz Kohut comes closest to interpreting the phenomenon with his concept of narcissistic rage, which I have related to the infant's reaction to the lack of availability of the primary care giver.

But we must go one step further if we are to understand the origins of a lifelong insatiable hatred such as consumed Adolf Hitler. We must leave the familiar territory of drive theory and address the question of what takes place in a child who is humiliated and demeaned by his parents on the one hand and on the other is commanded to respect and love those who treat him in this fashion and under no circumstances to give expression to his suffering. Although something so absurd would scarcely be expected of an adult (except in pronouncedly sadomasochistic relationships), this is exactly what parents expect of their children in most cases, and in previous generations they were rarely disappointed. In the earliest stage of life, it is possible for a child to forget about the extreme acts of cruelty he or she has endured and to idealize their perpetrator. But the nature of the subsequent enactment reveals that the whole history of early persecution was stored up somewhere; the drama now unfolds in front of the spectators with an amazing resemblance to the original situation but under another guise: in the reenactment, the child who was once persecuted now becomes the persecutor. In psychoanalytic treatment, the story is enacted within the framework of transference and countertransference.

If psychoanalysis could only free itself of its stubborn belief in the death instinct, it would be able to begin to answer the question of why wars occur, on the basis of material available on early childhood conditioning. Unfortunately, however, most psychoanalysts are not interested in what parents did to their children, leaving this question to family therapists. Since the latter in turn do not work with transference but concentrate primarily on modifying interactions among family members, they seldom gain the access to events of early childhood possible in a thoroughgoing analysis.

In order to show how the early debasement, mistreatment, and psychological rape of a child expresses itself throughout later life, I would need only to recount the history of a single analysis down to the last detail, but considerations of discretion make this impossible. Hitler's life, on the other hand, was observed and recorded so exactly by so many witnesses up to the very last day that this material can easily be used to demonstrate the enactment of the early childhood situation. In addition to the testimony of witnesses and the historical events in which his deeds are documented, his thoughts and feelings were expressed, albeit in coded form, in his many speeches and in his book *Mein Kampf.* It would be a highly instructive and rewarding task to make Hitler's entire political career comprehensible from the perspective of the history of his persecution in early childhood. But to pursue this task is far beyond the scope of this book, since my sole interest here is in showing examples of the effects of "poisonous pedagogy." For this reason I shall restrict myself to a few highlights in his biography; in so doing, I shall attribute particular significance to certain childhood experiences that until now have received little attention from his biographers. Because historians by profession concern themselves with external facts, and psychoanalysts with the Oedipus complex, few seem to have seriously raised the question: What did this child *feel,* what did he *store up* inside when he was beaten and demeaned by his father every day from an early age?

On the basis of available documents, we can easily gain an impression of the atmosphere in which Adolf Hitler grew up. The family structure could well be characterized as the prototype of a totalitarian regime. Its sole, undisputed, often brutal ruler is the father. The wife and children are totally subservient to his will, his moods, and his whims; they must accept humiliation and injustice unquestioningly and gratefully. Obedience is their primary rule of conduct. The mother, to be sure, has her own sphere of authority in the household, where she rules over the children when the father is not at home; this means that she can to some extent take out on those weaker than herself the humiliation she has suffered. In the totalitarian state, a similar function is assigned to the security police. They are the overseers of the slaves, although they are slaves themselves, carrying out the dictator's wishes, serving as his deputies in his absence, instilling fear in his name, meting out punishment, assuming the guise of the rulers of the oppressed.

Within this family structure, the children are the oppressed. If they have younger siblings, they are provided with a place to abreact their own humiliation. As long as there are even weaker, more helpless creatures than they, they are not the lowest of slaves. Sometimes, however, as was the case with Christiane F., the child is ranked below the dog, for the dog need not be beaten if a child is available.

This hierarchy, which can be observed in the way concentration camps were organized (with their ranking of guards, etc.) and which is legitimized by "poisonous pedagogy," is probably still maintained in many families today. The possible consequences for a sensitive child can be traced in detail in the case of Adolf Hitler. . . .

For many people it is very difficult to accept the sad truth that cruelty is usually inflicted upon the innocent. Don't we learn as small children that all the cruelty shown us in our upbringing is a punishment for our wrongdoing? A teacher told me that several children in her class, after seeing the *Holocaust* film, said, "But the Jews must have been guilty or they wouldn't have been punished like that."

With this in mind, we can understand the attempts of all Hitler's biographers to attribute every possible sin, especially laziness, obstinacy, and dishonesty, to little Adolf. But is a child born a liar? And isn't lying the only way to survive with such a father and retain a remnant of one's dignity? Sometimes deception and bad grades in school provide the only means for secretly developing a shred of autonomy for a person so totally at the mercy of another's whims as was Adolf Hitler (and not he alone!). We can assume on this basis that Hitler's later descriptions of an open battle with his father over a choice of career were doctored versions, not because the son was a coward "by nature," but because his father was unable to permit any discussion. It is more likely that the following passage from *Mein Kampf* reflects the true state of affairs.

> I had to some extent been able to keep my private opinions to myself; I did not always have to contradict him immediately. My own firm determination never to become a civil servant sufficed to give me complete inner peace.

It is significant that when Konrad Heiden quotes this passage in his Hitler biography he remarks at the end, "In other words, a little sneak." We expect a child in a totalitarian setting to be open and honest but at the same time to obey implicitly, bring good grades home from school, not contradict his father, and always fulfill his duty.

Another biographer, Rudolf Olden, writing about Hitler's problems at school, says:

> Apathy and poor performance soon become more pronounced. With the loss of a stern guiding hand upon the sudden death of his father, a crucial stimulus disappears.

The beatings are here considered a "stimulus" to learning. This is written by the very same biographer who has just presented this picture of Alois:

> Even after he retired, he retained the typical pride of a bureaucrat and insisted on being addressed as "Herr," followed by his title, whereas the farmers and laborers used the informal form of address ["Du"] with one another. By showing him the respect he demanded, the local people were really making fun of this outsider. He was never on good terms with the people he knew. To make up for it he had established a nice little dictatorship in his own home. His wife looked up to him, and he treated the children with a hard hand. Adolf in particular he had no understanding for. He tyrannized him. If he wanted the boy to come to him, the former noncommissioned officer would whistle on two fingers.

This description, written in 1935 when many Braunau acquaintances of the Hitler family were still living and it was not yet so difficult to gather information of this sort, is not repeated, to my knowledge, in the postwar biographies. The image of a man who calls his child to him by whistling as though he were a dog is so strongly reminiscent of reports of the concentration camps that it is not surprising if present-day biographers have been reluctant to make the connection. In addition, all the biographies share the tendency to play down the father's brutality with the observation that beatings were quite normal in those days or even with complicated arguments against "vilifying" the father, such as those presented by Jetzinger. Sadly enough, Jetzinger's careful research provides an important source for later biographies, even though his psychological insights are not far removed from those of an Alois.

The way Hitler unconsciously took on his father's behavior and displayed it on the stage of world history is indicative of how the child must really have seen his father: the snappy, uniformed, somewhat ridiculous dictator, as Charlie Chaplin portrayed him in his film and as Hitler's enemies saw him, is the way Alois appeared in the eyes of his critical son. The heroic Führer, loved and admired by the German people, was the other Alois, the husband loved and admired by his subservient wife, Klara, whose awe and admiration Adolf no doubt shared when he was still very little. These two internalized aspects of his father can be identified in so many of Adolf's later enactments (in connection with the "heroic" aspect, we need only think of the greeting "Heil Hitler," of the adoration of the masses, etc.) that we receive the impression that throughout his later life his considerable artistic talents impelled him to reproduce his earliest—deeply imprinted, though unconscious—memories of a tyrannical father. His portrayal is unforgettable for everyone who was alive at the time; some of his contemporaries experienced the dictator from the perspective of the horror felt by a mistreated child, and others from the perspective of an innocent child's complete devotion and acceptance. Every great artist draws on the unconscious contents of childhood, and Hitler's energies could have gone into creating works of art instead of destroying the lives of millions of people, who would then not have had to bear the brunt of this unresolved suffering, which he warded off in grandiosity. Yet, in spite of his grandiose identification with the aggressor, there are passages in *Mein Kampf* that show the way Hitler experienced his childhood.

> In a basement apartment, consisting of two stuffy rooms, dwells a worker's family of seven. Among the five children there is a boy of, let us assume, three. . . . The very narrowness and overcrowding of the room does not lead to favorable conditions. Quarreling and wrangling will very frequently arise. . . . But if this battle is carried on between the parents themselves, and almost every day, in forms which in vulgarity often leave nothing to be desired, then, if only very gradually, the results of such visual instruction must ultimately become apparent in the children. The character they will inevitably assume if the quarrel takes the form of brutal attacks by the father against the mother, of drunken beatings, is hard for anyone who does not know this milieu to imagine. At the age of six the pitiable little boy suspects the existence of things which can fill even an adult with nothing but horror. . . . All the other things that the little fellow hears at home do not tend to increase his respect for his dear fellow men.

It ends badly if the man goes his own way from the very beginning and the woman, for the children's sake, opposes him. Then there is fighting and quarreling, and as the man grows estranged from his wife, he becomes more intimate with alcohol. When at length he comes home on Sunday or even Monday night, drunk and brutal, but always parted from his last cent, such scenes often occur that God have mercy!

I have seen this in hundreds of instances.

Although the deep and lasting damage it would have done to his dignity prevented Hitler from admitting the situation of the "let us assume, three-year-old boy" to be his own in the first-person account of *Mein Kampf,* the content of his description leaves no doubt whose childhood is meant.

A child whose father does not call to him by name but by whistling to him as though the child were a dog has the same disenfranchised and nameless status in the family as did "the Jew" in the Third Reich.

Through the agency of his unconscious repetition compulsion, Hitler actually succeeded in transferring the trauma of his family life onto the entire German nation. The introduction of the racial laws forced every citizen to trace his or her descent back to the third generation and to bear the ensuing consequences. At first, the wrong ancestry, or an uncertain one, meant disgrace and degradation; later it meant death—and this during peacetime, in a country that called itself civilized. There is no other example of such a phenomenon in all of history. The Inquisition, for example, persecuted the Jews because of their religion, but they were offered the chance to survive if they accepted baptism. In the Third Reich, however, neither behavior nor merit nor achievement were of any avail; on the basis of descent alone a Jew was condemned, first to be demeaned and later to die. Is this not a twofold reflection of Hitler's fate?

1. It was impossible for Hitler's father, in spite of all his efforts, successes, and advances in career from shoemaker to chief customs inspector, to remove the "stain" in his past, just as it was later forbidden the Jews to remove the stigma of the yellow star they were forced to wear. The stain remained and oppressed Alois all his life. It may be that his frequent moves (eleven, according to Fest) had another cause beside a professional one—to obliterate his traces. This tendency is also very clear in Adolf's life. "When he was told in 1942 that there was a memorial marker in the village of Spital [in the region where his father was born] he went into one of his wild rages," Fest reports.

2. At the same time, the racial laws represented the repetition of

the drama of Hitler's own childhood. In the same way that the Jew now had no chance to escape, the child Adolf at one time could not escape his father's blows, which were caused, not by the child's behavior, but by the father's unresolved problems, such as his resistance to mourning over his own childhood. It is fathers such as this who are likely to drag their sleeping child out of bed if they cannot come to terms with a mood (perhaps having just felt insignificant and insecure on some social occasion) and beat the child in order to restore their narcissistic equilibrium (cf. Christiane F.'s father).

The Jews fulfilled the same function in the Third Reich—which attempted to recover from the disgrace of the Weimar Republic at their expense—as this sleeping child. This was Adolf's function throughout his childhood; he had to accept the fact that at any moment a storm could break over his helpless head without his being able to find any way to avert or escape it.

Since there were no bonds of affection between Adolf and his father (it is significant that in *Mein Kampf* he refers to Alois as "Herr Vater"), his burgeoning hatred was constant and unequivocal. It is different for children whose fathers have outbursts of rage and can then, in between times, play good-naturedly with their children. In this case the child's hatred cannot be cultivated in such a pure form. These children experience difficulties of another sort as adults; they seek out partners with a personality structure that, like their fathers', tends toward extremes. They are bound to these partners by a thousand chains and cannot bring themselves to leave them, always living with the hope that the other person's good side will finally win out; yet at every fresh outburst they are plunged into new despair. These sadomasochistic bonds, which go back to the equivocal and unpredictable nature of a parent, are stronger than a genuine love relationship; they are impossible to break, and signal permanent destruction of the self.

Little Adolf could be certain of receiving constant beatings; he knew that nothing he did would have any effect on the daily thrashings he was given. All he could do was deny the pain, in other words, deny himself and identify with the aggressor. No one could help him, not even his mother, for this would spell danger for her too, because she was also battered (cf. Toland).

This state of constant jeopardy is reflected very clearly in the fate of the Jews in the Third Reich. Let us try to imagine the following scene. A Jew is walking down the street, perhaps on his way home from buying milk, when a man wearing an SA armband attacks him; this man has the right to do anything to the Jew he wants, anything his fantasy happens to dictate and that his unconscious craves at the moment. The Jew can do nothing to alter this; he is in the same position as little Adolf once was. If the Jew tries to defend himself, there is nothing to prevent his being trampled to death. He is like the eleven-year-old Adolf, who in desperation once ran away from home with three friends, planning to float down the river on a homemade raft and thus flee from his violent father. Just for the very thought of trying to escape, he was nearly beaten to death (cf. Stierlin). It is just as impossible for the Jew to escape; all roads are cut off and lead to death, like the railroad tracks that simply came to an end at Treblinka and Auschwitz—signifying the end of life itself. This is the way any child feels who is beaten day in and day out and who is very nearly killed for daring to think of escape.

In the scene I have just described, which occurred countless times between 1933 and 1945 in many variations, the Jew has to endure everything like a helpless child. He must submit to having this creature with the SA armband, who has been transformed into a screaming, berserk monster, pour the milk over his head and summon others to the scene to share his amusement (the way Alois laughed at Adolf's "toga"). He must endure having the SA man feel big and strong alongside someone who is completely at his mercy, completely in his power. If this Jew loves his life, he will not risk it now just for the sake of proving to himself that he is tough and courageous. Instead, he will remain passive yet inwardly full of revulsion and scorn for this man, just as Adolf had been when he gradually came to see through his father's weakness and began to pay him back, at least a little, by doing poorly in school, which he knew upset his father. . . .

There is probably no more reliable common tie among the peoples of Europe than their shared hatred of the Jews. Those in power have always been able to manipulate this hatred for their own purposes; for example, it seems to be remarkably well suited to unite conflicting interests, with the result that even groups extremely hostile to one another can be in complete agreement about how dangerous and obnoxious the Jews are. Hitler realized this and once said to Rauschning that "if the Jews didn't exist they would have to be invented."

Where does anti-Semitism's perpetual ability to renew itself come from? The answer is not difficult to find. A Jew is not hated for doing or being something specific. Everything Jews do or the way they are applies to other groups as well. Jews are hated because people harbor a forbidden hatred and are eager to legitimate it. The Jewish people are particularly well-suited objects of this need. Because they have been persecuted for two thousand years by the highest authorities of church and state, no one ever needs to feel ashamed for hating the Jews, not even if one has been raised according to the strictest moral principles and is made to feel ashamed of the most natural emotions of the soul in other regards. A child who has been required to don the armor of "virtue" at too early an age will seize upon the only permissible discharge; he will seize upon anti-Semitism (i.e., his right to hate), retaining it for the rest of his life. It is possible that Hitler did not have easy access to this discharge, however, because it would have touched upon a family taboo. Later, in Vienna, he was happy to shed this silent prohibition, and when he came to power he needed only to proclaim this one legitimate hatred in the Western tradition as the highest Aryan virtue. . . .

I have dwelt so long on Hitler's problems at school because their causes and their later ramifications are typical of millions of other cases as well. The fact that Hitler had so many enthusiastic followers proves that they had a personality structure similar to his, i.e., that they had had a similar upbringing. The contemporary biographies demonstrate how far we still are in our thinking from the realization that a child has a right to be respected. Fest, who took immense and exhaustive pains to depict Hitler's life, cannot believe the son's claim that he suffered greatly because of his father and thinks Adolf is only "dramatizing" these difficulties—as if anyone were more qualified to judge the situation than Adolf Hitler himself.

Fest's tendency to spare the parents is scarcely surprising when we consider the extent to which psychoanalysis itself is captive to this approach. Insofar as its followers still consider it their main goal to fight for the free expression of sexuality, they are overlooking other crucial matters. We can see what a child who has not been shown respect and therefore lacks self-respect does with "liberated" sexuality when we consider child prostitution and the current drug scene. Here we can learn, among other things, about the disastrous dependency (on other people and on heroin) that can result from children's "liberation," which does not deserve the name if it is accompanied by self-degradation.

Both child abuse and its consequences are so well integrated into our lives that we are scarcely struck by their absurdity. Adolescents' "heroic willingness" to fight one another in wars and (just as life is beginning!) to die for someone else's cause may be a result of the fact that during puberty the warded-off hatred from early childhood becomes reintensified. Adolescents can divert this hatred from their parents if they are given a clear-cut enemy whom they are permitted to hate freely and with impunity. This may be why so many young painters and writers volunteered for the front in World War I. The hope of freeing themselves from the constraints imposed by their family enabled them to take pleasure in marching to the music of a military band. One of heroin's roles is to replace this function, with the difference that in the case of drugs the destructive rage is directed against one's own body and self.

Lloyd de Mause, who as a psychohistorian is particularly interested in motivation and in describing the group fantasies underlying it, once did a study of the dominant fantasies among aggressor nations. Looking through his material, he noticed that again and again statements by the leaders of these nations employed images relating to the birth process. With striking frequency they speak of their nation as being strangled, a situation they hope the war will finally rectify. De Mause believes that this fantasy reflects the actual situation of the infant during birth, which results in a trauma for every human being and thus is subject to the repetition compulsion. . . .

In spite of these considerations, it is possible to imagine that the birth fantasy does play a role here. For children who are beaten every day and must remain silent about it, birth may be the only childhood event where they emerged the victor, not only in fantasy but in actuality; otherwise, they would not have survived. They fought their way through a narrow passage and were allowed to scream afterwards, in spite of which they were taken care of by helping hands. Can this bliss be compared to what came later? It would not be surprising if we wanted to use this great triumph to help ourselves get over the defeats and loneliness of later years. Seen from this perspective, associations between the birth trauma and the declaration of war could be interpreted as a denial of the actual, hidden trauma, which is never taken seriously by society and therefore requires enactment. In Hitler's life, the "Boer wars" of his schooldays, *Mein Kampf,* and World War II belong to the visible tip of the iceberg. The hidden explanation for why he developed the way he did cannot be sought in the experience of emerging from the womb, an experience Hitler shares with all human beings. Not all human beings, on the other hand, were tormented the way he was as a child.

What didn't the son do to forget the trauma of the beatings his father gave him: he subjugated Germany's ruling class, won over the masses, and bent the governments of Europe to his will. He possessed nearly limitless power. At night, however, in his sleep, when the unconscious lets us know about our early childhood experiences, there was no escape: then his father came back to frighten him, and his terror was boundless. Rauschning writes:

Hitler, however, has states that approach persecution mania and a dual personality. His sleeplessness is more than the mere result of excessive nervous strain. He often wakes up in the middle of the night and wanders restlessly to and fro. Then he must have light everywhere. Lately he has sent at these times for young men who have to keep him company during his hours of manifest anguish. At times his condition must have been dreadful. A man in the closest daily association with him gave me this account: Hitler wakes at night with convulsive shrieks. He shouts for help. He sits on the edge of his bed, unable to stir. He shakes with fear, making the whole bed vibrate. He mutters confused, totally unintelligible phrases. He gasps, as if imagining himself to be suffocating.

My informant described to me in full detail a remarkable scene—I should not have credited the story if it had not come from such a reliable source. Hitler stood swaying in his room, looking wildly about him. "It was he! It was he! He's been here!" he gasped. His lips were blue. Sweat streamed down his face. Suddenly he began to reel off figures, and odd words and broken phrases, entirely devoid of sense. It sounded horrible. He used strangely constructed and entirely un-German word formations. Then he stood quite still, only his lips moving. He was massaged and offered something to drink. Then he suddenly burst out—

"There, there! In the corner! Who's that?"

He stamped and shrieked in the familiar way. He was shown that there was nothing out of the ordinary in the room, and then he gradually grew calm. After that he lay asleep for many hours, and then for some time things were endurable again.

Although (or because) most of the people surrounding Hitler had once been battered children themselves, no one grasped the connection between his panic and the "unintelligible" numbers. The feelings of fear he had repressed in his childhood when counting his father's blows now overtook the adult at the peak of his success in the form of nightmares, sudden and inescapable, in the loneliness of the night.

Had he made the entire world his victim, he still would not have been able to banish his introjected father from his bedroom, for one's own unconscious cannot be destroyed by destroying the world. Yet, in spite of this fact, the world would still have had to pay dearly if Hitler had lived any longer, for the springs of his hatred flowed unceasingly— even in his sleep.

Those who have never experienced the power of the unconscious may find it naïve to try to explain Hitler's deeds as an outgrowth of his childhood experiences. There are still many men and women who are of the opinion that "childhood matters are merely childish matters" and that politics is something serious, something for adults, and not child's play. These people think connections between childhood and later life farfetched or ridiculous, since they would like, for good reason, to forget completely the reality of those early years. A life such as Hitler's is especially instructive here because in it the continuity between earlier and later can be traced so clearly. Even as a small boy he expressed his longing to be free from his father's yoke in the war games he played. First he led the Indians and then the Boers into battle against the oppressors. "It was not long before the great heroic struggle [the Franco-German War of 1870–71] had become my greatest inner experience," he writes in *Mein Kampf,* and in the same passage we can detect the fateful connection between those games that reflected his childhood unhappiness and the deadly seriousness to come: "From then on, I became more and more enthusiastic about everything that was in any way connected with war or, for that matter, with soldiering." . . .

I have no doubt that behind every crime a personal tragedy lies hidden. If we were to investigate such events and their backgrounds more closely, we might be able to do more to prevent crimes than we do now with our indignation and moralizing. Perhaps someone will say: But not everyone who was a battered child becomes a murderer; otherwise, many more people would be murderers. That is true. However, human-kind is in dire enough straits these days that this should not remain an academic question. Moreover, we never know how a child will and must react to the injustice he or she has suffered—there are innumerable "techniques" for dealing with it. We don't yet know, above all, what the world might be like if children were to grow up without being subjected to humiliation, if parents would respect them and take them seriously as persons. In any case, I don't know of a single person who enjoyed this respect* as a child and then as an adult had the need to put other human beings to death.

---

* By respect for a child, I don't mean a "permissive" upbringing, which is often a form of indoctrination itself and thus shows a disregard for the child's own world.

We are still barely conscious of how harmful it is to treat children in a degrading manner. Treating them with respect and recognizing the consequences of their being humiliated are by no means intellectual matters; otherwise, their importance would long since have been generally recognized. To empathize with what a child is feeling when he or she is defenseless, hurt, or humiliated is like suddenly seeing in a mirror the suffering of one's own childhood, something many people must ward off out of fear while others can accept it with mourning. People who have mourned in this way understand more about the dynamics of the psyche than they could ever have learned from books.

The persecution of people of Jewish background, the necessity of proving "racial purity" as far back as one's grandparents, the tailoring of prohibitions to the degree of an individual's demonstrable "racial purity"—all this is grotesque only at first glance. For its significance becomes plain once we realize that in terms of Hitler's unconscious fantasies it is an intensified expression of two very powerful tendencies. On the one hand, his father was the hated Jew whom he could despise and persecute, frighten and threaten with regulations, because his father would also have been affected by the racial laws if he had still been alive. At the same time—and this is the other tendency—the racial laws were meant to mark Adolf's final break with his father and his background. In addition to revenge, the tormenting uncertainty about the Hitler family was an important motive for the racial laws: the whole nation had to trace its "purity" back to the third generation because Adolf Hitler would have liked to know with certainty who his grandfather was. Above all, the Jew became the bearer of all the evil and despicable traits the child had ever observed in his father. In Hitler's view, the Jews were characterized by a specific mixture of Lucifer-like grandeur and superiority (world Jewry and its readiness to destroy the entire world) on the one hand and ugliness and ludicrous weakness and infirmity on the other. This view reflects the omnipotence even the weakest father exercises over his child, seen in Hitler's case in the wild rages of the insecure customs official who succeeded in destroying his son's world.

It is common in analysis for the first breakthrough in criticizing the father to be signaled by the surfacing of some insignificant and ludicrous trait of his that the patient's memory has repressed. For example, the father—big out of all proportion in the child's eyes—may have looked very funny in his short nightshirt. The child had never been close to his father, had been in constant fear of him, but with this memory of the skimpy nightshirt, the child's imagination provides a weapon, now that ambivalence has broken through in the analysis, which enables him to take revenge on a small scale against the godlike, monumental paternal figure. In similar fashion, Hitler disseminates his hatred and disgust for the "stinking" Jew in the pages of the Nazi periodical *Der Stürmer* in order to incite people to burn books by Freud, Einstein, and innumerable other Jewish intellectuals of great stature. The breakthrough of this idea, which made it possible for him to transfer his pent-up hatred of his father to the Jews as a people, is very instructive. It is described in the following passage from *Mein Kampf.*

> Since I had begun to concern myself with this question and to take cognizance of the Jews, Vienna appeared to me in a different light than before. Wherever I went, I began to see Jews, and the more I saw, the more sharply they became distinguished in my eyes from the rest of humanity. Particularly the Inner City and the districts north of the Danube Canal swarmed with a people which even outwardly had lost all resemblance to Germans. . . .
>
> All this could scarcely be called very attractive; but it became positively repulsive when, in addition to their physical uncleanliness, you discovered the moral stains on this "chosen people." . . .
>
> Was there any form of filth or profligacy, particularly in cultural life, without at least one Jew involved in it?
>
> If you cut even cautiously into such an abscess, you found, like a maggot in a rotting body, often dazzled by the sudden light—a kike!
>
> Gradually I began to hate them.

Once he succeeds in directing all his bottled-up hatred toward an object, the first reaction is one of great relief ("Wherever I went, I began to see Jews"). Forbidden, long-avoided feelings can now be given free rein. The more they had filled and pressed in upon one, the happier one feels at having finally found an ersatz object. Now there is no need to hate his own father; now Adolf can allow the dam to burst without being beaten for it.

Yet this ersatz satisfaction merely whets the appetite—nothing illustrates this better than the case of Adolf Hitler. Although there probably had never before been a person with Hitler's power to destroy human life on such a scale with impunity, all this still could not bring him

peace. His last will and testament, which calls for the continued persecution of the Jews, is impressive proof of this.

When we read Stierlin's description of Hitler's father, we see how
closely the son resembled his father in personality.

> It appears, however, that his social rise was not without cost to
> himself and others. While he was conscientious and hard-work-
> ing, he was also emotionally unstable, inordinately restless, and
> perhaps at times mentally disturbed. According to one source,
> he possibly once entered an asylum. Also, in the opinion of at
> least one analyst, he combined an overriding determination
> with a flexible conscience, shown especially in how he manipu-
> lated rules and records to his own ends, while maintaining a
> facade of legitimacy. (For example, in applying for papal ap-
> proval to marry his legal cousin Klara, he stressed his two small
> motherless children, needing Klara's care, but failed to men-
> tion her pregnancy.)

Only a child's unconscious can copy a parent so exactly that every
characteristic of the parent can later be found in the child. This phenomenon, however, is one that usually escapes the attention of biographers. . . .

SUMMARY

Readers who interpret my treatment of Hitler's early childhood as
sentimental or even as an attempt to excuse his deeds naturally have
every right to construe what they have read as they see fit. People who,
for example, had to learn at a very early age "to keep a stiff upper lip"
identify with their parents to the extent that they consider any form of
empathy with a child as emotionalism or sentimentality. As for the question of guilt, I chose Hitler for the very reason that I know of no other
criminal who is responsible for the death of so many human beings. But
nothing is gained by using the word *guilt*. We of course have the right
and the duty to lock up murderers who threaten our life. For the time
being, we do not know of any better solution. But this does not alter the
fact that the need to commit murder is the outcome of a tragic childhood and that imprisonment is the tragic sequel to this fate.

If we stop looking for new facts and focus on the significance within
the total picture of what we already know, we will come upon sources of
information in our study of Hitler that have thus far not been properly

evaluated and therefore are not readily or widely accessible. As far as I know, for example, little attention has been paid to the important fact that Klara Hitler's hunchbacked and schizophrenic sister, Adolf's Aunt Johanna, lived with the family throughout his childhood. At least in the biographies I have read, I have never found a connection made between this fact and the Third Reich's euthanasia law. To find any significance in this connection, a person must be able and willing to comprehend the feelings that arise in a child who is exposed daily to an extremely absurd and frightening form of behavior and yet at the same time is forbidden to articulate his fear and rage or his questions. Even the presence of a schizophrenic aunt can be positively dealt with by a child, but only if he can communicate freely with his parents on the emotional level and can talk with them about his fears.

Franziska Hörl, a servant in the Hitler household when Adolf was born, told Jetzinger in an interview that she had not been able to put up with this aunt any longer and left the family on her account, stating simply that she refused to be around "that crazy hunchback" any longer.

The child of the family is not allowed to say such a thing. Unable to leave, he must put up with everything; not until he has grown up can he take any action. When Hitler was grown and came to power, he was finally able to avenge himself a thousandfold on this unfortunate aunt for his own misfortune. He had all the mentally ill in Germany put to death, because he felt they were "useless" for a "healthy" society (i.e., for him as a child). As an adult, Hitler no longer had to put up with anything; he was even able to "liberate" all of Germany from the "plague" of the mentally ill and retarded and was not at a loss to find ideological embellishments for this thoroughly personal act of revenge.

I have not gone into the background of the euthanasia law in this book because it has been my main concern to describe the consequences of actively humiliating a child, by presenting a striking example. Since such humiliation, combined with prohibiting a child's verbal expression, is a constant and universally encountered factor in child-rearing, the influence of this factor in the child's later development is easily overlooked. The claim that child beating (including spanking) is common, to say nothing of the conviction that it is necessary in order to spur the child on to learn, completely ignores the dimensions of childhood tragedy. Because the relationship of child beating to subsequent criminality is not perceived, the world reacts with horror to the crimes it sees committed and overlooks the conditions giving rise to them, as if murderers fell out of a clear blue sky.

I have used Hitler as an example to show that:

1. Even the worst criminal of all time was not born a criminal.

2. Empathizing with a child's unhappy beginnings does not imply exoneration of the cruel acts he later commits. (This is as true for Alois Hitler as it is for Adolf.)

3. Those who persecute others are warding off knowledge of their own fate as victims.

4. Consciously experiencing one's own victimization instead of trying to ward it off provides a protection against sadism; i.e., the compulsion to torment and humiliate others.

5. The admonition to spare one's parents inherent in the Fourth Commandment and in "poisonous pedagogy" encourages us to overlook crucial factors in a person's early childhood and later development.

6. We as adults don't get anywhere with accusations, indignation, or guilt feelings, but only by understanding the situations in question.

7. True emotional understanding has nothing to do with cheap sentimental pity.

8. The fact that a situation is ubiquitous does not absolve us from examining it. On the contrary, we must examine it for the very reason that it is or can be the fate of each and every one of us.

9. Living out hatred is the opposite of experiencing it. To experience something is an intrapsychic reality; to live it out, on the other hand, is an action that can cost other people their lives. If the path to experiencing one's feelings is blocked by the prohibitions of "poisonous pedagogy" or by the needs of the parents, then these feelings will have to be lived out. This can occur either in a destructive form, as in Hitler's case, or in a self-destructive one, as in Christiane F.'s. Or, as in the case of most criminals who end up in prison, this living out can lead to the destruction both of the self and of others.

Part II
THE AGENTS: REFLECTIONS ON VICTIMS AND MURDERERS

While we possess an enormous amount of factual knowledge about the experiences of the victims and the murderers, we still must question what those experiences mean. The following six selections seek not to enlarge our knowledge but to challenge our understanding. Terence Des Pres describes aspects of the consciousness of survivors of the camps, asking what type of personal strengths help a person survive this inhuman world. By helping us think ourselves into the desperate situation of the times, Abigail Rosenthal challenges the myth of Jewish complicity. Joan Ringelheim's and Myrna Goldenberg's essays, springing from recent accomplishments of feminist theory, question the role of gender in the experience of the Holocaust: What difference did it make if you were a man or woman? Why is this an important question to ask? Jean-Paul Sartre and Robert J. Lifton help us understand the psychology of the murderers. Sartre's classic essay focuses on the anti-semitism which surfaced during the Nazi occupation of France, but is applicable to the entire period of the Holocaust. Sartre identifies anti-semitism with a fundamentally dishonest choice to escape responsibility for one's fate. Lifton's contribution comes from his lengthy study of the doctors who performed torturous experiments on camp inmates, and suggests that distance from one's own deepest impulses allows for this monstrous behavior.

Terence Des Pres

US AND THEM

All around and beneath her she could hear strange submerged sounds, groaning, choking and sobbing: many of the people were not dead yet. The whole mass of bodies kept moving slightly as they settled down and were pressed tighter by the movements of the ones who were still alive. . . . Then she heard people walking near her, actually on the bodies . . . , occasionally firing at those which showed signs of life. . . . One SS man . . . shone his torch on her, . . . but she . . . gave no signs of life.

A. KUZNETSOV
Babi Yar

That corpse you planted last year in
    your garden,
Has it begun to sprout? Will it
    bloom this year?
Or has the sudden frost disturbed
    its bed?

T. S. ELIOT
The Waste Land

In 1959 Stanley M. Elkins put forward his slave-as-sambo thesis in *Slavery*, arguing that the personality of the American slave had been fundamentally regressive and infantile. Elkins does not examine direct evidence; he uses a "comparative" method, and his main comparison is with inmates of the German concentration camps. To identify the Southern plantation with Auschwitz is senseless, of course; but the comparison is still significant, not for what it tells us of either slave or survivors, but for the assumptions that are made about behavior in extremity. Elkins takes it for granted that in the camps men and women

109

lost their capacity to act as morally responsible adults, and the point of his comparison is to demonstrate that this also happened to American slaves. Specifically, he states that "old prisoners," by which he means the survivors, suffered "deep disintegrative effects" (107); that the "most immediate aspect of the old inmates' behavior . . . was its *childlike* quality" (111); and finally that "all" survivors were "reduced to complete and childish dependence upon their masters" (113). Elkins goes on to say that regression began with the abandonment of previous ethical standards, and to make his point he quotes as representative a brief statement by a survivor of Auschwitz. In Elkins' context, here is her remark:

> One part of the prisoner's being was thus, under sharp stress, brought to the crude realization that he must thenceforth be governed by an entire new set of standards in order to live. Mrs. Lingens-Reiner puts it bluntly: "Will you survive or shall I? As soon as one sensed that this was at stake everyone turned egotist" (109–10).

In extremity, in other words, everyone fights alone; and the "entire new set of standards" comes from the camp system itself. But is there not a contradiction here? Childlike behavior is not the same as rapacious battle in one's best self-interest. The former entails passivity and preference for illusion; the latter demands intelligent calculation and a capacity for quick, objective judgment. All the same, that survivors suffered regression to infantile stages, *and* that they were amoral monsters, are very widespread notions. They constitute nothing less than the prevailing view of survival behavior. Not surprisingly, in *Death in Life* Robert Lifton has used the same quotation—"Will you survive, or shall I?"—as a representative expression of the "competition for survival" which, in his view, lies at the root of the "guilt" survivors are supposed to feel (490). What, then, are we to make of the Lingens-Reiner statement? Is it a fair summation of her own view?

In *Prisoners of Fear* she aims to tell the very worst; and the most striking thing about her testimony is the double vision we have already noted in reports by survivors. The viciousness and horror are certainly there, but also examples of morally intelligent behavior, and many references to resistance and solidarity among camp inmates. There is the moment when the narrator exposes herself by taking action to get another prisoner's name off a death list. She does this, all the time calling herself a fool for taking the risk, because she sees an opportunity: there was a *way* to save someone and that decided her. The incident takes four

pages to describe (79–82) and is not an example of "survival egotism" or
of "infantile regression." It is one instance among many of men and
women acting with courage and intelligence to help others. The following are typical:

> There were girls among them who lived through a typhus at-
> tack without staying in bed. Two of their friends would take the
> sick comrade between them, when she had a temperature of
> 103° F. and saw everything as a blur, and drag her along with
> their labour gang; out in the fields they would lay her down
> under a shrub, and in the evening they would march her back
> to camp—all to avoid her being sent to the hospital hut and so
> being exposed to the danger of a selection (122).

> The camp doctor would line up all the Jewish patients. . . . All
> those who were too ill to get out of bed were lost from the
> outset. . . . The rest of the prisoners did everything in their
> power to obstruct the doctor and to save one or other of the
> victims; I do not think that a single one among us withheld her
> help. We would hide women somewhere in the hut. . . . We
> would smuggle them into "Aryan" huts. . . . We would put
> their names on the list of patients due for release (76–7).

> Under the pressure of a concentration camp you grew more
> closely attached to people than you would have done otherwise
> in such a short time (162).

The pursuit of self-interest was certainly a determinant of behavior
in the camps, but it was everywhere countered by an unsuppressible
urge toward decency and care, a multitude of small deeds against the
grain of one's "best" interest. Prisoners looked out for themselves first
of all, but also for one another when and however they could. In the
whole body of testimony by survivors there is no better description of
this contradiction than in the book by Lingens-Reiner:

> Ena Weiss, our Chief Doctor—one of the most intelligent,
> gifted and eminent Jewish women in the camp—once defined
> her attitude thus, in sarcastic rejection of fulsome flattery and
> at the same time with brutal frankness: "How did I keep alive in
> Auschwitz? My principle is: myself first, second and third. Then
> nothing. Then myself again—and then all the others." This
> formula expressed the only principle which was possible for

Jews who intended—almost insanely intended—to survive
Auschwitz. Yet, because this woman had the icy wisdom and
strength to accept the principle, she kept for herself a position
in which she could do something for the Jews. Hardly anybody
else in the camp did as much for them and saved so many lives
as she did (118).

At least in this instance, Elkins' thesis is not borne out by the
evidence from which he quotes, and if for a time his "sambo" theory of
slave behavior was accepted, that was not because he had offered solid
evidence but because by comparing slavery to the camp experience he
was able to mobilize the deeply disturbing and largely uncontrolled
range of reaction which attends our idea of the concentration camps.
Here is how he sums it up:

> Daily life in the camp, with its fear and tensions, taught over
> and over the lesson of absolute power. It prepared the person-
> ality for a drastic shift in standards. It crushed whatever anxi-
> eties might have been drawn from prior standards; such stan-
> dards had become meaningless. It focused the prisoner's
> attention constantly on the moods, attitudes, and standards of
> the only man who mattered [the SS guard]. A truly childlike
> situation was thus created: utter and abject dependency. . . . It
> is thus no wonder that their obedience became unquestioning,
> that they did not revolt, that they could not "hate" their mas-
> ters (122).

Elkins is simply reiterating accepted ideas. But power is never absolute, especially over time, and it is not true that the SS guard was the
"one significant other" on whom the prisoners' needs depended. Social
bonding among prisoners themselves was a universal phenomenon in
the camps. And of course it is not true that survivors were morally
crushed, that they lost all sense of prior standards, that moral sanity was
meaningless. Certainly it is not true that they did not revolt; to live was to
resist, every day, all the time, and in addition to dramatic events like the
burning of Treblinka and Sobibor there were many small revolts in
which all perished. Prisoners who were capable, furthermore, of organizing an underground and of systematically subverting SS intentions
were not behaving "as children." And it is not true, finally, that hatred
was absent. Survivors seethed with it, they speak of it often, they describe terrible acts of revenge. In *Prisoners of Fear* the author praises one
of her comrades for "the ice-cold self-control by which she hid her

abysmal hatred of the German rulers" (123) in order to exploit them. Ella Lingens-Reiner's own rage rings through her prose on every page.

No, most of this was not true, not for many survivors in many camps. Hence these disturbing questions: Why do we insist that prisoners died "like sheep"? Why is it easy to believe, despite the contradiction, that survivors were infantile *and* that they were cunning manipulators using every kind of betrayal and base trick to stay alive? Why, in short, do we insist that survivors did not really survive: that they suffered "death in life" and that if they are alive in body their spirit was destroyed beyond salvaging? Here is how one psychoanalytic commentator summed up the opinions of his colleagues in a symposium on the camp experience: "To one degree or another, they all stifled their true feelings, they all denied the dictates of conscience and social feeling in hope of survival, and they were all warped and distorted as a result" (Hope, 83). That word "all"—its assurance, its contempt—must be accounted for.

To date, serious study of the concentration-camp experience has been done almost exclusively from the psychoanalytic point of view. Elkins takes the bulk of his evidence from Elie Cohen and Bruno Bettelheim, both of whom employ the psychoanalytic approach, both of whom offer much valuable insight, but both of whom, in the end, are led by their method to mistaken conclusions. The psychoanalytic approach is misleading because it is essentially a theory of culture and of man in the civilized state. Its analytic power—which is considerable—is maximized when turned upon behavior which is symbolic, mediated, and therefore at a sufficient remove from necessity. To be of use, the psychoanalytic method, which is that of interpretation, must be applied to actions which have more than one meaning *on the level of meaning*. But that is not the case with extremity. When men and women must respond directly to necessity—when defilement occurs at gun-point and the most undelayable of needs determines action, or when death itself is the determinant —then behavior has no "meaning" at all in a symbolic or psychological sense.

The purpose of action in extremity is to keep life going; the multiplicity is lost. We have seen that life in the camps depended on a duality of behavior, but this duality—this layering of behavior—is very different from the kind of layering which psychoanalysis probes. In extremity, action splits into "primary" and "secondary" levels of adjustment, each of which is real and separate in itself. Precisely here the psychoanalytic approach misleads us: in its search for a second meaning on the first or primary level, it overlooks the secondary level. For psychoanalysis, covert behavior is implicit behavior. But for survivors it becomes explicit, actual, necessary in an immediately practical way.

I am assuming, with Freud, that the phenomenon of civilization, no matter how advanced or primitive, is based first of all on processes of sublimation and symbolization. Taken in this broad sense, civilization as a condition can be described as the transcendence of primal needs and crude necessities through systems of technical and symbolic mediation. Thereby a realm of freedom comes into being which is not governed immediately by the necessities which constitute extremity. Prisoners in a concentration camp would eat anything, at any time they could get it, in almost any state of rawness or decay. We, on the other hand, eat the kind of food we choose, when we choose, after it has been transformed aesthetically through cooking, and upon occasions rich in ritual observance. And thus too, the dead in the camps were stacked naked in piles, rammed into ovens, tossed every which way into ditches and pits. But the man or woman who dies in normal circumstances becomes the object of complicated ritual procedures which confer meaning and dignity upon his or her death and thereby humanize it. The primacy of death is denied symbolically, the immediate facts are overlaid with solemn meaning and removed from the center of consciousness. Death is no longer *thought of* as death, just as animal flesh is no longer thought of as animal flesh after it has been transformed by cooking and table rites.

Freedom to mediate facts and instill new significance, to create and multiply meanings, is the essence of civilization. And here the psychoanalytic method correctly assumes that nothing is to be taken at face value. Our actions are invested with memories, wishes and values reaching far beyond the performance itself, and no act is simply and wholly significant in its immediate, concrete function. Historically, psychoanalysis originated just as the *symboliste* movement was occurring in the arts, and it is tempting to see in both a common pursuit. Both read facts as symbols, both search out the mysteries of an invisible drama, and both take it for granted that in any act or situation there is more than meets the eye. Survivors act as they do because they must—the issue is always life or death—and at every moment the meaning and purpose of their behavior is fully known. We, on the other hand, act for all kinds of reasons, some known and others unconscious, some practical and others governed by an internal will that can only be guessed at. For us behavior requires interpretation; indeed, interpretation validates experience, and hence the usefulness of the psychoanalytic approach.

But only for us. Attempts to interpret the survivor's experience—to see it in terms other than its own—have done more harm than good. The outstanding spokesman, in this respect, has been Bruno Bettelheim, whose application of the psychoanalytic model to survival behavior has been definitive. Bettelheim was in Buchenwald and Dachau for a year, at a time when prisoners could still hope for release, and before systematic destruction became fixed policy, but he was there and speaks with that authority. His first analysis of the camp experience—"Individual and Mass Behavior in Extreme Situations"—appeared in 1943, adding the weight of precedence to a position which has never been challenged and which has influenced all subsequent study. Even among laymen his ideas are known and accepted. His version is *the* version, and in *The Informed Heart* it takes its final, polemical form. Bettelheim argues that prisoners in the camps exhibited the following general traits: they became "incompetent children"; they identified with the SS, "willing and able to accept SS values and behavior"; they fell into an "anonymous mass," without social base or organization; and they possessed no "autonomy," by which he means the capacity for dramatic acts of self-assertion.

Bettelheim's view differs sharply from that of other survivors—Ernst Wiechert and Ernest Rappaport, for example—who were in Buchenwald at the same time. His claims are not substantiated in the bulk of testimony by survivors, including the comprehensive report by Eugen Kogon, who was a member of the underground and was in Buchenwald from the beginning to the end. Bettelheim's attack on Anne Frank and her family is perhaps the essential expression of his outlook. He suggests that their decision to stay together and go into hiding was stupid—a judgment which disregards the situation in Holland, where the population at large helped many Jews to escape in this way. Rather, he argues, they should have abandoned their commitment to each other: each should have fought alone, each shooting down the Germans as they came. Where the guns were to come from, or how scattered individuals were to succeed when nations failed, he does not say.

Bettelheim develops his argument in terms of a dramatic contrast between the individual, who possesses "autonomy," and the masses, who do not possess "autonomy." In many cases this becomes a contrast between Bettelheim himself and "others":

> They appeared to be pathological liars, were unable to restrain themselves, unable to separate clearly between reality and their wishful or anxious day-dreams. So to the old worries, a new one was added, namely, "How could I protect myself from becoming as they are?" (114).

This may refer to prisoners during the stage of initial collapse, but Bettelheim does not say so. He is describing what appears to him to be the general situation, and this contrast between himself and other prisoners is in fact the theme of this book. It is evident not only in the sense of isolation and superiority which attends references to himself, but also in an animus toward other prisoners generally. At one point he attacks camp functionaries by suggesting that inmates with "privileged" positions had "a greater need to justify themselves":

> This they did as members of ruling classes for centuries have done—by pointing to their greater value to society because of their power to influence, their education, their cultural refinement (186).

His specific example is Eugen Kogon:

> Kogon's attitudes are fairly representative. For example, he took pride that in the stillness of the night he enjoyed reading Plato or Galsworthy, while in an adjacent room the air reeked of common prisoners, while they snored unpleasantly. He seemed unable to realize that only his privileged position, based on participation in human experiments, gave him the leisure to enjoy culture, an enjoyment he then used to justify his privileged position (186).

That sounds convincing, but let us look at Kogon's description of the same event:

> In the winter of 1942–43 a succession of bread thefts in Barracks 42 at Buchenwald made it necessary to establish a nightwatch. For months on end I volunteered for this duty, taking the shift from three to six o'clock in the morning. It meant sitting alone in the day room, while the snores of the comrades came from the other end. For once I was free of the ineluctable companionship that usually shackled and stifled every individual activity. What an experience it was to sit quietly by a shaded lamp, delving into the pages of Plato's *Dialogues,* Galsworthy's *Swan Song,* or the works of Heine, Klabund, Mehring! (132).

One of the anomalies of Nazi rule was that books unobtainable in the whole of the Reich were available in the camps. Kogon goes on: "Yes, they could be read illegally in camp. They were among books retrieved from the nation-wide wastepaper collections. The Nazis impounded many libraries of 'enemies of the state,' and turned them over to these collections" (132). There is perhaps a sense of amusement in Kogon's recounting of such details—a *Swan Song* in Buchenwald?—but not a trace of what Bettelheim calls the "need to justify."

Kogon's book, *The Theory and Practice of Hell,* is an extensive record of the achievements of the political underground in Buchenwald, including methods of organization, strategic use of functionary positions, and a detailed account of the take-over of the camp by the prisoners. The episode Bettelheim singles out is, in Kogon's view, just another small example of resistance in action. As a member of the underground, Kogon is simply doing his job. The reason he is there is not to read Plato and Mehring, but to enforce the bread law and thereby help keep a sense of moral order alive among the prisoners. He does not, as Bettelheim says, refer to air which "reeked of common prisoners," but to his "comrades." His private enjoyment is a by-product of responsibility, and if there had been no books Kogon would have volunteered all the same, going without sufficient sleep "for months on end" to do his duty as a man committed to the general struggle.

Bettelheim did not know Kogon in camp, and the incident cited above (one of several he takes from Kogon's report) occurred after his release. Yet this is not a matter of ignorance merely. To reduce Kogon's act to "privilege," and further to declare that it was "based on participation in human experiments," is a grave misrepresentation of basic facts. Bettelheim's obsession with "autonomy," his concept of transcendental selfhood, blinds him to collective action and mutual aid. After reading Kogon's book he remains unaware of organized resistance and of the enormous benefits which the camp population received through covert operations of the underground. He goes on to criticize prisoners who did not, at some point, assert their "autonomy" by openly risking their lives (Kogon's was on the line for nine years but never, if he could help it, openly). Bettelheim tells us that the act he himself performed by talking back to an SS officer, thereby risking his life in a dramatic assertion of self, was the kind of behavior all survivors should have displayed. And that is the heart of the matter. Bettelheim's critique of camp behavior is rooted in the old heroic ethic. Heroism, for him, is an isolated act of defiance through which the individual *as* an individual confronts death. Bettelheim's position is clear from the kind of action he praises:

> Once, a group of naked prisoners about to enter the gas chamber stood lined up in front of it. In some way the commanding SS officer learned that one of the women prisoners had been a dancer. So he ordered her to dance for him. She did, and as she danced, she approached him, seized his gun,

and shot him down. She too was immediately shot to death
(264–65).

"She was willing to risk her life," Bettelheim concludes, "to achieve
autonomy once more" (265). But this is not an example of risking life.
The act he celebrates is suicide. It is courageous, beautiful, and under
the circumstances the only alternative to passive surrender. It is heroic,
but it is still suicide. What can "autonomy" at the cost of personal
destruction amount to? How effective would underground activities, or
any of the forms of resistance, have been on such a principle? Bettelheim's argument comes down to this: "manhood" requires dramatic
self-confirmation, and in the camps this could only be achieved through
some moment of open confrontation with death. Insofar as the struggle
for life did not become overtly rebellious, prisoners were "childlike."
    Bettelheim's polemical objective, in *The Informed Heart,* is to com-
pare the survivor's experience with the predicament of modern man in
"mass society," in order to arrive at a critique of the latter. The comparison itself is invalid. No matter how disconcerting conditions become for
us, they do not hinge at every moment on the issue of life and death;
pain is not constant, options abound, the rule of terror and necessity is
far from total. Life for us does not depend on collective action—not
directly, that is; nor is death the price of visibility. Bettelheim wishes to
rouse us from our sense of victimhood; but by claiming that pressure
reduces men and women to children, and by praising a heroism based on
death, he tends instead to support what he fears.

    Whatever his conclusions, Bettelheim's argument for "autonomy"
is a defense of human dignity, a call to that principle in man which resists
determination by otherness. His fear is not only that human beings can
be made helpless, but that prevailing tendencies in modern thinking
have accepted the condition of victimhood as final. A primary assumption of his own discipline is that the self is forever in painful bondage to
its past. And much of social, economic and political theory—conserva-
tive as well as radical—takes it for granted that external forces shape
internal being, or finally that the self is constituted by forces it neither
controls nor understands but only suffers. Perhaps the case for man-as-
victim has been put most strongly by behaviorism, which assumes outright that environment is omnipotent and that the human self is ever and
always a unilateral function of the world in which it finds itself. Applied
to the concentration camps, the conclusion can only be that monstrosity
breeds monstrosity, and therefore that no one survived. Those not killed
in body most surely perished in spirit, for men and women could not

long endure such inhumanity without themselves becoming inhuman. One sees why B. F. Skinner, in his attack on freedom, also finds it necessary to attack dignity; as long as people persist in their refusal to be determined by forces external to themselves, the belief in freedom will likewise persist as a by-product of this basic recalcitrance.

That the concentration camps were a kind of "experiment" has often been noted. Their aim was to reduce inmates to mindless creatures whose behavior could be predicted and controlled absolutely. The camps have so far been the closest thing on earth to a perfect Skinner Box. They were a closed, completely regulated environment, a "total" world in the strict sense. Pain and death were the "negative reinforcers," food and life the "positive reinforcers," and all these forces were pulling and shoving twenty-four hours a day at the deepest stratum of human need. And yet, survivors are proof that the "experiment" did not succeed.

Their behavior was of course determined by camp conditions, but not in the way behaviorism or current theories of victimhood assume. The distinction overlooked is between responses to necessity which are really unilateral and therefore at one with necessity, and responses which are strategic and therefore provoked by, but opposed to, the same necessity. Facing extreme pressure, human beings either acquiesce or resist or do both. Like the psychoanalytic approach, behaviorism does not take into account the duality of action in extremity. It too fixes attention on the "primary" level of adjustment, precisely on those activities which are informed by, and expressive of, camp logic. On this level it appears that prisoners succumbed to their environment (and life depended on the success of this deception). But on the "secondary" level, as we have seen, prisoners were pushing hard against camp controls. And it is perhaps worth noting, finally, that the behaviorist assumption was held in practice by the SS themselves, who never doubted that force and fear could break anyone, could reduce all behavior to a function of their world.

In a way at first surprising, Bettelheim's idea of heroism dovetails with the view of man as victim—just as psychoanalysis and behaviorism, based on opposite principles, agree in the case of extremity. But in fact, the celebration of man's "indomitable spirit" and our acceptance of victimhood are rooted in the single belief, as old as Western culture, that human bondage can be transcended only in death. Death is at once the entrance to a world of fulfilment unobtainable on earth and the proof of a spirit unvanquished by fear or compromise. Neither is possible to men and women getting by as best they can from day to day; and a life not ready, at any moment, to give itself for something higher is life enchained, life cowed and disgraced by its own gross will to persist. Survival in itself, not dedicated to something *else*, has never been held in high esteem and often has been viewed with contempt. This complex of attitudes is at the heart of the Christian worldview; it had already been expounded in detail by Plato, and before that invested with grandeur by Homer. In the *Iliad*, the progress of a Greek advance is stopped by sudden mist and darkness; whereupon the great Ajax prays aloud for Zeus to send light to continue the battle, even if light should bring death. Many centuries later, in *On the Sublime*, Longinus remarked: "That is the true attitude of an Ajax. He does not pray for life, for such a petition would have ill beseemed a hero" (67).

Just so; when we say of someone that he or she "merely" survives, the word "merely" carries real if muted moral objection. And we say it all the time, as if to be alive, or simply to struggle for life, were not in itself enough. For "meaning" and "significance" we look elsewhere—to ideals and ideologies, to religion and other metaphysical systems; to anything, any *higher* cause or goal which defines life in terms other than its own and thereby justifies existence. Survivors are suspect because they are forced to do openly, without a shred of style or fine language to cover themselves, what the rest of us do by remote control. The bias against "mere survival" runs deep, and derives its force from the fact that all of us think and act in terms of survival, but at a crucial remove and with all the masks and stratagems which cultivated men and women learn to use—of which there would seem to be no end. As Nietzsche observed, man would rather will nothingness than have nothing to will, nothing with which to push life beyond itself. But as Nietzsche implies, the problem with these symbolic superstructures is that they redeem life by negating it.

One of the side-effects of civilization is that life is enhanced by denigrating actual life processes. But is this a side-effect merely? Might it not be the paradox of civilization itself—a direct result of, or even a condition for, the split between mind and body which characterizes the structure of civilized existence as we know it? Surely Descartes was not original when he declared that mind and matter are separate entities, nor was his "I think therefore I am" anything more than the commonplace bias of culture itself. Within the framework of civilization, experience has always been divided into physical and spiritual realms, immediate and mediated modes, concrete and symbolic forms, lower and higher activities. And all things "higher," as we know, are by definition *not* concerned with life itself; not, that is, with life in its physical concreteness.

In *The Presentation of Self in Everyday Life* Erving Goffman has observed that human activities take place either in "front" or in "back" regions. We "present" ourselves (our idealized selves) to ourselves and others in "front regions," while keeping our props, especially those which attend our biological needs, out of sight in "back regions":

> The line dividing front and back regions is illustrated every-where in our society. As suggested, the bathroom and bedroom . . . are places from which the downstairs audience can be excluded. Bodies that are cleansed, clothed, and made up in these rooms can be presented to friends in others. In the kit-chen, of course, there is done to food what in the bathroom and bedroom is done to the human body (123).

Goffman is talking about American society, but the compartmenta-lization of existence to which he points can be found everywhere, most dramatically at events which have a religious or an official function, places and ceremonies associated with power or the sacred. In all such instances, a division between front and back, higher and lower, is strictly upheld. And as far as ritual and technology permit, everything "lower" is kept out of sight—and thereby out of mind. Mary Douglas has called this "the purity rule":

> A natural way of investing a social situation exerts pressure on persons involved in it, the more the social demand for confor-mity tends to be expressed by a demand for physical control. Bodily processes are more ignored and more firmly set outside the social discourse, the more the latter is important. A natural way of investing a social occasion with dignity is to hide organic processes (12).

The division between body and mind, between lower and higher, is a structural component of civilization as such. Freud's concept of subli-mation is helpful here; it refers to the process through which immediate bodily needs are delayed, set at a distance or denied, and finally trans-formed into the "higher" accomplishments of mind and culture. That which *is* is negated in pursuit of that which *will* be or *should* be. Taken to its religious extreme, this principle results in the negation of this life in favor of another life, higher, purer, elsewhere. Actual existence is "death," whereas death becomes the entrance to "life," or so St. Paul would have us believe. The meaning of life is found *in* death, and the greatest action an individual can perform is to give his life for some "higher" cause.

The trouble with survivors, in our eyes, is that they do not live by the rules. Their needs cannot be delayed, cannot be transformed or got out of sight. Nor do they seek ideal justification for their struggle. Survivors fight merely to live, certain that what counts is life and the sharing of life. And through this experience of radical de-sublimation they come, as Nadezhuda Mandelstam puts it, very "close to earth":

> Our way of life kept us firmly rooted to the ground, and was not conducive to the search for transcendental truths. Whenever I talked of suicide, M. used to say: "Why hurry? The end is the same everywhere, and here they even hasten it for you." Death was so much more real, so much simpler than life, that we all involuntarily tried to prolong our earthly existence, even if only for a brief moment—just in case the next day brought some relief! In war, in the camps and during periods of terror, people think much less about death (let alone suicide) than when they are living normal lives. Whenever at some point on earth mortal terror and the presence of utterly insoluble problems are present in a particularly intense form, general questions about the nature of being recede into the background. . . . In a strange way, despite the horror of it, this also gave a certain richness to our lives. Who knows what happiness is? Perhaps it is better to talk in more concrete terms of the fullness or intensity of existence, and in this sense there may have been something more deeply satisfying in our desperate clinging to life than in what people generally strive for (261).

For years the Mandelstams lived at life's edge: they saw the tree in winter outline, barren against a barren land, and saw the strength of its shape. David Rousset, who passed through several Nazi camps, likewise insists upon a "positive side" to the experience of survival:

> Dynamic awareness of the strength and beauty of the sheer fact of living, in itself, brutal, entirely stripped of all superstructures—living through even the worst of cataclysms and most disastrous setbacks. A cool, sensual thrill of joy founded on the most complete understanding of the wreckage, and consequently incisiveness in action and firmness in decisions, in short, a broader and more intensely creative vigor (171).

Certainly one does not have to survive the concentration camps in order to arrive at awareness of life's immanent value. It can come abruptly, with the shock of death-encounter, or gradually after passing through a period of protracted death-threat, and sometimes in a moment of character-changing revelation. Dostoevsky is a wonderful example. As a young man he was arrested for mildly revolutionary activities, condemned to death, and taken to the place of execution; his sentence was commuted to imprisonment only after the ritual of execution had been carried up to the actual point of shooting. He genuinely thought he would die, and later that same day he wrote an extraordinary letter to his brother:

> Brother, I'm not depressed and haven't lost spirit. Life everywhere is life, life is not ourselves and not in the external. . . . This idea has entered into my flesh and blood. Yes, it's true! That head which created, lived by the highest life of art, which acknowledged and had come to know the highest demands of the spirit, that head has been cut from my shoulders. . . . But my heart is left me, and the same flesh and blood which likewise can love and suffer and desire and remember, and this is, after all, life. *On voit le soleil!* (Mochulsky, 141).

His awakening had nothing to do with belief, and in his letter he thanks neither God nor the Tsar. He has simply realized what he did not know before. Life's fundamental goodness is now clear, and he wants his brother to know that through the years in prison this knowledge will be his strength. Using exactly the same details of the letter, Dostoevsky re-described his mock execution nearly twenty years later in *The Idiot*. The Prince is obsessed by two images of man-condemned: one is executed, the other pardoned. Myshkin's desire is to conduct his life in terms of what they, the condemned, know. So too with Father Zosimo, and finally Alyosha and Mitya, in *The Brothers Karamazov*. They know that "life is in ourselves and not in the external."

Survivors develop a faith in life which seems unwarranted to others. Dostoevsky did, and so did Bertrand Russell, to take a final example from *our* world. While in Peking during the winter of 1920–21, Russell came down with double pneumonia. Complications set in and "for a fortnight," as he tells us, "the doctors thought every evening that I should be dead before morning" (180). But with the coming of spring his health returned, and at some point during recovery Russell had an extraordinary experience, which he describes in Volume Two of the *Autobiography:*

Lying in my bed feeling that I was not going to die was surprisingly delightful. I had always imagined until then that I was fundamentally pessimistic and did not greatly value being alive. I discovered that in this I had been completely mistaken, and that life was infinitely sweet to me. Rain in Peking is rare, but during my convalescence there came heavy rains bringing the delicious smell of damp earth through the windows, and I used to think how dreadful it would have been to have never smelt that smell again. I had the same feeling about the light of the sun, and the sound of the wind. Just outside my windows were some very beautiful acacia trees, which came into blossom at the first moment when I was well enough to enjoy them. I have known ever since that at bottom I am glad to be alive (181–82).

That is the survivor's special grace. He or she is glad to be alive. For camp survivors this affirmation was seldom so joyous or easily won, and often it was made in stubborn bitterness. A survivor of the Nazi camp at Neubrandenberg speaks of having "no right to be unhappy." She goes on to stress the one solid insight which her experience gave birth to, a vision distilled from such masses of suffering as to bear the force of ethical imperative:

Be happy, you who live in fine apartments, in ugly houses or in hovels. Be happy, you who have your loved ones, and you also who sit alone and dream and can weep. Be happy, you who torture yourself over metaphysical problems, and . . . you the sick who are being cared for, and you who care for them, and be happy, oh, how happy, you who die a death as normal as life, in hospital beds or in your homes (Maurel, 140).

BIBLIOGRAPHY

Bettelheim, Bruno. *The Informed Heart* (Glencoe, Ill.: Free Press, 1960; London: Thames & Hudson, 1961).

Cohen, Elie A. *Human Behavior in the Concentration Camp,* tr. M.H. Braaksma (New York: Norton, 1953; London: Jonathan Cape, 1954).

Elkins, Stanley M. *Slavery* (Chicago: University of Chicago, 1959; 2d ed., Chicago and London: University of Chicago, 1969).

Goffman, Erving. *The Presentation of Self in Everyday Life* (Garden City: Doubleday, Anchor Books 1959; London: Allen Lane, 1969).

Kogon, Eugen. *The Theory and Practice of Hell,* tr. Heinz Norden (New York: Farrar, Straus, 1953; London: Secker & Warburg, 1950).

Lifton, Robert Jay. *Death in Life: Survivors of Hiroshima* (New York: Random House, 1967; London: Weidenfeld & Nicolson, 1968).

Lingens-Reiner, Ella. *Prisoners of Fear* (London: Victor Gollancz, 1948).

Mandelstam, Nadezhda. *Hope Against Hope,* tr. Max Hayward (New York: Atheneum, 1970; London: Harvill, 1971).

Maurel, Micheline. *An Ordinary Camp,* tr. Margaret S. Summers (New York: Simon & Schuster, 1958). Under the title *Ravensbruck* (London: Blond, 1958).

Mochulsky, Konstantin. *Dostoevsky: His Life and Work,* tr. Michael A. Minihan (Princeton: Princeton University, 1971).

Rappaport, Erners A. "Beyond Traumatic Neurosis," *International Journal of Psycho-Analysis,* XLIX, Part 4, 1968, pp. 719–31.

———. "Survivor Guilt," *Midstream,* XVII, August–September 1971, pp. 41–47.

Wiechert, Ernst. *Forest of the Dead,* tr. Ursula Stechow (New York: Greenberg, 1947).

Abigail Rosenthal

THE RIGHT WAY TO ACT: INDICTING THE VICTIMS

It is clear that our moral and dramatic landscape, the narrative look of the twentieth century, would be far different if we could imaginatively erase the Nazi from that landscape. He occupies it with us. He is a kind of measuring rod of our relation to the category of evil. But the Nazi's outstandingness in that department has also been challenged. One of the challenges to the consensus about Nazi villainy has involved redirecting a part of it to the Jew, as the victim who obviously suffers the fullest impact of that villainy. Questions of the most serious kind have been raised about the integrity of the Jewish victims, or the "purity" of their victimization. Holocaust victims have been charged with various kinds of moral default, ranging from passivity to complicity, charges that make it hard to see them clear, for the purposes of the whole moral analysis.

If the Nazi's victim *is* in complicity, then we get instead the picture of an odd sort of morbid human interaction, a shared sickness, an epidemic if you like, where clear lines between poisoners, carriers, and felled members of the healthy population can no longer be drawn. A responsible physician would withhold praise and blame alike from his patients. But the task of a responsible moral being is rather different. It belongs to the latter to bestow praise and blame, whether on oneself or on another, in the right way. If we do not know where the victim as victim begins, we will not be able to make out sufficiently clearly where his victimizer in turn begins. It will then become a tricky thing, theoretically and practically, to make any use at all of the category of evil in what is generally held to be its most salient context. Accordingly, my task in this essay will be to help make the category of evil serviceable again in this context by pointing out that the Jewish Holocaust had approximately six million genuine victims, victims in the pure sense of the term. Said that way, it sounds almost too obvious to be worth saying. How, then, did the point get to be so inobvious?

In May 1960, in Buenos Aires, Israeli agents seized SS Lieutenant Colonel Adolf Eichmann, head of the variously initialed and named Gestapo Section IV D4, B4, and IV A4, on "Jewish Affairs and Deportations," and removed him clandestinely to Jerusalem to stand trial before the District Court of Jerusalem for, among other charges, five counts of "Crimes against the Jewish People." It was the first time that the Holocaust had been brought to the attention of the world as a single, planned crime of immense scope, with many stages. That there had been slaughters of terrifying magnitude and thoroughness was a fact that had sunk into consciousness with the liberation of the camps. Evidences of these mass murders had figured prominently in the Nuremberg trials, but always among others. But here a case that the planning and carrying out of *this particular project of genocide* in all its broad ramifications and details had occurred was to be made in a court of law, with the kind of evidence acceptable in a proper court of law, original documentary evidence or attested copies and eyewitness testimony, and safeguarding the right of the accused to hear the charges against him, to defend himself, and to introduce evidence that he did not do it—or evidence of an exculpatory nature.

It was one of those moments of contemporary history where the opportunity to see justice done that was opened by a court proceeding also opened a channel to conscience and stock taking in the world. Into that moment stepped Hannah Arendt, with a report on the Jerusalem trial that—more than any other report—captured the moral imagination of the intellectual community. The thesis of Arendt's *Eichmann in Jerusalem* was threefold: (1) Eichmann was administratively subordinate and psychologically free of malevolence, or "ordinary"—a sort of boring clerk or mailman; (2) *the Jewish victims were in crucial ways in complicity with their Nazi executioners;* (3) the jurisdiction of the Jerusalem court and its findings were legally and morally questionable. Arendt's case against the Jews (point 2 above) is the one that will be reexamined here.[1]

Arendt's case against the Jews was not a report of the trial at all—which incidentally gave quite a different picture. It was largely a condensation of Raul Hilberg's far more carefully worked through evidence, as presented in his historic work, *The Destruction of the European Jews,* which came out in 1961, after the conclusion of the trial.[2] The case for Jewish complicity (popularized by Arendt) is one that I will accordingly try to evaluate in Arendt's source, working from Hilberg's revised and expanded three-volume 1985 edition, and comparing that study with some other materials, including testimony given at the Eichmann trial. My purpose, in evaluating Hilberg's case, will not be to counter it with empirical evidences of Jewish noncooperation and resistance. I am not a historian. I have opinions here, but the dispute is not exactly on my territory. My purpose will be rather to get clearer about how moral judgments ought to work in such a case, what factors are relevant, what factors irrelevant, and what standards ought to guide the moral thinker.

The problem of Jewish complicity needs, I think, now to be viewed in the widest possible context, that of "world history." I have said elsewhere (in *A Good Look at Evil*) that there is no such thing as "world history," if by that is meant a single, universally agreed-upon narrative making collective sense of the stories of all individuals in their respective *genē* (plural of the Greek *genos,* meaning tribe or race), and of all *genē* together. The myth of such a common narrative, already emplaced, is what gives ideologues their spurious authorization to overthrow real stories, of real people and of real *genē.* Nevertheless, such a universally agreed-upon story is not logically impossible. It is what happens, writ small, when any two individuals, who have lived a certain course of experience together, agree as to the factual content of what happened and as to its significance. Such an agreement *can* come about, without any necessary sacrifice of the uniqueness of the parties, or the indissoluble otherness of each one's particular perspective. If individuals can do this (and if doing it is crucial to the ratification of their experiences), and call the doing of it "friendship," then larger groups might in principle also do it. In utopian or millenarian vision, what is at best pictured is all individuals and all *genē* getting a sort of shared (in the Quaker sense) "sense of the meeting," and getting it in an unforced way. This state of universal, unforced friendship, lifted free of empty platitudes, embedded in each person's real story, may be a kind of "regulative ideal," horizoning the goodness of each of us. When one thinks of how difficult it is for any single person to get his own story straight, one has a dim notion of the real obstacles that will delay indefinitely the actualizing of this regulative ideal. But, as long as we know that this ideal is what we are talking about, we *can* talk about "world history."

In the context, then, of "world history," what should we suppose was really happening in the course of the Holocaust, from start to end? At the very least, here was a whole people seeking to erase another people from its history, and from world history altogether. The German people worked as a team to get this done, and to let it get done. They looked away at the right times and they pitched in at the right times. The implementation of Nazi orders affecting Jewry required the active or passive consent of virtually all of the adult German population.[3] Whatever economic gains the targeted people could have voluntarily offered the genocidal people were feared, precisely because they might have deflected the genocidal people from its course.[4] On the other hand, whatever spoils the targeted people could *involuntarily* have yielded up to the genocidal people were relished, precisely because these were evidences that the planned genocide was indeed running its course.[5] Set in the world-historical context of German ambitions with regard to Jewry, plundering the strengthless dead loses its base character. Rather, the fact that one *can* do it becomes proof of the success of the original mission.

In sum, on the German side, everything functioned as if this was indeed, as it was self-styled at the time, an act of the national will—if there ever was such a thing in the world's "history." Orders did not have to be given. Far-reaching interpretations and creative implementations welled up from every stratum of the national life. The omissions and the lookings away, the differentiated (not blanket) failures of empathy, were all functional—as they were intended to be.

To that German context in which, world-historically, alleged Jewish complicity has to be viewed, we should add two other important factors. One concerns the non-German part of the world. The other concerns the internal character of Jewish culture—itself also a factor in world history.

As regards the non-German part of the world, there was the fact that rescue was largely unavailable from the lands and people surrounding the victimized Jews. "Where were we supposed to go," said the guide at the United Nations exhibit on Auschwitz, pointing to a map. "The North Sea?"[6] The distribution of such rescue efforts as were made was largely invidious where Jews were concerned.[7] This seems a point crucial to the correct valuation of the Jewish responses. In Denmark, which might be said to have offered a "control" on the Holocaust experiment where the effectiveness of Jewish leadership is concerned, the Jewish community went smartly to its own aid, full on the mark, having people and lands available for its rescue.[8]

It is hard to get a purchase on Jewish culture, as it affected the beliefs and behavior patterns of individuals caught in the Holocaust. Diffused within the divergent host cultures where Jews lived, the effects of Jewish culture took multiple variegated forms. But Jewish culture has been, for thousands of years, permeated by religious convictions and traditions. So it is appropriate to consult these relatively stable components, even when attempting to guess at the passions of secular Jews.

What is peculiar to Jewish religious culture is the belief that a whole *genos* (as opposed to an individual saint, disciple, or prophet) has been singled out as a vehicle of the Providential purpose. The Providential purpose is to accomplish human redemption in man's physical, national, and international setting.[9] There are no precise eschatalogical blueprints for history, as fundamentalist or secular millenarism has them. There is no militant wing of Judaism, committed to organizing cadres for a Jewish world takeover, as anti-Semitic imagination has it.[10] The story of history is pictured rather as a hidden story, for God to see as a whole and to unfold, and for man to enact bit by bit as the divine intent becomes clearer.

That being the Jewish religious frame of reference, any live occurrence of anti-Semitism does not merely strike a raw nerve, evoking its antecedents in the long train of such incidents. It also recharges a profound theological anxiety, from which only the most pious are wholly free, an anxiety on behalf of God's purposes. And for the secularized Jew, for whom God's purposes are quite out of it, it remains a given that justice and mercy *must* be done in human history. To take the extraordinarily long view remains second nature. It is not even necessarily a conscious thing. But an urgent sense of concern for mankind, and—in the same breath and by the same token—concern for or about the Jewish people, gets manifested by the secular Jew in all kinds of ways, big and little. Both concerns have a common, theological essence. What the Holocaust struck at, then, was the system of meaning internal to Jewish culture.

That being the world-historical context, German, non-German non-Jewish, and Jewish, how shall we view the alleged "complicity" of the Jewish people in their own destruction?

Hilberg, perhaps the most articulate and historically careful spokesman for this view, cites a number of evidences of Jewish complicity. They vary in scope and moral gravity. Included are fatalism about the end (pp. 841, 969; these and future page references in this paragraph are from Hilberg's *Destruction of the European Jews*) and mass compliance (e.g., with ghettoization) without actual force having to be used (p. 773). They further include giving administrative assistance to the Germans in supplying lists and other information (pp. 187, 434f), and in manufacture and distribution of such instruments in the isolation of the Jewish people as yellow star armbands (p. 216). They include cooperating, often under armed threat, by self-denigrating words and gestures (pp. 456, 471). They include providing assistance in actual roundups (pp. 460, 463f). They include popular opposition to the armed resistance movement (pp. 385, 500, 503 and note 69, p. 504). They include blindly self-deceived reliance on German information (pp. 459, 696, 1040), and blocked awareness or fatal absence of awareness (pp. 314f, 707). They include decisions by Jewish leaders to withhold information from the rank and file on misguidedly humane grounds (pp. 461, 639). They include sectarian divisions between potential resistance groups (p. 385). Included too are instances of self-aggrandizement of the leadership at the expense of the community (pp. 580, 589) or ready use of class and wealth distinctions to favor the privileged in the struggle for survival (pp. 218, 230, 262f, 439, 448f, 577, 778). Of all the accusations, the most grave concern the activity of Jewish leaders in the Selection of successive detachments of Jews for Nazi deportation to the death camps. That Jews were also put to work in the killing centers, in readying the condemned and stripping the dead, is sometimes mentioned, but less often recently, since it has somehow become common knowledge that actual concentration camp inmates were up against overwhelming force.

Let us take these charges one by one, not of course to assess the conduct of individuals (that would be a case-by-case matter, and a matter either for evidence in a court of law or for the God's-eye view), nor certainly to array on the other side the many well-attested instances of Jewish resistance at every point of the Nazi operation and from every stratum of the community. Our purpose is rather to try to see the *moral* sense of these charges, as they are applied to human behaviors of which a moral assessment is due.

Perhaps my own biases should be stated at this point. My childhood was colored by the knowledge that there was a man across the sea named Hitler, who had got under way a project to "kill us all." If he won the war, he would come over here to our walk-up apartment at Park Avenue and 86th Street, and simply finish the job. Since that outcome was by no means unimaginable in Yorkville, many of my preoccupations were horizoned by the question, "Would we all behave well *when that happened?* Would we go through that furnace *in the right way?* Would we die correctly, as one should, rather than incorrectly, as one shouldn't?" It was a childish conviction with me (the conviction seems subsequently to have been shared by many adults) that one had to behave *correctly* during one's Holocaust. Courage is grace under pressure, and all that.

Our question is, then, what is the right way to act during one's Holocaust? Let us take the wrong ways alleged by Hilberg (or some of them), and consider these one by one. The reader will be the Jew, and I will be, if you please, the philosopher.

Fatalism. You are the Jew, standing somewhere on the map of Europe. A whole people, armed and effective, wants to erase you from history. The surrounding peoples, some of them also armed and effective, having some conscious relation to your place in their history, stand by and they let it happen. Fatalism, under the circumstances, strikes *me* as a form of sanity. A preliminary form, to be sure. But you may not get much beyond the preliminaries. Meantime, to be sane, you must see that this is indeed happening, and not deny it. To understand that it "is" happening is also to understand that it "will" happen. That is, there is precious little you can do to stop it. *Except,* of course, hope and expect that the Allies will at last win the war and, by dint of doing that, take you off the back burner.

Anticipatory Compliance. In the somewhat ritualized struggles between male wolves in a pack, it is sometimes found that baring the throat, or making some other gesture of anticipatory compliance, will deter the victor from moving in for the kill. Analogous gestures of disarming submission are met with in other species. The instincts to make such gestures go very deep. There are few among us who, finding ourselves to be weaker in a natural struggle (e.g., between females and males, children and parents, weaker and stronger schoolmates, subordinates and bosses), have made no gestures of anticipatory compliance.

The more ferociously it seems we are menaced, the more we may hope or reason that it is the aggressor's primitive "needs" or "fears" that must have prompted him to threaten us, and that we ought merely to redouble our efforts to allay those needs and fears. After all (in the Nazi case), the aggressor is not merely moving to tear us apart boisterously and laughingly (though he does that too). Overall, he is moving to tear us apart with moral seriousness, with enraged *accusations.* If we can only prove to him that he need not hate us, or fear us, or absolutely despise us by his own moral lights, perhaps, perhaps, he will desist in time. He will not go the whole distance.

Now, in this kind of judgment there is a mixture of animal instinct and the common sense of the species. It is no more than an extension of the judgments we make for our survival every day. (Hannah Arendt, for example, told me of having been menaced by a young mugger in an elevator. Without a second's hesitation, she told him not to be afraid, just to calm down, that he would get his money. He did, got the money, and decamped forthwith. Her survival instincts, for quick compliance, had been sound and sure, and they worked. When I had asked her, earlier in the conversation, how she personally had managed to understand in time that the Nazis would be resistant to normal human appeals, she cited not her instincts but her *political theorist's* grasp of German culture, her educated realization that the Nazis were an element unlike any other.)

If survival is possible and desired, and escape impossible, then ordinarily this judgment (for anticipatory compliance) is the one to make. Nor is the compliance to be understood as gratuitously "anticipatory." The Nazis made no secret of the disproportionate violence of their reprisals. In these situations they always held hostages. Noncooperativeness was interpreted as active resistance and was punished in the same way, namely, by killing a disproportionate number of other Jews.[11] The *morality* of thus indirectly causing their deaths is unclear to me. A split-second practical judgment, hard to make in an armchair, is what is involved.

Administrative and Executive Support. This has the same basic motive as anticipatory compliance, except that often enough it is given in response to even more direct and credible threats.

Popular Opposition to Armed Resistance. This has the same motive as administrative support and anticipatory compliance.

Self-Deception. As a Jew, you want to live the best life you can, in history, in the human theater. That your values have been so patterned that the reach toward the transcendent is rerouted, as it were, toward immanence, is something of which you may or may not be consciously aware. But that patterning is shared by other members of your culture, across the spectrum from extreme orthodoxy to assimilationist humanism. All of a sudden, important numbers of your fellow actors in the human theater, actors within other cultures but on the same stage, want you out of it. Out of it, with all that was Egypt, and with all that was not Egypt. Out of it, without a footstep left on the sandy floor. This desire, to have you out of it, gives evidence of its existence on many hands—but you persist in deceiving yourself as to the real character of these evidences.

Now it is over. You have survived, although a great many of your fellow Jews did not. You survive, having been, it seems, as horribly hated and as callously neglected or disdained by members of brother cultures as it is possible for a human being to be. You are now told that you should not have deceived yourself about this. You should have known that confiscation of goods and jobs, and residential concentration—the ripping out of phones, the prohibition on talking to Gentiles—all that meant that you would be ripped out of the social organism. You should have known that those were death trains, not bound for resettlement areas. You should have known that those were gas chambers, not showers.

But in fact you *did* know. Not quite consciously, it is charged, you knew. And there is your real moral lapse. That you did not bring it all up to consciousness. That you tampered with your fatalism. That you were therefore in bad faith. By contrast, the killers seem models of psychic

transparency. They *knew* what they were about. You alone give an unpleasant opacity to this psychic terrain.

As I was penning these lines, in a museum café, two middle-aged
women tried persistently to enter and take seats, having been told by the
young manager that the café was closed. They did nevertheless sit down
at a table, promising him that they would stay only "two minutes," and
that they would order nothing. They sat surrounded by other patrons,
who were finishing their cups of coffee and so on at a leisurely pace,
while the staff cleaned up. I saw the thwarted young manager pause and
then gather himself up for a more concerted try. He strode to the
women's table and told them that he was *ordering* them out. Unmoved,
they smilingly remonstrated with him. In support of the young manager,
other waiters came over. A security guard was summoned and added her
point. At last the two women left, to the sounds of mimicry from the
staff who, from the look of them, were possibly in the arts. What the two
women had not been able to believe was that—in that small, diffuse
informal community ruled by the café staff—*they were not wanted.*

For good people, the thing is the more implausible as it becomes
more global. Good people have a necessary residuum of optimism that
enables them, so to speak, to get their goodness done.

Such a thing is conceivable (always presupposing your goodness)
only if you believe, being for example religiously a Hassid, or in secular
faith a Bundist, or a Zionist, that, as Elisha said, "they that be with us are
more than they that be with them" (2 Kings 6:16). Membership in some
such outgunning or outnumbering community, supernatural, international, or national, makes it psychologically possible to see clearly
that you are not wanted in another, more restricted or eccentric
community.[12]

But imagine that, for one reason or another, you are not able
psychologically to postulate your membership in that kind of an outnumbering community. (It must be admitted that, in the 1933–45 case,
such membership would have had to have been an article of faith, not an
evidence of things seen.) What would follow, from your inability to
postulate such membership, would be the admission that all your good
works and all your affections would come to nothing, would be kept in
no human repository.

*It is a central contention of this essay that such an admission is radically
incompatible with human goodness.*

Self-Aggrandizement, Corruption, Class Privilege. "The world," Léo
Bronstein used to say, "prefers a murderer to a petty-petty thief," indicating as he said so the aesthetically plausible but morally abysmal "pu-

rity" of the murderer.[13] We should perhaps take some care not to share the world's preference. But here again, the context has to be borne in mind for the purpose of a moral analysis. If what you "buy" with your bribe or payment to the extortionist is sufficient food for your own child, while another child starves, and the *fair* result would be that both children got to be equally malnourished, and you have greater natural affection for your own child than for another's—and there is no actual and coherent army of the beleaguered Jews, allocating strictly equal rations and duties, able to enforce its orders and to deliver release from the present state of nature—why, then the claims of natural affection do have some natural right.

It is to be remembered that the Nazi machinery had already broken up the old organizational lines of traditional Jewry and, more significantly, had broken Jewish communication lines with the outside communities, of other Jews and of non-Jews. (This included communication through participation in the wider work of the world, communication by speaking, writing, telephoning, use of public transportation, and the like.) Concomitantly, "Jewish Councils" were formed at gunpoint. In spirit and purpose, these were not "Jewish" and they were not "councils." They were formed as part of the German destruction process, to distribute the inadequate rations and laughable medical provisions to terrified people, recently rendered jobless and crowded into unfamiliar, often walled-off, concentration areas for Jews. The "Jewish Councils" were also to distribute the work cards that were the tormented community's only means of staving off deportation, and to transmit the orders by which that community could learn what its kidnappers wanted of it. We have gone over the point that at every stage noncooperation was interpreted as active resistance and was met by overwhelming force. In these circumstances, personal corruption was probably a sign of some kind of natural health. The organism was fighting back—not by fair means but by any means available. ("Prisoner's dilemma" reasoning doesn't apply here. All the prisoners were going to be killed whatever they did.)

However, there were paths open to those who wanted to escape personal corruption—and we have looked down some of them.[14] There were the partisan groups, dedicated to a political redemption, and you could join them if you were young or able bodied, and if you had no more family being held hostage. There were also the pious, which only a certain prior acculturation would have placed you among, and for them it was forbidden to save your son's life if the life of another's son would be forfeited in consequence.

Both kinds of self-exemption from corruption were *willed* departures from a real and prevailing state of nature, in the light of an unseen "world to come." But even if you were in a position to make such metaphysical wagers, they could not be made at every juncture. If a crust of stolen bread came into your palm, presumably you would want to share it with your best buddy, not crumb it into equal bits for the whole barracks.[15] And given the metaphysical wager, on the coming classless society, or Zion, or God, there could not be Kantian fairness in getting there. If the biological *genos* in whatever future form it would take needed the young and the able, and if God needed whoever best served His Providential purposes, then, even from a standpoint of the "world to come," there was favoritism. There was a selection.

It is not clear to me that the moment-to-moment selection that natural affection performs in favor of those whom it loves is *morally* worse.

Selection. The gravest of the accusations leveled against the so-called Jewish Councils is that, at German gunpoint, they made the actual selections of those who were to be deported from the slower death of the German-made ghettos to the quicker death of the killing centers. Acting in this way, some of them saved some of their own relatives; some saved some of those who were already privileged; some saved groups they thought politically more vital; some saved, or tried to save, some of the children; some (but by no means all) saved themselves. Many who participated in the Selections withheld from the deportees the information or educated guesses they possessed as to what "resettlement in the East" really meant.

It seems to me that the moral objections taken here fail fully to picture the nature and scale of this emergency. Rabbinic casuistry was not unfamiliar with the situation of a whole community taken hostage. The traditional rulings had been to the effect that a *guilty* fugitive may be surrendered by such a community if he is demanded by name (thus absolving the community of the moral taint of making a selection among the innocents). In a still more extreme case, even an innocent fugitive who is named may be surrendered if, failing to surrender him, his death and the community's would otherwise be certain. But if there is any doubt as to the fatality of the outcome, or it is demanded of the community that it make a selection among innocents, then, the rabbis ruled, the whole community must rather perish.[16]

Now let us alter the picture that the rabbis had in view. We no longer have one town, say third-century Lydda threatened by the Romans, or a twelfth-century legally imposed "Jewish Quarter" in the Maghreb, threatened by the dominant Arabs. Without needing to suppose that every "Jewish Council" member participating in a Selection saw clearly the scope of the German program, it will be admitted that what could be seen was, in its thoroughness, rapacity, and brutal orderliness, like nothing that had ever been seen or heard of before. If the "Jewish Council" member was not thinking, "they are going to kill us all," he was at least trying hard *not* to think that.

What were his options? He could save his own honor—but only by suicide. Noncooperation would bring down the full force of the Holocaust on his family and neighbors forthwith. Suicide is honorable—for a Stoic. But it is not usually honorable in Jewish religious thought. It is not even religiously honorable for one individual to offer his life for another single individual, since each person's life is considered to be his on trust, not a personal possession to be disposed of at will. God is not considered to allow any individual to decide that his own life is less valuable than another's.[17]

In sum, the honor that is saved by suicide is pagan honor, not honor as it is understood in the system of meaning internal to Jewish culture. Furthermore, as witness after witness testified in the Eichmann trial, as memoirists and historians have alike recorded, survival was felt to be an obligation in that realm of the Jewish psyche where history and the supernatural "world to come" are indistinguishable. It was felt to be an obligation in the Kantian sense. It overrode personal inclination. The duty was twofold: to preserve some remnant of the biological *genos* considered as a divine vehicle, and to preserve the memory, incorporating the latter into human memory itself, also considered as a divine vehicle.[18]

Now, considering that no escape routes were provided, that the program of liquidation was encompassing and relentless, *it was clear that survival would be an accident.* Whoever could survive, however he could, had however a twofold obligation to do so. He was not to live, in the collapse of his affections and his hopes, because it felt good. He was not to keep a diary, keep his memories intact, be prepared to tell and retell the story, because it was a great pleasure to do so. Rather, he was to do all that because it was the only appropriate rejoinder to a program of erasing his *genos* from what *both he and his liquidators* understood to be world history. (It cannot be said that the Nazis ignored the big picture. It cannot be said that the Jews were, by acculturated temperament, indifferent to it.)

If I am still, according to our earlier literary conceit, the philosopher, and the reader is still the Jew, the reader might at this point want to ask me, indignantly, "Are you recommending that we take part in a *Selection?*" I am not recommending anything, since my recommendations would presuppose that you have been placed, ethically, culturally, and physically, in a genocidal situation. But, if you are put in a genocidal situation, genocidal without remainder, which heaven forfend, then yes, I am recommending that you take part in Selections. It may be that not everyone selected will actually be killed. Some may be used for slave labor and will somehow survive the war. It may be that not everyone whose Selection is thus postponed will eventually be rounded up and deported. It may be that some will outlast the Final Solution, one way or another. What is virtually certain is that your whole community will be machine-gunned to death in your hundreds of thousands tomorrow morning if you do not "voluntarily" participate. Your neighbors will look on. There are no forests, or, if there are forests, the young who morally *can* get there—perhaps because they have no more families to suffer reprisals—will in large numbers be killed anyway, as a result of peasant informers, or by the bullets of non-Jewish partisans. And your old and your infants cannot make their way to forests. To cooperate in Selections, is—for the *genos* as a whole—to stall. Yes, cooperate. Yes, stall. Do what they tell you. Whoever survives, will survive by accident.

There are those who study Zen Buddhism in order to learn how, appropriately, to peel a potato, or how, appropriately, to succor the homeless. There is also a minutely appropriate way to undergo one's Holocaust. The appropriate way is to survive it, or to try to.

We are of course not trying to find out about the Holocaust victims, or about any other group of people similarly picked up at random (that is to say, picked up without regard to their wishes), how many were sinners, how many saints, how many heroes, sung and unsung, and how all that interesting stuff is to be measured. We were simply trying to figure out whether, in any sense that is morally intelligible, these victims of genocide were in actual complicity with it. We have not found that they were. If our analysis is correct, then it will be possible in this context to draw the moral lines, between those who have done evil and those who have suffered it, without undue ambiguity.

NOTES

1. Hannah Arendt's point 1 about the banality of evil in the Nazi, and her point 3 partly delegitimating that trial and other such trials, are discussed at length in my *A Good Look at Evil* (Philadelphia: Temple University Press, 1987), Chap. 6, "Banality and Originality," from which this article is adapted. Note, however, that when evil is redefined as "banal," it does not necessarily retain all its usefulness as a moral cate-

gory. Likewise, only if the trials are legitimate can that moral discourse *proceed* to which the trials have supplied the attested evidence. A foundation of fact, properly come by, must be supplied first. Then one can moralize.

2. Hannah Arendt, *Eichmann in Jerusalem: A Report on the Banality of Evil* (New York: Viking, 1964), p. 282.

3. Raul Hilberg, *The Destruction of the European Jews,* 3 vols. (New York: Holmes and Meier, 1985), pp. 993–1007.

4. Ibid., pp. 1006f.

5. Ibid., pp. 947–61.

6. Mrs. Rosa Goldstein of the International Auschwitz Committee, Brussels, to the author, January 29, 1986. The exhibition, "Auschwitz —A Crime against Mankind," was organized by the International Auschwitz Committee together with the Auschwitz State Museum in Poland.

7. David S. Wyman, *The Abandonment of the Jews: America and the Holocaust, 1941–1945* (New York: Pantheon, 1984), pp. 338ff.

8. Hilberg, *Destruction,* pp. 558–68.

9. See Michael Wyschogrod, *The Body of Faith: Judaism as Corporeal Election* (New York: Seabury, 1983), p. 68.

10. This should go without saying, and would have, had I not noticed that there were more catalogue entries for *The Protocols of the Elders of Zion* in the New York Public Library, in more languages, than for any other text that I came across.

11. For an example of the actual cost to the uninvolved of other people's resistance, see Lucy S. Dawidowicz, *The War against the Jews 1933–1945* (New York: Holt, Rinehart & Winston, 1975), p. 328. For an example of the threatened cost of noncooperation, see pp. 282ff. That such threats were incessantly carried out was made clear by eyewitness after eyewitness at the Eichmann trial. The line between active resistance and passive noncooperation was not respected by the Nazis, despite Arendt's contrary suggestion that Jews should have acted as if it would be; *Eichmann in Jerusalem,* p. 124.

12. See Dawidowicz, *War against the Jews,* chaps. 12 and 13.

13. Quoted in the author's preface to Léo Bronstein, *Kabbalah and Art* (Hanover, N.H.: Brandeis University Press and University Press of New England, 1980).

14. The political paths are explored in chap. 6 of my *A Good Look at Evil,* under the subhead "Sectarian Divisions," where another of Hilberg's charges is reexamined.

15. Cf. Primo Levi, "Last Christmas of the War," *New York Review of Books* 33, no. 1 (January 30, 1986): 5f.

16. See Robert Kirschner, ed. and trans., *Rabbinic Responsa of the Holocaust Era* (New York: Schocken, 1985), pp. 76ff.; and Dawidowicz, *War against the Jews,* pp. 284f.

17. See Kirschner, *Rabbinic Responsa,* pp. 119ff.; and Adin Steinsaltz, *The Essential Talmud,* trans. Chaya Galai (New York: Basic Books, 1976), pp. 203f.

18. "In December 1941, when the German police entered the Riga ghetto to round up the old and sick Jews, Simon Dubnow, the venerable Jewish historian, was said to have called out as he was being taken away: 'Brothers, write down everything you see and hear. Keep a record of it all.' " Lucy S. Dawidowicz, *The Holocaust and the Historians* (Cambridge, Mass.: Harvard University Press, 1981), p. 125. Cf. the testimony of Avraham Aviel, about his thoughts prior to a mass shooting: "Q. What did mother say?" "A. She said, 'Say Shamah Yisrael—die as Jews.' . . . I repeated the words after her but I had inner resistance. . . . Because my thoughts—my thought was always: 'One must survive—*überleben*— . . . and tell what happened.' " Eichmann Trial, *Israel v. Eichmann: The Attorney-General of the Government of Israel v. Adolf, the Son of Adolf Karl Eichmann,* Criminal Case no. 40/61, District Court, Jerusalem (Washington, D.C.: Microcard Editions, 1962), session 29.

Joan Ringelheim

THOUGHTS ABOUT WOMEN
AND THE HOLOCAUST

The past is never dead, it is not even past.

FAULKNER

. . . it is the past's function to haunt us . . . the world we live in
at any moment *is* the world of the past . . .[1]

ARENDT

The past is alive in our present, but connections with it are opaque
rather than transparent. The past as lived is chaotic and confusing; the
past as written is a refinement of this disorderliness. What is identified as
the historical past has been shaped, reconstructed, and muted to serve
various scholarly and political interests. While written history is continually reconstructed, portions of the past wait to be revealed. Thus, *the*
past doesn't exist in the present; *many* pasts do.

These simple observations present us with a set of questions and
problems: Whose memory will be respected? Whose memory will be
hidden or undermined? What will be considered the truth? Who will
decide? Who controls the identity of the past? In other words, since
decisions are always being made about what will be emphasized in history as written, we must always ask: "Was *that* all there was?"

Like other historical events, the Holocaust has been focused in our
minds by the selectivity of many interested parties: scholars, survivors,
politicians, novelists, journalists, filmmakers, perpetrators, and revi-
sionists. Each emphasize certain features and in the process hide, even
lose others.

Two of the most common perspectives on the Holocaust are problematic. One tells us that the Holocaust is exclusively and uniquely
Jewish. A sharp division, not only a differentiation, is thereby established between Jewish experiences and those of Gypsies, Russian
P.O.W.s, Communists, Jehovah's Witnesses, homosexuals, political

prisoners, Poles, Ukrainians, the mentally ill, "anti-socials," etc. While this first perspective emphasizes differences between Jews and "others," the second one tells us that there are no significant differentiations to be made about Jews or their experiences. On this view possible variations in treatment, response or perception are collapsed into an unrelenting story of terror, brutality, and death, and "the Jewish experience" is structured in a monolithic or univocal way. Not surprisingly, neither perspective acknowledges, let alone respects, the experiences and perceptions of women during the Holocaust.

These two views (uniqueness/exclusivity, and the sameness of the Jewish experience) are symbiotically tied to each other. Unravel one and the other disintegrates. The protection of this relationship has a disabling effect on Holocaust history.

The first perspective comes from a need to ward off the denial of the Jewish tragedy or the assimilation of Jewish experience to that of other groups. This need has produced, in one way or another, the parochial conclusion that only the Jewish experience is important, or that only the Jewish experience exists. If the Holocaust is perceived as singularly Jewish, however, it won't be integrated into general history. And unless it is so integrated, the Holocaust will become more and more a concern to Jews alone. That will insulate its meanings, submerge its implications, and in time effectively erase the experience from the consciousness of the rest of the world.

With uniqueness and exclusivity as a guide, the Holocaust is characterized as a metaphysical evil. This further excises Jews from history as it removes the Holocaust from the possibility of human explanation or understanding—beyond speech or rationality. The Holocaust is then seen as ontologically separate from human history; at the same time, it is used to make "relatively trivial" other events or other people's experience prior to, during, or even after the Holocaust. Under these conditions, it is difficult to reveal the many contours and crevices of Holocaust experiences, both Jewish and Gentile. It is as if a decision was made to revise Plato's "Divided Line": instead of the Form of the Good, there is the Form of Evil made identical with the Jewish experience of the Holocaust.

Jews, however, were not victims in a vacuum. Their lives intersected those of perpetrators, bystanders, and other victims. All these intertwined create the picture of the Holocaust. The Holocaust is not only a picture of unrestrained power over and terror against the Jews. Yet somehow political prisoners, homosexual men, Gypsies, Communists, Jehovah's Witnesses, the "mentally defective," Poles, Ukrainians, and "anti-socials" have been identified as "others"—victims with no names in much of the literature and the public perception. This has created an implausible silence about them.[2]

The term "Holocaust" ought to include the sufferings of everyone singled out by the Nazis. It is understood that the argument for exclusivity and uniqueness hinges on the fear that such universalization is tantamount to anti-semitism because it sometimes denies the experiences of Jews. Still, not every argument against exclusivity and uniqueness is anti-semitic. Differences among victims should not be ignored or denied. Certainly the attempt to exterminate the Jews and the Gypsies must be distinguished from the murder of three million Poles, from the starvation and killing of millions of Russian P.O.W.s, from the internment of political prisoners, from the murder of the resistance fighters. But there also must be an appreciation for the experiences of people whose suffering and trauma were so great that they cannot be measured any more than can the suffering of the Jews. Thus, the perspective of the Holocaust as a uniquely and exclusively Jewish event must be transformed into a more complex picture which can incorporate and not denigrate the experiences and sufferings of other peoples.

The second problematic view concerns the sameness of the Jewish experience—that is, the view that what happened to the Jews can be captured in singular and sharp images of victimization (for example, the extermination camps with their gas chambers and crematoria). Such a view seems to ignore the complexities of that Jewish experience just as the exclusivity/uniqueness view ignores the complexities of the experiences of victims who were not Jewish.

At a most basic level, this narrow view misses the fact that no two Jews experienced what is called the Holocaust in quite the same way, even if they were in the same place at the same time. There is no time, there is no place that is the same for everyone, not even Auschwitz. A woman who went to Auschwitz from Slovakia in 1942 was in a different place than a woman who came from Hungary or Lodz in 1944. If a woman worked in the camp offices in Auschwitz, her experiences and knowledge differed from those of a fifteen-year-old prisoner in Lager C. In the ghetto of Lodz, the men of the Judenrat were in a different position than someone on welfare. Those who hid or passed as Aryans, who escaped, who resisted, who were in labor camps, all had different experiences of the Holocaust. Yet all these different experiences have been submerged within the horrible picture of the extermination camps. Such a picture does not reveal the variations of death, more the differentials of survival, let alone the minutia of everyday life. Many Jews who were killed or died were not even in the extermination camps—some died of starvation or disease; some were shot; some died of old age; some were killed as members of the ghetto underground or as partisans.

Within such coordinates of time and place, there are other differentiations: age, economic class, nationality, occupation, education, political and religious affiliation, and sex. In spite of the differentiations among Jews, Jewishness has become the only significant description relevant to the Holocaust. Until recently, it didn't matter to Holocaust scholarship whether they were rich or poor, educated or uneducated, skilled or unskilled, female or male, because the Nazis intended to exterminate all Jews. However, if in the gas chambers or before firing squads all Jews seemed to be alike, the path to this end was not always the same. The end, namely extermination, does not describe or explain the process.

The most obvious and pronounced difference is sex, although it is usually ignored or trivialized, sometimes feared. Let me offer some examples. At a Holocaust conference in 1979, I casually asked two women I had just met: "What about women?" Helen Fagin, survivor and Holocaust scholar, responded quite angrily as she quickly backed away: "I don't want the Holocaust to be made secondary to feminism." That was the first time I asked the question. It was nearly the last. A year later, Cynthia Ozick responded to an inquiry about a conference on women and the Holocaust in a more deeply disturbing fashion:

> I think you are asking the wrong question. Not simply the wrong question in the sense of not having found the right one; I think you are asking a *morally* wrong question, a question that leads us still further down the road of eradicating Jews from history. You are—I hope inadvertently—joining up with the likes of [the Revisionists] who [say] that if it happened to Jews it never happened. You insist that it didn't happen to "just Jews." It happened to the women, and it is only a detail that the women were Jewish. It is not a detail. It is everything, the whole story. Your project is, in my view, an ambitious falsehood. . . . The Holocaust happened to victims who were not seen as men, women, or children, but *as Jews.*[3]

The views of Fagin and Ozick complement each other. The purity of the Jewish experience must be preserved in the reconstruction of the Holocaust. The Holocaust is Jewish, and that is that. Anything else defiles and/or negates what the Holocaust was really about. The Holocaust is to remain the supreme oppression or event against which the suffering of others must be measured. No other suffering can be judged approximate to or worse than that of the Holocaust. Jewishness must remain the criteria of suffering during the Holocaust. Thus, to speak about women and the Holocaust, even Jewish women, is either a denial that Jews were exterminated or an elevation of sexism to a position more important than anti-semitism in its genocidal form. However misguided these construals are, Fagin and Ozick are not alone in their conclusions. Similar responses were generated in 1986 when I gave a series of lectures at Hunter College on women and the Holocaust: "Of course sexism is everywhere. But why do you have to use the Holocaust to prove it? There are other events you can use."

All of these sorts of comments fall under the heading of what might be called "the banality of sexism": they suggest that taking account of sexism adds nothing to our understanding of the Holocaust because the oppression of women is so commonplace. Since it is part of everyday life, it must have been part of the Holocaust. It is asserted that the sole purpose of such a study of women and the Holocaust is to demonstrate the continuity of sexism in history. The underlying presumption is that the oppression of women is an insignificant matter. The conclusion is that such a study trivializes the Holocaust.

If sexism or the oppression of women is banal, that hardly implies that it is unimportant or unable to compete with the venality of anti-semitism in its genocidal forms. A study of women and the Holocaust demonstrates the continuities of women's oppression and puts into question some of the claims about the uniqueness of the Holocaust. Unquestionably, that is one purpose of such a study. However, there is a deeper and more difficult task: to reveal the ignored and complex relationship between anti-semitism (as a form of racism against Jews) and sexism prior to and during the Holocaust. While it appears that anti-semitism contains a monolithic view of Jews, in fact it looks at and treats Jews who are male and female quite differently. Our ignorance of these differences creates blind spots in the memories and reconstructions of the Holocaust.

Anti-semitic propaganda and literature prior to and during the Holocaust rarely mention women. Men are the targets. They are the Jews who are feared and abhorred. The stereotypes of Jews concerning usury, ritual murder, deicide, and sex speak about men, not women. Jewish women are primarily identified by their femaleness. The Jewish woman is the "other" when it comes to understanding anti-semitism. Whether Jewish or Aryan, women are reduced to their femininity. The male is still "the essential." Even when despised, men remain persons of a variety of attributes.

This being the case, anti-semitism against Jewish women may only make sense if it is understood as a form of sexism. That is to say, men are the real Jews. Women are peripheral Jews to anti-semites—similarly, women are peripheral Jews within Judaism itself. Jewish women are the targets of the Nazis because they are Jews, but they are attacked and used as women—as mothers, as objects of sexual derision and exploitation, as persons less valuable than men because of the curious and damaging sexual division of labor.

There is a reciprocity between sex and race in Nazi thinking. The presumptive biological basis of sexism complements and supports that of racism. As Claudia Koonz writes in *Mothers in the Fatherland:*

> To a degree unique in Western history, Nazi doctrine created a society structured around "natural" biological poles . . . race and sex as the immutable categories of human nature. The habit of taking psychological differences between men and women for granted reinforced assumptions about irrevocable divisions between Jew and "Aryan." In place of class, culture, religious divisions, race and sex became the predominant social markers.[4]

The Nazi view of women is a paradigm of misogyny in the form of an extreme reduction of woman to her biological capacities and functions. Hitler said:

> The woman has her own battlefield. With every child that she brings into the world, she fights the battle for the nation. The man stands up for the Volk, exactly as the woman stands up for the family.[5]

Goebbels added: "The mission of women is to be beautiful and to bring children into the world."[6] Although these descriptions only refer to certain "Aryan" women, they are applicable to Jewish women.

For the Nazis, the *functions* of Jewish and Aryan women were the same (reproduction and nurturance of family). However, the *value* of each was different. Simply, when Aryan and considered biologically superior, they were valued as women; when Jews, they were not. It is impossible that the deeply held sexism within the Nazis' ideology did not affect their beliefs about and treatment of Jewish women. If the Nazis identified women by their reproductive functions, then Jewish women cannot be allowed to be Jews because they are *women.* Jewish men cannot be allowed to be Jews because they are *Jews*—the authentic Jews. The lives of women became more precarious than those of men because of sexism, not only because of anti-semitism. If anti-semitism were all that mattered, men and women would have been similarly endangered and victimized. Thus, the question is not whether being male or female mattered during the Holocaust. The real question is: How did it matter? It is blind, if not malicious, to subsume and hide women's experiences under those of men when there are significant differences.

There was a direct link in Nazi policy between anti-semitism and sexism. Jewish women suffered both as Jews and as women from anti-semitism and sexism in their genocidal forms. More women were deported than men. More women were killed than men. Women's chances for survival were simply not equivalent to those of men. As Leon Wells writes in *The Death Brigade:* "Only infants and children, the old, the sick and, for the most part, women, could be certain the German would kill them as soon as they arrived at [the] Janowska [concentration camp]. For these there was for the most part no respite."[7] The sexism of the Nazis reverberated with the sexism within the Jewish community. A Jewish woman survivor once told me: "I had two enemies: Nazis and men."

Perhaps it isn't surprising to learn that women were less valuable than men and hence more victimized. The problem with such a response is that we then often miss the deeper issue: namely, women and men suffer from oppression in different ways even in its genocidal forms. When we miss this point, we universalize men's lives and in the process lose the lives of women for a second time. Women's perceptions and experiences as women become denigrated and are allowed to pass into the periphery of oblivion—into the banality of sexism. Jewish women were the victims of the Nazis as women and as Jews.

Jewish women and men were caught between two groups: the Nazis, who wanted to kill all Jews and had no tendency to protect women and children; and the Jewish leadership, who wanted to save as many Jews as possible. Survival rather than resistance became the goal around which most Jews tried to maneuver; cooperation with Nazi demands rather than non-compliance characterized their behavior. Active and/or armed resistance was seen as either impossible or too dangerous. On the whole, it was thought that resistance would make things worse. This conclusion was based either on ignorance about the extermination camps or on the refusal to believe that Jews were being murdered in unprecedented numbers even when evidence was available.

It became obvious (even to those who refused to admit what the Nazis were really doing) that it was not possible to help or save all Jews. Some Jews had to be sacrificed to Nazi demands if other Jews were to be saved. But *who* was to be saved? What were the criteria? Some Jews were more valuable and hence more protected than others. Certain men were more valuable than other men. On the whole women were less valuable than men. While men had little control over their choices, women had even less control. Women were not in positions of authority. They had to negotiate with Jewish men if not prostitute themselves in order to acquire some measure of the resources to which men had more access.

The Jewish leadership tried to use various strategies: bribery, petitions, requests. However, the strategy that seemed to fit Nazi needs best and was consequently used more (when it was possible) was that of "rescue through work." The strategy presumed that usefulness to the Nazis would save the lives of Jews. But the strategy did not benefit women. If it benefited anyone, it was Jewish men. The skills the Nazis needed were those of men, not women. Ghetto Chief Jacob Gens of the Vilna Ghetto summed this up most succinctly:

> I want to avert the end through work. Through work by healthy men. Thanks to that the ghetto exists. . . . The Germans wouldn't keep a ghetto for women and children for very long; they wouldn't give them food for one extra day.[8]

The Nazis did not want so-called women's skills (childbearing, etc.) if the women were Jewish. Jewish men tried to comply with Nazi demands and couldn't protect Jewish women. More than ever, "women and children first" was not an act of chivalry. The division of labor by sex, by sexual function, was nearly an immediate death sentence for women. Clearly women were systematically endangered as Jews and as women. To make the most sense of their experiences, their situation as women can no longer be obscured.

While all Jews were supposed to share the death sentence established by the Nazis, men and women did not all share it in the same way, at the same time, or for the same reasons. Women's modes of survival and resistance do not necessarily take the same shape as those of men. Their lives and deaths, their experiences and memories, their death and survival rates were different in significant ways from those of men.

NOTES

1. Hannah Arendt, "Home to Roost," *The New York Review of Books,* June 26, 1975, p. 6.

2. As an example see *The Holocaust Commission Report*, September 27, 1979, p. 3.

3. From a 1980 letter to the author.

4. Claudia Koonz, *Mothers in the Fatherland* (New York: St. Martin's Press, 1987), pp. 5–6.

5. From a speech to the Nationalist Socialist Congress published in the *Volkischer Beobacheer*, September 15, 1935 (Wiener Library Clipping Collection) reproduced in George L. Mosse, *Nazi Culture* (New York: Universal Library, 1966), p. 40. This Nazi view is hardly unique in Western Civilization. They may have used it with even greater effect than others.

6. From Joseph Goebbels, *Michael: Ein Deutsches Schicksal in Tagebuchblatten* (Munich: Zentralverlag der NSDAP Frx. Eher Nachf., 1929), p. 41 (Wiener Library Clipping Collection), reproduced in Mosse, *Nazi Culture*, p. 41.

7. Leon W. Wells, *The Death Brigade (The Janowska Road)* (New York: Holocaust Library, 1978), p. 133. I thank Irene Eber for this reference.

8. Leonard Tushnet, *The Pavement of Hell* (New York: St. Martin's Press, 1972), p. 186.

Myrna Goldenberg

DIFFERENT HORRORS, SAME HELL: WOMEN REMEMBERING THE HOLOCAUST

> And children someday will plant flowers in Auschwitz, where
> the sun couldn't crack through the smoke of burning flesh.
>
> ISABELLA LEITNER

Flames, ashes, soot, mud, cold, heat, barbed wire, watery excuses for soup, rancid synthetic coffee, lice, thirst, hunger, dysentery, beatings, roll calls, chimneys, *Canada* barracks, festering wounds, typhus, shaved heads and bodies, naked "parades," forced marches, random shootings, survival as an act of resistance and resistance as an act of sabotage— these are the terrible realities and images that haunt the pages of Holocaust witness literature.[1] They are all the more terrible because survivor narratives contain not one or a few but rather a full catalogue of such abominations, thereby assaulting our cultured imaginations and our untested morality. Thus, these narratives affect their readers in significant ways. Each narrative presents a paradox, an unimaginable set of horrors that were an unbearable reality forged of industrialized bestiality and brutality. Each narrative also transforms abstract cruelty into unique personal experiences that, individually and collectively, portray a cataclysmic event. These survivor narratives are invaluable because they provide a major source of historical evidence about the social context that has become both the setting for Holocaust fiction and the human expression of Holocaust history and philosophy. In other words, these narratives not only generate fiction about the Holocaust, but they also validate such fiction and verify historical accounts.[2]

English language audiences know Holocaust literature primarily through male writers and have generalized those experiences to represent the whole. For the most part, these excellent works have endured, remaining accessible through successive printings and continued inclusion in standard anthologies.[3] Narratives by women survivors, however, form a group that differs significantly from those by men. First, in both the labor and the death camps, women and men were separated, and they "operated in radically separated spheres." Brutalized "separately and equally," men and women had similar though different experiences.[4] Consequently, the women's narratives differ from those of men primarily because they are set in a female context and thus portray a women's *Lager* experience. Inescapably, they include material about experiences that are unique to women because of their biology, i.e. as childbearers, and their socialization, i.e. as nurturers and homemakers.

Facts and generalizations about the barracks, diet, clothing, and work assignments for women in the concentration camps can be deduced from historical documents and archival files. Survivor narratives provide a different type of information. Portrayed through the prism of women's eyes and sensibilities, they are impressionistic records of women's physical and psychic agonies as *Haftlings*. Though filtered by protective memory, they are accounts that explore the events that comprised everyday existence and the impact of those events on the narrators. Thus, these narratives both stimulate and support the works of historians and novelists and, as a group, suggest the pattern of women's lives in Auschwitz and other camps.[5] The memoirs of Charlotte Delbo, Livia Bitton Jackson, Ilona Karmel, Gerda Klein, Isabella Leitner, Olga Lengyel, Sarah Nomberg-Przytyk, Frances Penney, and Gisela Perl—corroborated by the testimony of other women—detail the specifics of these women's experiences.[6]

Repetition of several themes and incidents distinguish women's narratives from those of men. For example, women's narratives frequently acknowledge their vulnerability as sexual beings, and especially as menstruating or pregnant women. Moreover, they repeatedly link and often attribute survival to relationships with other women. Women write of their bonding, even of their re-creation of families and familial structures, and of the significance of maintaining their links with women. They describe extraordinary caring among women, particularly in contrast to the men who, they argue, competed against one another for survival but lacked essential skills necessary to survive in the "surrealistic nightmare" of the concentration camp.[7] Women survivors and scholars refer to the "feminization" of male survivors—males who had to learn to trust and share in the manner of women; in other words, women survivors compare themselves favorably to men who had "to learn behaviors that women already knew." Indeed, one Belsen survivor's intrepretation is unequivocally patronizing: "Men are far weaker and far less able to stand up to the hardship than the women—physically and often morally as well. Unable to control themselves, they display such a lack of moral fiber that we cannot but be sorry for them." She concludes by explaining that women and men behaved in the concentration camps as they had before.[8] Women's behavior includes their habits of cleanliness and housekeeping, attitudes toward food, and caretaker skills. Men, on the other hand, point to acts of kindness and nurturing as the exception and, in the words of one prisoner/survivor, only "when they became hardened to the necessity of the task."[9]

A gender study of Holocaust literature, however, is fraught with risks, not the least of which is the fear that such an approach trivializes the Holocaust or politicizes it or even eclipses historical, philosophical, sociological, and theological interpretations. Such assertions, however, ignore the fact that gender studies, and a variety of other studies rooted in the specific, enhance our knowledge and illuminate our understanding of the dimensions of the Final Solution. For example, we study each concentration camp as a separate entity because each differed from the next; we track the experiences of Jews according to their country of origin and avoid generalizations that disregard their separate trials and fates; we examine the behavior and attitudes of religious and secular Jews, of urban and rural Jews, of heterosexuals and homosexuals, and of Jew and non-Jews. In the same way, we are obligated to examine, separately, the lives of women and of men to determine the differences and the similarities in the way they were treated as well as in the way they responded.

Women's socialization as nurturers in the context of the Holocaust also raises a complex set of serious questions. If we accept their explanations that tie survival to relationships, are we not at the same time accepting an ethic that values relationships above autonomy, or a traditionally feminine characteristic over a traditionally masculine characteristic? Are the testimonies of these survivors confirming, directly or indirectly, the work of contemporary feminist theorists such as Nancy Chodorow and Carol Gilligan who have suggested that women are "oriented toward attachment and 'connectedness' to others" in contrast to men who are "inclined toward individuation and 'separateness' from others"?[10] Did the behavior of women in the extermination camps anticipate a new morality based on caring rather than justice? Did the unjust and irrational Auschwitz reality disorient men to the point of dysfunction? Did men, whose identity was (and is) traditionally dependent upon their public or communal role (the workplace or the synagogue), lose their ability to cope in a situation that reduced them to slaves or numbers? Did they also become dysfunctional when they lost their role as protectors, heads of families, entrepreneurs, professionals? Did women, who speak of re-creating a family and thus of the opportunity to nurture and be nurtured, instinctively adapt to their new situations? Stated succintly, is this "connectedness" an expression of a different morality, one that was—and is—instrumental to survival?

Indeed, it has been suggested that "ways of resisting and surviving are, in fact, differentiated by gender." From her early conversations and correspondence with survivors and historians, Joan Ringelheim reports their impressions that women were "better able to survive the loss of children and other members of their family than men" and quotes Des Pres:

> In places like Auschwitz and Ravensbruck [women] made bet-ter survivors. . . . They knew how to sew, for one thing (cul-tural); they were more at ease in matters of intimate help (also probably cultural); they seemed to care more for life (cultural but also biological?); and being less dependent on inflated egos, as men were, when these egos cracked and were swept away women recovered faster and with less bitterness.[11]

Suggesting that women's traditional roles contributed substantively to their ability to survive, Sybil Milton explains:

> Women had significantly different survival skills and tech-niques than men . . . [which] included doing housework as a kind of practical therapy and of gaining control over one's space, bonding and networks, religious and political convic-tions, and possibly even sex.
>
> Women appear to have been more resilient than men, both physically and psychologically, to malnutrition and star-vation. Clinical research . . . confirmed . . . and brought proof to the assertion that women were less vulnerable to the effects of short-term starvation and famine. Women in Gurs, There-sienstadt, and Bergen-Belsen reported that men "were selfish and undisciplined egoists, unable to control their hungry stom-achs, and revealed a painful lack of courage." Women also shared and pooled their limited resources better than men. . . .
> In the camps, women swapped recipes and ways of extending limited quantities of food. Men could be overheard discussing their favorite banquets and restaurants.[12]

Several sources report substantially lower mortality rates for women inmates than for men. At Ravensbruck, for example, in 1943, the rate of men dying was three times that of women. Women's higher survival rates in that camp have been attributed to greater skills in preserving life, "such as nursing sick inmates, refashioning clothing . . . and stretching limited food supplies." In Auschwitz, too, women apparently withstood incarceration better than men did in spite of Commandant Hoss' comments that camp conditions were "incomparably worse for women" than for men. The women, he said, were "far more tightly packed-in and the sanitary and hygienic conditions were notably inferior." The women's camp had considerably less drinking water and severe drainage problems which caused endless mud and, in the winter, dangerous patches of ice, which were even pictured in a survivor's watercolor of a section being supervised by Irma Griese.[13]

Although Jewish men were victims of Nazi violence far more often than women were, women were vulnerable to the unrelenting Nazi machine in a different way. Before systematic deportations began in 1941, Jewish women, having committed no crime, did not expect women to be rounded up, questioned, beaten, or incarcerated even though they were quick to feel the sting of Nazi anti-semitism. In Germany, in the early thirties, they were ostracized from women's groups and forced to comfort their victimized schoolchildren. Violence against women in the thirties "was still relatively rare," and women were not usually incarcerated or beaten in the thirties.[14] As the Nazi hold grew firmer, Jewish women "linked growing misogyny to rising anti-semitism," and at first redoubled their efforts at interfaith relations but soon abandoned "building bridges" in favor of "revitalizing" Jewish community life and "retreating" from their public roles, a confusing stance at best.[15]

Witness literature, both from the ghettos and the camps, offers example after example of women who trace their reactions and inaction to their inability to believe that the Nazis would breach the tradition of civility toward women and children. One women survivor testified that she "did not believe that the Nazis would stoop to murdering children. We women were lulled into the false hope that while we were working our children would be taken care of separately."[16] Indeed, after leaving the cattle car at Auschwitz, Olga Lengyel convinced the S.S. officer that her twelve year old son was merely "big for his age." To spare him hard labor that faced her group, Lengyel pushed him into the children's group and then urged her mother to join that group to care for her sons while she herself went with the group assigned for work (p. 27). Acts of futile self-sacrifice like Lengyel's, intended to save children, only hastened the murder of these same children. Tragically, many women were unsuspecting and thus unprepared for the horrors that followed sincere attempts to save old and young family members.

Jewish women, particularly observant Jewish women, were subject to still another level of abuse.[17] Judaism separates religious women from adult men (including, to a degree, their own husbands) and places a very high value on chastity, modesty, and obedience. In the hands of the Nazis, observant women were, therefore, particularly defenseless against the astonishing range of degradations: verbal abuse, untended menstruation, public nakedness, and head and body shavings by men, and internal body searches. That is, their religious isolation and parochial socialization left them even more vulnerable to humiliations caused by violations of their privacy and assaults to their dignity than would be the case with urbane women. Sheltered or urbane, Jewish women were targeted for nefarious degradation. Gisela Perl recalls with disgust having to watch the Gestapo "while they seized [in the ghetto] one woman after another and with dirty fingers searched the depths of her body for treasures" (p. 18). Livia Bitton Jackson portrays the women's incredulity at being told to undress in a room "swarming with S.S. men" who shouted, "Those having any clothes on in five minutes will be shot." She worries about her mother's feelings and, never having seen her mother nude, avoids looking at her (pp. 58–59). In fact, we are told that, in 1944, Hungarian women in Auschwitz often "had no clothes whatever."[18]

Unable to conceal her bitterness forty years after Kaiserweld, Frances Penney describes her reactions to Nazi abuse:

> It is, with hindsight, hard to comprehend what a blow to our morale this German tactic of shaving off women's hair, the symbol of their womanhood, was. Hard to comprehend, I repeat, since each of us, at any minute of the day, could have been annihilated in a variety of fashions. We could have been shot, gassed, or put into the ovens. And yet, this single act of German brutality constituted a sacrilegious act on our bodies, our only possessions.
>
> I was terrorized when my turn came to get under the hand of a "prosecutor with a shaver."
>
> I refrained from biting my lips. I was sure that this scheme was deliberately planned to break our will to survive. . . . I would not let them think that they had defeated me. . . . As long as there was a breath of life in me, they would not succeed in robbing me of my hope to see the day of redemption.
>
> Meanwhile, walking around us with a shaver in his hand and a malicious, delighted grin on his face, was our German Commandant. Examining every head, he would track down every single hair left by oversight and add his personal touch to this hideous operation by clipping it off (p. 107).

Sara Nomberg-Pryztyk's picture of women being shaved reflects her
pain and her sense of loss:

> [We were shaved] to the accompaniment of shouts and blows,
> which fell thickly on our heads and shoulders. . . . We were not
> allowed any modesty in front of these strange men. We were
> nothing more than objects on which they performed their
> duties, non-sentient things that they could examine from all
> angles. It did not bother them that cutting hair close to the skin
> with dull scissors was excruciatingly painful. It did not bother
> them that we were women and that without our hair we felt
> totally humiliated. In a few hours we were robbed of everything
> that had been ours personally. We were shown that here
> in Auschwitz we were just numbers, without faces or souls
> (pp. 14–15).

Jackson summarizes her emotional pain after being shaved: "Individuals
became a mass of bodies. . . . In a matter of minutes even the physical
aspect of our numbers seems reduced—there is less of a substance to
our dimensions" (p. 59). She interprets the verbal abuse heaped on
them by the S.S.:

> From *blode Lumpen,* "idiotic whores," we became *blode
> Schweine,* "idiotic swine." Easier to despise. And the epithet
> changed only occasionally to *blode Hunde,* "idiotic dogs." Eas-
> ier to handle (p. 60).

Perhaps women's narratives depict vivid scenes of cruelty because
they, even after incarceration, were unable to reconcile or even accommodate the contrast between their pre-concentration camp life and
their lives as *Haftlings.* Scenes of cruelty and sadism scarred their consciousness. Gerda Klein, Charlotte Delbo, and Isabella Leitner as well as
Perl, Klein, Lengyel, Penney, and Nomberg-Przytyk horrify readers with
their depictions of the brutality of the S.S., the *kapos,* and the Ukrainian
and Hungarian guards as well as the Darwinism of the inmates. Women
narrators vividly recall women guards as "worse than men," more vicious and cruel than S.S. men. In fact, the small number of S.S. women
was outweighed by their large measure of sadism.[19] Irma Griese, inextricably linked to such sadism, is described as the "most depraved, cruel,
imaginative sexual pervert" who, with "her bejewelled whip poised,
picked out the most beautiful young women and slashed their breasts
open with the braided wire end of her whip." To satisfy her perversions,

Perl tells us, Griese watched the subsequent breast surgery on her victims, "kicking the victim if her screams interfered with her pleasure and giving herself completely to the orgastic spasms which shook her entire body and made saliva run down from the corner of her mouth" (pp. 60–61).

Nomberg-Przytyk's despair at the "animalistic struggle for existence, a battle for a little watery soup, even for a little bit of water" leads her to plan suicide (p. 22). She is rescued by a former comrade who introduces her to the active communist underground in Auschwitz and saves her life by bringing her into a group of caring women. Consequently, Nomberg-Przytyk's verbal portraits focus on the relationships women formed with other women, often to avoid the brutality of other *kapos, blochowas,* or the S.S. Her understated short chapter on the burning of live children at Auschwitz shatters any reader's suspicion about the human capacity for bestiality:

> Suddenly the stillness was broken by the screaming of children, as if a single scream had been torn out of hundreds of mouths, a single scream of fear and unusual pain, a scream repeated a thousand times in the single word, "Mama," a scream that increased in intensity every second, enveloping the whole camp and every inmate. . . .
>
> On the block we could still hear the screams of the children who were being murdered, then only sighs, and at the end everything was enveloped in death and silence. The next day the men told us that the SS men loaded the children into wheelbarrows and dumped them into the fiery ravines. Living children burned like torches (pp. 81–82).

Terrorized by their vulnerability as sexual beings, women also feared the possibility of never bearing any (more) children. Their narratives reflect their fear of menstruation, amenorrhea, pregnancy, and permanent sterility. Klein's concern about menstruation and sterility are at the center of her narrative:

> We had heard that in some camps girls had been forcibly sterilized. That thought filled me with unspeakable horror. Many girls in our camp no longer had their monthly periods because of their poor nutrition. Few of them seemed concerned. . . . I spoke to other girls about my fears but they shrugged it off. Survival had become their most important thought, shutting out all else. Yet the thought of sterility did worry me. More

forcibly . . . the idea returned that someday I must have a baby of my own. I felt that I would endure anything willingly so long as that hope was not extinguished (pp. 155–156).

Leitner complains, "We haven't menstruated for a long time" (p. 14). Jackson is shocked at the sight of blood on a girl's legs during roll call:

Oh, my God, she must have been shot! . . . She is menstruating. . . . Of course, we have no underwear. . . . There are no pads . . . the blood simply flows. Down her legs. . . . This is horrible. . . . She might even be shot for reporting that she is bleeding. Does menstruating constitute sabotage? (p. 72).

Images and metaphors, too, focus on the family and women's traditional interests and preoccupations. Delbo describes screaming victims as "a flower bed of twisted mouths" (p. 56). When a friend calls to her to prevent her from surrendering to fatigue and despair, Delbo cries, "It is the voice of my mother that I hear. . . . And I feel I cling to Viva as much as a child clings to its mother" (p. 73). In a rainstorm, the S.S. allow Delbo's *kommando* to take shelter in a house left empty when its Jewish owners were liquidated. The women "look at the house as though [they] had forgotten and were rediscovering words." Delbo reports snatches of their conversation, "I would put a couch here next to the fireplace."—"Some cottage prints would look nice. You know those prints." They "provide the house with all its furniture, polished, comfortable, familiar. It is complete except for a few details" (p. 88). In Ilona Karmel's *Estate of Memory,* grief "was like gifts from home sent to the one who somewhere in the frozen dark was still struggling on, but growing smaller, more shadowy with each step" (p. 321). Another one of Kermel's female characters describes a moment in the labor camp: "The air was quiet except when at times—like a hostess who, guests gone, sets her home aright and then rests—the breeze stirred, erased the footprints, restored the road to its damask smoothness, then ceased" (p. 104). Later she depicts the work site, "As in a home tables for refreshments are set out at the guests' arrival, so here stones, here bricks and planks were being piled . . ." (p. 195).

The women's hunger triggers conversations and fantasies about recipes, table settings, and kitchen matters—ironically bizarre scenes in the context of extreme filth and food deprivations. "We would talk about the past, about the future, and lots of times about recipes, about the cooking skills one remembered and about the wonderful recipes one used to make or taste," remembers Susan Cernyak-Spatz, who explained that these memories mitigated the despair at their everyday life.[20] Karmel's inmates evoke memories of "eating red sherbet out of silver cups" (p. 156) and ". . . apples. When had she eaten such apples, sweet with sugar, with cinnamon and cloves" (p. 218). These women fantasize about life "after the war" when they will have an abundance of "cakes, bowls of broth or fruit" (p. 300). Delbo dreams that she was given tea with an orange section: "It gives between my teeth and it is really an orange section. . . . I have the taste of an orange in my mouth, the juice seeps under my tongue, touches my palate, my gums, trickles down my throat. It is a slightly sour orange and wonderfully cool. This taste of orange and the sensation of cold wake me up. The awakening is dreadful" (p. 85). In the disorder of the chaotic evacuation of Auschwitz in late January 1945, Leitner's sister finds and smashes a chicken against a wall to make chicken soup: "Chicken soup—no matter where, no matter how—is a cure for everything. That is the old adage, and it works. Our spirits soar at the smell of it. My mother would be happy" (p. 87). Later Leitner wryly says, "Is there food enough on this planet to satiate the remnants of Auschwitz?" (p. 90). Gerda Klein relates an afternoon of women daydreaming about ideal husbands: "One voice, unforgettable, boomed, 'Give me a Grocer!' " (p. 156).

Women's narratives also alert us to the significance of gender-specific behaviors and attitudes. The relative mobility of women in and out of the ghetto, the preoccupation with futile attempts at cleanliness and with keeping up one's personal appearance, and again, most important, the bonding between women form a context and sometimes a structure of several stories by women survivors. Women speak about their "domestic instinct" to clean and about their toleration for hunger that came from the custom of serving the family before they themselves sat down to eat.[21] These strategies not only permitted women to hold onto their former identities, but it is quite likely that they influenced women's ability to survive the concentration camps. Oral testimony yields graphic descriptions that illustrate the behavior and perceptions of women *Haftlings:*

> [Women were] picking each other like monkeys [for lice]. . . .
> Never remember seeing the men do it. The minute they had
> lice they just left it alone; the women have a different instinct.
> Housewives. We want to clean. . . . Somehow the men . . . the
> [lice] ate them alive. . . . [During roll call] the women holding
> each other and keeping each other warm. . . . Someone puts
> their arm around you and you remember. . . . Men were
> crouching into themselves—maybe five feet apart. . . . I think

more women survived. . . . As much as I saw in Auschwitz, the men were falling like flies. The women were somehow stronger. . . . Women friendship is different than men friendship. . . . We have these motherly instincts, friend instinct more. . . . Men were friends too. They talked to each other but they didn't, wouldn't, sell their bread for an apple for another guy. They wouldn't sacrifice nothing. See, that was the difference.[22]

In the works of women survivors, women devote much of their energy and ingenuity to creating and maintaining family connections. Women who were assigned to a commando with "access to some non-camp food" liberated

such food at considerable risk and shared it with the group. Women had the managerial capacity to ration and apportion the little food available. Men had a tendency to hoard for themselves and to consume whatever they had at once to appease the never-ending hunger at least temporarily.[23]

Indeed, women survivors often tend to attribute their survival to their connections with other women in the family or in their surrogate family.

We witness women motivating other women to stay alive in a universe created for their annihilation. "If you are sisterless, you do not have the pressure, the absolute responsibility to end the day alive" (p. 44), sighs Leitner whose "sisters came every night [to the infirmary] to pump spirit into my near-death body" (p. 70). Delbo's unequivocal need for trustworthy friends is pragmatic:

We protect each other. Everyone wants to stay close to a friend. One woman to stay in front of a weaker one to take the blows for her, another to stay behind a woman who can no longer run to steady her if she falls (p. 103).

Separated temporarily from her companions, Delbo remains "alone at the bottom of this ditch." She laments:

I am overcome with despair. The presence of others, their words, made return possible. They went away and I am afraid. I do not believe in the return when I am alone. With them, since they seem to believe in it so firmly, I believe in it too. The minute they leave me, I am afraid. No one believes in the return when she is alone (p. 115).

Cernyak-Spatz describes her bout with typhoid fever in the spring of 1943 which went undetected because her "group of German-Jewish women held [her] upright." Never forgetting that she owes her life to this group, she explains:

> My group, for at least a week, took me in the center of the row of five prisoners, the prescribed formation, and practically carried me through the gate, so that it would look like I was marching in step, though my feet barely touched the ground.[24]

Penney describes a similar incident. Beaten by kapos, her friend Roza was unable to lift her "battered body." Yet "the next morning and for many mornings after . . . we women had to drag the debilitated Roza down to the courtyard, for roll call. Since she was unable to stand on her feet, we supported her and propped her up, so that her weakness would not be noticed by the German Commandant" (p. 103). Karmel describes women during a punishment *appell* on a winter day, futilely trying to warm one another, "huddling together, then by kneeling back to back, but it was just pressing cold against cold, and soon they drew apart, each doubled up" (p. 210). In contrast, men survivors analyze the consequences of maintaining or severing ties with other men and portray nurturing relationships as the exception, not the rule. A sense of duty or obligation rather than love or tenderness ties them to another human being.

Childbirth, when it did occur, took on ironic dimensions of risk and danger and turned mothers into murderers, forcing them to kill their newborns in order to prevent reprisals to the women in their barracks. The Nazis' "unrelenting decision," writes Lengyel, was to send mother and newborn to the gas chambers. To foil their "monstrous" and immoral intentions and save the mother, the infirmary staff delivered the babies and instantly killed them, leaving them to be counted as stillborn (pp. 110–113). Nomberg-Przytyk quotes Mengele's twisted explanation for killing Jewish mothers with their newborns. He explained that such babies had to be spared camp life *and* the inhumaneness of being sent to the ovens "without permitting the mother to be there to witness the child's death." Esther, a friend of Nomberg-Przytyk who delivers a son, loses her hold on reality and, at a selection three days after she gave birth, parades her son past Mengele who sends them both to the gas chambers (p. 69). Karmel's women, however, manage to collude with a young sympathetic S.S. man and with non-Jewish Poles in Krakow to save the baby of Aurelia, one of the four women whose lives comprise the book. Karmel's childbirth event, however, is the exception. Motherhood, in other words, was both the cause of and excuse for physical violence or death.

As absorbing and repellant as these women's narratives are as works of literature, they pose many interesting, unanswered issues for philosophy, psychology, sociology, and education. First there are the disturbing questions about the nature of evil as it relates to sex and gender. Holocaust literature and testimony prove that it is impossible to assign qualities of relative goodness or evil exclusively to one or the other sex. Survivors recall criminal *kapos, blochowas,* and *anweiserins* with revulsion and never fail to mention Irma Griese's capricious cruelty. We need, therefore, to examine the relationship of socially acquired traits not only to gender but also to survival.

Women tended to maintain familial (natural or surrogate) ties and to function as part of a family even in this forsaken environment. Indeed, the first Commandant of Ravensbruck understood the significance of relationships among women and supported his request to build detention cells by pointing out that women cannot survive "strict confinement, since no more severe punishment can be used in a women's camp. Denial of food does not suffice for discipline and order in a women's camp."[25] If, as has been suggested, this type of cultural conditioning is more significant for survival than the presence or absence of autonomy or any other high-sounding principle, then women's Holocaust narratives support the work of feminist scholars and have major implications for education and public policy today.[26] We must recognize the value of nurturing to any society that is growing more and more fragmented and violent.

Women's Holocaust literature presents other issues to consider. The context of Holocaust narratives is alien and extreme. It is the context of another world, "planet Auschwitz," in Leitner's term, one which did not live by the rules and customs of civil or civilized society. Therefore, we need to be cautious about applying analytical tools and developmental theory which emerge from a normal context to an environment that was created to perform genocide.[27] Although it is natural to begin to examine women's bonding in the concentration camps from the perspectives of Nancy Chodorow and Carol Gilligan, we must ask ourselves whether it is valid to use traditional cultural norms, psychoanalytic theory, or feminist theory to understand the context of the concentration camp, let alone the death camp. "I imagine," says Vera Laske ironically, "that you form certain bonds in prisons that are different from some bonds that you form joining the ladies' auxiliary or a bridge club or what-have-you."[28] Are we thus ultimately presented with a body of literature that requires another language, as Primo Levi insisted, as well as another psychology and sociology? If the Holocaust presents us with a new kind of norm (the term *norm* is actually a disturbing paradox in this context), are we not also faced with the challenge of developing new theoretical approaches to race, gender, genocide, and morality?

The Nazi propaganda machine created an illusion of traditional family values that in reality masked an odious mechanized, legalized sadism practiced in sites dedicated to atrocity: Auschwitz, Belzec, Bergen-Belsen, Buchenwald, Chelmo, Dachau, Mauthausen, Maidanek, Ravensbruck, Sachenhausen, Sobibor, Treblinka, Stutthof, Babi Yar, Rumboli, and so on. Predicated on authority in the form of brutality, the concentration camp was an ultimate expression of the extreme masculinity and misogyny that undergirded Nazi ideology. The female death camp, a "warehouse destructive of life" for women who are naturally life-giving,[29] reflected "one of the most women-hating regimes of the modern world."[30] This perverted patriarchical bureaucracy is depicted in women's Holocaust narratives which differ from one another primarily in the characterization of the narrator but not in the events portrayed. In many of these narratives, childbirth is the centerpiece in a context of incremental and unremitting loss. In these works, the delivery of a live baby in the death camp is both a result of and an act of women's collaboration and resistance. Placed at the center of these stories, the delivery of a live baby is an act of triumph and affirmation. Indeed, while they have not denied Hitler his millions of victims, these women have denied him his Final Solution.

NOTES

1. By witness literature, I am referring to autobiographical accounts of survivors of their periods of confinement to ghettos or incarceration in Nazi concentration camps. I use the term *witness literature* interchangeably with survivor narrative and narrative.

2. See, for example, Terence Des Pres, *The Survivor: An Anatomy of Life in the Death Camp* (NY: Pocket Books, 1977), p. vi; Sidra Ezrahi, *By Words Alone: The Holocaust in Literature* (Chicago: U. of Chicago, 1980), p. 22; Kenneth Harper, "The Literature of Witness," *Holocaust Studies Annual* 3 (1985): 249; Raul Hilberg, *The Destruction of European Jews* (Chicago: Quadrangle, 1961), frequent references to Gisela Perl's narrative. See also John Hersey, *The Wall* (NY: Knopf, 1950); Herman Wouk, *War and Remembrance* (Boston: Little, Brown, 1978); and many other novels based on Holocaust diaries or history.

3. Joan Ringelheim, "The Unethical and the Unspeakable: Women

and the Holocaust," *Simon Wiesenthal Center Annual* 1 (1984): 69–70; see also major works of Elie Wiesel, Primo Levi, Tadeusz Borowski, Alexander Donat; and two major anthologies, Albert Friedlander, *Out of the Whirlwind* (NY: UAHC, 1968); and Jacob Glatstein et al., *Anthology of Holocaust Literature* (Philadelphia: JPS, 1969).

4. Claudia Koonz, *Mothers in the Fatherland* (NY: St. Martin's Press, 1987), pp. 420, 406; Sybil Milton, "Women and the Holocaust," in *When Biology Became Destiny,* eds. Renate Bridenthal, Atina Grossman, Marion Kaplan (NY: Monthly Review Press, 1984), p. 298; Joan Ringelheim, "Women and the Holocaust: A Reconsideration of the Research," *Signs* 10, no. 4 (1985): 745. See also Marlene Heinemann, *Gender and Destiny: Women Writers of the Holocaust* (Westport, CT: Greenwood, 1986), pp. 2–5.

5. Conversations with Joan Ringelheim, May 16, 1989, and with Susan Cernyak-Spatz, May 19, 1989, dealt with the problem with narratives that are historically inaccurate, particularly with respect to specific names and dates. I am convinced that though these narratives may be "flawed" or highly selective or incomplete, they are valuable. Their value lies in the events they describe, their singular focus on women, and their validation of one another. Some are inconsistent with historical facts but all describe the same type of experiences, especially about bonding with and caring for other women, violence, atrocious camp conditions, punishments, food, and so on.

6. Charlotte Delbo, *None of Us Will Return* (Boston: Beacon, 1968); Livia Bitton Jackson, *Elli: Coming of Age in the Holocaust* (NY: Times, 1980); Ilona Karmel, *Estate of Memory* (NY: Feminist Press, 1986); Gerda Klein, *All But My Life* (NY: Hill and Wang, 1957); Isabella Leitner, *Fragments of Isabella* (NY: Crowell, 1978); Olga Lengyel, *Five Chimneys* (NY: Ziff and Davis, 1947); Sara Nomberg-Przytyk, *Auschwitz: True Tales from a Grotesque Land* (Chapel Hill, NC: UNC, 1985); Frances Penney, *I Was There* (NY: Shengold, 1988); Gisela Perl, *I Was a Doctor at Auschwitz* (1948, Tamarac, FL: Yale Garber, 1987).

7. Susan Cernyak-Spatz, Lecture. Woman Reach Convention, Charlotte, NC. October 24, 1987; conversation, May 19, 1989.

8. Koonz, p. 381, quoting Hannah Levy-Haas, *Inside Belsen* (Totowa, NJ: Barnes and Noble, 1982; see also Helene Celmina, *Women in Soviet Prisons* (NY: Paragon, 1985), pp. 151–152, for similar discussions about men and women survival in Soviet prison camps; for example, "Men were dying as fast as if death were stalking through the camps, mowing grass. The women did the same work in the woods on the same food in the same circumstances, but showed much greater endurance."

9. Germaine Tillion, *Ravensbruck* (NY: Doubleday, 1975), p. 230 commenting on Eugene Kogon; see also Heinemann, pp. 4–6; Ringelheim, 1985, p. 747; Viktor Frankl, *Man's Search for Meaning*, 3rd ed. (NY: Simon and Schuster, 1984), p. 75.

10. Mary Roth Walsh, ed. *The Psychology of Women: Ongoing Debates* (New Haven: Yale, 1987), pp. 274–75. See also Nancy Chodorow, *The Reproduction of Mothering* (Berkeley: U of Calif, 1978), p. 167: "Girls emerge from this [oedipal] period with a basis for 'empathy' built into their primary definition of self in a way that boys do not. Girls emerge with a stronger basis for experiencing another's needs or feelings as one's own," and p. 207: "Women define and experience themselves relationally"; also see pp. 173ff. See also Carol Gilligan, *In a Different Voice* (Cambridge, MA: Harvard, 1982), p. 73: "The logic underlying an ethic of care is a psychological logic of relationships, which contrasts with the formal logic of fairness that informs the justice approach," and p. 104: "The blind willingness to sacrifice people to truth, however, has always been the danger of an ethics abstracted from life," and p. 105: "The abortion study suggests that women impose a distinctive construction on moral problems, seeing moral dilemmas in terms of conflicting responsibilities. . . . The sequence of women's moral judgment proceeds from an initial concern with survival to a focus on goodness and finally to a reflective understanding of care as the most adequate guide to the resolution of conflicts in human relationships."

11. Ringelheim, 1984, p. 70. Ringelheim is now investigating survival rates; her preliminary research suggests that, by May 1945, fewer women than men survived. Conversation, May 16, 1989.

12. Milton, pp. 311–312.

13. Milton, pp. 307–308, 313; Koonz, illustrations.

14. Esther Katz and Joan Miriam Ringelheim, *Proceedings of the Conference, Women Surviving the Holocaust* (NY: Institute for Research in History, 1983), pp. 11–21, 79, 106, 109.

15. Koonz, pp. 355–358, 363–373.

16. Esther Garfinkel in Glatstein, pp. 257–258.

17. Milton, p. 312.

18. Hilberg, p. 581.

19. Koonz, pp. 404–405; Tillion, pp. 67–70; Milton, pp. 308–309.

20. Cernyak-Spatz, Lecture.

21. Katz and Ringelheim, pp. 17–19.

22. Ringelheim, 1985, pp. 748–749.

23. Cernyak-Spatz, Lecture.

24. Cernyak-Spatz, Lecture.

25. Milton, pp. 306–307; see also Katz and Ringelheim, pp. 16–17.

26. Heinemann, pp. 112–113.

27. Ringelheim, 1985, pp. 758–761.

28. Katz and Ringelheim, p. 62.

29. Ruth Angress, Lecture. University of Maryland, College Park, MD. April 11, 1988.

30. Linda Gordon, "Nazi Feminists?" Review of *Mothers in the Fatherland,* by Claudia Koonz. *Tikkun,* July/August 1987, p. 76.

Jean-Paul Sartre
THE ANTI-SEMITE

If a man attributes all or part of his own misfortunes and those of his country to the presence of Jewish elements in the community, if he proposes to remedy this state of affairs by depriving the Jews of certain of their rights, by keeping them out of certain economic and social activities, by expelling them from the country, by exterminating all of them, we say that he has anti-Semitic *opinions.*

This word *opinion* makes us stop and think. It is the word a hostess uses to bring to an end a discussion that threatens to become acrimonious. It suggests that all points of view are equal; it reassures us, for it gives an inoffensive appearance to ideas by reducing them to the level of tastes. All tastes are natural; all opinions are permitted. Tastes, colors, and opinions are not open to discussion. In the name of democratic institutions, in the name of freedom of opinion, the anti-Semite asserts the right to preach the anti-Jewish crusade everywhere.

At the same time, accustomed as we have been since the Revolution to look at every object in an analytic spirit, that is to say, as a composite whose elements can be separated, we look upon persons and characters as mosaics in which each stone coexists with the others without that coexistence affecting the nature of the whole. Thus anti-Semitic opinion appears to us to be a molecule that can enter into combination with other molecules of any origin whatsoever without undergoing any alteration. A man may be a good father and a good husband, a conscientious citizen, highly cultivated, philanthropic, *and* in addition an anti-Semite. He may like fishing and the pleasures of love, may be tolerant in matters of religion, full of generous notions on the condition of the natives in Central Africa, *and* in addition detest the Jews. If he does not like them, we say, it is because his experience has shown him that they are bad, because statistics have taught him that they are dangerous, because certain historical factors have influenced his judgment. Thus this opinion seems to be the result of external causes, and those who wish to

study it are prone to neglect the personality of the anti-Semite in favor
of a consideration of the percentage of Jews who were mobilized in
1914, the percentage of Jews who are bankers, industrialists, doctors,
and lawyers, or an examination of the history of the Jews in France since
early times. They succeed in revealing a strictly objective situation that
determines an equally objective current of opinion, and this they call
anti-Semitism, for which they can draw up charts and determine the
variations from 1870 to 1944. In such wise anti-Semitism appears to be
at once a subjective taste that enters into combination with other tastes
to form a personality, and an impersonal and social phenomenon which
can be expressed by figures and averages, one which is conditioned by
economic, historical, and political constants.

I do not say that these two conceptions are necessarily contradictory. I do say that they are dangerous and false. I would admit, if
necessary, that one may have an opinion on the government's policy in
regard to the wine industry, that is, that one may decide, *for certain
reasons,* either to approve or condemn the free importation of wine from
Algeria: here we have a case of holding an opinion on the administration
of things. But I refuse to characterize as opinion a doctrine that is aimed
directly at particular persons and that seeks to suppress their rights or to
exterminate them. The Jew whom the anti-Semite wishes to lay hands
upon is not a schematic being defined solely by his function, as under
administrative law; or by his status or his acts, as under the Code. He is a
Jew, the son of Jews, recognizable by his physique, by the color of his
hair, by his clothing perhaps, and, so they say, by his character. Anti-
Semitism does not fall within the category of ideas protected by the right
of free opinion.

Indeed, it is something quite other than an idea. It is first of all a
passion. No doubt it can be set forth in the form of a theoretical proposition. The "moderate" anti-Semite is a courteous man who will tell you
quietly: "Personally, I do not detest the Jews. I simply find it preferable,
for various reasons, that they should play a lesser part in the activity of
the nation." But a moment later, if you have gained his confidence, he
will add with more abandon: "You see, there must be *something* about
the Jews; they upset me physically."

This argument, which I have heard a hundred times, is worth examining. First of all, it derives from the logic of passion. For, really now,
can we imagine anyone's saying seriously: "There must be something
about tomatoes, for I have a horror of eating them"? In addition, it
shows us that anti-Semitism in its most temperate and most evolved
forms remains a syncretic whole which may be expressed by statements
of reasonable tenor, but which can involve even bodily modifications.

Some men are suddenly struck with impotence if they learn from the woman with whom they are making love that she is a Jewess. There is a disgust for the Jew, just as there is a disgust for the Chinese or the Negro among certain people. Thus it is not from the body that the sense of repulsion arises, since one may love a Jewess very well if one does not know what her race is; rather it is something that enters the body from the mind. It is an involvement of the mind, but one so deep-seated and complete that it extends to the physiological realm, as happens in cases of hysteria.

This involvement is not caused by experience. I have questioned a hundred people on the reasons for their anti-Semitism. Most of them have confined themselves to enumerating the defects with which tradition has endowed the Jews. "I detest them because they are selfish, intriguing, persistent, oily, tactless, etc."—"But, at any rate, you associate with some of them?"—"Not if I can help it!" A painter said to me: "I am hostile to the Jews because, with their critical habits, they encourage our servants to insubordination." Here are examples a little more precise. A young actor without talent insisted that the Jews had kept him from a successful career in the theater by confining him to subordinate roles. A young woman said to me: "I have had the most horrible experiences with furriers; they robbed me, they burned the fur I entrusted to them. Well, they were all Jews." But why did she choose to hate Jews rather than furriers? Why Jews or furriers rather than such and such a Jew or such and such a furrier? Because she had in her a predisposition toward anti-Semitism.

A classmate of mine at the lycée told me that Jews "annoy" him because of the thousands of injustices that "Jew-ridden" social organizations commit in their favor. "A Jew passed his *agrégation** the year I was failed, and you can't make me believe that that fellow, whose father came from Cracow or Lemberg, understood a poem by Ronsard or an eclogue by Virgil better than I." But he admitted that he disdained the *agrégation* as a mere academic exercise, and that he didn't study for it. Thus, to explain his failure, he made use of two systems of interpretation, like those madmen who, when they are far gone in their madness, pretend to be the King of Hungary but, if questioned sharply, admit to being shoemakers. His thoughts moved on two planes without his being in the least embarrassed by it. As a matter of fact, he will in time manage to justify his past laziness on the grounds that it really would be too stupid to prepare for an examination in which Jews are passed in preference to good Frenchmen. Actually he ranked twenty-seventh on the

---

* Competitive state teachers' examination.

official list. There were twenty-six ahead of him, twelve who passed and fourteen who failed. Suppose Jews had been excluded from the competition; would that have done him any good? And even if he had been at the top of the list of unsuccessful candidates, even if by eliminating one of the successful candidates he would have had a chance to pass, why should the Jew Weil have been eliminated rather than the Norman Mathieu or the Breton Arzell? To understand my classmate's indignation we must recognize that he had adopted in advance a certain idea of the Jew, of his nature and of his role in society. And to be able to decide that among twenty-six competitors who were more successful than himself, it was the Jew who robbed him of his place, he must a priori have given preference in the conduct of his life to reasoning based on passion. Far from experience producing his idea of the Jew, it was the latter which explained his experience. If the Jew did not exist, the anti-Semite would invent him.

That may be so, you will say, but leaving the question of experience to one side, must we not admit that anti-Semitism is explained by certain historical data? For after all it does not come out of the air. It would be easy for me to reply that the history of France tells us nothing about the Jews: they were oppressed right up to 1789; since then they have participated as best they could in the life of the nation, taking advantage, naturally, of freedom of competition to displace the weak, but no more and no less than other Frenchmen. They have committed no crimes against France, have engaged in no treason. And if people believe there is proof that the number of Jewish soldiers in 1914 was lower than it should have been, it is because someone had the curiosity to consult statistics. This is not one of those facts which have the power to strike the imagination by themselves; no soldier in the trenches was able on his own initiative to feel astonishment at not seeing any Jews in the narrow sector that constituted his universe. However, since the information that history gives on the role of Israel depends essentially on the conception one has of history, I think it would be better to borrow from a foreign country a manifest example of "Jewish treason" and to calculate the repercussions this "treason" may have had on contemporary anti-Semitism.

In the course of the bloody Polish revolts of the nineteenth century, the Warsaw Jews, whom the czars handled gently for reasons of policy, were very lukewarm toward the rebels. By not taking part in the insurrection they were able to maintain and improve their position in a country ruined by repression.

I don't know whether this is true or not. What is certain is that many Poles believe it, and this "historical fact" contributes not a little to their bitterness against the Jews. But if I examine the matter more closely, I discover a vicious circle: The czars, we are told, treated the Polish Jews well whereas they willingly ordered pogroms against those in Russia. These sharply different courses of action had the same cause. The Russian government considered the Jews in both Russia and Poland to be unassimilable; according to the needs of their policy, they had them massacred at Moscow and Kiev because they were a danger to the Russian empire, but favored them at Warsaw as a means of stirring up discord among the Poles. The latter showed nothing but hate and scorn for the Jews of Poland, but the reason was the same: For them Israel could never become an integral part of the national collectivity. Treated as Jews by the czar and as Jews by the Poles, provided, quite in spite of themselves, with Jewish interests in the midst of a foreign community, is it any wonder that these members of a minority behaved in accordance with the representation made of them?

In short, the essential thing here is not an "historical fact" but the idea that the agents of history formed for themselves of the Jew. When the Poles of today harbor resentment against the Jews for their past conduct, they are incited to it by that same idea. If one is going to reproach little children for the sins of their grandfathers, one must first of all have a very primitive conception of what constitutes responsibility. Furthermore one must form his conception of the children on the basis of what the grandparents have been. One must believe that what their elders did the young are capable of doing. One must convince himself that Jewish character is inherited. Thus the Poles of 1940 treated the Israelites in the community as *Jews* because their ancestors in 1848 had done the same with their contemporaries. Perhaps this traditional representation would, under other circumstances, have disposed the Jews of today to act like those of 1848. It is therefore the *idea* of the Jew that one forms for himself which would seem to determine history, not the "historical fact" that produces the idea.

People speak to us also of "social facts," but if we look at this more closely we shall find the same vicious circle. There are too many Jewish lawyers, someone says. But is there any complaint that there are too many Norman lawyers? Even if all the Bretons were doctors would we say anything more than that "Brittany provides doctors for the whole of France"? Oh, someone will answer, it is not at all the same thing. No doubt, but that is precisely because we consider Normans as Normans and Jews as Jews. Thus wherever we turn it is the *idea of the Jew* which seems to be the essential thing.

It has become evident that no external factor can induce anti-Semitism in the anti-Semite. Anti-Semitism is a free and total choice of oneself, a comprehensive attitude that one adopts not only toward Jews but toward men in general, toward history and society; it is at one and the same time a passion and a conception of the world. No doubt in the case of a given anti-Semite certain characteristics will be more marked than in another. But they are always all present at the same time, and they influence each other. It is this syncretic totality which we must now attempt to describe.

I noted earlier that anti-Semitism is a passion. Everybody understands that emotions of hate or anger are involved. But ordinarily hate and anger have a *provocation:* I hate someone who has made me suffer, someone who contemns or insults me. We have just seen that anti-Semitic passion could not have such a character. It precedes the facts that are supposed to call it forth; it seeks them out to nourish itself upon them; it must even interpret them in a special way so that they may become truly offensive. Indeed, if you so much as mention a Jew to an anti-Semite, he will show all the signs of a lively irritation. If we recall that we must always *consent* to anger before it can manifest itself and that, as is indicated so accurately by the French idiom, we "put ourselves" into anger, we shall have to agree that the anti-Semite has *chosen* to live on the plane of passion. It is not unusual for people to elect to live a life of passion rather than one of reason. But ordinarily they love the *objects* of passion: women, glory, power, money. Since the anti-Semite has chosen hate, we are forced to conclude that it is the *state* of passion that he loves. Ordinarily this type of emotion is not very pleasant: a man who passionately desires a woman is impassioned because of the woman and in spite of his passion. We are wary of reasoning based on passion, seeking to support by all possible means opinions which love or jealousy or hate have dictated. We are wary of the aberrations of passion and of what is called monoideism. But that is just what the anti-Semite chooses right off.

How can one choose to reason falsely? It is because of a longing for impenetrability. The rational man groans as he gropes for the truth; he knows that his reasoning is no more than tentative, that other considerations may supervene to cast doubt on it. He never sees very clearly where he is going; he is "open"; he may even appear to be hesitant. But there are people who are attracted by the durability of a stone. They wish to be massive and impenetrable; they wish not to change. Where, indeed, would change take them? We have here a basic fear of oneself and of truth. What frightens them is not the content of truth, of which they have no conception, but the form itself of truth, that thing of indefinite approximation. It is as if their own existence were in continual suspension. But they wish to exist all at once and right away. They do not want any acquired opinions; they want them to be innate. Since they are afraid of reasoning, they wish to lead the kind of life wherein reasoning and research play only a subordinate role, wherein one seeks only what he has already found, wherein one becomes only what he already was. This is nothing but passion. Only a strong emotional bias can give a lightninglike certainty; it alone can hold reason in leash; it alone can remain impervious to experience and last for a whole lifetime.

The anti-Semite has chosen hate because hate is a faith; at the outset he has chosen to devaluate words and reasons. How entirely at ease he feels as a result. How futile and frivolous discussions about the rights of the Jew appear to him. He has placed himself on other ground from the beginning. If out of courtesy he consents for a moment to defend his point of view, he lends himself but does not give himself. He tries simply to project his intuitive certainty onto the plane of discourse. I mentioned awhile back some remarks by anti-Semites, all of them absurd: "I hate Jews because they make servants insubordinate, because a Jewish furrier robbed me, etc." Never believe that anti-Semites are completely unaware of the absurdity of their replies. They know that their remarks are frivolous, open to challenge. But they are amusing themselves, for it is their adversary who is obliged to use words responsibly, since he believes in words. The anti-Semites have the *right* to play. They even like to play with discourse for, by giving ridiculous reasons, they discredit the seriousness of their interlocutors. They delight in acting in bad faith, since they seek not to persuade by sound argument but to intimidate and disconcert. If you press them too closely, they will abruptly fall silent, loftily indicating by some phrase that the time for argument is past. It is not that they are afraid of being convinced. They fear only to appear ridiculous or to prejudice by their embarrassment their hope of winning over some third person to their side.

If then, as we have been able to observe, the anti-Semite is impervious to reason and to experience, it is not because his conviction is strong. Rather his conviction is strong because he has chosen first of all to be impervious.

He has chosen also to be terrifying. People are afraid of irritating him. No one knows to what lengths the aberrations of his passion will carry him—but he knows, for this passion is not provoked by something external. He has it well in hand; it is obedient to his will: now he lets go the reins and now he pulls back on them. He is not afraid of himself, but he sees in the eyes of others a disquieting image—his own—and he makes his words and gestures conform to it. Having this external model, he is under no necessity to look for his personality within himself. He has chosen to find his being entirely outside himself, never to look within, to be nothing save the fear he inspires in others. What he flees even more than Reason is his intimate awareness of himself. But someone will object: What if he is like that only with regard to the Jews? What if he otherwise conducts himself with good sense? I reply that that is impossible. There is the case of a fishmonger who, in 1942, annoyed by the competition of two Jewish fishmongers who were concealing their race, one fine day took pen in hand and denounced them. I have been assured that this fishmonger was in other respects a mild and jovial man, the best of sons. But I don't believe it. A man who finds it entirely natural to denounce other men cannot have our conception of humanity; he does not see even those whom he aids in the same light as we do. His generosity, his kindness are not like our kindness, our generosity. You cannot confine passion to one sphere.

The anti-Semite readily admits that the Jew is intelligent and hard-working; he will even confess himself inferior in these respects. This concession costs him nothing, for he has, as it were, put those qualities in parentheses. Or rather they derive their value from the one who possesses them: the more virtues the Jew has the more dangerous he will be. The anti-Semite has no illusions about what he is. He considers himself an average man, modestly average, basically mediocre. There is no example of an anti-Semite's claiming individual superiority over the Jews. But you must not think that he is ashamed of his mediocrity; he takes pleasure in it; I will even assert that he has chosen it. This man fears every kind of solitariness, that of the genius as much as that of the murderer; he is the man of the crowd. However small his stature, he takes every precaution to make it smaller, lest he stand out from the herd and find himself face to face with himself. He has made himself an anti-Semite because that is something one cannot be alone. The phrase, "I hate the Jews," is one that is uttered in chorus; in pronouncing it, one attaches himself to a tradition and to a community—the tradition and community of the mediocre.

We must remember that a man is not necessarily humble or even modest because he has consented to mediocrity. On the contrary, there is a passionate pride among the mediocre, and anti-Semitism is an attempt to give value to mediocrity as such, to create an elite of the ordinary. To the anti-Semite, intelligence is Jewish; he can thus disdain it in all tranquillity, like all the other virtues which the Jew possesses. They are so many ersatz attributes that the Jew cultivates in place of that balanced mediocrity which he will never have. The true Frenchman, rooted in his province, in his country, borne along by a tradition twenty centuries old, benefiting from ancestral wisdom, guided by tried customs, does not *need* intelligence. His virtue depends upon the assimilation of the qualities which the work of a hundred generations has lent to the objects which surround him; it depends on property. It goes without saying that this is a matter of inherited property, not property one buys. The anti-Semite has a fundamental incomprehension of the various forms of modern property: money, securities, etc. These are abstractions, entities of reason related to the abstract intelligence of the Semite. A security belongs to no one because it can belong to everyone; moreover, it is a sign of wealth, not a concrete possession. The anti-Semite can conceive only of a type of primitive ownership of land based on a veritable magical rapport, in which the thing possessed and its possessor are united by a bond of mystical participation; he is the poet of real property. It transfigures the proprietor and endows him with a special and concrete sensibility. To be sure, this sensibility ignores eternal truths or universal values: the universal is Jewish, since it is an object of intelligence. What his subtle sense seizes upon is precisely that which the intelligence cannot perceive. To put it another way, the principle underlying anti-Semitism is that the concrete possession of a particular object gives as if by magic the meaning of that object. Maurras said the same thing when he declared a Jew to be forever incapable of understanding this line of Racine:

*Dans l'Orient désert, quel devint mon ennui.**

But the way is open to me, mediocre me, to understand what the most subtle, the most cultivated intelligence has been unable to grasp. Why? Because I possess Racine—Racine and my country and my soil. Perhaps the Jew speaks a purer French than I do, perhaps he knows syntax and grammar better, perhaps he is even a writer. No matter; he has spoken this language for only twenty years, and I for a thousand years. The correctness of his style is abstract, acquired; my faults of French are in conformity with the genius of the language. We recognize here the reasoning that Barrès used against the holders of scholarships. There is no occasion for surprise. Don't the Jews have all the scholarships? All that intelligence, all that money can acquire one leaves to them, but it is as empty as the wind. The only things that count are irrational values, and it is just these things which are denied the Jews forever. Thus the anti-Semite takes his stand from the start on the ground of irrationalism. He is opposed to the Jew, just as sentiment is to intelligence, the particular to the universal, the past to the present, the

---

* *Bérénice.*

concrete to the abstract, the owner of real property to the possessor of negotiable securities.

Besides this, many anti-Semites—the majority, perhaps—belong to the lower middle class of the towns; they are functionaries, office workers, small businessmen, who possess nothing. It is in opposing themselves to the Jew that they suddenly become conscious of being proprietors: in representing the Jew as a robber, they put themselves in the enviable position of people who could be robbed. Since the Jew wishes to take France from them, it follows that France must belong to them. Thus they have chosen anti-Semitism as a means of establishing their status as possessors. The Jew has more money than they? So much the better: money is Jewish, and they can despise it as they despise intelligence. They own less than the gentleman-farmer of Périgord or the large-scale farmer of the Beauce? That doesn't matter. All they have to do is nourish a vengeful anger against the robbers of Israel and they feel at once in possession of the entire country. True Frenchmen, good Frenchmen are all equal, for each of them possesses for himself alone France whole and indivisible.

Thus I would call anti-Semitism a poor man's snobbery. And in fact it would appear that the rich for the most part exploit this passion for their own uses rather than abandon themselves to it—they have better things to do. It is propagated mainly among the middle classes, because they possess neither land nor house nor castle, having only some ready cash and a few securities in the bank. It was not by chance that the petty bourgeoisie of Germany was anti-Semitic in 1925. The principal concern of this "white-collar proletariat" was to distinguish itself from the real proletariat. Ruined by big industry, bamboozled by the Junkers, it was nonetheless to the Junkers and the great industrialists that its whole heart went out. It went in for anti-Semitism with the same enthusiasm that it went in for wearing bourgeois dress: *because* the workers were internationalists, because the Junkers possessed Germany and it wished to possess it also. Anti-Semitism is not merely the joy of hating; it brings positive pleasures too. By treating the Jew as an inferior and pernicious being, I affirm at the same time that I belong to the elite. This elite, in contrast to those of modern times which are based on merit or labor, closely resembles an aristocracy of birth. There is nothing I have to do to merit my superiority, and neither can I lose it. It is given once and for all. It is a *thing*.

We must not confuse this precedence the anti-Semite enjoys by virtue of his principles with individual merit. The anti-Semite is not too anxious to possess individual merit. Merit has to be sought, just like truth; it is discovered with difficulty; one must deserve it. Once acquired, it is perpetually in question: a false step, an error, and it flies away. Without respite, from the beginning of our lives to the end, we are responsible for what merit we enjoy. Now the anti-Semite flees responsibility as he flees his own consciousness, and choosing for his personality the permanence of rock, he chooses for his morality a scale of petrified values. Whatever he does, he knows that he will remain at the top of the ladder; whatever the Jew does, he will never get any higher than the first rung.

We begin to perceive the meaning of the anti-Semite's choice of himself. He chooses the irremediable out of fear of being free; he chooses mediocrity out of fear of being alone, and out of pride he makes of this irremediable mediocrity a rigid aristocracy. To this end he finds the existence of the Jew absolutely necessary. Otherwise to whom would he be superior? Indeed, it is vis-à-vis the Jew and the Jew alone that the anti-Semite realizes that he has rights. If by some miracle all the Jews were exterminated as he wishes, he would find himself nothing but a concierge or a shopkeeper in a strongly hierarchical society in which the quality of "true Frenchman" would be at a low valuation, because everyone would possess it. He would lose his sense of rights over the country because no one would any longer contest them, and that profound equality which brings him close to the nobleman and the man of wealth would disappear all of a sudden, for it is primarily negative. His frustrations, which he has attributed to the disloyal competition of the Jew, would have to be imputed to some other cause, lest he be forced to look within himself. He would run the risk of falling into bitterness, into a melancholy hatred of the privileged classes. Thus the anti-Semite is in the unhappy position of having a vital need for the very enemy he wishes to destroy.

The equalitarianism that the anti-Semite seeks with so much ardor has nothing in common with that equality inscribed in the creed of the democracies. The latter is to be realized in a society that is economically hierarchical, and is to remain compatible with a diversity of functions. But it is in protest *against* the hierarchy of functions that the anti-Semite asserts the equality of Aryans. He does not understand anything about the division of labor and doesn't care about it. From his point of view each citizen can claim the title of Frenchman, not because he co-operates, in his place or in his occupation, with others in the economic, social, and cultural life of the nation, but because he has, in the same way as everybody else, an imprescriptible and inborn right to the indivisible totality of the country. Thus the society that the anti-Semite conceives of is a society of juxtaposition, as one can very well imagine, since his ideal of property is that of real and basic property. Since, in point of fact, anti-Semites are numerous, each of them does his part in constituting a community based on mechanical solidarity in the heart of organized society.

The degree of integration of each anti-Semite with this society, as well as the degree of his equality, is fixed by what I shall call the temperature of the community. Proust has shown, for example, how anti-Semitism brought the duke closer to his coachman, how, thanks to their hatred of Dreyfus, bourgeois families forced the doors of the aristocracy. The equalitarian society that the anti-Semite believes in is like that of mobs or those instantaneous societies which come into being at a lynching or during a scandal. Equality in them is the product of the non-differentiation of functions. The social bond is anger; the collectivity has no other goal than to exercise over certain individuals a diffused repressive sanction. Collective impulsions and stereotypes are imposed on individuals all the more strongly because none of them is defended by any specialized function. Thus the person is drowned in the crowd, and the ways of thinking and reacting of the group are of a purely primitive type. Of course, such collectivities do not spring solely from anti-Semitism; an uprising, a crime, an injustice can cause them to break out suddenly. But those are ephemeral formations which soon vanish without leaving any trace.

Since anti-Semitism survives the great crises of Jew-hatred, the society which the anti-Semites form remains in a latent state during normal periods, with every anti-Semite celebrating its existence. Incapable of understanding modern social organization, he has a nostalgia for periods of crisis in which the primitive community will suddenly reappear and attain its temperature of fusion. He wants his personality to melt suddenly into the group and be carried away by the collective torrent. He has this atmosphere of the pogrom in mind when he asserts "the union of all Frenchmen." In this sense anti-Semitism is, in a democracy, a covert form of what is called the struggle of the citizen against authority. Question any one of those turbulent young men who placidly break the law and band together to beat up a Jew in a deserted street: He will tell you that he wants a strong authority to take from him the crushing responsibility of thinking for himself. Since the Republic is weak, he is led to break the law out of love of obedience. But is it really strong authority that he wishes? In reality he demands rigorous order for others, and for himself disorder without responsibility. He wishes to place himself above the law, at the same time escaping from the consciousness of his liberty and his isolation. He therefore makes use of a subterfuge: The Jews take part in elections; there are Jews in the government; therefore the legal power is vitiated at its base. As a matter of fact, it no longer exists, so it is legitimate to ignore its decrees. Consequently there is no disobedience—one cannot disobey what does not exist. Thus for the anti-Semite there is a *real* France with a government *real* but diffused and without special organs, and an abstract France, official, Jew-ridden, against which it is proper to rebel.

Robert J. Lifton

DOUBLING: THE FAUSTIAN BARGAIN

Not only will you break through the paralysing difficulties of
the time—you will break through time itself . . . and dare to be
barbaric, twice barbaric indeed.

THOMAS MANN

Any of us could be the man who encounters his double.

FRIEDRICH DURRENMAT

The key to understanding how Nazi doctors came to do the work of
Auschwitz is the psychological principle I call "doubling": the division
of the self into two functioning wholes, so that a part-self acts as an
entire self. An Auschwitz doctor could, through doubling, not only kill
and contribute to killing but organize silently, on behalf of that evil
project, an entire self-structure (or self-process) encompassing virtually
all aspects of his behavior.

Doubling, then, was the psychological vehicle for the Nazi doctor's
Faustian bargain with the diabolical environment in exchange for his
contribution to the killing; he was offered various psychological and
material benefits on behalf of privileged adaptation. Beyond Auschwitz
was the larger Faustian temptation offered to German doctors in general: that of becoming the theorists and implementers of a cosmic
scheme of racial cure by means of victimization and mass murder.

One is always ethically responsible for Faustian bargains—a responsibility in no way abrogated by the fact that much doubling takes
place outside of awareness. In exploring doubling, I engage in psychological probing on behalf of illuminating evil. For the individual Nazi
doctor in Auschwitz, doubling was likely to mean a choice for evil.

Generally speaking, doubling involves five characteristics. There is,
first, a dialectic between two selves in terms of autonomy and connection. The individual Nazi doctor needed his Auschwitz self to function

psychologically in an environment so antithetical to his previous ethical standards. At the same time, he needed his prior self in order to continue to see himself as humane physician, husband, father. The Auschwitz self had to be both autonomous and connected to the prior self that gave rise to it. Second, doubling follows a holistic principle. The Auschwitz self "succeeded" because it was inclusive and could connect with the entire Auschwitz environment: it rendered coherent, and gave form to, various themes and mechanisms, which I shall discuss shortly. Third, doubling has a life-death dimension: the Auschwitz self was perceived by the perpetrator as a form of psychological survival in a death-dominated environment; in other words, we have the paradox of a "killing self" being created on behalf of what one perceives as one's own healing or survival. Fourth, a major function of doubling, as in Auschwitz, is likely to be the avoidance of guilt: the second self tends to be the one performing the "dirty work." And, finally, doubling involves both an unconscious dimension—taking place, as stated, largely outside of awareness—and a significant change in moral consciousness. These five characteristics frame and pervade all else that goes on psychologically in doubling.

For instance, the holistic principle differentiates doubling from the traditional psychoanalytic concept of "splitting." This latter term has had several meanings but tends to suggest a sequestering off of a portion of the self so that the "split off" element ceases to respond to the environment (as in what I have been calling "psychic numbing") or else is in some way at odds with the remainder of the self. Splitting in this sense resembles what Pierre Janet, Freud's nineteenth-century contemporary, originally called "dissociation," and Freud himself tended to equate the two terms. But in regard to sustained forms of adaptation, there has been confusion about how to explain the autonomy of that separated "piece" of the self—confusion over (as one thoughtful commentator has put it) "What splits in splitting?"[1]*

---

* This writer seemed to react against the idea of a separated-off piece of the self when he ended the article by asking, "Why should we invent a special intrapsychic act of splitting to account for those phenomena as if some internal chopper were at work to produce them?"[2] Janet meant by "dissociation" the hysteric's tendency to "sacrifice" or "abandon" certain psychological functions, so that these become "dissociated" from the rest of the mind and give rise to "automatisms," or segmented-off symptom complexes.[3] Freud spoke, in his early work with Josef Breuer, of "splitting of consciousness," "splitting of the mind," and "splitting of personality" as important mechanisms in hysteria.[4] Edward Glover referred to the psychic components of splitting or dissociation as "ego nuclei."[5] And, beginning with the work of Melanie Klein, splitting has been

"Splitting" or "dissociation" can thus denote something about Nazi doctors' suppression of feeling, or psychic numbing, in relation to their participation in murder.* But to chart their involvement in a continuous routine of killing, over a year or two or more, one needs an explanatory principle that draws upon the entire, functioning self. (The same principle applies in sustained psychiatric disturbance, and my stress on doubling is consistent with the increasing contemporary focus upon the holistic function of the self.)[8]

Doubling is part of the universal potential for what William James called the "divided self": that is, for opposing tendencies in the self. James quoted the nineteenth-century French writer Alphonse Daudet's despairing cry "*Homo duplex, homo duplex!*" in noting his "horrible duality"—as, in the face of his brother Henri's death, Daudet's "first self wept" while his "second self" sat back and somewhat mockingly staged the scene for an imagined theatrical performance.[9] To James and Daudet, the potential for doubling is part of being human, and the process is likely to take place in extremity, in relation to death.

But that "opposing self" can become dangerously unrestrained, as it did in the Nazi doctors. And when it becomes so, as Otto Rank discovered in his extensive studies of the "double" in literature and folklore, that opposing self can become the usurper from within and replace the original self until it "speaks" for the entire person.[10] Rank's work also suggests that the potential for an opposing self, in effect the potential for evil, is *necessary* to the human psyche: the loss of one's shadow or soul or "double" means death.

In general psychological terms, the adaptive potential for doubling is integral to the human psyche and can, at times, be life saving: for a soldier in combat, for instance; or for a victim of brutality such as an Auschwitz inmate, who must also undergo a form of doubling in order to survive. Clearly, the "opposing self" can be life enhancing. But under certain conditions it can embrace evil with an extreme lack of restraint.

The Nazi doctor's situation resembles that of one of Rank's examples (taken from a 1913 German film, *The Student of Prague*): a student fencing champion accepts an evil magician's offer of great wealth and the chance for marriage with his beloved in return for anything the old magician wishes to take from the room; what he takes is the student's

---

associated with polarization of "all good" and "all bad" imagery within the self, a process that can be consistent with normal development but, where exaggerated, can become associated with severe personality disorders now spoken of as "borderline states."[6]

* Henry V. Dicks invokes this concept in his study of Nazi killers.[7]

mirror image, a frequent representation of the double. That double eventually becomes a killer by making use of the student's fencing skills in a duel with his beloved's suitor, despite the fact that the student (his original self) has promised the woman's father that he will not engage in such a duel. This variation on the Faust legend parallels the Nazi doctor's "bargain" with Auschwitz and the regime: to do the killing, he offered an opposing self (the evolving Auschwitz self)—a self that, in violating his own prior moral standards, met with no effective resistance and in fact made use of his original skills (in this case, medical-scientific).[11]*

Rank stressed the death symbolism of the double as "symptomatic of the disintegration of the modern personality type." That disintegration leads to a need for "self-perpetuation in one's own image"[13]—what I would call a literalized form of immortality—as compared with "the perpetuation of the self in work reflecting one's personality" or a creative-symbolic form of immortality. Rank saw the Narcissus legend as depicting both the danger of the literalized mode and the necessity of the shift to the creative mode (as embodied by the "artist-hero").† But the Nazi movement encouraged its would-be artist-hero, the physician, to remain, like Narcissus, in thralldom to his own image. Here Mengele comes immediately to mind, his extreme narcissism in the service of his quest for omnipotence, and his exemplification to the point of caricature of the general situation of Nazi doctors in Auschwitz.[15]

The way in which doubling allowed Nazi doctors to avoid guilt was not by the elimination of conscience but by what can be called the *transfer of conscience*. The requirements of conscience were transferred to the Auschwitz self, which placed it within its own criteria for good (duty, loyalty to group, "improving" Auschwitz conditions, etc.), thereby freeing the original self from responsibility for actions there. Rank spoke

---

* Rank's viewing of *The Student of Prague*, during a revival in the mid-1920s, was the original stimulus for a lifelong preoccupation with the theme of the double. Rank noted that the screenplay's author, Hanns Heinz Ewers, had drawn heavily on E.T.A. Hoffmann's "Story of the Lost Reflection."[12]

† In his earlier work, Rank followed Freud in connecting the legend with the concept of "narcissism," of libido directed toward one's own self. But Rank gave the impression that he did so uneasily, always stressing the issue of death and immortality as lurking beneath the narcissism. In his later adaptation, he boldly embraced the death theme as the earlier and more fundamental one in the Narcissus legend and spoke somewhat disdainfully of "some modern psychologists [who] claimed to have found a symbolization of their self-love principle" in it.[14] By then he had broken with Freud and established his own intellectual position.

similarly of guilt "which forces the hero no longer to accept the responsibility for certain actions of his ego, but to place it upon another ego, a double, who is either personified by the devil himself or is created by making a diabolical pact"[16]: that is, the Faustian bargain of Nazi doctors mentioned earlier. Rank spoke of a "powerful consciousness of guilt" as initiating the transfer;[17] but for most Nazi doctors, the doubling maneuver seemed to fend off that sense of guilt prior to its developing, or to its reaching conscious dimensions.

There is an inevitable connection between death and guilt. Rank equates the opposing self with a "form of evil which represents the perishable and mortal part of the personality."[18] The double is evil in that it represents one's own death. The Auschwitz self of the Nazi doctor similarly assumed the death issue for him but at the same time used its evil project as a way of staving off awareness of his own "perishable and mortal part." It does the "dirty work" for the entire self by rendering that work "proper" and in that way protects the entire self from awareness of its own guilt and its own death.

In doubling, one part of the self "disavows" another part. What is repudiated is not reality itself—the individual Nazi doctor was aware of what he was doing via the Auschwitz self—but the meaning of that reality. The Nazi doctor knew that he selected, but did not interpret selections as murder. One level of disavowal, then, was the Auschwitz self's altering of the meaning of murder; and on another, the repudiation by the original self of *anything* done by the Auschwitz self. From the moment of its formation, the Auschwitz self so violated the Nazi doctor's previous self-concept as to require more or less permanent disavowal. Indeed, disavowal was the life blood of the Auschwitz self.*

DOUBLING, SPLITTING, AND EVIL

Doubling is an active psychological process, a means of *adaptation to extremity*. That is why I use the verb form, as opposed to the more usual noun form, "the double." The adaptation requires a dissolving of "psychic glue"[20] as an alternative to a radical breakdown of the self. In Auschwitz, the pattern was established under the duress of the individual doctor's transition period. At that time the Nazi doctor experienced

---

* Michael Franz Basch speaks of an interference with the "union of affect with percept without, however, blocking the percept from consciousness."[19] In that sense, disavowal resembles psychic numbing, as it alters the *valencing* or emotional charge of the symbolizing process.

his own death anxiety as well as such death equivalents as fear of disintegration, separation, and stasis. He needed a functional Auschwitz self to still his anxiety. And that Auschwitz self had to assume hegemony on an everyday basis, reducing expressions of the prior self to odd moments and to contacts with family and friends outside the camp. Nor did most Nazi doctors resist that usurpation as long as they remained in the camp. Rather they welcomed it as the only means of psychological function. If an environment is sufficiently extreme, and one chooses to remain in it, one may be able to do so *only* by means of doubling.

Yet doubling does not include the radical dissociation and sustained separateness characteristic of multiple or "dual personality." In the latter condition, the two selves are more profoundly distinct and autonomous, and tend either not to know about each other or else to see each other as alien. The pattern for dual or multiple personality, moreover, is thought to begin early in childhood, and to solidify and maintain itself more or less indefinitely. Yet in the development of multiple personality, there are likely to be such influences as intense psychic or physical trauma, an atmosphere of extreme ambivalence, and severe conflict and confusion over identifications[21]—all of which can also be instrumental in doubling. Also relevant to both conditions is Janet's principle that "once baptized"—that is, named or confirmed by someone in authority —a particular self is likely to become more clear and definite.[22] Though never as stable as a self in multiple personality, the Auschwitz self nonetheless underwent a similar baptism when the Nazi doctor conducted his first selections.

A recent writer has employed the metaphor of a tree to delineate the depth of "splitting" in schizophrenia and multiple personality—a metaphor that could be expanded to include doubling. In schizophrenia, the rent in the self is "like the crumbling and breaking of a tree that has deteriorated generally, at least in some important course of the trunk, down toward or to the roots." In multiple personality, that rent is specific and limited, "as in an essentially sound tree that does not split very far down."[23] Doubling takes place still higher on a tree whose roots, trunk, and larger branches have previously experienced no impairment; of the two branches artificially separated, one grows fetid bark and leaves in a way that enables the other to maintain ordinary growth, and the two intertwine sufficiently to merge again should external conditions favor that merging.

Was the doubling of Nazi doctors an antisocial "character disorder"? Not in the classical sense, in that the process tended to be more a form of adaptation than a lifelong pattern. But doubling can include elements considered characteristic of "sociopathic" character impairment: these include a disorder of feeling (swings between numbing and rage), pathological avoidance of a sense of guilt, and resort to violence to overcome "masked depression" (related to repressed guilt and numbing) and maintain a sense of vitality.[24] Similarly, in both situations, destructive or even murderous behavior may cover over feared disintegration of the self.

The disorder in the type of doubling I have described is more focused and temporary and occurs as part of a larger institutional structure which encourages or even demands it. In that sense, Nazi doctors' behavior resembles that of certain terrorists—and members of the Mafia, of "death squads" organized by dictators, or even of delinquent gangs. In all these situations, profound ideological, family, ethnic, and sometimes age-specific ties help shape criminal behavior. Doubling may well be an important psychological mechanism for individuals living within any criminal subculture: the Mafia or "death squad" chief who coldly orders (or himself carries out) the murder of a rival while remaining a loving husband, father, and churchgoer. The doubling is adaptive to the extreme conditions created by the subculture, but additional influences, some of which can begin early in life, always contribute to the process.* That, too, was the case with the Nazi doctors.

In sum, doubling is the psychological means by which one invokes the evil potential of the self. That evil is neither inherent in the self nor foreign to it. To live out the doubling and call forth the evil is a moral choice for which one is responsible, whatever the level of consciousness involved.† By means of doubling, Nazi doctors made a Faustian choice for evil: in the process of doubling, in fact, lies an overall key to human evil.

VARIETIES OF DOUBLING

While individual Nazi doctors in Auschwitz doubled in different ways, all of them doubled. Ernst B., for instance, limited his doubling; in

---

* Robert W. Rieber uses the term "pseudopsychopathy" for what he describes as "selective joint criminal behavior" within the kinds of subculture mentioned here.[25]

† James S. Grotstein speaks of the development of "a separate being living within one that has been preconsciously split off and has an independent existence with independent motivation, separate agenda, etc.," and from which can emanate "evil, sadism, and destructiveness" or even "demoniacal possession." He calls this aspect of the self a "mind parasite" (after Colin Wilson) and attributes its development to those elements of the self that have been artificially suppressed and disavowed early in life.[26]

avoiding selections, he was resisting a full-blown Auschwitz self. Yet his conscious desire to adapt to Auschwitz was an accession to at least a certain amount of doubling: it was he, after all, who said that "one could react like a normal human being in Auschwitz only for the first few hours"; after that, "you were caught and had to go along," which meant that you had to double. His own doubling was evident in his sympathy for Mengele and, at least to some extent, for the most extreme expressions of the Nazi ethos (the image of the Nazis as a "world blessing" and of Jews as the world's "fundamental evil"). And despite the limit to his doubling, he retains aspects of his Auschwitz self to this day in his way of judging Auschwitz behavior.

In contrast, Mengele's embrace of the Auschwitz self gave the impression of a quick adaptive affinity, causing one to wonder whether he required any doubling at all. But doubling was indeed required in a man who befriended children to an unusual degree and then drove some of them personally to the gas chamber; or by a man so "collegial" in his relationship to prisoner doctors and so ruthlessly flamboyant in his conduct of selections. Whatever his affinity for Auschwitz, a man who could be pictured under ordinary conditions as "a slightly sadistic German professor" had to form a new self to become an energetic killer. The point about Mengele's doubling was that his prior self could be readily absorbed into the Auschwitz self; and his continuing allegiance to the Nazi ideology and project probably enabled his Auschwitz self, more than in the case of other Nazi doctors, to remain active over the years after the Second World War.

Wirths's doubling was neither limited (like Dr. B.'s) nor harmonious (like Mengele's): it was both strong and conflicted. We see Auschwitz's chief doctor as a "divided self" because both selves retained their power. Yet his doubling was the most successful of all from the standpoint of the Auschwitz institution and the Nazi project. Even his suicide was a mark of that success: while the Nazi defeat enabled him to equate his Auschwitz self more clearly with evil, he nonetheless retained responsibility to that Auschwitz self sufficiently to remain inwardly divided and unable to imagine any possibility of resolution and renewal—either legally, morally, or psychologically.

Within the Auschwitz structure, significant doubling included future goals and even a sense of hope. Styles of doubling varied because each Nazi doctor created his Auschwitz self out of his prior self, with its particular history, and with his own psychological mechanisms. But in all Nazi doctors, prior self and Auschwitz self were connected by the overall Nazi ethos and the general authority of the regime. Doubling was a shared theme among them.

DOUBLING AND INSTITUTIONS

Indeed, Auschwitz as an *institution*—as an atrocity-producing situation—ran on doubling. An atrocity-producing situation is one so structured externally (in this case, institutionally) that the average person entering it (in this case, as part of the German authority) will commit or become associated with atrocities. Always important to an atrocity-producing situation is its capacity to motivate individuals psychologically toward engaging in atrocity.[27]

In an institution as powerful as Auschwitz, the external environment could set the tone for much of an individual doctor's "internal environment." The demand for doubling was part of the environmental message immediately perceived by Nazi doctors, the implicit command to bring forth a self that could adapt to killing without one's feeling oneself a murderer. Doubling became not just an individual enterprise but a shared psychological process, the group norm, part of the Auschwitz "weather." And that group process was intensified by the general awareness that, whatever went on in other camps, Auschwitz was the great technical center of the Final Solution. One had to double in order that one's life and work there not be interfered with either by the corpses one helped to produce or by those "living dead" (the *Muselmänner*) all around one.

Inevitably, the Auschwitz pressure toward doubling extended to prisoner doctors, the most flagrant examples of whom were those who came to work closely with the Nazis—Dering, Zenkteller, Adam T., and Samuel. Even those prisoner doctors who held strongly to their healing ethos, and underwent minimal doubling, inadvertently contributed to Nazi doctors' doubling simply by working with them, as they had to, and thereby in some degree confirmed a Nazi doctor's Auschwitz self.

Doubling undoubtedly occurred extensively in nonmedical Auschwitz personnel as well. Rudolf Höss told how noncommissioned officers regularly involved in selections "pour[ed] out their hearts" to him about the difficulty of their work (their prior self speaking)—but went on doing that work (their Auschwitz self directing behavior). Höss described the Auschwitz choices: "either to become cruel, to become heartless and no longer to respect human life [that is, to develop a highly functional Auschwitz self] or to be weak and to get to the point of a nervous breakdown [that is, to hold onto one's prior self, which in Auschwitz was nonfunctional]."[28] But in the Nazi doctor, the doubling was particularly stark in that a prior healing self gave rise to a killing self that should have been, but functionally was not, in direct opposition to it. And as in any atrocity-producing situation, Nazi doctors found themselves in a psychological climate where they were virtually certain to choose evil: they were propelled, that is, toward murder.

DOUBLING—NAZI AND MEDICAL

Beyond Auschwitz, there was much in the Nazi movement that promoted doubling. The overall Nazi project, replete with cruelty, required constant doubling in the service of carrying out that cruelty. The doubling could take the form of a gradual process of "slippery slope" compromises: the slow emergence of a functional "Nazi self" via a series of destructive actions, at first agreed to grudgingly, followed by a sequence of assigned tasks each more incriminating, if not more murderous, than the previous ones.

Doubling could also be more dramatic, infused with transcendence, the sense (described by a French fascist who joined the SS) of being someone entering a religious order "who must now divest himself of his past," and of being "reborn into a new European race."[29] That new Nazi self could take on a sense of mystical fusion with the German *Volk*, with "destiny," and with immortalizing powers. Always there was the combination noted earlier of idealism and terror, imagery of destruction and renewal, so that "gods . . . appear as both destroyers and culture-heroes, just as the Führer could appear as front comrade and master builder."[30] Himmler, especially in his speeches to his SS leaders within their "oath-bound community,"[31] called for the kind of doubling necessary to engage in what he considered to be heroic cruelty, especially in the killing of Jews.

The degree of doubling was not necessarily equivalent to Nazi Party membership; thus, Hochhuth could claim that "the great divide was between Nazis [meaning those with well-developed Nazi selves] and decent people, not between Party members and other Germans."[32] But probably never has a political movement demanded doubling with the intensity and scale of the Nazis.

Doctors as a group may be more susceptible to doubling than others. For example, a former Nazi doctor claimed that the anatomist's insensitivity toward skeletons and corpses accounted for his friend Hirt's grotesque "anthropological" collection of Jewish skulls. While hardly a satisfactory explanation, this doctor was referring to a genuine pattern not just of numbing but of medical doubling. That doubling usually begins with the student's encounter with the corpse he or she must dissect, often enough on the first day of medical school. One feels it necessary to develop a "medical self," which enables one not only to be relatively inured to death but to function reasonably efficiently in relation to the many-sided demands of the work. The ideal doctor, to be sure, remains warm and humane by keeping that doubling to a minimum. But few doctors meet that ideal standard. Since studies have suggested that a psychological motivation for entering the medical profession can be the overcoming of an unusually great fear of death, it is possible that this fear in doctors propels them in the direction of doubling when encountering deadly environments. Doctors drawn to the Nazi movement in general, and to SS or concentration-camp medicine in particular, were likely to be those with the greatest previous medical doubling. But even doctors without outstanding Nazi sympathies could well have had a certain experience with doubling and a proclivity for its further manifestations.

Certainly the tendency toward doubling was particularly strong among *Nazi* doctors. Given the heroic vision held out to them—as cultivators of the genes and as physicians to the *Volk,* and as militarized healers combining the life-death power of shaman and general—any cruelty they might perpetrate was all too readily drowned in hubris. And their medical hubris was furthered by their role in the sterilization and "euthanasia" projects within a vision of curing the ills of the Nordic race and the German people.

Doctors who ended up undergoing the extreme doubling necessitated by the "euthanasia" killing centers and the death camps were probably unusually susceptible to doubling. There was, of course, an element of chance in where one was sent, but doctors assigned either to the killing centers or to the death camps tended to be strongly committed to Nazi ideology. They may well have also had greater schizoid tendencies, or been particularly prone to numbing and omnipotence-sadism, all of which also enhance doubling. Since, even under extreme conditions, people have a way of finding and staying in situations they connect with psychologically, we can suspect a certain degree of self-selection there too. In these ways, previous psychological characteristics of a doctor's self had considerable significance—but a significance in respect to tendency or susceptibility, and no more. Considerable doubling occurred in people of the most varied psychological characteristics.

We thus find ourselves returning to the recognition that most of what Nazi doctors did would be within the potential capability—at least under certain conditions—of most doctors and of most people. But once embarked on doubling in Auschwitz, a Nazi doctor did indeed separate himself from other physicians and from other human beings. Doubling was the mechanism by which a doctor, in his actions, moved from the ordinary to the demonic. (I discuss the factors in this process later in this book.)

DOUBLING AS GERMAN?

Is there something especially German in doubling? Germany, after all, is the land of the *Doppelgänger*, the double as formalized in literature and humor. Otto Rank, while tracing the theme back to Greek mythology and drama, stresses its special prominence in German literary and philosophical romanticism, and refers to the "inner split personality, characteristic of the romantic type."[33] That characterization, not only in literature but in political and social thought, is consistent with such images as the "torn condition" (*Zerrissenheit*), or "cleavage," and the "passages and galleries" of the German soul.[34] Nietzsche asserted that duality in a personal way by depicting himself as both "the antichrist" and "the crucified"; and similar principles of "duality-in-unity" can be traced to earlier German writers and poets such as Hölderlin, Heine, and Kleist.[35]

Indeed, Goethe's treatment of the Faust legend is a story of German doubling:

> Two souls, alas, reside within my breast
> And each withdraws from and repels its brother.[36]

And the original Faust, that doctor of magic, bears more than a passing resemblance to his Nazi countrymen in Auschwitz. In Goethe's hands, Faust is inwardly divided into a prior self responsible to worldly commitments, including those of love, and a second self characterized by hubris in its quest for the supernatural power of "the higher ancestral places."* In a still earlier version of the legend, Faust acknowledges the

---

* The passage concerning the "two souls" continues:

One with tenacious organs holds in love
And clinging lust the world within its embraces.
The other strongly sweeps this dust above
Into the higher ancestral places.

The historian of German literature Ronald Gray finds patterns of "polarity and synthesis" in various spheres of German culture: Luther's concept of a God who "works by contraries," the Hegelian principle of thesis and antithesis, and the Marxist dialectic emerging from Hegel. In all of these, there is the "fusion of

hegemony of his evil self by telling a would-be spiritual rescuer, "I have gone further than you think and have pledged myself to the devil with my own blood, to be his in eternity, body and soul."[38] Here his attitude resembles the Auschwitz self's fidelity to evil. And Thomas Mann's specific application of the Faust legend to the Nazi historical experience captures, through a musician protagonist, the diabolical quest of the Auschwitz self for unlimited "creative power": the promise of absolute breakthrough, of conquering time and therefore death; if the new self will "dare to be barbaric, twice barbaric indeed."[39]*

Within German psychological and cultural experience, the theme of doubling is powerful and persistent. Moreover, German vulnerability to doubling was undoubtedly intensified by the historical dislocations and fragmentations of cultural symbols following the First World War. Who can deny the Germanic "feel" of so much of the doubling process, as best described by a brilliant product of German culture, Otto Rank?

Yet the first great poet to take up the Faust theme was not Goethe but the English playwright Christopher Marlowe. And there has been a series of celebrated English and American expressions of the general theme of the double, running through Edgar Allan Poe's "William Wilson," Robert Louis Stevenson's *The Strange Case of Dr. Jekyll and Mr. Hyde,* Oscar Wilde's *Picture of Dorian Gray,* and the comic strip *Superman.* Indeed, the theme penetrates the work of writers of all nationalities: for instance, Guy de Maupassant's *Le Horla* and Dostoevski's novel *The Double.*[41]

Clearly, the Nazis took hold of a universal phenomenon, if one given special emphasis by their own culture and history. But they could not have brought about widespread doubling without the existence of certain additional psychological patterns that dominated Auschwitz behavior. These internalized expressions of the environment of the death camp came to characterize the Auschwitz self, and have significance beyond that place and time.

---

opposites," the rending of the individual as well as the collective self, and the passionate quest for unity.[37] One could almost say that the German apocalyptic tradition—the Wagnerian "twilight of the gods" and the general theme of the death-haunted collective end—may be the "torn condition" extended into the realm of larger human connectedness and disconnectedness.

* Mann also captures the continuity in doubling by speaking of the "implicit Satanism" in German psychology, and by having the devil make clear to the Faust figure that "we lay upon you nothing new . . . [but] only ingeniously strengthen and exaggerate all that you already are."[40]

NOTES

1. Paul W. Pruyser, "What Splits in Splitting?," *Bulletin of the Menninger Clinic* 39 (1975): 1–46.

2. Ibid., p. 46. See also Jeffrey Lustman, "On Splitting," in Kurt Eissler et al., eds., *The Psychoanalytic Study of the Child,* vol. 19 (1977), pp. 19–54; Charles Rycroft, *A Critical Dictionary of Psychoanalysis* (New York: Basic Books, 1968), pp. 156–57.

3. See Pierre Janet, *The Major Symptoms of Hysteria* (New York: Macmillan, 1907) and *Psychological Healing* (New York: Macmillan, 1923). See also Leston Havens, *Approaches to the Mind* (Boston: Little, Brown, 1973), pp. 34–62; and Henri F. Ellenberger, *The Discovery of the Unconscious* (New York: Basic Books, 1970), pp. 364–417.

4. Sigmund Freud and Josef Breuer, *Studies on Hysteria,* in *Standard Edition of the Works of Sigmund Freud,* James Strachey, ed. (London: Hogarth Press, 1955 [1893–95]), vol. II, pp. 3–305.

5. Edward Glover, *On the Early Development of Mind: Selected Papers on Psychoanalysis* (New York: International Universities Press, 1956 [1943]), vol. I., pp. 307–23.

6. Melanie Klein, "Notes on Some Schizoid Mechanisms," *International Journal of Psychoanalysis* 27 (1946): 99–110; and Otto F. Kernberg, "The Syndrome," in *Borderline Conditions and Pathological Narcissism* (New York: Jason Aronson, 1973), pp. 3–47.

7. Henry V. Dicks, *Licensed Mass Murder: A Socio-Psychological Study of Some SS Killers* (New York: Basic Books, 1972).

8. See, for example, Erik H. Erikson, *Identity: Youth and Crisis* (New York: W. W. Norton, 1968); Heinz Kohut, *The Restoration of the Self* (New York: International Universities Press, 1977); Henry Guntrip, *Psychoanalytic Theory, Therapy and the Self* (New York: Basic Books, 1971); and Robert Jay Lifton, *The Broken Connection: On Death and the Continuity of Life* (New York: Basic Books, 1983 [1979]).

9. William James, *The Varieties of Religious Experience: A Study in Human Nature* (New York: Collier, 1961 [1902]), p. 144.

10. Rank's two major studies of this phenomenon are *The Double: A Psychoanalytic Study* (Chapel Hill: University of North Carolina Press, 1971 [1925]); and "The Double as Immortal Self," in *Beyond Psychology* (New York: Dover, 1958 [1941]), pp. 62–101.

11. Rank, *Double* [10], pp. 3–9; Rank, *Beyond Psychology* [10], pp. 67–69. On "Der Student von Prag," see Siegfried Kracauer, *From Caligari to Hitler: A Psychological History of the German Film* (Princeton: Princeton University Press, 1947), pp. 28–30.

12. E. T. A. Hoffmann, "Story of the Lost Reflection," in J. M. Cohen, ed., *Eight Tales of Hoffmann* (London, 1952).

13. Rank, *Beyond Psychology* [10], p. 98.

14. Ibid.

15. On Rank's "artist-hero," see Rank, *Beyond Psychology* [10], pp. 97–101.

16. Rank, *Double* [10], p. 76.

17. Ibid.

18. Rank, *Beyond Psychology* [10], p. 82.

19. Michael Franz Basch, "The Perception of Reality and the Disavowal of Meaning," *Annual of Psychoanalysis*, 11 (New York: International Universities Press, 1982): 147.

20. Ralph D. Allison, "When the Psychic Glue Dissolves," *HYPNOS-NYTT* (December 1977).

21. The first two influences are described in George B. Greaves, "Multiple Personality: 165 Years After Mary Reynolds," *Journal of Nervous and Mental Disease* 168 (1977): 577–96. Freud emphasized the third in *The Ego and the Id*, in the *Standard Edition of the Works of Sigmund Freud*, James Strachey, ed. (London: Hogarth Press, 1955 [1923]), vol. XIX, pp. 30–31.

22. Ellenberger, *Unconscious* [3], pp. 394–400.

23. Margaretta K. Bowers et al., "Theory of Multiple Personality," *International Journal of Clinical and Experimental Hypnosis* 19 (1971): 60.

24. See Lifton, *Broken Connection* [8], pp. 407–9; and Charles H. King, "The Ego and the Integration of Violence in Homicidal Youth," *American Journal of Orthopsychiatry* 45 (1975): 142.

25. Robert W. Rieber, "The Psychopathy of Everyday Life" (unpublished manuscript).

26. James S. Grotstein, "The Soul in Torment: An Older and Newer View of Psychopathology," *Bulletin of the National Council of Catholic Psychologists* 25 (1979): 36–52.

27. See Robert Jay Lifton, *Home From the War: Vietnam Veterans, Neither Victims Nor Executioners* (New York: Basic Books, 1984 [1973]).

28. Rudolf Höss, quoted in Karl Buchheim, "Command and Compliance," in Helmut Krausnick et al., *Anatomy of the SS State* (New York: Walker, 1968 [1965]), p. 374.

29. Christian de La Mazière, *The Captive Dreamer* (New York: Saturday Review Press, 1974), pp. 14, 34.

30. John H. Hanson, "Nazi Aesthetics," *The Psychohistory Review* 9 (1981): 276.

31. Sociologist Werner Picht, quoted in Heinz Höhne, *The Order of*

the Death's Head: The Story of Hitler's S. S. (New York: Coward-McCann, 1970 [1966]), pp. 460–61.

32. Rolf Hochhuth, *A German Love Story* (Boston: Little, Brown, 1980 [1978]), p. 220.

33. Rank, *Beyond Psychology* [10], p. 68.

34. Koppel S. Pinson, *Modern Germany: Its History and Civilization* (2nd ed.; New York: Macmillan, 1966), pp. 1–3 (last phrase is from Nietzsche's *Beyond Good and Evil*).

35. Ronald Gray, *The German Tradition in Literature, 1871–1945* (Cambridge: Cambridge University Press, 1965), pp. 3, 79.

36. *Faust,* quoted in Pinson, *Germany* [34], p. 3.

37. Gray, *Tradition* [35], pp. 1–3.

38. Walter Kaufmann, *Goethe's Faust* (New York: Doubleday, 1961), p. 17.

39. Thomas Mann, *Doctor Faustus: The Life of the German Composer Adrian Leverkühn as Told by a Friend* (New York: Alfred A. Knopf, 1948 [1947]), p. 243.

40. Ibid., pp. 249, 308.

41. Rank, *Double* [10]; see also Robert Rogers, *A Psychoanalytic Study of the Double in Literature* (Detroit: Wayne State University Press, 1970).

Part III
THE HOLOCAUST
AND SPIRITUAL LIFE

Faith, prayer, religious observance, our sense of God's presence in the world—are all these irrevocably altered by the Holocaust? The next five authors explore these questions, working with and beyond our initial shock and despair and toward a spiritual existence in which faith in the spiritual dimension of human life coexists with full recognition of its terrors.

In two painfully autobiographical selections, Elie Wiesel asks what meaning Judaism's traditional observance of death and obligation to repent can have in a concentration camp. For Eliezer Berkovits, this genocidal universe confirms rather than suspends traditional Jewish life. Emile Fackenheim searches for the cultural and religious significance of the Holocaust for those who are creating Jewish life after the war. John Pawlikowski, a Catholic priest, challenges Christianity to take note of its role in the Holocaust and study the bitter lessons it must learn from the event. Finally, Abraham Heschel challenges us to find the roots of the tragedy in our common, everyday acceptances of evil.

Elie Wiesel

"THE DEATH OF MY FATHER"
AND "YOM KIPPUR"

"THE DEATH OF MY FATHER"

The anniversary of the death of a certain Shlomo ben Nissel falls on the eighteenth day of the month of *Shvat.* He was my father, the day is tomorrow; and this year, as every year since the event, I do not know how to link myself to it.

Yet, in the *Shulchan Aruch,* the great book of precepts by Rabbi Joseph Karo, the astonishing visionary-lawmaker of the sixteenth century, precise, rigorous rules on the subject do exist. I could and should simply conform to them. Obey tradition. Follow in the footsteps. Do what everyone does on such a day: go to the synagogue three times, officiate at the service, study a chapter of *Mishna,* say the orphan's *Kaddish* and, in the presence of the living community of Israel, proclaim the holiness of God as well as his greatness. For his ways are tortuous but just, his grace heavy to bear but indispensable, here on earth and beyond, today and forever. May his will be done. Amen.

This is undoubtedly what I would do had my father died of old age, of sickness, or even of despair. But such is not the case. His death did not even belong to him. I do not know to what cause to attribute it, in what book to inscribe it. No link between it and the life he had led. His death, lost among all the rest, had nothing to do with the person he had been. It could just as easily have brushed him in passing and spared him. It took him inadvertently, absent-mindedly. By mistake. Without knowing that it was he; he was robbed of his death.

Stretched out on a plank of wood amid a multitude of blood-covered corpses, fear frozen in his eyes, a mask of suffering on the bearded, stricken mask that was his face, my father gave back his soul at Buchenwald. A soul useless in that place, and one he seemed to want to give back. But, he gave it up, not to the God of his fathers, but rather to the impostor, cruel and insatiable, to the enemy God. They had killed his

God, they had exchanged him for another. How, then, could I enter the sanctuary of the synagogue tomorrow and lose myself in the sacred repetition of the ritual without lying to myself, without lying to him? How could I act or think like everyone else, pretend that the death of my father holds a meaning calling for grief or indignation?

Perhaps, after all, I should go to the synagogue to praise the God of dead children, if only to provoke him by my own submission.

Tomorrow is the anniversary of the death of my father and I am seeking a new law that prescribes for me what vows to make and no longer to make, what words to say and no longer to say.

In truth, I would know what to do had my father, while alive, been deeply pious, possessed by fervor or anguish of a religious nature. I then would say: it is my duty to commemorate this date according to Jewish law and custom, for such was his wish.

But, though he observed tradition, my father was in no way fanatic. On the contrary, he preached an open spirit toward the world. He was a man of his time. He refused to sacrifice the present to an unforeseeable future, whatever it might be. He enjoyed simple everyday pleasures and did not consider his body an enemy. He rarely came home in the evening without bringing us special fruits and candies. Curious and tolerant, he frequented Hasidic circles because he admired their songs and stories, but refused to cloister his mind, as they did, within any given system.

My mother seemed more devout than he. It was she who brought me to *heder* to make me a good Jew, loving only the wisdom and truth to be drawn from the Torah. And it was she who sent me as often as possible to the Rebbe of Wizsnitz to ask his blessing or simply to expose me to his radiance.

My father's ambition was to make a man of me rather than a saint. "Your duty is to fight solitude, not to cultivate or glorify it," he used to tell me. And he would add: "God, perhaps, has need of saints; as for men, they can do without them."

He could be found more often in government offices than in the synagogue—and, sometimes, in periods of danger, even more often than at home. Every misfortune that befell our community involved him directly. There was always an impoverished, sick man who had to be sent in an emergency to a clinic in Kolozsvar or Budapest; an unfortunate shopkeeper who had to be bailed out of prison; a desperate refugee who had to be saved. Many survivors of the Polish ghettos owed their lives to him. Furnished with money and forged papers, thanks to him and his friends, they were able to flee the country for Rumania and from there to the United States or Palestine. His activities cost him three months in a Hungarian prison cell. Once released, he did not utter a word of the tortures he had undergone. On the very day of his release, he took up where he had left off.

My mother taught me love of God. As for my father, he scarcely spoke to me about the laws governing the relations between man and his creator. In our conversations, the *Kaddish* was never mentioned. Not even in camp. Especially not in camp.

So I do not know what he would have hoped to see me do tomorrow, the anniversary of his death. If only, in his lifetime, he had been a man intoxicated with eternity and redemption.

But that is not the problem. Even if Shlomo ben Nissel had been a faithful servant of the fierce God of Abraham, a just man, of demanding and immaculate soul, immune against weakness and doubt, even then I would not know how to interpret his death.

For I am ignorant of the essentials: what he felt, what he believed, in that final moment of his hopeless struggle, when his very being was already fading, already withdrawing toward that place where the dead are no longer tormented, where they are permitted at last to rest in peace, or in nothingness—what difference does it make?

His face swollen, frightful, bloodless, he agonized in silence. His cracked lips moved imperceptibly. I caught the sounds, but not the words of his incoherent memory. No doubt, he was carrying out his duty as father by transmitting his last wishes to me, perhaps he was also entrusting me with his final views on history, knowledge, the world's misery, his life, mine. I shall never know. I shall never know if he had the name of the Eternal on his lips to praise him—in spite of everything— or, on the contrary, because of everything, to free himself from him.

Through puffy, half-closed eyelids, he looked at me and, at times, I thought with pity. He was leaving and it pained him to leave me behind, alone, helpless, in a world he had hoped would be different for me, for himself, for all men like him and me.

At other times, my memory rejects this image and goes its own way. I think I recognize the shadow of a smile on his lips: the restrained joy of a father who is leaving with the hope that his son, at least, will remain alive one more minute, one more day, one more week, that perhaps his son will see the liberating angel, the messenger of peace. The certitude of a father that his son will survive him.

In reality, however, I do not hesitate to believe that the truth could be entirely different. In dying, my father looked at me, and in his eyes where night was gathering, there was nothing but animal terror, the demented terror of one who, because he wished to understand too much, no longer understands anything. His gaze fixed on me, empty of meaning. I do not even know if he saw me, if it was me he saw. Perhaps he mistook me for someone else, perhaps even for the exterminating angel. I know nothing about it because it is impossible to grasp what the eyes of the dying see or do not see, to interpret the death rattle of their last breath.

I know only that that day the orphan I became did not respect tradition: I did not say *Kaddish*. First, because no one there would have heard and responded "Amen." Also because I did not yet know that beautiful and solemn prayer. And because I felt empty, barren: a useless object, a thing without imagination. Besides there was nothing more to say, nothing more to hope for. To say *Kaddish* in that stifling barracks, in the very heart of the kingdom of death, would have been the worst of blasphemies. And I lacked even the strength to blaspheme.

Will I find the strength tomorrow? Whatever the answer, it will be wrong, at best incomplete. Nothing to do with the death of my father.

The impact of the holocaust on believers as well as unbelievers, on Jews as well as Christians, has not yet been evaluated. Not deeply, not enough. That is no surprise. Those who lived through it lack objectivity: they will always take the side of man confronted with the Absolute. As for the scholars and philosophers of every genre who have had the opportunity to observe the tragedy, they will—if they are capable of sincerity and humility—withdraw without daring to enter into the heart of the matter; and if they are not, well, who cares about their grandilo-quent conclusions? Auschwitz, by definition, is beyond their vocabulary.

The survivors, more realistic if not more honest, are aware of the fact that God's presence at Treblinka or Maidanek—or, for that matter, his absence—poses a problem which will remain forever insoluble.

I once knew a deeply religious man who, on the Day of Atonement, in despair, took heaven to task, crying out like a wounded beast. "What do you want from me, God? What have I done to you? I want to serve you and crown you ruler of the universe, but you prevent me. I want to sing of your mercy, and you ridicule me. I want to place my faith in you, dedicate my thought to you, and you do not let me. Why? Why?"

I also knew a free-thinker, who, one evening, after a selection, suddenly began to pray, sobbing like a whipped child. He beat his breast, became a martyr. He had need of support, and, even more, of certitude: if he suffered, it was because he had sinned; if he endured torment, it was because he had deserved it.

Loss of faith for some equaled discovery of God for others. Both answered to the same need to take a stand, the same impulse to rebel. In both cases, it was an accusation. Perhaps some day someone will explain how, on the level of man, Auschwitz was possible; but on the level of God, it will forever remain the most disturbing of mysteries.

Many years have passed since I saw my father die. I have grown up and the candles I light several times a year in memory of departed members of my family have become more and more numerous. I should have acquired the habit, but I cannot. And each time the eighteenth day of the month of *Shvat* approaches, I am overcome by desolation and futility: I still do not know how to commemorate the death of my father, Shlomo ben Nissel, a death which took him as if by mistake.

Yes, a voice tells me that in reality it should suffice, as in previous years, to follow the trodden path: to study a chapter of *Mishna* and to say *Kaddish* once again, that beautiful and moving prayer dedicated to the departed, yet in which death itself figures not at all. Why not yield? It would be in keeping with the custom of countless generations of sages and orphans. By studying the sacred texts, we offer the dead continuity if not peace. It was thus that my father commemorated the death of his father.

But that would be too easy. The holocaust defies reference, analogy. Between the death of my father and that of his, no comparison is possible. It would be inadequate, indeed unjust, to imitate my father. I should have to invent other prayers, other acts. And I am afraid of not being capable or worthy.

All things considered, I think that tomorrow I shall go to the synagogue after all. I will light the candles, I will say *Kaddish,* and it will be for me a further proof of my impotence.

"YOM KIPPUR"

With a lifeless look, a painful smile on his face, while digging a hole in the ground, Pinhas moved his lips in silence. He appeared to be arguing with someone within himself and, judging from his expression, seemed close to admitting defeat.

I had never seen him so downhearted. I knew that his body would not hold out much longer. His strength was already abandoning him, his movements were becoming more heavy, more chaotic. No doubt he knew it too. But death figured only rarely in our conversations. We preferred to deny its presence, to reduce it, as in the past, to a simple allusion, something abstract, inoffensive, a word like any other.

"What are you thinking about? What's wrong?"

Pinhas lowered his head, as if to conceal his embarrassment, or his sadness, or both, and let a long time go by before he answered, in a voice scarcely audible: "Tomorrow is Yom Kippur."

Then I too felt depressed. My first Yom Kippur in the camp. Perhaps my last. The day of judgment, of atonement. Tomorrow the heavenly tribunal would sit and pass sentence: "And like unto a flock, the creatures of this world shall pass before thee." Once upon a time—last year—the approach of this day of tears, of penitence and fear, had made me tremble. Tomorrow, we would present ourselves before God, who sees everything and who knows everything, and we would say: "Father, have pity on your children." Would I be capable of praying with fervor again? Pinhas shook himself abruptly. His glance plunged into mine.

"Tomorrow is the Day of Atonement and I have just made a decision: I am not going to fast. Do you hear? I am not going to fast."

I asked for no explanation. I knew he was going to die and suddenly I was afraid that by way of justification he might declare: "It is simple, I have decided not to comply with the law anymore and not to fast because in the eyes of man and of God I am already dead, and the dead can disobey the commandments of the Torah." I lowered my head and made believe I was not thinking about anything but the earth I was digging up under a sky more dark than the earth itself.

We belonged to the same Kommando. We always managed to work side by side. Our age difference did not stop him from treating me like a friend. He must have been past forty. I was fifteen. Before the war, he had been *Rosh-Yeshiva,* director of a rabbinical school somewhere in Galicia. Often, to outwit our hunger or to forget our reasons for despair, we would study a page of the Talmud from memory. I relived my childhood by forcing myself not to think about those who were gone. If one of my arguments pleased Pinhas, if I quoted a commentary without distorting its meaning, he would smile at me and say: "I should have liked to have you among my disciples."

And I would answer: "But I am your disciple, where we are matters little."

That was false, the place was of capital importance. According to the law of the camp I was his equal; I used the familiar form when I addressed him. Any other form of address was inconceivable.

"Do you hear?" Pinhas shouted defiantly. "I will not fast."

"I understand. You are right. One must not fast. Not at Auschwitz. Here we live outside time, outside sin. Yom Kippur does not apply to Auschwitz."

Ever since Rosh Hashana, the New Year, the question had been bitterly debated all over camp. Fasting meant a quicker death. Here everybody fasted all year round. Every day was Yom Kippur. And the book of life and death was no longer in God's hands, but in the hands of the executioner. The words *mi yichye umi yamut,* "who shall live and who shall die," had a terrible real meaning here, an immediate bearing. And all the prayers in the world could not alter the *Gzar-din*, the inexorable movement of fate. Here, in order to live, one had to eat, not pray.

"You are right, Pinhas," I said, forcing myself to withstand his gaze. "You *must* eat tomorrow. You've been here longer than I have, longer than many of us. You need your strength. You have to save your strength, watch over it, protect it. You should not go beyond your limits. Or tempt misfortune. That would be a sin."

Me, his disciple? I gave him lessons, I gave him advice, as if I were his elder, his guide.

"That is not it," said Pinhas, getting irritated. "I could hold out for one day without food. It would not be the first time."

"Then what is it?"

"A decision. Until now, I've accepted everything. Without bitterness, without reservation. I have told myself: 'God knows what he is doing.' I have submitted to his will. Now I have had enough, I have reached my limit. If he knows what he is doing, then it is serious; and it is not any less serious if he does not. Therefore, I have decided to tell him: 'It is enough.' "

I said nothing. How could I argue with him? I was going through the same crisis. Every day I was moving a little further away from the God of my childhood. He had become a stranger to me; sometimes, I even thought he was my enemy.

The appearance of Edek put an end to our conversation. He was our master, our king. The Kapo. This young Pole with rosy cheeks, with the movements of a wild animal, enjoyed catching his slaves by surprise and making them shout with fear. Still an adolescent, he enjoyed possessing such power over so many adults. We dreaded his changeable moods, his sudden fits of anger: without unclenching his teeth, his eyes half-closed, he would beat his victims long after they had lost consciousness and had ceased to moan.

"Well?" he said, planting himself in front of us, his arms folded. "Taking a little nap? Talking over old times? You think you are at a resort? Or in the synagogue?"

A cruel flame lit his blue eyes, but it went out just as quickly. An aborted rage. We began to shovel furiously, not thinking about anything but the ground which opened up menacingly before us. Edek insulted us a few more times and then walked off.

Pinhas did not feel like talking anymore, neither did I. For him the die had been cast. The break with God appeared complete.

Meanwhile, the pit under our legs was becoming wider and deeper.

Soon our heads would hardly be visible above the ground. I had the weird sensation that I was digging a grave. For whom? For Pinhas? For myself? Perhaps for our memories.

On my return to camp, I found it plunged in feverish anticipation: they were preparing to welcome the holiest and longest day of the year. My barracks neighbors, a father and son, were talking in low voices. One was saying: "Let us hope the roll-call does not last too long." The other added: "Let us hope that the soup is distributed before the sun sets, otherwise we will not have the right to touch it."

Their prayers were answered. The roll-call unfolded without incident, without delay, without public hanging. The section-chief hurriedly distributed the soup; I hurriedly gulped it down. I ran to wash, to purify myself. By the time the day was drawing to a close, I was ready.

Some days before, on the eve of Rosh Hashana, all the Jews in camp—Kapos included—had congregated at the square where roll was taken, and we had implored the God of Abraham, Isaac, and Jacob to end our humiliation, to change sides, to break his pact with the enemy. In unison we had said *Kaddish* for the dead and for the living as well. Officers and soldiers, machine guns in hand, had stood by, amused spectators, on the other side of the barbed wire.

Now, we did not go back there for *Kol Nidre*. We were afraid of a selection: in preceding years, the Day of Atonement has been turned into a day of mourning. Yom Kippur had become *Tisha b'Av*, the day the Temple was destroyed.

Thus, each barracks housed its own synagogue. It was more prudent. I was sorry, because Pinhas was in another block.

A Hungarian rabbi officiated as our cantor. His voice stirred my memories and evoked that legend according to which, on the night of Yom Kippur, the dead rise from their graves and come to pray with the living. I thought: "Then it is true; that is what really happens. The legend is confirmed at Auschwitz."

For weeks, several learned Jews had gathered every night in our block to transcribe from memory—by hand, on toilet paper—the prayers for the High Holy Days. Each cantor received a copy. Ours read in a loud voice and we repeated each verse after him. The *Kol Nidre*, which releases us from all vows made under constraint, now seemed to me anachronistic, absurd, even though it had been composed in similar circumstances, in Spain, right near the Inquisition stakes. Once a year the converts would assemble and cry out to God: "Know this, all that we have said is unsaid, all that we have done is undone." *Kol Nidre*? A sad joke. Here and now we no longer had any secret vows to make or to deny: everything was clear, irrevocable.

Then came the *Vidui,* the great confession. There again, everything rang false, none of it concerned us anymore. *Ashamnu,* we have sinned. *Bagadnu,* we have betrayed. *Gazalnu,* we have stolen. What? Us? *We* have sinned? Against whom? by doing what? *We* have betrayed? Whom? Undoubtedly this was the first time since God judged his creation that victims beat their breasts accusing themselves of the crimes of their executioners.

Why did we take responsibility for sins and offenses which not one of us could ever have had the desire or the possibility of committing? Perhaps we felt guilty despite everything. Things were simpler that way. It was better to believe our punishments had meaning, that we had deserved them; to believe in a cruel but just God was better than not to believe at all. It was in order not to provoke an open war between God and his people that we had chosen to spare him, and we cried out: "You are our God, blessed be your name. You smite us without pity, you shed our blood, we give thanks to you for it, O Eternal One, for you are determined to show us that you are just and that your name is justice!"

I admit having joined my voice to the others and implored the heavens to grant me mercy and forgiveness. At variance with everything my lips were saying, I indicted myself only to turn everything into derision, into farce. At any moment I expected the Master of the universe to strike me dumb and to say: "That is enough—you have gone too far." And I like to think I would have replied: "You, also, blessed be your name, you also."

Our services were dispersed by the camp bell. The section-chiefs began to yell: "Okay, go to sleep! If God hasn't heard you, it's because he is incapable of hearing."

The next day, at work, Pinhas joined another group. I thought: "He wants to eat without being embarrassed by my presence." A day later, he returned. His face even more pale, even more gaunt than before. Death was gnawing at him. I caught myself thinking: "He will die because he did not observe Yom Kippur."

We dug for several hours without looking at each other. From far off, the shouting of the Kapo reached us. He walked around hitting people relentlessly.

Toward the end of the afternoon, Pinhas spoke to me: "I have a confession to make."

I shuddered, but went on digging. A strange, almost child-like smile appeared on his lips when he spoke again: "You know, I fasted."

I remained motionless. My stupor amused him.

"Yes, I fasted. Like the others. But not for the same reasons. Not out of obedience, but out of defiance. Before the war, you see, some

Jews rebelled against the divine will by going to restaurants on the Day of Atonement; here, it is by observing the fast that we can make our indignation heard. Yes, my disciple and teacher, know that I fasted. Not for love of God, but against God."

He left me a few weeks later, victim of the first selection.

He shook my hand: "I would have liked to die some other way and elsewhere. I had always hoped to make of my death, as of my life, an act of faith. It is a pity. God prevents me from realizing my dream. He no longer likes dreams."

Nonetheless, he asked me to say *Kaddish* for him after his death, which, according to his calculations, would take place three days after his departure from camp.

"But why?" I asked, "since you are no longer a believer?"

He took the tone he always used when he explained a passage in the Talmud to me: "You do not see the heart of the matter. Here and now, the only way to accuse him is by praising him."

And he went, laughing, to his death.

Eliezer Berkovits
AUTHENTICITY OF BEING

The concept of authenticity of being was introduced into modern existentialist philosophy by Martin Heidegger. He meant by this the form of human existence that is not determined by external conditions and whose values do not derive from "them," from the standard bearers of the established social order in the midst of which a human being may find himself. Jean-Paul Sartre developed the thought further when he spoke of freedom as a condition to which man is "condemned," meaning that no matter in what situation a person may find himself, he is always free to make his choices and, indeed, he always does choose between different possibilities of behavior. The decision is always his. When the Gestapo tortured a member of the Maquis to get him to betray his comrades, he was still free to choose to die or to reveal. His betrayal might be understandable; it is not a matter of condemning him. But in all circumstances the decision is his.

Sartre's position is no mere theory. His understanding of human freedom is based on his actual experiences in the French underground. Similarly Frankl, basing himself on his observations in the concentration camps, affirms the reality of human freedom even in extreme conditions. He writes: "The experiences of camp life show that man does have a choice of action. . . . Man can preserve a vestige of spiritual freedom, of independence of mind, even in such terrible conditions of psychic and physical stress." There were always choices to make, and it was your decision that "determined whether you would or would not submit to those powers which threatened to rob you of your very self, your inner freedom . . ."[1]

For the Jew there is no surprise in these discoveries of Sartre and Frankl. He has made his choices all through history and the Jewish people have survived to this day because there were always Jews who knew that no matter what the conditions and circumstances, it was always up to them to make the decision. We are not only thinking of the

209

untold martyrs who made their choice, in the supreme freedom of the spirit, to die rather than to surrender, but also—and perhaps chiefly—of the ordinary daily life of the Jewish masses through the ages. They lived in confrontation with cultures and civilizations whose values they often rejected and whose lifestyles they mostly did not share. The Jew has been the nonconformist of history and has lived in authenticity of selfhood through many centuries.

Though living through a persecution radically more severe than anything experienced previously, the Jews who suffered under the Nazis in essence continued the historic lifestyle of the Jewish people. To be sure, this lifestyle, as embodied in the *halakhah*, is a style of living. It does not consider physical existence unworthy of its concern. On the contrary, it is concerned with existence in its entirety. But human life is not limited to physical or biological existence; its physical and biological components are not a bit more "real" than its spiritual, value-oriented and meaning-seeking aspects. In the same sense, external reality, whose determination has been the preoccupation of modern philosophy for generations, is no more real than the internal life of the person. A thought, an idea, a concept, is no less of this world than a cell, a molecule, or a biological drive. The human being, as a potentiality, and the world that he encounters, are the raw material out of which selfhood emerges. The reality of man is never given; he has to shape it for himself out of what is given to him. How he does it, that alone determines the quality of his humanity.

The significance of what we have called authentic Jewish behavior is that even in the ghettos and the death camps there were numerous Jews who determined their own lifestyles. In the midst of the filth of the SS kingdom they established their own realm of Jewish continuity, giving structure to the wilderness into which they were cast. What did this mean in terms of the actual, daily camp situation?

In a moving passage, Frankl describes one of his personal experiences that could have occurred on any ordinary day:

> Almost in tears from pain (I had terrible sores on my feet from wearing torn shoes), I limped a few kilometers with our long column of men from the camp to our work site. Very cold, bitter winds struck. I kept thinking of the endless little problems of our miserable life. What should there be to eat tonight? If a piece of sausage came as extra ration, should I exchange it for a piece of bread? Should I trade my last cigarette, which was left from a bonus I received a fortnight ago, for a bowl of soup? How could I get a piece of wire to replace the fragment

which served as one of my shoelaces? Would I get to our work
site in time to join my usual working party or would I have to
join another, which might have a brutal foreman . . . ?

Unlike the mass of prisoners, Frankl, having been able to safeguard a
high measure of personal dignity, became disgusted with a situation that
compelled him to think "daily and hourly . . . of only such trivial things."
Fighting off the onslaught of the trivia, he found relief in falling back on
his professional interest. Suddenly, as if in a vision, he saw himself
standing "on the platform of a well-lit, warm and pleasant lecture
room." In front of him sat "an attentive audience on comfortable
upholstered seats," to whom Frankl lectured on the psychology of the
concentration camp. Thus the daily camp experience became objectified
as a phenomenon for scientific examination. Frankl then explains: "By
this method I succeeded somehow in rising above the situation, above
the sufferings of the moment, and I observed them as if they were
already of the past."[2] Needless to say, matters which in normal conditions would be considered mere trivia received extraordinary importance in the camps. Hosts of prisoners found themselves in the predicament of having to limp many kilometers from the camp to their work site
and back in pain because of their sore feet. What would authentic Jews
be thinking of during such a march? Probably of the very same trivial
needs that so preoccupied Frankl. But they would not be thinking of
these things "daily and hourly," and their concern was not only with
"such trivial things." They would be no less deeply involved with problems of an entirely different nature: would they be able to find a corner
in their barracks where they might be able to pray Ma'ariv (the evening
service) with the prescribed quorum of at least ten men? How could they
get their hands on a pair of tefillin? How many rations of bread would it
cost? Or, if Purim was approaching, where could they get a megillah (the
Scroll of Esther)? Would it be another Pesaḥ without matzah? How could
they minimize the need for eating the hot soup of the camp, which was
terefah? How could they make a menorah for Ḥanukkah and smuggle it
into the camp? And once it was there, how could they light it without it
being discovered? Innumerable problems of this nature, and the devis-
ing of possible solutions for them, were among the foremost of their
"daily and hourly" concerns. Viktor Frankl had the strength of character to create his scientific vision and thus to escape the degrading misery
of the death camps. These Jews, however, were not escaping. They
imposed another rhythm on that raw reality to which they were subjected and thus drew out its dehumanizing poison. They lived their lives
as Jews.

Trying to understand, trying to empathize with the suffering of Frankl, his feet covered with sores, limping along with his fellow prisoners from the hell of the camp to the hell of the work site and back, I see in my mind's eye another long column of men, marching perhaps along the same road, in all kinds of chafing footwear, their torn rags exposing them to the elements, many of them limping along supported by their comrades; and the same long column returning exhausted in the evening, usually dragging along a few lifeless bodies with them. But somewhere there, intentionally lost in that same column, is a group of Jews, keeping close together. In their midst there walks one, a *Talmid Hakham,* who knows large sections of the Talmud by heart. He teaches Talmud, he teaches Torah. The others are listening; they interrupt with questions or to make their own contribution to the discussion. And of course there are other roads, other threadbare marchers, and other intense groups of Jews studying Talmud, or perhaps Mishnah, or reciting chapters from the Psalms by memory.

The camps had their own geographic pattern, designed to serve the goals of the extermination squads. But for these Jews, some of the roads were not paths of SS-prescribed misery, but were transformed by them into paths of daily renewal. The authentic Jewish lifestyle superimposed a space-structure of meaningfulness on the camp geography of humiliation and degradation. Similarly, the occupants of the *Tahara Bretter* (the boards of purity) at Buchenwald changed the space structure of the camp in their immediate area, establishing a focal point of direction for the Jews all around them, and not only for those who were still practicing Judaism. In that section, the map of the camp received the impact of a humanizing purpose. Or think of the deathpit turned into the *Bet Medreshel,* a place of prayer and study; the various spots in the Holocaust kingdom where *sukkot* were built secretly; the hiding places for *tefillin,* for a *Hanukkah menorah,* for a *shofar* to blow on *Rosh haShanah*—all points of a conspiratorial changing of space structure, a reorientation of directions in the camps.

Nowhere did this autonomous restructuring of camp reality achieve a more penetrating influence than in the dimension of time. Using the example of Bernard Malamud's *The Fixer,* Terence Des Pres effectively discusses the trying experience of unstructured time that was the lot of the prisoners in the concentration camps. He writes: ". . . in extremity the forms of time dissolve, the rhythms of change and motion are lost. Days pass, seasons, years pass and the fixer has no idea how long his ordeal will go on." There is "an emptiness complete in itself, a suspension in the sameness of identical days which could last a year or a lifetime."[3] What was true for the fixer was even more oppressive and demoralizing for those in the German death camps.[4] However, for the Jews whose lifestyle we are examining, the "suspension in the sameness of identical days," the complete emptiness of endless duration, did not exist. Their time was not the SS-imposed structureless sameness; their time was structured by the Jewish calendar. Calendars were handwritten in the ghettos and camps, and even where they were not available, there were always Jews who could calculate and compute the necessary dates on the basis of the scanty information that was available. Thus, for the Jews, time was divided into days, weeks, months, seasons, and years. The division represented an experienced rhythm of sequence, each part of which carried its remembered and observed meaning and significance.

According to Frankl, the most ghastly moment of the day was "the awakening, when, at a still nocturnal hour, the three shrill blows of a whistle tore us pitilessly from our exhausted sleep and from the longings of our dreams." He tells the story of how a comrade beside him was having a nightmare. At first, instinctively, he meant to wake him; but then he decided not to disturb him, for no matter how frightening his nightmare might have been, the awakening would have been even worse. To Frankl, it was a wonder that prisoners got up at all. What was awaiting them? An endless day of torture, humiliation, exhaustion, and hunger. "Prisoners were driven awake by fear, by anxiety, and often by the blows of a whip or club."[5] But what was each new day in the structured time of the Jewish calendar? Needless to say the tortures, the humiliation, the fatigue were all there in it. But for those Jews who rose one or two hours before the general *appell* in order to put on *tefillin* for a few moments, and for the thousands who had no access to *tefillin* but who nevertheless rose before the other prisoners, without the three shrill blows of the whistle, in order to say their morning prayers, it was a day given by God, on which one praised him as the Creator of light. One got up, because one had to, not because of the whip and the club, but because the morning is the time for *Shaharit*, the daily morning service. The day of the camp was indeed endless misery, yet another daily order was superimposed on it. With the sun about to set, one had to find an inconspicuous spot for a quick *Minha* prayer. And at night, one did not drop with senseless exhaustion into one's bunk. One collected oneself. The order of the day called for its conclusion with *Ma'ariv*, the evening service. The week: for those who live in unstructured time there is no such thing as a week, but empty duration stretching infinitely. Only he who knows of the Sabbath knows of the week. Of course, the Sabbath could not be observed traditionally. One *had* to work; yet, one could, and did, celebrate the Sabbath even in the most extreme circumstances. This is how one survivor describes it:

Comes Sabbath we feel the *Neshama Yeterah,* the enrichment of our souls.[6] She sings in the depth of our being. How we love the Sabbath! We draw from her strength for all the days of the week. In the dim light of the descending evening we sing quietly . . . God is with us. *Imo Anokhi beZarah.* "I am with him in his trouble". . . *Shekhinta beGaluta,* yes, the Divine Presence itself is in exile with us.[7] We are not so lonely. A High Guest is staying with us. He, too, is now homeless, lonely without His people, suffering through our suffering. As the day is passing, in a darkening world we hold on to her, to our Sabbath. It is hard to take leave of her. We shall be alone again for such a long gray frightening week. Beginning with the first day of the week we start counting the days in our hearts till *Erev Shabbat,* till the sixth day. . . .[8]

A long week indeed, full of hardship and suffering. But on Monday it would be only five days till the next Sabbath; on Tuesday, only four; by Thursday they would have almost made it. And what is true of the day and the week in that calendar is also true for the months, the seasons, and the year. All along the road there are stations; one moves toward them, one prepares oneself for them. The time spent in the evenings studying, usually by heart, the talmudic tractate *Megillah* in anticipation of *Purim,* or going over the laws of *Pesaḥ* as that festival approached, or on studying the relevant Talmud passages in mental preparation for *Ḥanukkah*—all this was not time suspended in empty repetition of the same eternal misery; it was the ordered time of a lifestyle imposed on chaos.

Frankl makes the point that a human being must have a future to live for. But since in the camps one could not see an end to the incarceration, one could not aim at a future. Therefore, he saw his life as "provisional existence of unknown limit." This is one of the causes of so many losing their hold on life. Everything became pointless for them.[9] Future for them meant time beyond camp existence. But in the structured time sequence of the authentic Jew the future was also the next moment, with its demands and promises, waiting to be lived through as a Jew. His future was the continuous anticipation of the meaning and purpose of the next date in his calendar—*Pesaḥ,* the festival of liberation; *Shavu'ot,* the festival of the revelation at Sinai; *Rosh haShanah* and *Yom Kippur* were waiting for him.

One is deeply stirred by Frankl's words as he describes what the futureless existence in empty time meant for a sensitive prisoner who

told him that as he marched in that long column of new inmates from
the station to the camp he felt . . .

> as though he were marching at his own funeral. His life seemed
> to him absolutely without future. He regarded it as over and
> done, as if he had already died . . . The outside life, that is, as
> much as he could see of it, appeared to him almost as if it might
> have to a dead man who looked at the world from another
> planet.[10]

Now the authentic Jew never had his roots in that "outside life." In fact,
at all times he would look at it with a measure of reservation. Living in a
different dimension of the spirit, he indeed looked at that world as if
from another planet. The concentration camp was hell on earth. But
even in such a hell one lives, in the embracing context of historic Judaism, in the presence of God.

Frankl has a counterpart to the story of the man who felt as if he
were walking at his own funeral. It is the story of the human greatness of
a sick young woman who knew that she had only a few more days to live.
Yet, cheerful in spite of her knowledge, she told Frankl that she was
grateful for her fate. "In my former life," she said, "I was spoiled and
did not take spiritual accomplishments seriously." Then, pointing with
her finger through the window of the hut, she continued: "This tree
here is the only friend I have in my loneliness." All that could be seen
through the window was a single branch of a chestnut tree with two
blossoms on it. "I often talk to this tree," she confessed. At first Frankl
was startled, imagining that the woman might be delirious or that she
suffered from occasional hallucinations. But when he anxiously asked
her whether the tree replied, she said: "Yes! It said to me, 'I am here—I
am here—I am life, eternal life.' "[11] The woman's answer is very reminiscent of Martin Buber's I-Thou relationship. According to Buber, it is
possible to establish such a dialogically personal relationship even with a
tree. Through the finite Thou of that tree one might gain a glimpse of
the Eternal Thou. Quite clearly, this young woman did not feel that she
was seeing an outside world of unreality, as if she were dead or on
another planet. In fact, never previously had she been so much alive to
the reality of the world, never before so intimately close to it. Such are,
of course, the unique experiences of unique people. But it is remarkable
to what extent the authentic Jews remained in touch with the reality of
the world. Even though separated from the world of men, these Jews
were not alienated from God's creation. This resulted, in a way, directly

from their continued observance of the seasonal festivals. *Pesaḥ* does not only commemorate the Exodus, it is also *Ḥag haAviv,* the Spring festival; *Shavu'ot,* when the Torah was given, is also remembered as *Ḥag haBikurim,* the festival of the first fruits of the land that used to be offered in the Temple of Jerusalem; and *Sukkot,* the "season of our joy," is also the season of the harvest. They were not only memories of the past; the Jews knew very well that no matter what their personal fate might turn out to be, *Pesaḥ, Shavu'ot,* and *Sukkot,* as well as the other significant dates in the Jewish calendar, would outlast Nazi Germany. The structured time of the Jewish calendar preserved their contact with the world that brought to them the message of the eternal life of its source.

In the ghetto of Lodz a few young men were in hiding in order to be able to do nothing else but study *Torah.* We know the address. The place was in Radogshaz Street. We know their names: Moishe Podembizer, Leibel Rosenblat, Moishe Liss, and two Bornstein brothers, Naftoli and Falk. When the Gestapo discovered their hiding place they were accused of spying and sabotage and taken to a prison. There they were tortured in order to get them to reveal the "secrets of the underground." After one of these bloody "examinations," when the boys met for a short moment in a prison corridor, Moishe Liss called to the others: "Remember to start saying *Tal uMatar,* tomorrow evening," referring to a two-word seasonal change which is introduced into the *Shemoneh Esrei* (Eighteen Benedictions) prayer early in December each year. The exact date of this change varies between December 4 and 5, but since Jewish calendars were no longer printed in the ghetto, Moishe Liss must have known the calendar of that year by heart and thus could remind his friends not to forget to insert the change in their prayers the next evening.[12] Who cared about the Nazis! In the midst of the inferno, these young Jews, bruised and bleeding from German barbarism, could focus on such a small nuance of their prayers, reflecting the change in season.

If the festivals are chiefly seasonal, the Sabbath has its place in the cosmos. For God created the world in six days and He rested on the seventh. "And God blessed the seventh day and sanctified it."[13] The same survivor, whose words about the Sabbath in his bunker we quoted earlier, experiences the holy day in its cosmic context:

> At the time of sunset on the eve of the Sabbath it would seem as if the fields were being covered with plush carpets in honor of Queen Sabbath. The lights in the far-away little windows flicker as if they were Sabbath candles lit in universal space. Our

saintly mothers who kindled those lights hover above in the distant blue. They cover their faces with their hands . . . they put their hands on our hands and bless us. The stars across the sky twinkle . . . twinkling Sabbath candles. Soon they will fade and be extinguished. A Sabbath song is in the air, floating in from somewhere behind the woods. Oh, how we wish to sit at the hole of the bunker and let the song filter into us till the rise of the sun.[14]

A partisan. The battle has subsided. Quiet. His head fills with confusing thoughts. A maddening desire overcomes him: to smoke, to smoke. To take a piece of paper, to roll a cigarette and to forget. To forget everything.

Suddenly, a thought passes over my mind, cutting as if with a knife's edge. Shabbat! Shabbat?

Behind him a red sun ignites flames of fire at the end of the horizon and floods with purple some scattered and lonely greyish clouds. Far, far away, other clouds rise thickeningly above the trees, hastening to extinguish the conflagration. Roll that cigarette! The sun . . . Shabbat!

Raise your head and look at the sky—spoke a voice within me—it is already dark. The Sabbath has descended.

His fingers clasped the tobacco in his pocket as if it were some precious and desired treasure that one did not have the courage to bring out into the light of the day. Just to touch it gave him a pleasurable feeling.

I looked at the sky. As if there were something there before which I was ashamed . . . nor did I have the strength to pull my hand out of my pocket.

The partisan struggled against that voice on behalf of his consuming desire.

Gradually the dark cloud covered the last tongues of fire that were still spreading from the horizon. The sun was emitting some of its last weakening sparks. Then it disappeared as if it had never been. Shabbat! Shabbat!

His head sunk onto the soft earth. He closed his eyes and his thoughts took him away from the still unfinished battle and from everything around him.

> I did not sleep, nor did I see any visions in a dream. Only my eyes were closed. Suddenly, well-known faces of long ago, forgotten under the burden of the time, were flowing towards me. Sabbath evening! The *Shtiebel* is filled from one end to the other with Jews in black "kapotes" of silk, and velvet hats on their heads . . . long tables covered with white tablecloths . . . red-cheeked little children with long descending curly sidelocks squeeze themselves through the crowd. Heart-warming tunes are heard as some study the *Zohar* and others recite *Shir ha-Shirim.*[15] The wax candles are dripping from the warm atmosphere of the *Shtiebel.*
>   "L'kha Dodi . . . Come, my beloved to meet the Bride
>   Let us welcome the Shabbat."[16]
> It is the voice of my father who has been honored with *Kabbalat Shabbat,* to welcome the Shabbat. And I am assisting him . . . with a tune that inspires and caresses at the same time.

The Germans interrupt the silence; they tear apart the web of the dream. Bullets, flying like stars, erred in their paths and were whistling over his head. Quickly he emptied his pocket. Temptation had been conquered. The tobacco was swallowed up in the mud. He felt better; he breathed restfully, as if a heavy burden had been taken from off him.

> I felt light, refreshed; as if born anew. I sat on the trunk of a rotting tree. I looked up into the star-studded sky; I knew that the night was a Shabbat night. My lips were whispering . . . I did not know what . . . I thanked God for the loving kindness that he rendered unto me on that day . . .[17]

For this survivor the experience brought back the memory of a far-away, wondrous world, a world that had disappeared and no longer existed. And yet, it was speaking to him with the cosmic voice of a Shabbat night in the universe.

The authenticity of being reached its deepest validation when the Jew was confronted with the ultimate, when powers beyond his physical strength were about to put an end to his physical existence. The prototype of this autonomous Jew has been Rabbi Akiva, the story of whose death, as told in the Talmud, is well known. When the Romans were leading him to be executed it became time to recite the morning *Shema*. As he was being tortured, he said the *Shema*, taking upon himself the "yoke of the Heavens."[18]

Struggling intellectually with the nightmarish bequest of the destruction of European Jewry makes one think with awe of the majestic simplicity of the words in this story ". . . it was time to recite the morning *Shema*." It has been customary for many generations that when a Jew's life is threatened, or, on his sickbed when he feels that his end is approaching, he would use his last moments on earth to recite the first verse of the *Shema*. With a last effort and fervor he would call out the words: "Hear, O Israel . . ." There is a drama in this call that surpasses the mundane and is sounded in a transcendental realm at the border line between two worlds. It was, however, not like this that Rabbi Akiva said the *Shema*. There was nothing of drama in his words, nothing of the sublime that one might notice in the voice of a man who with his last breath affirms the meaning of his whole life. Rabbi Akiva did not say the *Shema* because they were taking him to his execution, not because the ultimate test was approaching. On the contrary, there was nothing extraordinary about his *Shema*. The reason he said it was very simple; ". . . it was time to recite the morning *Shema*. . . ." He said it just as on any other day, because that hour of the day had arrived when one was supposed to say it. It was totally irrelevant to what the Romans were about to do to his body. The soldiers of Rome, all the might and glory of the empire—Rabbi Akiva ignored them. They were of no consequence; he was busy with something else. It was time to recite the *Shema* and according to the law one should not delay saying it.

To be unconcerned with what others may do to you, even when your life is at stake, because you are committed to the truth of your own life, is the supreme act of personal autonomy. In the spirit of Rabbi Akiva such acts of autonomous being occurred not infrequently in the ghettos and the death camps. We are not thinking here of the tens of thousands who went to the gas chambers with the *Shema* or some other form of affirmation of faith on their lips, though this, too, was a majestic deed of devotion to the truth of one's life. We are thinking of those who showed that radical indifference to the external reality that had been imposed on them. Such for instance, was the behavior of a group of fifty *baḥurim* (young yeshiva students) who stood at the door to the gas chambers in Auschwitz on *Simḥat Torah* (the festival of the Rejoicing of the Law): "It is *Simḥat Torah* today. There are no scrolls of the Torah here; but surely God is here. Let us celebrate with Him." It was the same indifference, the same contempt for all the might of the oppressor that Rabbi Akiva showed so many centuries earlier to the Roman Empire.

There were many similar situations in which others acted no differently. One Friday, the Germans took Rabbi Ḥayyim Yeḥiel Rubin of Dambrowe to the cemetery, together with twenty other Jews of the city. There they ordered them to dig their graves. As so often on such occasions, the Germans were in no hurry. Standing in their graves, the Jews were able to welcome the Sabbath Queen with the traditional prayers. After the prayers, the Rebbe greeted the little congregation, as well as the regular Jewish grave diggers who were there, with the traditional "Good Shabbes" and started singing, as on every other Friday night, *Shalom Aleikhem*, "Peace unto you, angels of peace." He recited *Kiddush*, sanctified the Sabbath over two *ḥallot*, two Sabbath loaves which the Jewish grave diggers had smuggled in to them, and taught Torah, interpreting the twenty-two letters with which the contents of the Torah are written. In the midst of his teaching, he was overcome with religious fervor and began to sing. Influenced by Rabbi Rubin, the other Jews joined in with him and, singing and dancing, celebrated the Sabbath, completely ignoring the Germans who, their machine-guns at the ready, were surrounding the grave.[19]

In Baranowicz, Rabbi Nissan Scheinberg was a *Dayyan,* a member of the rabbinical court. On *Shushan Purim,* in 1942, the Germans prepared a blood bath in the town at which thousands of Jews were murdered. Dr. Nehemia Kroschinsky, a surviving eyewitness, tells this story:

> A group of Slonim ḥasidim, who were caught in the "selection," stood together, preparing themselves for the moment of *Kiddush Hashem,* "the sanctification of the Divine Name" in death. In the midst of the group stood the Dayyan, Rabbi Nissan, who called to the others: "Jews! Let us not forget that today is Purim. Let us drink *L'ḥayyim,* to life." He poured out a cupful and said again: "*L'ḥayyim!*" He got hold of a few other Jews and started dancing. His face was shining as he sang the traditional Purim song, *Shoshanat Ya'akov,* "Rose of Jacob," and he shouted with joy until a German bullet silenced him.[20]

This kind of contemptuous indifference to the enemy is the ultimate of human autonomy. Dov Sadan called it *haEmunah haAḥaronah,* the ultimate faith. He rightly said that it is superior to all the might of the enemy, for while this might is considered by the foe the essential substance of reality, for men of ultimate faith this reality does not exist at

all. Only such faith enables the human soul to rise to its highest exaltation, an experience so well-known to the Jew through his wanderings
because of the truth that he represents in the history of man.[21] Many a
survivor of the ghettos and camps speaks of such joyous exaltation. One
of the survivors of the Lodz ghetto recalls the past in these words:

> The truth is that often I am ashamed of myself. How I have
> fallen from *igra rama,* from the lofty heights of those days to
> the life of comforts and smallness of today. Woe is me! How far
> removed I am today even from the mere perception of the
> sublime of that time . . . What are our concepts of the ghetto
> today? *Gehinnom,* hell, graveyard! Dark and black abyss! Yet for
> us, for our group the ghetto was the furnace in which our
> unlimited commitment (*mesirut nefesh*) was purified and where
> one reached a purity of attachment to the divine than which
> nothing higher is conceivable.[22]

Another survivor, explaining how the Torah teachings of his father and
other pious Jews helped him cope with continually mounting suffering
in the ghetto, summed up his memories by observing: "Perhaps now
some will believe me when I say in full truth and seriousness that to this
day I have not tasted life as I did in those days of trouble."[23]

In one of the huts in a certain concentration camp some Jews were
celebrating the Passover *seder.* Suddenly the door was opened with
force. They all expected the worst. But the "guests" were Nohumze and
a few other young Jews. They all acted as if they were somewhat drunk,
although it was clear that not one of them had touched a drop of
alcohol. "What is the matter, Reb Itsche?" Nohumze demanded. "Is this
how one conducts a *seder!* Is this how one serves God with joy? And if
there is no wine for the 'Four Cups' a Jew cannot get inebriated . . . that
God has helped us to celebrate the *seder* even in a camp?" After that they
started singing with fervor the traditional *seder* songs.[24]

Many a Jew understood that the way they met the tribulations had
itself to be a form of divine service and one had to serve God with joy.
Leib Brikman, a survivor of Dachau, tells of a hard winter in a camp he
was in near Landsberg. Cold and hunger was gnawing at the prisoners
and wearing down what remained of their strength. These are Brikman's
words:

> I felt like a candle about to go out. All along the way . . . the
> snow was piled high. I skidded often and fell. The little will that

was still left in the dying body whispered to me: "Lie down on this soft pile of snow and don't get up again."

At this moment his friend, Notte Eibschitz, a young man of eighteen, stepped up to him and said:

What is the matter, my friend? True, we are walking to hell. (*Gehinnom*). But does not a Jew accept even suffering with love! Even to *Gehinnom* one has to walk in joy.

"It was then that I rose and stood on my feet," concludes Leib Brikman.[25]

NOTES

1. *Op. cit.*, pp. 65–66.
2. *Ibid.*, pp. 73–74.
3. *Op. cit.*, p. 12.
4. Cf. also what Frankl has to say on the crushing burden of unstructured time, *op. cit.*, p. 70.
5. *Op. cit.*, p. 75.
6. According to a mystical tradition, the Jew receives an "additional soul" on the Sabbath which leaves him at the Sabbath's conclusion.
7. Cf. Psalms 91:15; T.B. *Ta'anit* 16a; also T.B. *Sukkah* 45a and *Tosafot s.v. Ani veHoo.*
8. Eliav, p. 141; from Leib Rochman, *BeDamayikh Ḥayyee*, Jerusalem, 1961.
9. *Op. cit.*, pp. 69–70.
10. *Ibid.*, p. 71.
11. *Ibid.*, pp. 68–69.
12. Prager, I, p. 82.
13. Genesis 2:2.
14. Prager, I, p. 82.
15. The *Zohar*, the Book of Light, is the classic work of Jewish mysticism. *Shir haShirim*, the biblical *Song of Songs*, is often read in the synagogue by individuals prior to the communal Sabbath eve services.
16. A refrain from the Sabbath eve liturgy.
17. Eliav, pp. 75–76.
18. T. B. *Berakhot* 61b.
19. Unger, p. 135.
20. *Eleh Ezkerah*, VII, p. 196.

21. Dov Sadan in *Maḥanayim, Ḥanukkah* 5720 (1959).
22. Prager, II, p. 100.
23. *Ibid.*, p. 93.
24. Unger, p. 322.
25. Prager, II, p. 136.

Emil L. Fackenheim

JEWISH EXISTENCE AFTER
THE HOLOCAUST

A

What is a Jew? Who is a Jew? These questions have troubled Jews, ever since the Emancipation rendered problematic all the old answers—those of Gentiles and those given by Jews themselves. Today, however, these same old questions, when asked by Jews, bespeak a hidden dread. It is true that the old post-Emancipation answers are still with us: a "religious denomination," a "nationality," a "nation like other nations," or, currently most fashionably in North America, an "ethnic group." Also, the much older Halakhic answer—"a child born of a Jewish mother or a convert to Judaism"—has gained a new lease on life; and, whether it is admitted or not, this is very largely thanks to the existence of the State of Israel. Finally, the fact of Israel itself, a modern state in the modern world, has shaken and confused all the old answers, i.e., the old post-Emancipation ones and the still older Halakhic ones, lending the question of Jewish identity a new kind of urgency. (The state exists. It *is* a state. It has problems that brook no postponement.) All this is true. Not true, however, is that all the above definitions, whether taken separately or together, today either exhaust the depth of the question or even so much as touch a dimension that is now in it. As for conferences on Jewish identity conducted in such terms alone, in these the hidden dread is shut out.

A Jew today is one who, except for an historical accident—Hitler's loss of the war—would have either been murdered or never been born. One makes this statement at a conference on Jewish identity. There is an awkward silence. And then the conference proceeds as if nothing had happened.

Yet the truth of the statement is undeniable. To be sure, the heroism and sacrifices of millions of men and women made the Nazi defeat no mere accident. But victory was not inevitable. Thus without as brief a diversion as the Yugoslav campaign Russia might have been conquered.

Thus, too, Hitler might have won the war had he not attacked Russia at all when he did—a gratuitous, suicidal lapse into a two-front war that is surrounded by mystery to this day.

No mystery, however, surrounds the condition of a world following a Nazi victory—the "New Order," as it already was called, or the "Free New Order," as in due course it might have been called. (As it was, the Auschwitz gate already bore the legend *Arbeit macht Frei.*) Such are the names and the propaganda. The reality would have resembled a vast, worldwide concentration camp, ruled by a *Herrenvolk* assisted by dupes, opportunists, and scoundrels, and served by nations conditioned to slavery. We say "worldwide," although a few semi-independent satellite states, modelled, perhaps, after Vichy France, might have been tolerated at the fringes. Of these the United States would surely have been the most prominent.

Such is the outer shape of a worldwide Nazi "New Order." Its inner essence would have been a murder camp for Jews, for without Jews to degrade, torture, and "exterminate," the rulers could have spiritually conditioned neither themselves to mastery nor the world to slavery. (Had Julius Streicher not said: "Who fights the Jew, fights the devil; who masters the devil, conquers heaven"?) However, with all, or almost all, Jews long murdered, the New Order would have had to invent ever-new Jews for the necessary treatment. (Had not Hitler himself once remarked that, if there were no Jews, it would be necessary to invent them?) Or alternatively, in case such an inventing were impossible—who except *real* Jews are the devil?—one would have had to maintain the fiction that Jews long dead were still alive, a mortal threat to the world.* (Had not Goebbels declared in the Berlin *Sportpalast* that Jews alone of all peoples had not suffered in the war but only profited from it—this in

---

* Hitler's remark is reported by Hermann Rauschning and is integrated into the latter's "revolution of nihilism" thesis. In an attempt to refute that thesis Eberhard Jäckel's *Hitlers Weltanschauung* (Tübingen: Wunderlich, 1969) starts out by asserting that Hitler was no nihilist but rather had a coherent, if evil, *Weltanschauung* composed of "principles." The book ends up, however, with the unwitting demonstration that with Hitler all except Jew-hatred was compromisable, and that what is grandiloquently called Hitler's "coherent *Weltanschauung*"—indeed, no less than a "thought system" with "theoretical foundations"—amounts only to this, that the nineteenth-century anti-Semitic slogan "the Jews are our misfortune" is made into a cosmic principle. In *Mein Kampf* Hitler himself writes: "If, with the help of the Marxist creed, the Jew is victorious over the other peoples of the world, his crown will be the funeral wreath of humanity and this planet will, as it did thousands [second edition: millions] of years ago, move through the ether devoid of men . . ." (p. 60).

1944, when most Jews of Europe were dead?) We speak advisedly of *all*, or almost all, Jews being dead. A worldwide Nazi New Order that permits semi-independent satellite states at its fringes is conceivable; Jews permitted refuge in them are not. (Had not Professor Johann von Leers argued that, by the principle of hot pursuit, the Third Reich had the legal right and the moral duty to invade surrounding countries, for the purpose of "exterminating" the "Jewish vermin"?) And if nevertheless only *almost* all Jews were dead, if a *few* still survived, this would be due to the help of some Gentiles whose ingenuity, endurance, and righteousness will always pass understanding.

Such would be our world today if, by ill fortune, Hitler had won the war. But by good fortune he lost the war; then why, for the sake of a future Jewish identity, conjure up the spectre of his victory? The answer is simple. One survivor, a poet, rightly laments that, except for a few missing persons, the world has not changed. Another, this one a philosopher, charges just as rightly that the world refuses to change, that it views the reminding presence of such as himself as a malfunctioning of the machinery. Long before either Jewish plaint—long before the *Ereignis* itself—the Christian Sören Kierkegaard had spelled out the abstract principle—that a single catastrophic event of monumental import is enough to call all things into question ever after. We have cited such witnesses against others. As we now turn to our native realm of Jewish self-understanding, we can do no other than cite them against ourselves.

Even to do so only tentatively—preliminarily, as it were by way of experiment—is to discover, quite independently from all the previous complicated reflections and simply by looking at the facts, that to minimize, ignore, "overcome," "go beyond" the dark past for the sake of a happy and healthy future Jewish self-understanding is impossible. Empirically, to be sure, all this *is* possible: the phenomenon exists on every side. But morally, religiously, philosophically, humanly it is an impossibility. Shall we trust in God because we—though not they—were spared? Shall we trust in man because here and now—though not then and there—he bears traces of humanity? Shall we trust in ourselves—that we, unlike them, would resist being made into *Muselmänner*, the living dead, with the divine spark within us destroyed?

We can do none of these things; they are all insults, one hopes unwitting, to the dead. And behind these unintended insults lies the attempt to repress the hidden dread, to deny the rupture that is a fact. Above we asserted that philosophy and Christian theology can each find its respective salvation not by avoiding the great rupture, but only by confronting it. We must now turn this assertion against ourselves.

B

   The move from non-Jewish to Jewish post-Holocaust thought is not a step but a veritable leap. This is so by dint of a single fact the implications of which brook no evasion. "Aryan" victims of the Third Reich, though robbed, enslaved, subjected to humiliation, torture, and murder, were not *singled out* unless they *chose* to *single themselves* out; Jews, in contrast, were *being* singled out *without choice of their own*. We have already considered this difference as it was manifest during the Holocaust itself. We must now consider its implications for today.

   There are two such implications. First, whereas much of the post-Holocaust world is ruptured, the post-Holocaust *Jewish* world is *doubly* ruptured, divorced by an abyss not only from its own past tradition but also—except for such as Huber and Lichtenberg who, even then, bridged the gulf from the non-Jewish side—from the Gentile world. Second, whereas post-Holocaust philosophical and Christian thought finds a *Tikkun* in such as Huber and Lichtenberg, post-Holocaust Jewish thought finds itself situated after a world which spared no effort to make a *Jewish* Huber or Lichtenberg systematically impossible. For "Aryans," "crime," then as always, was a *doing,* so that in their case the Nazi tyranny, like other tyrannies, *created* the possibilities of heroism and martyrdom. For "non-Aryans," however, the crime was *being itself,* so that in *their* case—a *novum* in history, all previous tyrannies included—every effort was made to *destroy* the very possibility of both heroism and martyrdom, to make all such choosing, actions, and suffering into an irrelevancy and a joke, if indeed not altogether impossible. The Jewish thinker considers the choiceless children; their helpless mothers; and finally—the achievement most revelatory of the essence of the whole Nazi world—the *Muselmänner,* these latter once free persons, and then dead while still alive: and he is filled not only with human grief but also with a metaphysical, religious, theological terror. Ever since Abraham, the Jewish people were singled out, for life unto themselves, and for a blessing unto the nations. And again and again throughout a long history, this people, however weary, responded to this singling-out act with the most profound freedom. (No response is as profoundly free as that to a singling-out act of God.) Ever since 1933, this people was singled out for death, and no effort or ingenuity was spared to make it into a curse to all those befriending it, while at the same time robbing it of the most elementary, most animal freedom. (No freedom is either more elementary or more animal than to relieve the bowels at the time of need.) The Reich had a research institute on the "Jewish question." Its work included serious, scholarly, professorial studies. These can have had no higher aim than to discover the deepest roots of Jewish existence and, after four thousand years of uninterrupted life, destroy them. The Jewish thinker is forced to ask: Was the effort successful?*

C

It is unthinkable that the twofold rupture should win out. It is unthinkable that the age-old fidelity of the religious Jews, having persisted through countless persecutions and against impossible odds—Yehuda Halevi expressed it best†—should be destroyed forever. It is unthinkable that the far less ancient, no less noble fidelity of the secular Jew—he holds fast, not to God, but to the "divine spark in man"—should be smashed beyond repair. It is unthinkable that the gulf between Jews and Gentiles, created and legislated since 1933, should be unbridgeable from the Jewish side so that the few but heroic, saintly attempts to bridge it from the Gentile side—we shall never forget such as Lichtenberg and Huber—should come to naught. It is this unthinkability that caused in my own mind, on first confronting it, the perception of a "614th commandment," or a "commanding Voice of Auschwitz," forbidding the post-Holocaust Jew to give Hitler posthumous victories. (This is the only statement of mine that ever widely caught on, articulating, as one reviewer aptly put it, "the sentiments . . . of Jewish shoe salesmen, accountants, policemen, cab-drivers, secretaries.")

But we must now face the fact—and here my thinking is forced to move decisively beyond the earlier perception just mentioned—that the unthinkable has been real in our time, hence has ceased to be unthinkable; and that therefore the "614th commandment" or "commanding Voice of Auschwitz" may well be a moral and religious necessity, but also, and at the same time, an ontological impossibility. In his time, as sober a thinker as Immanuel Kant could argue that since moral freedom, while undemonstrable, is at any rate also irrefutable, we all *can* do that which we *ought* to do. On our part and in our time, we need but

---

* With this question we are forced to go beyond Buber's stance toward the Holocaust, see above, section 7. This is not to say, however, that it ceases to be relevant, or that there may not be ways of recovering it.

† In the *Kuzari* he asserts that the great Jewish virtue is not saintliness or humility but rather fidelity, and implies that this belongs not to some but to the whole people. Jews could "escape degradation by a word spoken lightly" (IV, pp. 22, 23). Only because they stay in fidelity at their singled-out Jewish posts do they exist as Jews at all.

visualize ourselves as victims of the Nazi logic of destruction in order to see this brave doctrine dissolve into the desperate cry, "I cannot be obligated to do what I no longer can do!" Indeed, such may well have been the last silent cry of many, just before, made into the living dead, they were no longer capable of crying even in silence.* Nor are we rescued in this extremity by the Jewish symbol of *Tikkun* in any of its pre-Holocaust uses, even when, as in the most radical of them, a rupture is admitted and confronted. We have seen that during the Holocaust the Nazi logic of destruction murdered kabbalistic no less than nonkabbalistic Jews—and their *Tikkun* with them. A would-be kabbalistic *Tikkun* of *our own* post-Holocaust rupture would inevitably be a flight from *that* rupture, and hence from our post-Holocaust situation as a whole, into an eternity that could only be spurious.

We are thus driven back to insights gained earlier in the present work: the moral necessity of the "614th commandment" or "commanding Voice of Auschwitz" must be "rootless and groundless" (*bodenlos*) unless it is an "ontological" possibility; and it *can* be such a possibility only if it rests on an "ontic" reality. With this conclusion all our Jewish thinking and seeking either comes to a dead halt or else finds a *novum* that gives it a new point of departure.

D

The Tikkun *which for the post-Holocaust Jew is a moral necessity is a possibility because during the Holocaust itself a Jewish* Tikkun *was already actual.* This simple but enormous, nay, world-historical truth is the rock on which rests any authentic Jewish future, and any authentic future Jewish identity. (As is gradually emerging, it is also the pivotal point of the developing argument of this whole work.) We have already seen that the singled-out Jewish resistance *in extremis* to the singling-out assault in its own extremity is ontologically ultimate. As we now turn from the Jewish past to a prospective Jewish future we perceive that this ontological Ultimate—a *novum* of inexhaustible wonder, just as the Holocaust itself is a *novum* of inexhaustible horror—is the sole basis, now and henceforth, of a Jewish existence, whether religious or secular, that is

---

* The careful reader will notice that, compared to my *Encounters* (in which all of ch. II is taken up with the Kantian "ought"), the role of Kantianism has diminished in the present work. This is so because of considerations which reach their climax in the present section.

not permanently sick with the fear that, were it then and there rather than here and now, *everything*—God and man, commandments and promises, hopes and fears, joys and sorrows, life itself, and even a human way of dying—would be *indiscriminately* prey to the Nazi logic of destruction. The witnesses cited earlier all crowd back into the mind. We recall those we named. We also think of many we did not name and, above all, of the countless ones whose memory can only be nameless. As we ponder—ever reponder—their testimony, we freely concede that we, or others before us, may have romanticized it. We also concede that, yielding to all sorts of delusions, they may have done much romanticizing themselves. (Both errors are human.) But such concessions reveal only the more clearly that the astounding fact is not that many succumbed to the Nazi logic of destruction but rather that there were *some* who did *not* succumb. Indeed, even one would suffice to warrant a unique astonishment—and deny the evil logic its total victory.

We have reached this conclusion before. Our task now is to consider its implications for an authentic Jewish future. Above we repudiated the belief—an outworn idealism then, a case of humanistic twaddle now—that there is a core of human goodness that is indestructible. Now we must repudiate the belief—an outworn theology then, a case of Jewish twaddle now—that there is a Jewish substance—an *inyan enoli,* as it were*—that cannot be destroyed. Rather than in any such terms, the Jewish resistance to the singling-out Holocaust assault must be thought of as a life-and-death, day-and-night struggle, forever threatened with collapse and in fear of it, and saved from actual collapse—if at all—only by acts the source of whose strength will never cease to be astonishing. Their resistance, in short, was the *Tikkun* of a rupture. *This* Tikkun *is the* ultimate *ground of our own.*

E

To this theme—*their Tikkun* as the basis of *our* present and future Jewish *Tikkun*—we shall turn in detail forthwith. For the present, it is

---

* An allusion to Yehuda Halevi's *Kuzari, II,* pp. 34 ff. Halevi attempts to establish the continuity of the Divine-Jewish covenant through the dubious doctrine of a "divine content" planted hereditarily into the Jewish people. That he does not embrace racism is proved by the fact that the whole work is addressed to a would-be convert. Nor is any respectable modern Jewish thinker a racist. However, not a few have affirmed an absolutely indestructible Jewish tradition—religious, moral, or, more vaguely, cultural.

necessary, for a last time, to hark back to the theme of post-Holocaust philosophy and Christianity. We have seen that when Huber and Lichtenberg made their momentous choices—had their momentous trials —they each created a *Tikkun,* the one for future philosophy, the other for future Christianity. But what if, treated like Jews, they had been robbed of all choice, denied any trial, and had been subjected to the Nazi logic of destruction? (Other "Aryans" were treated in just this way.) Would they—*could* they—have resisted the irresistible? We did not ask this question when we considered their testimony. (It would then have been out of place.) We must ask it now. And, remembering the *Muselmänner,* we cannot answer it. (The question is—will always be— unanswerable.) Moreover, if we *can* say that they *might* have resisted, it is solely and exclusively because the irresistible Nazi logic of destruction was *in fact* resisted by some who were subjected to it, i.e., by Jews and those many non-Jews who were treated as if they were Jews themselves.* Hence we must say of a philosophical and Christian future exactly what we said of a Jewish future: Were it not for the Jewish *Tikkun* then and there—and that of quasi- and honorary Jews of whom Pelagia Lewinska has served as our symbol in this exploration—all authentic future philosophers and Christians would be sick with a permanent fear—in this case, the fear that, were they then and there rather than here and now, they, their prayers, their philosophical thoughts, would all be indiscriminately prey to the Nazi logic of destruction. This is what was meant (or some of what was meant) by the above assertion that the Jewish *Tikkun* in the Holocaust world is not only enormous in significance but world-historical.

Directly, then, the *Tikkun* of such as Pelagia Lewinska, the Lublin and Buchenwald Hasidim, the Warsaw Ghetto fighters, is the basis of a future Jewish *Tikkun.* Indirectly, it is also a pillar—not, to be sure, the sole pillar, but indispensable—of a future philosophy and Christianity. We thus arrive at a strange, unexpected, even paradoxical conclusion. Then and there, no effort was spared to make the Jewish people into a curse for all those befriending it. Yet philosophers and Christians today and tomorrow—no other group of Gentiles can be considered within the limits of the present exploration—are reached by a blessing across the abyss, coming to them from the darkest Jewish night. It is a blessing the like of which the world has never seen.

---

* See the above argument (section 8B) to the effect that insofar as the Nazi logic of destruction aimed at the self-destruction of its victims, it can be understood in terms of the Nazi scheme of things only if these victims are Jews.

F

Christians after the Holocaust, we have seen, must be Zionist on behalf not only of Jews but also of Christianity itself. Jews after the Holocaust, it now emerges, must be Zionist on behalf not only of themselves but also of the whole post-Holocaust world. That a Jewish state is an authentic modern project without need for justification through the Holocaust has already been shown.* Yet to be shown in pages to come is its place within a post-Holocaust Jewish self-understanding. At stake in the present context is the role of a Jewish state in a post-Holocaust mending of Jewish-Gentile relations. Such a mending is needed after the Holocaust. During the Holocaust, Jewish powerlessness placed Jews absolutely at the mercy of Nazi enemies and democratic friends alike, encouraging murder among the first and among the second, half-heartedness in opposition, or even total indifference. After the Holocaust, the Jewish people owe the whole world the duty of not encouraging its vices—in the case of the wicked, murderous instincts, in the case of the good people, indifference mixed with hypocrisy—by continuing to tolerate powerlessness. Without a Jewish state there could be no post-Holocaust *Tikkun* of Jewish-Gentile relations, from the Jewish any more than from the Gentile side. The "Jewish emergence from powerlessness," occurring when it did, has been and continues to be a moral achievement of world-historical import.†

This, of course, is not universally recognized. The United Nations

---

* See above, ch. III, section 12. That Zionism and the State of Israel became thematic in this book before the Holocaust is, of course, not accidental.

† Persistent attempts to obscure or deny this fact arise from a combination of repressed guilt on the part of the good people, and a new form of Jew-hatred on the part of the wicked. Arnold Toynbee's equation of Israeli behavior toward Palestinian Arabs with Nazi behavior toward Jews is, one hopes, a case of the first. A case of the second is the PLO National Covenant's denial of the same right to self-determination to Jews that is claimed on behalf of Palestinian Arabs themselves. And the two combine whenever the wicked succeed in persuading the good that the State of Israel is a radical injustice—a punishment of the innocent (i.e., the Palestinian Arabs) for sins committed by others (i.e., the German Nazis). The British White Paper of 1939 that stopped Jewish immigration into Palestine at the time of greatest need was inspired by Arab protests. When the 1946 Anglo-American committee recommended, not a Jewish state but only the admission to Palestine of 100,000 Jewish survivors, the Arabs, by then fully aware what *these* were survivors *of,* flatly rejected the recommendation and declared a general strike. These two examples are sufficient proof to the effect that if any state or political leadership at the time was innocent of the shedding of Jewish blood, the Palestinian Arab leadership was not among them.

Organization condemns Zionism as a form of racism. Clerical councils exalt a "moderate" PLO that shows no signs of moderateness. A world indifferent to Jerusalem in Arab hands is greatly concerned when she is in Jewish hands. To go beyond Zionism and Israel in this melancholy litany, Nazi criminals are widely at large, unmolested. Anti-Jewish hate literature flourishes. Synagogues are bombed in Paris. There are even Jews who wish the State of Israel would "go away." And since Vietnamese boat-people now, much like Jewish boat-people then, roam the seas, one wonders whether today Hitler is not winning posthumous victories throughout the world. Despite the new reality that is Israel, one must therefore ask a radical question. *Jewish trust in the Gentile world was ruptured by the Holocaust: how, in the world of today, can it be mended?*

Of course one wants to avoid this question. Any Jew today wants to say that there *is* no such rupture any longer, and hence no need for a mending, and this in gratitude to Allied soldiers then (without whom no Jews would survive); in friendship with many Gentiles now; and also, perhaps above all, in simple fairness to a new generation of Germans that knows not Auschwitz and bears no guilt. (Not all anti-Zionists are anti-Semites; not all anti-Semites are murderers; and, above all, the post-Holocaust world is not the Holocaust world itself.) A Jew *wants* to say all this; but he cannot say it. For he remembers Kierkegaard—having cited him against others, we must also cite him against ourselves—and he is forced to spurn a course at once so easy and so obvious. The Holocaust ruptured Jewish-Gentile relations once. If unmended, the rupture would haunt Jewish-Gentile relations forever, even if learned professors could give proof absolute to the effect that a repetition is impossible. Thus a question arises for Jews and Gentiles alike that brooks no evasion. For Gentiles it is: If *per improbabibile aut impossibile* there *were* a repetition, could they trust themselves? (This question extends to Jews as well—just in the unlikely case that, next time, they were among the "Ayrans.") For Jews it is: Profoundly and radically rather than merely superficially, can they ever again trust the world? For four millennia of uninterrupted existence, the Jewish people, even when totally abandoned, has managed to keep a bond with the world, if only because it understood its existence as meant for a blessing. The post-Holocaust Jew must ask: Is this bond broken forever? Is Jewish existence henceforth condemned to utter solitariness?

Meant for a blessing, the Jewish people was treated time and again as though it were a curse. Yet except for moments of despair, its prophets and sages have never in turn wished a curse upon the nations. The tone was set by Lamentations, following the first fall of Jerusalem: "Let it not come unto you, all ye that pass by!" (1:12). Following the second fall of the City, a Midrashic author commented: "The community of Israel says to the nations of the world: 'May that not come upon you which has come upon me! May not happen to you what has happened to me!' " This Midrash is last and climactic in *Midrashim of Lament and Comfort,* an anthology published for German Jews in Germany by a German rabbi in 1935, the year of the Nuremberg laws.[1] So early was an attempt made, on the Jewish side, to narrow (if not close) the Jewish-Gentile abyss.

This was, of course, before the gulf had *become* an abyss. After that catastrophe Jews cannot speak the biblical words to unrepentant Nazis, accomplices, bystanders, for they cannot speak to them at all. They can and must speak to those upon whom it, or something resembling it, has come—starving African children, Gulag slave laborers, boat-people roaming the seas. But can the Jewish people speak to a world which, first, let it happen and, now, lets all this happen? Can there be a *Tikkun* of the ruptured Jewish trust?

From the Gentile side of the Jewish-Gentile relations, what will happen will happen. From the Jewish side, it is clear enough what ought to happen. Gentile friends, many or few, are spending themselves in the attempt to repair the great rupture of trust. Jews cannot abandon these efforts made on the Gentile side, but must respond to them on the Jewish side. This much, we say, is clear enough. It is even trivially clear, since not sharing in the mending of Jewish-Gentile relations would be handing posthumous victories to Hitler. Yet here as before we must ask whether what is morally necessary is also ontologically possible. For what haunts Jews and Gentiles alike in their search for mutual trust—what *cannot but* haunt them—is whether, if they were then and there rather than here and now, they could trust themselves—and, therefore, each other. It is the crucial question. And so long as it remains unasked, or if asked remains wholly without answer, every expression of "Never again," Jewish or Gentile, belongs into the realm of mere pious hopes, gestures, or prayers that, rather than mend the broken trust, are themselves untrusted.

A Tikkun *of Jewish-Gentile trust, genuine even if fragmentary, is possible from the Jewish side, here and now, because a corresponding* Tikkun *was already begun from the Gentile side then and there.* Above we came upon a blessing that reaches post-Holocaust philosophy and Christianity from the darkest Jewish night. We come upon a blessing now, no less unique, that reaches post-Holocaust Jewish life and thought from this same night. (This is no symmetry constructed by armchair philosophy. Coming as it does from the testimony of survivors, it is rather a stumbling block to all armchair understanding.) In other worlds, a hero or martyr serves, and is himself sustained by, a great and noble cause as, going beyond all ordinary decency, he risks or gives his life. In the Holocaust world, a Gentile's decency, if shown toward Jews, made him into something worse than a criminal—an outlaw, vermin—just as were Jews themselves; and, as he risked or gave his life, there was nothing in the world to sustain him, except ordinary decency itself. Above we saw, in Huber and Lichtenberg, a *Tikkun*, respectively, of the Idea of Man and the Christian Word. Now we have come upon something greater still: in the Holocaust world there occurred a *Tikkun* of ordinary decency. Those that performed this *Tikkun* may insist that they did nothing unusual. However, a post-Holocaust Jew—and the post-Holocaust world —can never cease to be amazed.*

This is by no means to say that ordinary decency has inherited the earth. Then and there, the number of the "righteous among the nations" was small. If *per improbabibile aut impossibile* there *were* a repetition, their number, for all the far-reaching efforts to learn lessons from the Holocaust, might be no larger. Conceivably—our age is grim—it might even be smaller, so that the "contracting logic" which Rosenzweig once found applicable to Jews might come to dominate the decency of humanity. Even so the post-Holocaust Jew must stake much—almost all—on the trust that it is these, many or few, who represent humanity; and that, like Rosenzweig's "eternal people," they will never vanish wholly from the earth.

G

What is a Jew? Who is a Jew? After *this* catastrophe, what is a Jew's relation to the Jewish past? We resume our original question as we turn from one rupture in post-Holocaust Jewish existence—of the bond with the Gentile world—to the other—of the bond with his own past history, past tradition, past God.

After all previous catastrophes ever since biblical times, a Jew could understand himself as part of a holy remnant. Not that the generation itself was holy, a presumptuous view, and one devoid of any real meaning. The generation was rather *heir* to holy ones—not to the many who

---

* Eliezer Berkowitz has rightly remarked that according to some Jewish writers "righteous Gentiles" were so numerous during the Holocaust that he must wonder how it could happen that most of his relatives were murdered. It is true that these righteous ones were few, that their number is depressing; the quality of these few, however, is an abiding wonder.

had fallen away but rather to the few that, whether in life or the death of martyrdom, had stayed in fidelity at their singled-out Jewish post. Was there ever a self-definition by a flesh-and-blood people that staked so much—staked *all*—on fidelity? It is the deepest definition of Jewish identity in all Jewish history.

It cannot, however, be the self-definition of this Jewish generation for, except for an accident, we, the Jews of today, would either have been murdered or never born. *We are not a holy remnant. We are an accidental remnant.* However we may wish to evade the grim fact, this is the core definition of Jewish identity today.

The result is that we, on our part, cannot consider ourselves heir to the few alone. (For the religious among us, the martyrs and their prayers; for the secularists, the heroes and their battles.) We are obliged to consider ourselves heir to the *whole* murdered people. We think of those made into *Muselmänner* by dint of neither virtue nor vice but some "banal incident." We think of the children; their mothers; of the countless saints, sinners, and ordinary folk who, unsuspecting to the end, were gassed in the twinkling of an eye. And what reaches us is nothing so much as *the cry of an innocence that shakes heaven and earth; that can never be stilled; that overwhelms our hopes, our prayers, our thought.* Maimonides is said to have ruled that any Jew murdered for no reason other than being a Jew is to be considered holy. Folk tradition, already existing, cites Maimonides to this effect and views *all* the Jewish victims of the Holocaust as *kedoshim*—as holy ones. Only in this and no other sense are we, the accidental remnant, also a holy remnant. *In this sense, however, our holiness is ineluctable and brooks no honest escape or refusal.*

This circumstance places us into a hermeneutical situation that, after all that has been said about a post-Holocaust *Tikkun*, is new and unique still. Indeed, the dilemma in which we are placed is so extreme, so unprecedented, so full of anguish as to seem to tear us in two; and as to cause us to wonder whether, at the decisive point where all comes to a head, a post-Holocaust *Tikkun* of any kind is not seen, after all, to be impossible.

The dilemma is as follows. If (as we must) we hold fast to the children, the mothers, the *Muselmänner,* to the whole murdered people and its innocence, then we must surely despair of any possible *Tikkun;* but then we neglect or ignore the few and select—those with the opportunity to resist, the will and strength to resist, deriving the will and strength we know not whence—whose *Tikkun* (as we have seen) precedes and makes mandatory our own. And if (as also we must) we hold fast to just these select and their *Tikkun,* then *our Tikkun,* made possible by *theirs,* neglects and ignores all those who performed no heroic or saintly deeds such as to merit holiness and who yet, murdered as they were in utter innocence, must be considered holy. Not accidentally, "Holocaust theology" has been moving toward two extremes—a "God-is-dead" kind of despair, and a faith for which, having been "with God in hell," either nothing has happened or all is mended.* However, post-Holocaust thought—it includes theological concerns but is not confined to them—must dwell, however painful and precariously, between the extremes, and seek a *Tikkun* as it endures the tension.

The *Tikkun* emerging from this tension is composed of three elements: (a) a recovery of Jewish tradition—a "going back into possibilities of [Jewish] *Dasein* that once was *da*";† (b) a recovery in the quite different sense of recuperation from an illness; and (c) a fragmentariness attaching to these two recoveries that makes them both ever-incomplete and ever-laden with risk. Without a recovered Jewish tradition—for the religious Jew, the Word of God; for the secular Jew, the word of man and his "divine spark"—there is no Jewish future. Without a recuperation from the illness, the tradition (and hence the Jewish future) must either flee from the Holocaust or be destroyed by it. And without the stern acceptance of both the fragmentariness and the risk, in both aspects of the recovery, *our* Jewish *Tikkun* lapses into unauthenticity by letting *theirs*, having "done its job," lapse into the irrelevant past.

To hold fast to the last of these three elements is hardest but also most essential. Once Schelling and Hegel spoke scathingly about theological contemporaries who were momentarily awakened from their dogmatic slumber by the Kantian philosophy but soon used that philosophy as a soporific: every old dogma, bar none, could become a "postulate of practical reason." Jewish thought today is in a similar danger. We remember the Holocaust; we are inspired by the martyrdom and the resistance: and then the inspiration quickly degenerates into this, that every dogma, religious or secular, is restored as if nothing had happened. However, the unredeemed anguish of Auschwitz must be ever-present *with* us, even as it is past *for* us. *Yom Ha-Shoah cannot now, or ever after, be assimilated to the ninth of Av.*

The attempt, to be sure, is widely made; but it is impossible. The

---

* The most influential expression of the first extreme is Richard Rubenstein's *After Auschwitz* (Indianapolis and New York: Bobbs-Merrill, 1966). A poignant expression of the second is Eliezer Berkowitz, *With God in Hell* (New York: Sanhedrin, 1979). As is clear from his *Faith after the Holocaust* (New York: Ktav, 1973), Berkowitz does not assert either that nothing has happened or all is mended. He does, however, affirm a *faith* for which this is true, i.e., one which, though deeply shaken by the Holocaust, is not altered in consequence.

† An allusion to Heidegger, see above, section 3.

age-old day of mourning is for catastrophes that are punishment for
Jewish sins, vicarious atonement for the sins of others, or in any case
meaningful, if inscrutable, divine decrees. The new day of mourning
cannot be so understood, for it is for the children, the mothers, the
Muselmänner—the whole murdered people in its utter innocence. Nor
has the *Yom Ha-Shoah* ceremonial any such content, for it commemo-
rates not Jewish sin but innocent Jewish suffering; not sins of others
vicariously atoned but such as are incapable of atonement; not an inscrutable decree to be borne with patience but one resisted then, and to
be resisted ever after. As for attempts to find a ninth-of-Av-meaning in
the Holocaust—punishment for the sins of Zionism; or of anti-Zionism;
or a moral stimulus to the world—their very perversity confirms a conclusion reached earlier in the present work: *Galut* Judaism, albeit most
assuredly not *Galut* itself, has come to an end.

Even so the attempt to assimilate *Yom Ha-Shoah* to the ninth of Av
must be viewed with a certain sympathy. The cycle of the Jewish liturgi-
cal year—Rosenzweig described it sublimely—is an experience antici-
pating redemption. The ninth of Av, though a note of discord, fits into
this cycle: but does *Yom Ha-Shoah*? The ninth of Av does not touch the
Yom Kippur—the Jewish "experience" of the "end" not through
"dying" but living. *Yom Ha-Shoah* cannot but touch it; indeed it threatens to overwhelm the Yom Kippur. Martin Buber has asked his post-
Holocaust Jewish question—not whether one can still "believe" in God
but whether one can still "speak" to Him. Can the Jew still speak to God
on Yom Kippur? If not how can he speak to Him at all? The Jewish fear
of *Yom Ha-Shoah*—the wish to assimilate it to the ninth of Av—is a fear,
in behalf not only of *Galut* Judaism but also of Judaism itself.

"Judaism and the Holocaust" must be the last, climactic question
not only of the present exploration but also of this whole work. Meanwhile we ask what ways of Jewish *Tikkun* there could be even if the
climactic question had to be indefinitely suspended. These ways are
many; their scope is universal. (The task is *Tikkun Olam*, to mend the
world.) Yet they would all become insubstantial without one *Tikkun* that
is a collective, particular Jewish response to history. This *Tikkun* may be
said to have begun when the first Jewish "DP" gave a radical response to
what he had experienced. Non-Jewish DPs, displaced though they were,
had a home to which to return. This Jewish DP did not—and even so was
barred by bayonets and laws from the land that had been home once,
and that Jewish labor was making into home once again. Understand-
ably, many of his comrades accepted these facts with a shrug of centuries, and waited for someone's charity that would give them the bless-
ings of refuge, peace, and oblivion. (They waited in camps, often the

very places of their suffering—and for years.) This Jewish DP took his destiny in his own hands, disregarded the legal niceties of a world that still classified him as Pole or German, still without Jewish rights, and made his way to the one place where there would be neither peace nor oblivion but which would be, without ifs and buts, home.

The *Tikkun* that is Israel is fragmentary. This fact need not be stressed, for it is reported almost daily in the newspapers. The power of the State is small, as is the State itself. It can offer a home to captive Jews but cannot force captors to set them free. Limited abroad, it is limited at home as well. It cannot prevent strife. It cannot even guarantee its Jewish citizens a culture or a strong Jewish identity. *Galut* Judaism may have ended; but there is no end to *Galut* itself, inside as well as outside the State of Israel.

If the *Tikkun* is fragmentary, the whole enterprise is laden with risk. (This too the papers report assiduously.) Within, *Yerida*—emigration of Israelis—threatens to rival or overtake *Aliyah,* the Ingathering. Without, for all the talk of a comprehensive peace, implacable enemies remain; and while enemies elsewhere seek to destroy a regime, or at most conquer a state, *these* enemies seek destruction of a state—and renewed exile for its Jewish inhabitants.

What then is the *Tikkun?* It is Israel itself. It is a state founded, maintained, defended by a people who—so it was once thought—had lost the arts of statecraft and self-defense forever. It is the replanting and reforestation of a land that—so it once seemed—was unredeemable swamps and desert. It is a people gathered from all four corners of the earth on a territory with—so the experts once said—not room enough left to swing a cat. It is a living language that—so even friends once feared—was dead beyond revival. It is a City rebuilt that—so once the consensus of mankind had it—was destined to remain holy ruins. And it is in and through all this, on behalf of the accidental remnant, after unprecedented death, a unique celebration of life.

It is true—so fragmentary and precarious is the great *Tikkun*—that many want no share of it, deny it, distort it, slander it. But slanders and denials have no power over those who are astonished—ever again astonished—by the fact that in this of all ages the Jewish people have returned—*have been* returned?—to Jerusalem. Their strength, when failing, is renewed by the faith that despite all, because of all, the "impulse from below" will call forth an "impulse from above."

NOTE

1. *Midraschim der Klage und des Zuspruchs,* ed. Max Dienemann (Berlin: Schocken, 1935); *Midrash Rabba,* Lamentation I 40.

John T. Pawlikowski

THE CHALLENGE OF THE HOLOCAUST FOR CHRISTIAN THEOLOGY

The reflections that follow are those of a Catholic trying to grasp the implications of the Nazi conflagration. They come as a response to the challenge posed by the church historian Franklin Littell. According to Professor Littell, the Holocaust is something that happened to Christians as well as to Jews. In his view, the Holocaust "remains the major event in recent church history—signalizing . . . the rebellion of the baptized against the Lord of History. . . . Christianity itself has been 'put to the question.' "[1] For a Catholic Christian, the following theological issues emerge from serious reflection concerning this epochal event.

Emil Fackenheim claims that it is immoral to search for meaning in the Holocaust.[2] In one sense he is correct. There is no way in which one can possibly make a positive affirmation about any aspect of the Holocaust without destroying all human sensibility. However, one cannot ignore evil and must confront what happened to the spirit of the human community as a result of Hitler's attempt at the "Final Solution." To fail in this task would be to endanger our humanity. In the final analysis, one must recognize the Holocaust as a *rational* event. This position denies the claim of those who interpret it as a fundamentally irrational event.[3] To place the Holocaust in the category of the irrational would offer some relief for the human spirit.

Irrationality has always been manifested in human experience. As tragic as its consequences can be, the challenge to the overall creative and hopeful image of the human person would not be as great if one were to opt for the irrationality hypothesis.

One must recognize the rational origins of the Holocaust. It was a planned event with roots in philosophies developed by thinkers still recognized as giants of liberal Western thought. In reflecting about the Holocaust, one must confront theological attitudes central to Christianity almost from its inception. The ideological parents of the Holocaust—Western philosophy and Christian theology—represent the mainstream of western culture and not its lunatic fringe.

TRANSFORMATION OF VALUES

Within a rationality perspective, what emerges from the Holocaust is the attempt to create "supermen," to develop that truly liberated epitome of universal humanity. To this end, all the "dregs of humanity" —the Jews, the Poles, gay people, the Gypsies, the mentally/physically handicapped—had to be eliminated as "polluters" of true humanity. The Nazis endeavored to realize the "new man" that Nietzsche had spoken of so forcefully in his writings. This "Final Solution" was not exclusively aimed at the elimination of the Jews. As Uriel Tal strongly maintains, the "Final Solution" was meant to answer a universal crisis of man. Its aim was the total transformation of values. It wished to free humankind from the shackles of a God concept and its attendant notions of moral responsibility, redemption, sin and revelation. It sought to transfer theological ideas into anthropological and political concepts. As Tal puts it,

> God became man, but not in the theological New Testament sense of the incarnation of the word . . . or in accordance with Paul's understanding of the incarnation of God in Christ in whom "the whole fulness of deity dwells bodily" (Col. 2:9). In the new conception, God becomes man in a political sense as a member of the Aryan race whose highest representative on earth is the Fuhrer. Communication with the Fuhrer became communion. This transfiguration took place through public mass meetings which were staged and celebrated as sacred cults as well as by means of education, indoctrination and inculcation of discipline. As a result, a personal identification with the Father was made possible in terms of the Father of the State, the Son of the race and the Spirit of the *Volk*.[4] . . .

GOD-HUMAN RELATIONSHIP REEXAMINED

In light of the Nazi experience, however, Christian theology cannot blindly or naively welcome the new sense of human liberation. In *After Auschwitz*, Rubenstein has correctly interpreted the Holocaust as a manifestation of what can happen when man senses his tremendous power and has no adequate theology with which to direct its use.[5] Therefore, the challenge addressed to theology today, both Christian and Jewish, is whether it can provide an understanding and experience of the God-human relationship which can guide this newly found power creatively and constructively. A mere emphasis on the scriptural understanding of human co-creatorship will not prove sufficient by itself. For Christian theology, re-incorporating the sense of this co-creatorship found in the Hebrew Scriptures would mark an important and unavoidable step in the right direction. Nevertheless, contemporary man still finds himself in a freer situation than biblical man; he perceives dimensions to his co-creatorship which far exceed the consciousness of the biblical world. Can post-Holocaust theology articulate an understanding of God and religion which will prevent the creative powers of man from being transformed into the destructive force we have seen exposed in all its ugliness in the Holocaust? That is the question before us.

Rubenstein further insists that after Auschwitz only paganism can guard against turning human creativity into destructiveness on a massive scale. He writes:

> . . . I would like to offer my own confession of faith after Auschwitz. I am a pagan. To be a pagan means to find once again one's roots as a child of earth and to see one's own existence as wholly and totally an earthly existence. It means once again to understand that for mankind the true divinities are the gods of earth, not the high gods of time; the gods of home and hearth, not the gods of wandering, though wanderers we must be. Though every single establishment Jewish theologian rejects this position, the Jewish people have given their assent—with their feet. They have gone home. The best part of that people has ceased to be wanderers. They have once again found a place of their own on this earth. That is paganism.[6]

Rubenstein claims the need to affirm strongly that the human community must once again find its roots in the earth. This claim, however, is an insufficient response to the Holocaust.

FRESH SENSE OF TRANSCENDENCE

Accompanying the new earthliness which Rubenstein seeks, there must also be the recovery of a fresh sense of transcendence. Devoid of such a sense of transcendence, the utilization of the tremendously more powerful dimensions of human creativity that we have stumbled across during the last two centuries will inevitably lead to the hideousness witnessed in the Holocaust. If one analyzes the attempts to create new societies within the context of philosophies where transcendence has been ignored or positively denied, one will find frequent attempts to suppress diversity in the name of creating the "universal person" and (in many cases) the destruction of human life on an unprecedented scale. Much of Western liberal thought has been guilty of the former. Whether in its European manifestation, where it could not fit Jewish self-identity into its universal scheme[7] or its American version where the universalizing attempt represented by the Melting Pot tried to squeeze Blacks, Jews, White ethnics, Native Americans and Chicanos into a basically Northern European cultural mold, modern Western thought signalled cultural and at times even physical death for those whose origins did not allow them to fit easily its pre-conceived matrix.[8] At least indirectly, Western liberal thought was responsible for the Holocaust. By breaking the tight hold the God-concept had on previous generations, it paved the way for greater human freedom and self-sufficiency without realistically assessing the potential of the destructive forces within mankind to pervert this freedom into the cruelty revealed by the Nazi experiment. Thus, the Holocaust shattered much of the grandeur of Western liberal thought. In some ways it represents the ultimate achievement of the person totally "liberated" from God.

The ultimate effects of an attempt to create the "new man," combined with an explicit rejection of transcendence, can be seen even more clearly in the creation of "new" societies such as the Soviet Union and the People's Republic of China where millions died in the struggle to create a so-called "heaven upon earth." One can perceive the identical pattern being repeated at the present moment in parts of the Third World.

Those of us who approach this question from a religious perspective must be totally honest. Past history has shown that many have been slaughtered at the instigation of religious groups which clearly affirmed a sense of transcendence. We need only look to the Crusades, to the slaughter of perhaps ten million Jews since the birth of Christianity, and to the annihilation of scores of Native Americans in the creation of a "new Zion" on this side of the Atlantic and the fertile ground traditional Christian anti-Semitism provided for the Nazi ideology, for a brutal confirmation of this view. The past history, however, should not prevent us from a forthright critique of the abuses and death that non- or anti-transcendence philosophies have inflicted upon society. We are not going to return to the world of the Crusades and the Inquisition. While it is important for Christians to know this history, it is not really the problem we face today. The threat before us is rather ovens and gas chambers manned by those who would claim to have the ultimate replacement for the religious perspective.

Rubenstein's paganism is not the answer. It fails to adequately combine the new sense of human freedom when it has been totally divorced from any guiding norms beyond mankind, something verified in the Holocaust and the other "universalizing" attempts of our time. The new theology of the world, currently fashionable in large segments of Christianity and best represented in the Latin American liberation theologians, also proves inadequate in the light of the Holocaust. While it has accurately captured some of the new spirit of human freedom, this new theology tries to ground its theological understanding of freedom too completely in the biblical tradition. It fails to consider seriously the extent to which contemporary human experience has actually shattered part of the worldview within which the biblical experience was framed. There has also been a deep and disturbing reluctance on the part of people connected with the liberal/left circle of Catholicism (in which the liberation theologies have their strongest foothold) to deal with an event like the Holocaust. They tend to view it as past history and hence dismiss it as not terribly relevant for present discussions. But in doing so they ignore the opportunity to come to grips with the tremendous potential for human destructiveness as the underside of human freedom that the Holocaust revealed. Any theology that fails to grapple seriously with this phenomenon of destructiveness will ultimately prove irrelevant for the current situation.

The task facing present-day theology is to find a way to articulate a notion of transcendence which can counterbalance the potential for destructiveness found in the contemporary human condition while guiding human freedom towards the creation of societies in which the dignity and diversity of individual persons is affirmed and maintained within the context of a deep commitment to communal responsibility on a national and international plane. Theology alone cannot develop this new sense of transcendence. It will have to emerge from experiments in religious experience in which persons genuinely experience contact with a personal power beyond themselves. It will have to be an experience that heals the destructive tendencies within all of us; it will have to provide contact with a loving presence which draws us beyond ourselves and in so doing provides a moral norm greater than ourselves which can guide and judge our conduct toward our fellow human beings and the earth we have been given. For the newly liberated person to be able to work consistently towards the creation of a just and humane society he/she must sense that there is a judgment upon their endeavors that goes beyond mere human judgment. This judgment however, can no longer be rooted in fear of punishment as it was in ages past. The modern experience of the human community is that man can perpetrate the worst atrocities with seeming impunity. The only norm that can curb such atrocities is one rooted in an experience of love and unity beyond the narrow dimensions of this earth and the concomitant realization that actions such as those which surfaced in the Holocaust and in the building of some of the "new societies" of the Marxist and Third World block the ultimate realization of such love and unity. This model must become a deeply felt perception of the human community and not merely a theological idea. Theology's role is simply, but very importantly, to try to express the reality of this experience, to speak of God and to address the human community, to describe their mutual relationship in a way which is faithful to the new understanding of human freedom that Nietzsche so dramatically brought to the modern consciousness.

PROVIDENCE, OMNISCIENCE, AND OMNIPOTENCE

How is theology to speak of transcendence and of God against the background of the new consciousness of human liberation? The answer at this juncture in history can be tentative and exploratory at best. However, one can insist that it will have to follow along the paths suggested by Gregory Baum, Paul Tillich and Teilhard de Chardin. Baum maintains the Church's view of God as Lord of history necessarily implies that somehow human sins and crimes are in keeping with God's permissive will. God was thought of as permitting evil in the present, for the sake of a greater good to be achieved in the future. Even Auschwitz, according to this theology, had a place in divine providence. Does not such a view make a monster out of God? Baum must ask.[9] Baum finds he must reject the traditional concepts of providence, omniscience and omnipotence:

God is not provident . . . in the sense that as ruler of the world he has a master plan for human history by which he provides help for the people in need, especially those who ask him for it, and by which he guides the lives of men, acknowledging their freedom . . . (or) in which God has permitted evil and . . . calculated its damaging effects and compensated for them in the final outcome. . . . (But God is provident in the sense that in whatever trap man falls, a summons continued to address him and offer him new life that makes him more truly human.

This leads Baum to conclude that

> God is omniscient (only) in the sense that there exists no human situation, however difficult, however obscure, however frightening, in which God remains silent or . . . in which a summons to greater insight is not available. . . . (Similarly) God is omnipotent (only) in the sense that there is . . . no situation, however destructive, in which an inner strength is not offered to man, allowing him to assume greater possession of his humanity.

With this understanding, Baum believes, we can affirm the radical opposition between God and evil. Evil is not permitted by him. Rather, "God is constantly at work among men, summoning them . . . to discern the evil in human life, to wrestle against it, to be converted away from it, to correct their environment, to redirect history, to transform the human community. The death that destroys is never the will of God. On the contrary God is the never-ending summons to life."[10]

According to Baum the expression "This is God's will" must never be taken to mean that God wants or even permits terrible calamities or injustices to occur. However, it can mean (for a person of great faith) continuing trust that God will summon forth new insights, and will create life out of death in new ways:

> Jewish men and women on the way to the extermination chambers may have said to themselves that this incomprehensible and groundless evil was in some mysterious way God's will—in the sense that they continued to trust in God. But on the lips of an observer such a statement would be a dreadful blasphemy.[11]

For Baum, God's power over the world can no longer be explained as the miraculous action by which he makes things happen as he pleases, but the redemptive action by which he enables men to deal with their own problems and by which he calls people to "resist evil and find ways of conquering it."[12]

GOD AFTER AUSCHWITZ

In struggling with the same issues as Baum, Paul Tillich spoke of a new understanding of divine providence along the following lines. Any notion of providence that implies even a vague promise that, with divine help, everything will result in a good outcome must be rejected in the light of events like Auschwitz. We cannot deny that there are many things that come to a bad end. More positively put, Tillich says that divine providence consists in this:

> . . . when death rains from heaven as it does now, when hunger and persecution drive millions from place to place as they do now, and when prisons and slums all over the world distort the humanity of the bodies and souls of men as they do now—we can boast in that time, and just in that time, that even all of this cannot separate us from the love of God. In this sense, and in this sense alone, all things work together for good, for the *ultimate* good, the eternal love and the kingdom of God. Faith in divine providence is the faith that nothing can prevent us from fulfilling the ultimate meaning of our existence. Providence does not mean a divine planning by which everything is predetermined, as in an efficient machine. Rather, providence means that there is a creative and saving possibility implied in every situation which cannot be destroyed by any event. Providence means that the demoniac and destructive forces within ourselves and our world can never have an unbreakable grasp upon us, and that the bond which connects us with the fulfilling love can never be disrupted.[13]

Finally, in this regard, Teilhard de Chardin has written that "The only God we can now adore 'in spirit and truth' is, in a phrase that appeals to me, the synthesis of the (Christian) God 'above,' the (Marxist) God of 'ahead.' "[14] One must take issue with those who have claimed that God died in Auschwitz, that we are obligated to forget about transcendence after the death camps. Blaming God for the horrors of Nazism is in many ways a "cop-out." Why blame God for the nightmare? To do so is to indulge in a blatant form of escapism. The real challenge of the Holocaust is whether we can say anything positive and constructive about the dignity of man after the exposure of the evil forces within humanity during this period of history. The present claim is that we can, but only if we continue to affirm the existence of a God who, with his presence, can heal the wounds of Auschwitz and re-kindle within humanity the potentialities for love which the Holocaust, because of the divine origins of this love force, could not completely eradicate. Nevertheless, it is correct to say that one notion of God died in Auschwitz. The post-Auschwitz God-human relationship will have to be one in which we clearly acknowledge God's utter and inescapable dependence upon man as a partner in bringing about the ultimate salvation of the world. The God whom we used to invoke through our prayers to intervene and correct the ills of this world died at Auschwitz. People begin wars; people began the Holocaust; people must stop them. God will not intercede to stop such perversions of true human freedom. As Franklin Sherman has correctly noted, the God who lives after Auschwitz is the God who participates in the sufferings of men.[15] For the humanity of man shares in the humanity of God in an intimate and profound way. God cannot be truly God until he has become fully reconciled with mankind in the final Kingdom. But what Auschwitz has taught us is that God will not, perhaps even cannot, effect the full redemption of that part of his being which he has graciously shared with man unless man assumes his role of co-creator.

In the act of creation God gave mankind freedom. The consequences of that act are irreversible. God learned what we too have come to know—that no one can fully develop apart from community. So God chose to create community by sharing what part of himself we term his humanity. But all meaningful sharing involves a risk and exposes one to hurt. In creating this sharing situation he opened himself to the potential for suffering that Auschwitz historically realized. The Holocaust has made it clear that God needs man as much as man needs God.

The Holocaust has likewise shown us that the need to retain some sense of transcendence whereby we continue to be touched by the gifts of grace and love of which Baum and Tillich have spoken. Unless that transcendence begins from within the human person and moves outward in the way Chardin has spoken of (in the need to forge Marxism and Christianity), then the world will continue to experience repetitions of human degradation. Though some antitranscendence philosophies like Marxism and Western liberal philosophies have produced a betterment of the quality of life on several levels, the abuses we have seen in both, as well as the potential for even greater destructiveness we have been shocked by in the Holocaust, cannot be curbed without some maintenance of a belief in a transcendent God. Contemporary people must once again come to know this transcendent God in an intimate, personal way through new forms of prayer, through art and dance, through meditation, liturgy and poetry.

The importance of this task—helping contemporary Catholics to once more develop personal contact with a loving God—cannot be overestimated. To the extent that Catholic theologians have rethought theology in light of the Holocaust, the concentration has tended to be on Christology and the Christian-Jewish relationship. While Christology certainly deserves scrutiny in this post-Auschwitz era with the "hermeneutics of suspicion" developed by David Tracy, Tracy is quite correct in faulting Catholic theologians for their general neglect in examining the even more fundamental God question:

> . . . as far as I am aware, the ultimate theological issue, the understanding of God, has yet to receive much reflection from Catholic theologians. And yet, as Schleirmacher correctly insisted, the doctrine of God can never be "another" doctrine for theology but must pervade all doctrines. Here Jewish theology, in its reflections on the reality of God since the *Tremendum* of the Holocaust, has led the way for all serious theological reflection.[16]

But if we are to take Tracy's call to heart we will need to look much more seriously at the phenomenon of human consciousness in light of the Freudian/Jungian revolutions. We must discover ways of genuine divine-human encounter appropriate for our time—hence the above emphasis on liturgy, music, poetry, and dance. It is this whole realm that Stanley Hauerwas misses in his criticism of my position on theology and the Holocaust. In an article dealing with theology after Auschwitz[17] he argues that my approach to Christology which sees this doctrine primarily in terms of humanity's discovery of its intimate link with the divine is really not Christology, but "Platonic soteriology," as Rosemary Ruether has said of my view. And such an approach has led in the opinion of both Hauerwas and Ruether to the abandonment of the realm of history as theologically important, an abandonment which helped pave the way for the inadequacy of Christian response to the Nazis. What both Ruether and Hauerwas fail to appreciate is the bond between historical consciousness and inner consciousness. It is my contention, contrary to Hauerwas and Ruether, that until Christianity recognizes this profound link we will continue to live with the devastating dichotomy between those who would espouse a political theology and those who would advocate a more "spiritual" way. The latter by itself will in fact lead to moral irresponsibility as it did in the Holocaust; the former by itself will not sufficiently satisfy the deeper yearnings of the human spirit nor provide the resources for the neutralizing of false notions of power and control that Hauerwas deems necessary, as I do as well (hence his opposition to my viewpoint on this score is misguided), for the prevention of future Holocausts. Neither Ruether nor Hauerwas adequately deals with the healing of the inner person that is necessary before people develop an adequate historical consciousness that will prevent further degradations of humanity on the scale of the Holocaust. Central to this inner healing is restoration of a link with the Parent God, though a link that will be understood in a significantly different light than it was pre-Holocaust. . . .

THE ISSUE OF EVIL

Another theological issue raised by the Holocaust, touched upon in the quotation from Gregory Baum given above, is that of evil. A. Roy Eckardt has written that in the final analysis it is impossible to understand the Holocaust except by attributing it to the work of the Devil.[18] One may agree with Eckardt that since the Holocaust confronts us with the reality of evil on such a massive and grotesque scale, simple explanations seem ludicrous. Yet, to place the origins of the evil outside the person fails to deal with the problem in its ultimate depths. Just as one may claim that the Holocaust was a *rational* event and in that fact lies its greatest devastation of the image of the human person, so to locate the root of the evil that was Auschwitz outside of man is an easier solution, for it leaves the dignity of man more intact. Following through on the rationality thesis proposed at the beginning of this essay, the evil perpetrated by the Nazis was ultimately due to forces at work within human consciousness since the time of the creation of man. For the act of creation constituted the liberation of humanity from its total enslavement by God. God realized he had to let go of part of himself in order to develop and become truly God. He granted newly made man the power of co-creatorship. But that part of God that now took on an independent existence was forced to work out a new relationship with the Godhead. At times, it even tried to supplant the Creator himself. For centuries, fear largely kept such desires in check. But with the dawning of the modern age man began to experience a new sense of freedom and to lose the fear he once had of the Creator. Since the problem of the new relationship between God and man had not been adequately developed and since the temptation to try to become God himself still lingered

within humanity, the new liberation of man opened the doors for catastrophe. That catastrophe was the Holocaust. Here the analysis of Uriel
Tal and the quotations from Nazi sources cited above are most germane.
There was a total reversal of meanings in Nazism in which man finally
tried to overpower the Creator.

It is vitally important to try to define the root cause of the evil of
Auschwitz, for without such knowledge we will be powerless to do anything about preventing its recurrence. A devil-origin theory makes it
almost impossible to sustain any hope of preventing another outbreak of
such evil. However, by understanding this evil as rooted in the centuries-long struggle of man to define his proper relationship to the
Creator, one is at least provided with some possibility of accomplishing
this goal. The final assertion of man's freedom from God in our time
may in fact be the beginning of the ultimate resolution of the conflict.
Man is beginning to understand, to more fully appreciate, the dimensions of co-creatorship that God has bestowed upon him. The fear and
the paternalism that characterized the God-human relationship in the
past has ended. Yet this relationship cannot finally be made aright unless
man develops along with his new sense of dignity and with his new grasp
of the power to shape himself and his environment a sense of profound
humility evoked by the presence of the ultimate Creator of these human
powers. Without this sense of humility, the potential for goodness and
love inherent in this new consciousness will become a reality that is one
long nightmare of hate and destruction. "Humility" is not a very popular word in contemporary religious or secular circles. "Power" and
"strength" dominate our contemporary vocabulary. While it must be
granted that much of the talk about humility in previous religious literature made the human person excessively subservient to God and perverted the dignity and power of man implicit in the concept of co-creatorship, a proper incorporation of humility into twentieth-century
consciousness is imperative for survival. This humility can only be realized by means of the experience of the transcendent God discussed
above. While we are discussing the importance of humility, it would also
be well to urge theologians to adopt a new stance of humility. Michael
Ryan puts it very well, when he says,

> . . . because of the Holocaust . . . I believe that theologians of
> the church should come down out of the Barthian "above" in
> theology and pursue with historians all along the way the truth
> question in regard to the whole history of the church, but
> especially the historical Jesus and the relationship of a chas-
> tened Christianity to Judaism. This is not to say that we theolo-

gians should stop speaking "as though" we had a special noetic access to the history of Jesus and the primitive church not available to the working historian as historian. Let us talk about faith within the limits that make faith intelligible as faith, namely, by the fact of our finitude, of our acknowledging creaturehood before God.[19]

To this point we have concentrated upon general theological reflections concerning the Holocaust. It is now necessary to look more closely at the specifically Catholic-Christian aspects of Auschwitz. In accepting the position of Uriel Tal, we approached the Holocaust as something more than the final, gruesome sequel in the long history of Christian anti-Semitism. However, this viewpoint in no way intends to undercut the blame Christian churches share for Hitler's Final Solution. In this regard, the words of Edward Flannery are very much to the point. While acknowledging the complexity of any investigation of the root causes of the Holocaust, he clearly affirms that

> . . . in the final analysis, some degree of the charge (against the Church) must be validated. Great or small, the apathy or silence was excessive. The fact remains that in the twentieth century of Christian civilization a genocide of six million innocent people was perpetrated in countries with many centuries of Christian traditions and by hands that were in many cases Christian. This fact in itself stands, however vaguely, as an indictment of the Christian conscience. The absence of reaction by those most directly implicated in the genocide only aggravates this broader indictment.

THE HOLOCAUST AND CHRISTIAN CONSCIENCE

Flannery continues to say that even if one accepts the view (as this essay has) that the Holocaust is primarily due to modern secularism, its architects found their targets well-primed for the formulation of their racist theories:

> The degraded state of the Jews, brought about by centuries of opprobrium and oppression, gave support to the invidious comparisons with which the racists built their theories. And in their evil design, they were able to draw moral support from traditional Christian views of Jews and Judaism.[20]

Endorsing the position of Urial Tal regarding the origins of the Holocaust, at least in its German form, is in no sense an exoneration of the church's responsibility for six million deaths. Tal himself insists that outside of the German leadership, Nazism was a direct response to deeply rooted anti-Semitic feelings. Thus, while the springboard for the Holocaust came from Western liberalism's distorted attempt to create the universal person, the satanic machinations of Hitler and his cohorts could never have attained the heights they did if it were not for the centuries-long tradition of anti-Semitism in Christian theology and preaching. The anti-Jewish laws devised by Hitler closely parallel the anti-Jewish laws instituted by Christians throughout the centuries.

The lessons of the Holocaust have not been learned very well by Christians up till now. In fact, the event has hardly been studied. We have been truly afraid to probe the significance of this tragedy for Christian self-identity. When the Holocaust issue did surface with the appearance of the play *The Deputy*[21] and the publication of Guenter Lewy's *The Catholic Church and Nazi Germany*,[22] the general posture in Catholic circles was one marked by extreme defensiveness and hostility towards the authors. In fact, the American Catholic community was generally successful in muffling the accusations made in these two works. Their appearance could have occasioned a serious exploration of the Holocaust by American Catholics. It did not; the dominant response was to bury rather than to probe.

The above situation is confirmed for Christianity generally by Alice Eckardt in her survey of Christian and Jewish responses to the Holocaust. She writes that there simply exists no comparison between the responses and reactions of the Christian and Jewish communities to the reality of Hitler's Final Solution:

> Whatever aspects of response one looks at—historical, theological, psychological, existential—it is overwhelmingly that of Jews, individually and collectively. If we say that this is to be expected and is quite normal, we are only giving away the very problem: that nothing normal should prevail after the most fearful abnormality in human history. It further assumes that the Holocaust is primarily a *Jewish* problem—whereas in fact it is, in far deeper respects, a Christian problem.[23]

Alice Eckardt strongly feels that Christianity has failed to recognize the crucial nature of the question the Holocaust has raised for the future of its theological enterprise in the same manner as it generally has refused to assume any responsibility for the death camps. This view concurs with that expressed by Elwyn Smith. Smith asks,

Was not the Holocaust a terrible test—which the church
failed? . . . It may be . . . that the question whether Christianity
is to remember the Holocaust or dismiss it is a question of the
ability and the right of Christianity to survive in a form in any
way conformable to the Scriptures.[24]

MORAL INTEGRITY OF THE CHURCH

Returning to Eckardt, her analysis has determined that "those
Christians who have grappled with the reality and implications of the
Holocaust see a church in vast apostasy, involved not only in the murder
of Jews but also of God through his people, still linked to a superses-
sionist theology that bears the genocidal germ, in danger of repeating its
complicity in criminal actions, and without credibility because of its
failure to understand that everything has been changed by Auschwitz."[25]
We are faced at this point with the inevitable question, why have American Catholics been so reticent to confront the implications of the Nazi
period? The answer is a complex one. The following factors have contributed to the silence. The first is the fact that the United States as a
nation, and therefore the American Catholic Church, was generally
removed from the physical ravages of World War II. Americans simply
did not feel its effects in the same existential way as the Europeans. The
American Catholic church in particular was not faced with the same type
of immediate and painful judgments about political allegiance or protest
that confronted many European Catholics. However, this is only a small
part of the total explanation. A residual anti-Semitism, which subcon-
sciously still regards Jewish life as expendable because of the Jewish
people's past "sins" and the general indifference to the extermination
of human beings that has developed in our day, also accounts in part for
the failure to deal with the Holocaust.

One of the principal reasons, perhaps *the* principal reason, for
silence about the Holocaust is to be found in a theological attitude that
has become deeply ingrained in Catholicism. In essence, this attitude
views the church as a holy and spotless institution incapable of any major
moral defect. Traditionally, it has been extremely difficult to suggest
to a believing Catholic even the possibility that his or her church could
have been guilty of serious moral irresponsibility in such an event as
the Holocaust. The initial reaction is usually hostility and extreme defensiveness.

The first specifically Christian theological challenge emanating
from Auschwitz is the question of the very definition and understanding

THE HOLOCAUST AND CHRISTIAN THEOLOGY

of the Church itself. The Holocaust has eliminated any possibility of retaining an ecclesiology which depicts the church as a wholly complete and perfect institution, existing essentially apart from this world though in contact with it. The only model of the church that can claim any authenticity and credibility after Auschwitz is one that envisions it as a group of men and women immersed in the flow of history who have experienced through Christ the love and healing of the transcendent God and are struggling as a result of this experience to exercise their co-creatorship in concert with non-Christians towards the attainment of that peace and that justice which are central to the ultimate salvation of mankind.[26]

It will prove trying for Catholics to face the challenge to the traditional Catholic notion of the church's basic moral integrity that is represented by the Holocaust. As difficult as it may be, a new ecclesiology will have to be created. As we begin to penetrate the veil of silence that has covered the Holocaust in Catholic circles, we can begin to see more clearly some of the theological postures which made at least indirect complicity with the Nazis a possible option for Roman Catholicism.

NEW TESTAMENT ANTI-SEMITISM

In *Faith and Fratricide: The Theological Roots of Anti-Semitism,*[27] Rosemary Ruether sees the Holocaust as ultimately rooted in the anti-Semitism that emerged from the New Testament itself, especially the Gospel of John, and which was given definite shape in the teachings of the Church Fathers. The myth of the Jew eventually underwent a social incorporation during the ensuing centuries, resulting in a legal status for Judaism inferior to that enjoyed by Christianity. This included a loss of all civil rights, as well as the imposition of an economic role that made the Jew vulnerable to violence from below and to arbitrary action from above. Finally we come to the situation of total vilification, rightlessness and ghettoization that characterized Jewish life in Western Christendom from the later Middle Ages to the emancipation following the French Revolution. According to Ruether Nazism arose as "the final repository of all this heritage of religious and secular anti-Semitism making Jews responsible for capitalism and communism simultaneously! The racial theory was new but the stereotypes of hatred were old. The mythical Jew, who is the eternal conspiratorial enemy of Christian faith, spirituality, and redemption, was being shaped to serve as the scapegoat for all the things in secular industrial society which the middle class had created and now feared and hated for their dissolution of traditional religion, culture, social hierarchy, and life style." European society saw a need to purge itself of a deep threat to its inner health, wealth and wisdom. "The mythical Jew," Ruether claims, "had long been fashioned in Christian history to serve as the symbol of this 'disease' from which the Christian must purge himself in order to save himself. Under the slogan 'the Jews are our misfortune' mass paranoia again gripped the soul of the European heartland."[28] Ruether believes that the Christian background of the Nazi "Final Solution" is well illustrated by an incident reported in Hitler's "Table Talk." The episode in question is one in which Hitler reports meeting two bishops who came to confront him on the issue of Nazi racial policy. Hitler's reply to their questioning was that he was only putting into effect what Christianity had been preaching and practicing for two thousand years.[29]

Ruether identifies a significant "advancement" in Hitlerian anti-Semitism that goes beyond the framework of the traditional Christian manifestation. Christian religious anti-Judaism aimed at making Jews miserable and at containing their lack of belief. Sharing the perspective that has been the main thrust of this essay, she claims that the Third Reich would not limit itself in this way: "Master of its own eschatology and creator of its own millennium the Third Reich took in hand that last judgment which Christianity had reserved for the returning Christ. In Hitler, the Fuhrer empowers himself with the ultimate work of Christ to execute the 'Final Solution' to the Jewish Question."[30]

Ruether's study has raised considerable controversy within the Christian community, even among those who have been deeply sensitive to the need for correcting Christianity's historical bias against Judaism. Her work basically centers around the issue of whether Christian anti-Semitism is due to an improper exegesis of the New Testament or whether it stems from the teaching of the New Testament itself (Ruether takes the latter position). While both theological positions are unwavering in their call for an end to Christian anti-Semitism, they see the remedy somewhat differently. The "improper exegesis" school would claim that the anti-Jewish passages in the New Testament are largely the result of an intra-Jewish struggle in the first century. The problem really arose only when those passages fell into the hands of a predominantly Gentile church. This group feels that sufficient background explanations, coupled with an emphasis on those parts of the New Testament where Paul especially stresses (Romans 9–11 in particular) his great love for the Jewish people, is the direction the cure should take. The other school would say that this solution is too simplistic, ignoring the deep contempt for Jews evident in particular in the Gospel of John. Even Romans 9–11, while it certainly would repudiate the persecution and murder of the Jews, does not in the final analysis, despite its evident positive sentiments towards the Jewish people, uphold the full validity of Judaism after Christ, ending in a conversionist note. An articulation of the first point of view can be found in the writings of Bruce Vawter,[31] Joseph Grassi[32] and Markus Barth,[33] to name only a few. In addition to Ruether, the second perspective is represented in the writings of Gregory Baum[34] and Joseph Stiassny.[35] While the present discussion cannot resolve this complicated scholarly dispute, it is sympathetic toward the position presented by Ruether, Baum and Stiassny. (This represents a change in the present author's perspective from *Catechetics and Prejudice* where the Vawter viewpoint is adopted.[36]) This is not to deny that better exegesis and more background material on the Jewish context of early Christianity can go a long way in improving the image of Judaism by correcting, for example, the distorted notion of the Pharisees, making it clear that the Romans were responsible for the death of Jesus on a political charge and showing that much of the vehement denunciation of the so-called "Judaizers" in Ephesians and Galatians may have been directed at non-Jews. One also must insist that Paul's general affection for Judaism would have led him to condemn the infliction of any suffering upon Jews despite their unbelief. But when we move to the Gospel of John and Jews begin to be depicted as the "very incarnation of the false apostate principle of the fallen world, alienated from its true being in God,"[37] we come very close to a contemptuous attitude that must be branded as anti-Semitic.[38] Certainly this type of teaching became explosive in the hands of later Christian preachers and teachers. Therefore, the Christian confrontation with the New Testament on the question of anti-Semitism must now move beyond mere background information and improved exegesis to a genuine soul-searching as to whether we can continue to proclaim parts of the Gospel of John as authentic teaching for our time.

PROPER EXEGESIS

Some Christians want too desperately to extract a positive portrait of the Jewish people from the New Testament because the type of challenge presented by the Ruether-Stiassny thesis has tried their personal faith too severely. They would find it too difficult to make the fundamental changes in their understanding of the nature of the church and the role and authority of the New Testament that this perspective demands. While it would be much easier and more reassuring for Christians to be able to endorse the "wrong exegesis" approach, one cannot do so and still remain honest to the data at hand. However, whatever position one takes on the New Testament basis for the legacy of anti-Semitic teaching in the church, it cannot be denied that interpretations of New Testament teachings by Christian teachers and preachers throughout the centuries created an atmosphere which contributed directly to the acceptance of Nazi attitudes towards the Jewish people. If the exegesis was improper, this still does not absolve the church; for such "improper" teaching was never corrected by its leadership on any widespread scale.

Another perspective on Christian compliance in the Holocaust is offered by Edward Flannery. Basing his presentation upon some of the psychological explanations of anti-Semitism, he suggests that many Christians harbor a deeply repressed death wish for the Jewish people that at its core may be a hatred of Christianity itself. The apathy manifested during the Nazi period, he believes, is explicable on the basis of this psychological understanding of anti-Semitism.[39] While such an interpretation must be approached with caution and needs considerably more research, enough reputable scholars have suggested it so that Christian theologians will have to treat it seriously.

A third avenue of thought regarding the church's inability to challenge more strongly the operations of the Third Reich is to be found in the works of Frederich Heer, who tries to place the phenomenon of anti-Semitism in a larger context. For him, Catholicism's failure to confront adequately the Holocaust is symptomatic of how Catholicism has reacted to all other evils, especially to war and to the possibility of a nuclear holocaust. For him, the main problem springs from the church's withdrawal from history:

> The withdrawal of the church from history has created that specifically Christian and ecclesiastical irresponsibility towards the world, the Jew, the other person, even the Christian himself, considered as a human being—which was the ultimate cause of past catastrophes and may be the cause of a final catastrophe in the future.[40]

For Heer, anti-Semitism has been the historical manifestation of a much deeper cancer in Christianity that was manifested in classical Christianity. The disregard of the fate of the Jewish people throughout history, especially between 1918 and 1945, can only be understood, he claims, as part of a general disregard of man and the world. He primarily attributes this disregard to the dominance in Christian theology of the so-called "Augustinian principle" which views the world under the aspect of sin and which ultimately leads to a sense of fatalism and despair about the world. According to Heer, this fatalistic tendency is a danger today as it was in the period of the incubation of Nazism, especially from 1933–45. In fact, he quite bluntly reports that millions of contemporary Christians share the responsibility for preparing the suicide of the Church and of mankind in a new holocaust which may be brought about by nuclear warfare while the church once more stands by in idle silence. He writes: "There is a straight line from the church's failure to notice Hitler's attempt at a 'Final Solution' of the Jewish problem to her failure to notice today's and tomorrow's endeavors to bring about a 'Final Solution' to the human problem. The murder of millions of Jews during the Hitler era anticipates the murder of millions and perhaps hundreds of millions of human beings who would die if the great war returned—a war that could only end in mass murder and genocide."[41] The only cure for this centuries-long pattern in Christianity, according to Heer, is to abandon the "Augustinian principle" and replace it with a return to the Hebrew Bible's roots of Christ's own piety and to even older roots— namely, to the original faith in which man felt himself to be both God's creature and his responsible partner.

CHANGING CONCEPT OF THE CHURCH

In his emphasis upon the fatalistic tendency in Christian theological thinking, Heer is on to something important. However, he does not carry his analysis quite far enough. A search for the origins of this destructive tendency is lacking in his work. These origins really lie in the assumption by the early Christian community that the coming of Christ had inaugurated the Messianic age, the end of history. When the expected characteristic of the Messianic age failed to materialize, the church's theology pushed the fulfillment to the inner, spiritual dimension. Rosemary Ruether has pin-pointed some of the serious problems created for the church's relationship with the world as a result of this "spiritualizing" of the eschatological era.[42] By means of baptism, a Christian could enter the so-called completed world, not visible to the naked eye within the context of ordinary human history.[43] This impulse eventually led to a theology of the world which saw the church as a wholly complete entity essentially existing apart from the world. As was indicated above, the Holocaust has shattered such an ecclesiology. The church now cannot be viewed as anything but an incomplete community, still struggling for salvation within the confines of the flow of history. An imperative therefore exists for Christian theologians to rethink the whole meaning of the Christ Event relative to the fulfillment of history. Some theologians have already begun this process.[44] Its completion still requires much work and research.

What these theologians are beginning to assert is that Christianity must take a fresh look at its contention that the Messianic age, the time of fulfillment, took place with the coming of Christ. It has become obvious that Catholic theology can no longer simply claim the Jewish notion of the Messianic age was realized in the Death-Resurrection of Christ. Such a conclusion does not imply a total discarding of traditional Christology, but it does demand significant restatement and clarification. Only by reversing the process of "spiritualizing of the eschatological" that took place in the first century can the church finally remove the fatalistic tendency identified by Heer and insure that it will not cause some future, far greater holocaust. Part of the process of sinking the church anew into the realm of the historical will involve the recovery of the Jewish sense of the human person as God's co-creator, as co-responsible for the salvation of the earth. The recovery of this idea alone will not suffice unless the church combines it with an adequate appreciation and affirmation of the new sense of human liberation that has infiltrated human consciousness in our day. A cautionary note must be sounded here, one that will lead us to another interpretation of the Holocaust experience from a Catholic perspective. We have talked a great deal in this essay about the absolute need for the church to rediscover its anchorage in history with the incompleteness and future growth that this implies. However, at the same time we cannot completely lose sight of the transcendent dimensions of the church. Great stress was placed at the outset of this essay on the human community's need to discover a new sense of transcendence for our time. This means that the community called "church" must experience an aspect of its existence that pulls it beyond the confines of the world as it now exists. The above call for historical involvement does not mean to restrict the church to the realm of present history alone. The danger in the latter is that the church becomes too identified with a given socio-political order. The Catholic sociologist Gorden Zahn who has extensively studied the Nazi experience, writes that

> if there is any single overriding lesson to be learned . . . it would seem to be that the religious community must never become so enmeshed in its support for a given socio-political order that it loses its potential to be a source of dissent and disobedience. In other more familiar terms, the church must recognize that it has a stake in maintaining a separation of

church and state as that separation is defined from its own perspective. It is a serious mistake to see that separation, as Americans are so prone to see it, only in terms of protecting the purity and independence of the secular order from unwarranted intrusions or domination by the spiritual. The problem as it developed in Germany (and as it may exist here to a greater degree than we are aware!) is also one of preserving the purity and independence of the spiritual community and its teaching from domination by the national state, with its definitions of situational needs and priorities.[45]

In short, what is called for in the light of the Holocaust is a vision of church as immersed in history, recognizing that it is only within history that its still incomplete nature can be realized. One must recognize that the salvation process is directly inhibited by regimes such as Nazi Germany and that the church can never reach its ultimate goals while non-Catholics suffer punishment and death. Only such an ecclesiology can have legitimacy after Auschwitz.

THE CHURCH AND RESISTANCE TO AUTHORITY

Zahn also believes that as a consequence of its experiences in Nazi Germany, the Church must reconsider its traditional position relative to the "just war" theory, that it must more thoughtfully grapple with resistance to authority as a possible Catholic imperative and take a new, hard look at the idea that as a temporal, social institution it can accommodate itself to any regime which affirms its willingness to respect church property and prerogatives, something that has been virtually an unchallengeable truism in Catholic political philosophy and Vatican diplomacy.[46] A similar analysis is to be found in Guenter Lewy's *The Catholic Church and Nazi Germany*.[47]

Another Christian theological perspective that has come to the fore links the Jewish sufferings during the Holocaust with the sufferings of Christ on the Cross. For example, Franklin Sherman claims that the only way we can possibly speak of God after Auschwitz is by recognizing that God participates in the sufferings of people while people are called to participate in the sufferings of God. "For Christianity," says Sherman, "the symbol of the agonizing God is the cross of Christ. It is tragic that this symbol should have become a symbol of division between Jews and Christians, for the reality to which it points is a Jewish reality as well, the reality of suffering and martyrdom."[48] For Sherman, the Cross reveals in the first instance a *Jewish* reality. The subsequent interpretations Christians have given to the cross of Christ are well-known, "but behind the interpretations surrounding this man who suffered as a Jew is the Jewish reality that should make Christians the first to identify with the sufferings of any Jews . . . we can speak of God after Auschwitz only as the one who calls us to a new unity as between brothers—not only between Jews and Christians, but especially between Jews and Christians."[49] Echoes of a similar perspective are in the writings of Marcel Dubois. While deeply conscious of the difficulty Christians face in setting the reality of Auschwitz within the context of a theology of the Cross, and recognizing that such a linkage may appear as an obscenity to Jews whose sufferings in the Holocaust the church helped to perpetrate, he nonetheless feels that this is the direction in which Christians must move:

> . . . in the person of the suffering servant there appears to take place an ineffable change. Our vision of Jewish destiny and our understanding of the Holocaust in particular depend on our compassion; the Calvary of the Jewish people whose summit is the Holocaust, can help us to understand a little better the mystery of the cross.[50]

Dubois is convinced that under the guidance of faith the Christian can truly affirm that Jesus fulfills Israel in her destiny of suffering servant and that Israel, in her experience of solitude and anguish, announces and represents even without knowing it the mystery of the Passion and of the Cross. The challenge of the massive annihilation which the Holocaust era ushered into the world stands before both Jews and Christians:

> They have learnt to be united in compassion; they must now learn to be united in hope, the hope . . . of the people that believes in the victory of life and in the fidelity of God, Christian hope that affirms the certitude of the victory of the cross.[51]

One may question the propriety of combining the theology of the Cross with the Auschwitz experience, as Sherman and Dubois do out of their awareness of Christian complicity in the Holocaust. The suitability of Dubois's notion that Israel is the precursor of the sufferings of Christ may be questioned. Insofar as both show that Auschwitz forces upon us a new understanding of the God-human person relationship, one in which there is greater communion and interdependence both in creativity and in suffering, and insofar as they stress that the Holocaust inextricably links the fate of Jews and Christians (as well as all other peoples), their interpretations help to lay the foundations for the new Christian theology that needs to be formulated.

PIUS XII AS SYMBOL

A final point that needs to be raised from a Christian perspective relative to the Holocaust concerns the verdict on the papacy of Pius XII. Was he guilty of an act of massive moral irresponsibility in not working more strenuously against Hitler and more directly aiding Jews in their struggle to survive? First of all, it should be noted that Edward Flannery's contention is essentially correct. He claims that

> the centralization of the charge on the Pope has unfortunately deflected attention from the scope of a silence that affected many churches, governments, and people. More recent research has shown that apathy towards the Jewish plight was a pervasive thing.[52]

Historians and popular writers have debated the morality and immorality of Pius' handling of Jewish extermination under the Nazis. Rolf Hochhuth's *The Deputy*[53] elicited a wide body of accusatory as well as defensive literature on the question.[54] Most Jewish writers have rendered a rather harsh verdict on Pius' actions (or better non-actions), though several have written in his behalf.[55] To some extent the issue of whether Pius could have done more can never be definitively answered because who can judge for certain the outcome of a more public defense of Jews on Pius' part? The preface to a new monograph in defense of Pius by the Vatican historian Fr. Robert Graham, S.J., claims that Pius was troubled by the inability to go public with a denunciation of the Nazi attack against the Jews, but was of the opinion that such action would have submitted the Jews to even more intense persecution.[56]

Certainly there is no doubt that Pius strongly disapproved of the Nazis' anti-Jewish plans and did undertake some concrete efforts to save Jews. Many of these actions are detailed by Graham in his new monograph based on data from the last volumes of the official Vatican documents from the period. They clearly render as totally prejudicial any simplistic judgment about Pius' lack of concern for all Jews. But this latest attempt to rehabilitate the Pope, though it has made his record much more positive than many scholars of the Holocaust have previously granted, does not totally answer the conclusions reached by Fr. John Morley in his study *Vatican Diplomacy and the Jews During the Holocaust, 1939–1943.*[57] Morley argues that the tone of Vatican diplomacy during this period, set by Pius himself, was marked by an attitude of prudence and reserve. It sought to refrain from "offending" any nation, especially Germany. This approach placed a straitjacket on Vatican diplomacy and in no way differentiated it from the posture of the civil states. Morley writes:

> The Pope, in defining and restraining Vatican diplomatic practice in this way, failed not only the Jews but also many members of the church who suffered brutal treatment from the Germans. . . . The nuncios could have vigorously protested the rationale behind the racial laws as a violation of justice. . . . The Pope did not give such direction to the Vatican diplomats. He chose reserve, prudence, and a diplomatic presence in all the capitals over any other goal or needs. This approach does not seem to have been motivated by malevolence or anti-Semitism but was caused by an inability to depart from cherished ecclesiastical or personal concepts to confront the evils besetting Europe and the Jewish People.[58]

In one sense Pius XII is a symbol, as Hochhuth observed in an interview:

> Pius is a symbol, not only for all leaders, but for all men— Christians, atheists, Jews. For all men who are passive when their brother is deported to death. Pius was at the top of the hierarchy and, therefore, he had the greatest duty to speak. But every man—the Protestants, the Catholics, the Jews, Eden, Cordell Hull, Churchill, all had the duty to speak.[59]

The words of Frederich Heer are also very much to the point in any evaluation of Pius XII. "Thus far," Heer observes, "he (Pius) has been surrounded by taboos, glorified as a plaster saint, dehumanized—and thus made to appear inhuman. But this would be a task for a truly Catholic investigation and historical writing, conscious of the duty of the *pontifex maximus* since Auschwitz, Maidaneck, Mauthausen, and Hiroshima: to portray the Pope bearing the cross of human guilt, of common guilt, up until this frightful agony; his solitary death, deprived of human communications. To such a Pope bearing the cross of human guilt, Christians and non-Christians would not give a false aura of holiness, but neither would they deny him a crown, the crown proper to a mortal who in times of Copernican revolution where Catholicism seeks to shake off the shackles of centuries, has to carry the burden which—as he admitted himself in a note found in an envelope before his death—was beyond his strength."[60]

Over and above a personal evaluation of Pius, it is more important for us to understand the theological framework that conditioned his mentality and guided him in his decision-making during this critical period of human history. Nora Levin's assessment in this regard approximates the truth:

> The Vatican . . . through the Holocaust was not only a prisoner of its own history of anti-Semitism but was the product of a historical conditioning as strong as that of any other human institution. It needed to find arenas of power in an era of shrinking religious response and had to weigh the political consequences of impulsively acting out of moral fervor. In the years of fateful concern to European Jews this institution was entrusted to a man who undoubtedly believed he was being scrupulously neutral in his appraisal of world-shattering events but who, admittedly, believed that national socialism was a lesser evil than communism. In this context alone, were no other considerations involved, how could Jews be viewed other than as unfortunate expendables? After all, it was the Nazis, not the Bolsheviks, who were destroying them.[61]

The real limitation of the papacy of Pius XII was that it was mired in the type of other worldly, perfectly fulfilled ecclesiology discussed above. This ecclesiology did not totally prevent actions in behalf of Jews and others persecuted by the Nazis. But it definitely made such actions a secondary goal that had to be abandoned when the threat to the existence of the church was too great. The study of the actions of Pius XII only confirms the dire need for Catholicism to bury such a self-understanding of the church once and for all. The goal was to keep the church alive no matter what the cost in non-Christian lives.

"NEVER AGAIN"

In light of the preceding discussion, one may insist that the present task for Catholicism is to join other Christians and Jews in truly making their own words inscribed on the international memorial sculpture at

Dachau, "Never Again." For this to happen, Catholic theology will have to:

1) come to understand the new dimensions of human liberation in our time and find ways of combining this new awareness of freedom with the biblical appreciation of the human person as God's co-creator within the context of a new experience of transcendence;

2) reinterpret its understanding of the meaning of the church and how the Christian community can truly reinsert itself into the historical flow; and

3) scrutinize anew the New Testament to see in what ways it may have been a source of anti-Semitic teachings.

If it is determined that this is due to improper exegesis, then corrective background material will have to be provided. If anti-Semitism is discovered to be actually inherent in part of the New Testament, then the church will have to grapple seriously with the possibility that such passages will have to be discarded as authentic teaching in the present and in the future. On the whole, one should remember that the new post-Holocaust theology of Catholicism is only in a nascent stage. The future, therefore, holds both the promise and the opportunity for a clearly developed post-Holocaust theology of Catholicism.

NOTES

1. Franklin Littell, "The Meaning of the Holocaust: A Christian Point of View," address at the University of Michigan, 3 November 1971 (unpublished manuscript). Also cf. F. Littell, "Christendom, Holocaust and Israel," *Journal of Ecumenical Studies* 10 (Summer 1973): 483–97.

2. Cf. Emil Fackenheim, "The People Israel Lives," *Christian Century* 87 (May 6, 1970): 563–568 and *God's Presence in History* (New York: New York University Press, 1970).

3. Cf. Emil Fackenheim, "Reflections on the Holocaust," remarks made to the National Council of Churches Faith & Order Study Group on Israel: Land, People, State, New York, 16 October 1970.

4. Uriel Tal, "Forms of Pseudo-Religion in the German *Kulturbereich* Prior to the Holocaust," *Immanuel* 3 (Winter 1973–74): 69–70. In light of the more "universal" approach of Tal and others, it is unfortunate that the stories of other victims of Nazi ideology have not entered

the theological discussions of the Holocaust. For one account of their sufferings, cf. Bohdan Wytwycky, *The Other Holocaust: Many Circles of Hell.* (Washington: The Novak Report, 1980).

5. Quoted by Frederich Heer in *God's First Love* (New York: Weybright and Talley, 1970), p. 401.

6. Richard Rubenstein, "Some Perspectives on Religious Faith After Auschwitz," in Littell and Locke (eds.), *op. cit.*, p. 267.

7. Cf. Arthur Hertzberg, *The French Enlightenment and the Jews* (New York: Schocken, 1968).

8. The Protestant and Catholic textbook studies give us good evidence of this. Cf. Bernhard E. Olson, *Faith and Prejudice* (New Haven: Yale University Press, 1963) and John T. Pawlikowski, *Catechetics and Prejudice* (New York: Paulist Press, 1973). Cf. also Eugene Fisher, *Faith Without Prejudice* (New York: Paulist Press, 1977).

9. Cf. Juan Luis Segundo, *A Theology For Artisans of a New Humanity,* 5 vols. (Maryknoll, NY: Orbis, 1973–74) and Gustavo Gutierrez, *Theology of Liberation* (Maryknoll, NY: Orbis, 1973).

10. Gregory Baum, *Man Becoming: God in Secular Experience* (New York: Herder and Herder, 1971), pp. ix, 245.

11. *Ibid.,* pp. 242–44.

12. *Ibid.,* pp. 248–49.

13. Paul Tillich, *The Shaking of the Foundations* (New York: Charles Scribner's Sons, 1948), pp. 106–107. Also cf. John T. Pawlikowski, *Epistle Homilies* (Milwaukee: Bruce, 1966), pp. 65–66.

14. As quoted in Claude Cuenot, *Teilhard de Chardin: A Biographical Study* (Baltimore: Helicon, 1965), p. 369.

15. Franklin Sherman, "Speaking of God After Auschwitz," *Worldview* 17, No. 9 (September 1974): 26–30.

16. David Tracy, "Religious Values After the Holocaust: A Catholic View," in Abraham J. Peck (ed.), *Jews and Christians After the Holocaust* (Philadelphia: Fortress, 1982), p. 101.

17. Stanley Hauerwas, "Jews and Christians Among the Nations," *Cross Currents* 31 (Spring 1981), p. 34.

18. The notion of the Holocaust as the work of the devil is part of Eckardt's basic thesis that all anti-Semitism is satanic in origin. Cf. A. Roy Eckardt, "The Devil and Yom Kippur," *Midstream* 20, no. 7 (August/September 1974): 67–75. In a collaborative volume with Alice L. Eckardt, Roy Eckardt tries to answer some of my objections and those of the late Anglican church historian James Parkes to his devil origins theory relative to the Holocaust. While he has clarified some points, I fear he still places the evil origin of the Nazi endeavor too much outside

of human consciousness and its struggle with its Parent God. Cf. A. Roy Eckardt and Alice L. Eckardt, *Long Night's Journey Into Day* (Detroit: Wayne State University Press, 1982), pp. 50–57.

19. Cf. Ryan, *op. cit.*, p. 164.

20. Edward Flannery, "Anti-Zionism and the Christian Psyche," *Journal of Ecumenical Studies* 6, No. 2 (Spring 1969): 174–75.

21. For essays on *The Deputy*, see, Eric Bentley (ed.), *The Storm Over The Deputy* (New York: Grove Press, 1964).

22. Guenter Lewy, *The Catholic Church and Nazi Germany* (New York: McGraw-Hill, 1964).

23. Alice Eckardt, "The Holocaust: Christian and Jewish Responses," *Journal of the American Academy of Religion* 42, No. 3 (September 1974): p. 453.

24. Elwyn Smith, "The Christian Meaning of the Holocaust," *Journal of Ecumenical Studies* 6 (Summer 1969): 421–22.

25. Eckardt, *op. cit.*, p. 454.

26. In light of this definition of the church I find it difficult to understand Stanley Hauerwas' contention that I fail to challenge the priority given to mere "survival" by Catholic ecclesiology during the Holocaust. This definition certainly challenges any simple "survival-first" mentality. Cf. Hauerwas, *op. cit.*, p. 34.

27. Rosemary Ruether, *Faith and Fratricide: The Theological Roots of Anti-Semitism* (New York: The Seabury Press, 1974).

28. *Ibid.*, pp. 22–23.

29. *Ibid.*, p. 224.

30. *Ibid.*, 224–25.

31. Bruce Vawter, "Are the Gospels Anti-Semitic?," *Journal of Ecumenical Studies* 5 (Summer 1968): 473–487.

32. Joseph Grassi, "Are the Roots of Anti-Semitism in the Gospels?" in Michael Zeik and Martin Siegel (eds.), *Root and Branch* (Williston Park, NY: Roth Publishing, 1973). pp. 71–88.

33. Markus Barth, "Was Paul an Anti-Semite?," *Journal of Ecumenical Studies*, 5 No. 1 (Winter 1968): 78–104. Also appears as Chapter 2 in the author's volume *Israel and the Church* (Richmond: John Knox Press, 1969).

34. In his introduction to R. Ruether's *Faith and Fratricide* Baum explains why he changed his position from that expressed in his previous work, *The Jews and the Gospel*. Cf. Ruether, *op. cit.*, pp. 2–5.

35. Joseph Stiassny, "Development of the Christian's Self-Understanding in the Second Part of the First Century." *Immanuel* 1 (Summer 1973): 32–34.

36. John T. Pawlikowski, *Catechetics and Prejudice.*

37. Cf. Ruether, *op. cit.,* p. 113.

38. The presence of some anti-Semitism in the gospel of John has been affirmed by the Johannine scholar Raymond Brown. Cf. *The Community of the Beloved Disciple* (New York: Paulist Press, 1979).

39. Flannery, *op. cit.,* pp. 182–183.

40. Heer, *op. cit.,* p. 406.

41. Frederich Heer, "The Catholic Church and the Jews Today," *Midstream* 17 (May 1971): 29.

42. Cf. Rosemary Ruether, "An Invitation to Jewish-Christian Dialogue: In What Sense Can We Say that Jesus was 'The Christ'?", *Ecumenist,* 10, No. 2 (January/February 1973): 17–24.

43. Cf. John T. Pawlikowski, "Pauline Baptismal Theology and Christian-Jewish Relations," in Zeik and Siegel (eds.), *op. cit.,* pp. 89–110.

44. Cf. John T. Pawlikowski, "The Contemporary Jewish-Christian Theological Dialogue Agenda," *Journal of Ecumenical Studies* 11 (Fall 1974): 602–606 and John T. Pawlikowski, "The Church and Judaism: The Thought of James Parkes," *Journal of Ecumenical Studies* 6 (Fall 1969): 573–97. Also John T. Pawlikowski, *Christ in Light of the Christian-Jewish Dialogue* (Ramsey, NJ: Paulist Press, 1982).

45. Gordon Zahn, "Catholic Resistance? A Yes and a No," in Littell and Locke (eds.), *op. cit.,* pp. 234–35.

46. Cf. Gordon Zahn, *German Catholics and Hitler's Wars* (New York: Sheed & Ward, 1962), pp. 208–224.

47. Guenter Lewy, *The Catholic Church and Nazi Germany* (New York: McGraw-Hill Book Co., 1964), pp. 325–41.

48. Franklin Sherman, "Speaking of God after Auschwitz," *Worldview* 17, no. 9 (September 1974), p. 29.

49. *Ibid.,* p. 30.

50. Marcel Dubois, "Christian Reflection on the Holocaust," *Sidic* 7 No. 2 (1974), p. 15.

51. *Ibid.*

52. Flannery, *op. cit.,* p. 175.

53. Rolf Hochhuth, *The Deputy* (New York: Grove Press, 1964).

54. Cf. Eric Bentley (ed.), *op. cit.*

55. Cf. Nora Levin, *The Holocaust* (New York: Schocken Books, 1973), pp. 687–693 and Joseph L. Lichten, *Pius XII: A Question of Judgment* (Washington: National Catholic Welfare Conference, 1963). Also, Pinchas Lapide, *Three Popes and the Jews* (New York: Hawthorne Books, Inc., 1967).

56. Robert A. Graham, SJ. *Pius XII's Defense of Jews and Others: 1944–45*. (Milwaukee: Catholic League for Religious and Civil Rights, 1982).

57. John F. Morley, *Vatican Diplomacy and the Jews During the Holocaust: 1939–1943* (New York: KTAV, 1980).

58. *Ibid.*, p. 209.

59. Cf. Bentley (ed), *op. cit.*, p. 43.

60. *Ibid.*, p. 173.

61. Levin, *op. cit.*, p. 693.

Abraham Joshua Heschel
THE MEANING OF THIS HOUR

Emblazoned over the gates of the world in which we live is the escutcheon of the demons. The mark of Cain in the face of man has come to overshadow the likeness of God. There has never been so much guilt and distress, agony, and terror. At no time has the earth been so soaked with blood. Fellow men turned out to be evil ghosts, monstrous and weird. Ashamed and dismayed, we ask: Who is responsible?

History is a pyramid of efforts and errors; yet at times it is the Holy Mountain on which God holds judgment over the nations. Few are privileged to discern God's judgment in history. But all may be guided by the words of the Baal Shem: If a man has beheld evil, he may know that it was shown to him in order that he learn his own guilt and repent; for what is shown to him is also within him.

We have trifled with the name of God. We have taken the ideals in vain. We have called for the Lord. He came. And was ignored. We have preached but eluded Him. We have praised but defied Him. Now we reap the fruits of our failure. Through centuries His voice cried in the wilderness. How skillfully it was trapped and imprisoned in the temples! How often it was drowned or distorted! Now we behold how it gradually withdraws, abandoning one people after another, departing from their souls, despising their wisdom. The taste for the good has all but gone from the earth. Men heap spite upon cruelty, malice upon atrocity.

The horrors of our time fill our souls with reproach and everlasting shame. We have profaned the word of God, and we have given the wealth of our land, the ingenuity of our minds and the dear lives of our youth to tragedy and perdition. There has never been more reason for man to be ashamed than now. Silence hovers mercilessly over many dreadful lands. The day of the Lord is a day without the Lord. Where is God? Why didst Thou not halt the trains loaded with Jews being led to slaughter? It is so hard to rear a child, to nourish and to educate. Why dost Thou make it so easy to kill? Like Moses, we hide our face; for we

271

are afraid to look upon *Elohim,* upon His power of judgment.[1] Indeed, where were we when men learned to hate in the days of starvation? When raving madmen were sowing wrath in the hearts of the unemployed?

Let modern dictatorship not serve as an alibi for our conscience. We have failed to fight for right, for justice, for goodness; as a result we must fight *against* wrong, *against* injustice, *against* evil. We have failed to offer sacrifices on the altar of peace; thus we offered sacrifices on the altar of war. A tale is told of a band of inexperienced mountain climbers. Without guides, they struck recklessly into the wilderness. Suddenly a rocky ledge gave way beneath their feet and they tumbled headlong into a dismal pit. In the darkness of the pit they recovered from their shock only to find themselves set upon by a swarm of angry snakes. For each snake the desperate men slew, ten more seemed to lash out in its place. Strangely enough, one man seemed to stand aside from the fight. When indignant voices of his struggling companions reproached him for not fighting, he called back: "If we remain here, we shall be dead before the snakes. I am searching for a way of escape from the pit for all of us."

Our world seems not unlike a pit of snakes. We did not sink into the pit in 1939, or even in 1933. We had descended into it generations ago, and the snakes have sent their venom into the bloodstream of humanity, gradually paralyzing us, numbing nerve after nerve, dulling our minds, darkening our vision. Good and evil, that were once as real as day and night, have become a blurred mist. In our everyday life we worshiped force, despised compassion, and obeyed no law but our unappeasable appetite. The vision of the sacred has all but died in the soul of man. And when greed, envy and the reckless will to power came to maturity, the serpents cherished in the bosom of our civilization broke out of their dens to fall upon the helpless nations.

The outbreak of war was no surprise. It came as a long expected sequel to a spiritual disaster. Instilled with the gospel that truth is mere advantage and reverence weakness, people succumbed to the bigger advantage of a lie—"the Jew is our misfortune"—and to the power of arrogance—"tomorrow the whole world shall be ours," "the peoples' democracies must depend upon force." The roar of bombers over Rotterdam, Warsaw, London, was but the echo of thoughts bred for years by individual brains, and later applauded by entire nations. It was through our failure that people started to suspect that science is a device for exploitation, parliaments pulpits for hypocrisy, and religion a pretext for a bad conscience. In the tantalized souls of those who had faith in ideals, suspicion became a dogma and contempt the only solace. Mistaking the abortions of their conscience for intellectual heroism, many thinkers employ clever pens to scold and to scorn the reverence for life, the awe for truth, the loyalty to justice. Man, about to hang himself, discovers it is easier to hang others.

The conscience of the world was destroyed by those who were wont to blame others rather than themselves. Let us remember. We revered the instincts but distrusted the prophets. We labored to perfect engines and let our inner life go to wreck. We ridiculed superstition until we lost our ability to believe. We have helped to extinguish the light our fathers had kindled. We have bartered holiness for convenience, loyalty for success, love for power, wisdom for information, tradition for fashion.

We cannot dwell at ease under the sun of our civilization as our ancestors thought we could. What was in the minds of our martyred brothers in their last hours? They died with disdain and scorn for a civilization in which the killing of civilians could become a carnival of fun, for a civilization which gave us mastery over the forces of nature but lost control over the forces of our self.

Tanks and planes cannot redeem humanity, nor the discovery of guilt by association nor suspicion. A man with a gun is like a beast without a gun. The killing of snakes will save us for the moment but not forever. The war has outlasted the victory of arms as we failed to conquer the infamy of the soul: the indifference to crime, when committed against others. For evil is indivisible. It is the same in thought and in speech, in private and in social life. The greatest task of our time is to take the souls of men out of the pit. The world has experienced that God is involved. Let us forever remember that the sense for the sacred is as vital to us as the light of the sun. There can be no nature without spirit, no world without the Torah, no brotherhood without a father, no humanity without attachment to God.

God will return to us when we shall be willing to let Him in—into our banks and factories, into our Congress and clubs, into our courts and investigating committees, into our homes and theaters. For God is everywhere or nowhere, the Father of all men or no man, concerned about everything or nothing. Only in His presence shall we learn that the glory of man is not in his will to power, but in his power of compassion. Man reflects either the image of His presence or that of a beast.

Soldiers in the horror of battle offer solemn testimony that life is not a hunt for pleasure, but an engagement for service; that there are things more valuable than life; that the world is not a vacuum. Either we make it an altar for God or it is invaded by demons. There can be no neutrality. Either we are ministers of the sacred or slaves of evil. Let the blasphemy of our time not become an eternal scandal. Let future generations not loathe us for having failed to preserve what prophets and saints, martyrs and scholars have created in thousands of years. The apostles of force have shown that they are great in evil. Let us reveal that we can be as great in goodness. We will survive if we shall be as fine and sacrificial in our homes and offices, in our Congress and clubs, as our soldiers are on the fields of battle.

There is a divine dream which the prophets and rabbis have cherished and which fills our prayers, and permeates the acts of true piety. It is the dream of a world, rid of evil by the grace of God as well as by the efforts of man, by his dedication to the task of establishing the kingship of God in the world. God is waiting for us to redeem the world. We should not spend our life hunting for trivial satisfactions while God is waiting constantly and keenly for our effort and devotion.

The Almighty has not created the universe that we may have opportunities to satisfy our greed, envy and ambition. We have not survived that we may waste our years in vulgar vanities. The martyrdom of millions demands that we consecrate ourselves to the fulfillment of God's dream of salvation. Israel did not accept the Torah of their own free will. When Israel approached Sinai, God lifted up the mountain and held it over their heads, saying: "Either you accept the Torah or be crushed beneath the mountain."[2]

The mountain of history is over our heads again. Shall we renew the covenant with God?

NOTES

1. The reference is to Exodus 3:6. In Jewish tradition, *Elohim* is the name of God denoting the attribute of judgment (while the name YHVH denotes mercy).

2. Babli, Shabbat 88a.

Part IV
TWO CENTRAL MORAL QUESTIONS: NAZI GUILT AND JEWISH RESISTANCE

Of the many moral questions raised by the Holocaust, two have been the focus of extended debate. The question of German guilt has been repeatedly raised as we try to measure moral responsibility for six million murders. Hannah Arendt argues that Adolf Eichmann, a Nazi bureaucrat who directed the deportation of hundreds of thousands of Jews to the gas chambers, was essentially a person whose conscience had been abandoned to his social role. Gershom Scholem responds to Arendt's controversial position, while A. Zvi Bar-On clarifies our understanding of the complicated and difficult concept of collective responsibility.

Were the Jews passive before the deadly assault? This question, which suggests that somehow Jews were guilty of their own murder, has plagued observers of the Holocaust for decades. Radically different views on this question are presented in a symposium on Jewish resistance by four well-known commentators on Jewish life and community. These views are followed by my analysis of some of the moral and political dimensions of our understanding of resistance.

Hannah Arendt
POSTSCRIPT TO *EICHMANN IN JERUSALEM*

Even before its publication, this book became both the center of a controversy and the object of an organized campaign. It is only natural that the campaign, conducted with all the well-known means of image-making and opinion-manipulation, got much more attention than the controversy, so that the latter was somehow swallowed up by and drowned in the artificial noise of the former. This became especially clear when a strange mixture of the two, in almost identical phraseology—as though the pieces written against the book (and more frequently against its author) came "out of a mimeographing machine" (Mary McCarthy)—was carried from America to England and then to Europe, where the book was not yet even available. And this was possible because the clamor centered on the "image" of a book which was never written, and touched upon subjects that often had not only not been mentioned by me but had never occurred to me before.

The debate—if that is what it was—was by no means devoid of interest. Manipulations of opinion, insofar as they are inspired by well-defined interests, have limited goals; their effect, however, if they happen to touch upon an issue of authentic concern, is no longer subject to their control and may easily produce consequences they never foresaw or intended. It now appeared that the era of the Hitler regime, with its gigantic, unprecedented crimes, constituted an "unmastered past" not only for the German people or for the Jews all over the world, but for the rest of the world, which had not forgotten this great catastrophe in the heart of Europe either, and had also been unable to come to terms with it. Moreover—and this was perhaps even less expected—general moral questions, with all their intricacies and modern complexities, which I would never have suspected would haunt men's minds today and weigh heavily on their hearts, stood suddenly in the foreground of public concern.

The controversy began by calling attention to the conduct of the

277

Jewish people during the years of the Final Solution, thus following up the question, first raised by the Israeli prosecutor, of whether the Jews could or should have defended themselves. I had dismissed that question as silly and cruel, since it testified to a fatal ignorance of the conditions at the time. It has now been discussed to exhaustion, and the most amazing conclusions have been drawn. The well-known historico-sociological construct of a "ghetto mentality" (which in Israel has taken its place in history textbooks and in this country has been espoused chiefly by the psychologist Bruno Bettelheim—against the furious protest of official American Judaism) has been repeatedly dragged in to explain behavior which was not at all confined to the Jewish people and which therefore cannot be explained by specifically Jewish factors. The suggestions proliferated until someone who evidently found the whole discussion too dull had the brilliant idea of evoking Freudian theories and attributing to the whole Jewish people a "death wish"—unconscious, of course. This was the unexpected conclusion certain reviewers chose to draw from the "image" of a book, created by certain interest groups, in which I allegedly had claimed that the Jews had murdered themselves. And why had I told such a monstrously implausible lie? Out of "self-hatred," of course.

Since the role of the Jewish leadership had come up at the trial, and since I had reported and commented on it, it was inevitable that it too should be discussed. This, in my opinion, is a serious question, but the debate has contributed little to its clarification. As can be seen from the recent trial in Israel at which a certain Hirsch Birnblat, a former chief of the Jewish police in a Polish town and now a conductor at the Israeli Opera, first was sentenced by a district court to five years' imprisonment, and then was exonerated by the Supreme Court in Jerusalem, whose unanimous opinion indirectly exonerated the Jewish Councils in general, the Jewish Establishment is bitterly divided on this issue. In the debate, however, the most vocal participants were those who either identified the Jewish people with its leadership—in striking contrast to the clear distinction made in almost all the reports of survivors, which may be summed up in the words of a former inmate of Theresienstadt: "The Jewish people as a whole behaved magnificently. Only the leadership failed"—or justified the Jewish functionaries by citing all the commendable services they had rendered before the war, and above all before the era of the Final Solution, as though there were no difference between helping Jews to emigrate and helping the Nazis to deport them.

While these issues had indeed some connection with this book, although they were inflated out of all proportion, there were others which had no relation to it whatsoever. There was, for instance, a hot discussion of the German resistance movement from the beginning of the Hitler regime on, which I naturally did not discuss, since the question of Eichmann's conscience, and that of the situation around him, relates only to the period of the war and the Final Solution. But there were more fantastic items. Quite a number of people began to debate the question of whether the victims of persecution may not always be "uglier" than their murderers; or whether anyone who was not present is entitled "to sit in judgment" over the past; or whether the defendant or the victim holds the center of the stage in a trial. On the latter point, some went so far as to assert not only that I was wrong in being interested in what kind of person Eichmann was, but that he should not have been allowed to speak at all—that is, presumably, that the trial should have been conducted without any defense.

As is frequently the case in discussions that are conducted with a great show of emotion, the down-to-earth interests of certain groups, whose excitement is entirely concerned with factual matters and who therefore try to distort the facts, become quickly and inextricably involved with the untrammeled inspirations of intellectuals who, on the contrary, are not in the least interested in facts but treat them merely as a springboard for "ideas." But even in these sham battles, there could often be detected a certain seriousness, a degree of authentic concern, and this even in the contributions by people who boasted that they had not read the book and promised that they never would read it.

Compared with these debates, which wandered so far afield, the book itself dealt with a sadly limited subject. The report of a trial can discuss only the matters which were treated in the course of the trial, or which in the interests of justice should have been treated. If the general situation of a country in which the trial takes place happens to be important to the conduct of the trial, it too must be taken into account. This book, then, does not deal with the history of the greatest disaster that ever befell the Jewish people, nor is it an account of totalitarianism, or a history of the German people in the time of the Third Reich, nor is it, finally and least of all, a theoretical treatise on the nature of evil. The focus of every trial is upon the person of the defendant, a man of flesh and blood with an individual history, with an always unique set of qualities, peculiarities, behavior patterns, and circumstances. All the things that go beyond that, such as the history of the Jewish people in the dispersion, and of anti-Semitism, or the conduct of the German people and other peoples, or the ideologies of the time and the governmental apparatus of the Third Reich, affect the trial only insofar as they form the background and the conditions under which the defendant committed his acts. All the things that the defendant did not come into contact with, or that did not influence him, must be omitted from the proceedings of the trial and consequently from the report on it.

It may be argued that all the general questions we involuntarily raise as soon as we begin to speak of these matters—why did it have to be the Germans? why did it have to be the Jews? what is the nature of totalitarian rule?—are far more important than the question of the kind of crime for which a man is being tried, and the nature of the defendant upon whom justice must be pronounced; more important, too, than the question of how well our present system of justice is capable of dealing with this special type of crime and criminal it has had repeatedly to cope with since the Second World War. It can be held that the issue is no longer a particular human being, a single distinct individual in the dock, but rather the German people in general, or anti-Semitism in all its forms, or the whole of modern history, or the nature of man and original sin—so that ultimately the entire human race sits invisibly beside the defendant in the dock. All this has often been argued, and especially by those who will not rest until they have discovered an "Eichmann in every one of us." If the defendant is taken as a symbol and the trial as a pretext to bring up matters which are apparently more interesting than the guilt or innocence of one person, then consistency demands that we bow to the assertion made by Eichmann and his lawyer: that he was brought to book because a scapegoat was needed, not only for the German Federal Republic, but also for the events as a whole and for what made them possible—that is for anti-Semitism and totalitarian government as well as for the human race and original sin.

I need scarcely say that I would never have gone to Jerusalem if I had shared these views. I held and hold the opinion that this trial had to take place in the interests of justice and nothing else. I also think the judges were quite right when they stressed in their verdict that "the State of Israel was established and recognized as the State of the Jews," and therefore had jurisdiction over a crime committed against the Jewish people; and in view of the current confusion in legal circles about the meaning and usefulness of punishment, I was glad that the judgment quoted Grotius, who, for his part, citing an older author, explained that punishment is necessary "to defend the honor or the authority of him who was hurt by the offence so that the failure to punish may not cause his degradation."

There is of course no doubt that the defendant and the nature of his acts as well as the trial itself raise problems of a general nature which go far beyond the matters considered in Jerusalem. I have attempted to go into some of these problems in the Epilogue, which ceases to be simple reporting. I would not have been surprised if people had found my treatment inadequate, and I would have welcomed a discussion of the general significance of the entire body of facts, which could have been all the more meaningful the more directly it referred to the concrete events. I also can well imagine that an authentic controversy might have arisen over the subtitle of the book; for when I speak of the banality of evil, I do so only on the strictly factual level, pointing to a phenomenon which stared one in the face at the trial. Eichmann was not Iago and not Macbeth, and nothing would have been farther from his mind than to determine with Richard III "to prove a villain." Except for an extraordinary diligence in looking out for his personal advancement, he had no motives at all. And this diligence in itself was in no way criminal; he certainly would never have murdered his superior in order to inherit his post. He *merely,* to put the matter colloquially, *never realized what he was doing.* It was precisely this lack of imagination which enabled him to sit for months on end facing a German Jew who was conducting the police interrogation, pouring out his heart to the man and explaining again and again how it was that he reached only the rank of lieutenant colonel in the S.S. and that it had not been his fault that he was not promoted. In principle he knew quite well what it was all about, and in his final statement to the court he spoke of the "revaluation of values prescribed by the [Nazi] government." He was not stupid. It was sheer thoughtlessness—something by no means identical with stupidity—that predisposed him to become one of the greatest criminals of that period. And if this is "banal" and even funny, if with the best will in the world one cannot extract any diabolical or demonic profundity from Eichmann, that is still far from calling it commonplace. It surely cannot be so common that a man facing death, and, moreover, standing beneath the gallows, should be able to think of nothing but what he has heard at funerals all his life, and that these "lofty words" should completely becloud the reality of his own death. That such remoteness from reality and such thoughtlessness can wreak more havoc than all the evil instincts taken together which, perhaps, are inherent in man—that was, in fact, the lesson one could learn in Jerusalem. But it was a lesson, neither an explanation of the phenomenon nor a theory about it.

Seemingly more complicated, but in reality far simpler than examining the strange interdependence of thoughtlessness and evil, is the question of what kind of crime is actually involved here—a crime, moreover, which all agree is unprecedented. For the concept of genocide, introduced explicitly to cover a crime unknown before, although applicable up to a point is not fully adequate, for the simple reason that massacres of whole peoples are not unprecedented. They were the order of the day in antiquity, and the centuries of colonization and imperialism provide plenty of examples of more or less successful attempts of that sort. The expression "administrative massacres" seems better to fill the bill. The term arose in connection with British imperialism; the English deliberately rejected such procedures as a means of maintaining their rule over India. The phrase has the virtue of dispelling the prejudice that such monstrous acts can be committed only against a foreign nation or a different race. There is the well-known fact that Hitler began his mass murders by granting "mercy deaths" to the "incurably ill," and that he intended to wind up his extermination program by doing away with "genetically damaged" Germans (heart and lung patients). But quite aside from that, it is apparent that this sort of killing can be directed against any given group, that is, that the principle of selection is dependent only upon circumstantial factors. It is quite conceivable that in the automated economy of a not-too-distant future men may be tempted to exterminate all those whose intelligence quotient is below a certain level.

In Jerusalem this matter was inadequately discussed because it is actually very difficult to grasp juridically. We heard the protestations of the defense that Eichmann was after all only a "tiny cog" in the machinery of the Final Solution, and of the prosecution, which believed it had discovered in Eichmann the actual motor. I myself attributed no more importance to both theories than did the Jerusalem court, since the whole cog theory is legally pointless and therefore it does not matter at all what order of magnitude is assigned to the "cog" named Eichmann. In its judgment the court naturally conceded that such a crime could be committed only by a giant bureaucracy using the resources of government. But insofar as it remains a crime—and that, of course, is the premise for a trial—all the cogs in the machinery, no matter how insignificant, are in court forthwith transformed back into perpetrators, that is to say, into human beings. If the defendant excuses himself on the ground that he acted not as a man but as a mere functionary whose functions could just as easily have been carried out by anyone else, it is as if a criminal pointed to the statistics on crime—which set forth that so-and-so many crimes per day are committed in such-and-such a place —and declared that he only did what was statistically expected, that it was mere accident that he did it and not somebody else, since after all somebody had to do it.

Of course it is important to the political and social sciences that the essence of totalitarian government, and perhaps the nature of every bureaucracy, is to make functionaries and mere cogs in the administrative machinery out of men, and thus to dehumanize them. And one can debate long and profitably on the rule of Nobody, which is what the political form known as bureaucracy truly is. Only one must realize clearly that the administration of justice can consider these factors only to the extent that they are circumstances of the crime—just as, in a case of theft, the economic plight of the thief is taken into account without excusing the theft, let alone wiping it off the slate. True, we have become very much accustomed by modern psychology and sociology, not to speak of modern bureaucracy, to explaining away the responsibility of the doer for his deed in terms of this or that kind of determinism. Whether such seemingly deeper explanations of human actions are right or wrong is debatable. But what is not debatable is that no judicial procedure would be possible on the basis of them, and that the administration of justice, measured by such theories, is an extremely unmodern, not to say outmoded, institution. When Hitler said that a day would come in Germany when it would be considered a "disgrace" to be a jurist, he was speaking with utter consistency of his dream of a perfect bureaucracy.

As far as I can see, jurisprudence has at its disposal for treating this whole battery of questions only two categories, both of which, to my mind, are quite inadequate to deal with the matter. These are the concepts of "acts of state" and of acts "on superior orders." At any rate, these are the only categories in terms of which such matters are discussed in this kind of trial, usually on the motion of the defendant. The theory of the act of state is based on the argument that one sovereign state may not sit in judgment upon another, *par in parem non habet jurisdictionem*. Practically speaking, this argument had already been disposed of at Nuremberg; it stood no chance from the start, since, if it were accepted, even Hitler, the only one who was really responsible in the full sense, could not have been brought to account—a state of affairs which would have violated the most elementary sense of justice. However, an argument that stands no chance on the practical plane has not necessarily been demolished on the theoretical one. The usual evasions—that Germany at the time of the Third Reich was dominated by a gang of criminals to whom sovereignty and parity cannot very well be ascribed—were hardly useful. For on the one hand everyone knows that the analogy with a gang of criminals is applicable only to such a limited extent that it is not really applicable at all, and on the other hand these crimes undeniably took place within a "legal" order. That, indeed, was their outstanding characteristic.

Perhaps we can approach somewhat closer to the matter if we realize that back of the concept of act of state stands the theory of *raison d'état*. According to that theory, the actions of the state, which is responsible for the life of the country and thus also for the laws obtaining in it, are not subject to the same rules as the acts of the citizens of the country. Just as the rule of law, although devised to eliminate violence and the war of all against all, always stands in need of the instruments of violence in order to assure its own existence, so a government may find itself compelled to commit actions that are generally regarded as crimes in order to assure its own survival and the survival of lawfulness. Wars are frequently justified on these grounds, but criminal acts of state do not occur only in the field of international relations, and the history of civilized nations knows many examples of them—from Napoleon's assassination of the Duc d'Enghien, to the murder of the Socialist leader Matteotti, for which Mussolini himself was presumably responsible.

Raison d'état appeals—rightly or wrongly, as the case may be—to *necessity*, and the state crimes committed in its name (which are fully criminal in terms of the dominant legal system of the country where they occur) are considered emergency measures, concessions made to the stringencies of *Realpolitik,* in order to preserve power and thus assure the continuance of the existing legal order as a whole. In a normal political and legal system, such crimes occur as an exception to the rule and are not subject to legal penalty (are *gerichtsfrei,* as German legal theory expresses it) because the existence of the state itself is at stake, and no outside political entity has the right to deny a state its existence or prescribe how it is to preserve it. However—as we may have learned from the history of Jewish policy in the Third Reich—in a state founded upon criminal principles, the situation is reversed. Then a non-criminal act (such as, for example, Himmler's order in the late summer of 1944 to halt the deportation of Jews) becomes a concession to necessity imposed by reality, in this case the impending defeat. Here the question arises: what is the nature of the sovereignty of such an entity? Has it not violated the parity (*par in parem non habet jurisdictionem*) which international law accords it? Does the *"par in parem"* signify no more than the paraphernalia of sovereignty? Or does it also imply a substantive equality or likeness? Can we apply the same principle that is applied to a governmental apparatus in which crime and violence are exceptions and borderline cases to a political order in which crime is legal and the rule?

Just how inadequate juristic concepts really are to deal with the criminal facts which were the subject matter of all these trials appears perhaps even more strikingly in the concept of acts performed on superior orders. The Jerusalem court countered the argument advanced by the defense with lengthy quotations from the penal and military lawbooks of civilized countries, particularly of Germany; for under Hitler the pertinent articles had by no means been repealed. All of them agree on one point: manifestly criminal orders must not be obeyed. The court, moreover, referred to a case that came up in Israel several years ago: soldiers were brought to trial for having massacred the civilian inhabitants of an Arab village on the border shortly before the beginning of the Sinai campaign. The villagers had been found outside their houses during a military curfew of which, it appeared, they were unaware. Unfortunately, on closer examination the comparison appears to be defective on two accounts. First of all, we must again consider that the relationship of exception and rule, which is of prime importance for recognizing the criminality of an order executed by a subordinate, was reversed in the case of Eichmann's actions. Thus, on the basis of this argument one could actually defend Eichmann's failure to obey certain of Himmler's orders, or his obeying them with hesitancy: they were manifest exceptions to the prevailing rule. The judgment found this to be especially incriminating to the defendant, which was certainly very understandable but not very consistent. This can easily be seen from the pertinent findings of Israeli military courts, which were cited in support by the judges. They ran as follows: the order to be disobeyed must be "manifestly unlawful"; unlawfulness "should fly like a black flag above [it], as a warning reading, 'Prohibited.' " In other words, the order, to be recognized by the soldier as "manifestly unlawful," must violate by its unusualness the canons of the legal system to which he is accustomed. And Israeli jurisprudence in these matters coincides completely with that of other countries. No doubt in formulating these articles the legislators were thinking of cases in which an officer who suddenly goes mad, say, commands his subordinates to kill another officer. In any normal trial of such a case, it would at once become clear that the soldier was not being asked to consult the voice of conscience, or a "feeling of lawfulness that lies deep within every human conscience, also of those who are not conversant with books of law . . . provided the eye is not blind and the heart is not stony and corrupt." Rather, the soldier would be expected to be able to distinguish between a rule and a striking exception to the rule. The German military code, at any rate, explicitly states that conscience is not enough. Paragraph 48 reads: "Punishability of an action or omission is not excluded on the ground that the person considered his behavior required by his conscience or the prescripts of his religion." A striking feature of the Israeli court's line of argument is that the concept of a sense of justice grounded in the depths of every man is presented solely as a substitute for familiarity with the law. Its plausibility rests on the assumption that the law expresses only what every man's conscience would tell him anyhow.

If we are to apply this whole reasoning to the Eichmann case in a meaningful way, we are forced to conclude that Eichmann acted fully within the framework of the kind of judgment required of him: he acted in accordance with the rule, examined the order issued to him for its "manifest" legality, namely regularity; he did not have to fall back upon his "conscience," since he was not one of those who were unfamiliar with the laws of his country. The exact opposite was the case.

The second account on which the argument based on comparison proved to be defective concerns the practice of the courts of admitting the plea of "superior orders" as important extenuating circumstances, and this practice was mentioned explicitly by the judgment. The judgment cited the case I have mentioned above, that of the massacre of the Arab inhabitants at Kfar Kassem, as proof that Israeli jurisdiction does not clear a defendant of responsibility for the "superior orders" he received. And it is true, the Israeli soldiers were indicted for murder, but "superior orders" constituted so weighty an argument for mitigating circumstances that they were sentenced to relatively short prison terms. To be sure, this case concerned an isolated act, not—as in Eichmann's case—an activity extending over years, in which crime followed crime. Still, it was undeniable that he had always acted upon "superior orders," and if the provisions of ordinary Israeli law had been applied to him, it would have been difficult indeed to impose the maximum penalty upon him. The truth of the matter is that Israeli law, in theory and practice, like the jurisdiction of other countries cannot but admit that the fact of "superior orders," even when their unlawfulness is "manifest," can severely disturb the normal working of a man's conscience.

This is only one example among many to demonstrate the inadequacy of the prevailing legal system and of current juridical concepts to deal with the facts of administrative massacres organized by the state apparatus. If we look more closely into the matter we will observe without much difficulty that the judges in all these trials really passed judgment solely on the basis of the monstrous deeds. In other words, they judged freely, as it were, and did not really lean on the standards and legal precedents with which they more or less convincingly sought to justify their decisions. That was already evident in Nuremberg, where the judges on the one hand declared that the "crime against peace" was the gravest of all the crimes they had to deal with, since it included all the other crimes, but on the other hand actually imposed the death penalty only on those defendants who had participated in the new crime of administrative massacre—supposedly a less grave offense than conspiracy against peace. It would indeed be tempting to pursue these and similar inconsistencies in a field so obsessed with consistency as jurisprudence. But of course that cannot be done here.

There remains, however, one fundamental problem, which was implicitly present in all these postwar trials and which must be mentioned here because it touches upon one of the central moral questions of all time, namely upon the nature and function of human judgment. What we have demanded in these trials, where the defendants had committed "legal" crimes, is that human beings be capable of telling right from wrong even when all they have to guide them is their own judgment, which, moreover, happens to be completely at odds with what they must regard as the unanimous opinion of all those around them. And this question is all the more serious as we know that the few who were "arrogant" enough to trust only their own judgment were by no means identical with those persons who continued to abide by old values, or who were guided by a religious belief. Since the whole of respectable society had in one way or another succumbed to Hitler, the moral maxims which determine social behavior and the religious commandments—"Thou shalt not kill!"—which guide conscience had virtually vanished. Those few who were still able to tell right from wrong went really only by their own judgments, and they did so freely; there were no rules to be abided by, under which the particular cases with which they were confronted could be subsumed. They had to decide each instance as it arose, because no rules existed for the unprecedented.

How troubled men of our time are by this question of judgment (or, as is often said, by people who dare "sit in judgment") has emerged in the controversy over the present book, as well as the in many respects similar controversy over Hochhuth's *The Deputy*. What has come to light is neither nihilism nor cynicism, as one might have expected, but a quite extraordinary confusion over elementary questions of morality—as if an instinct in such matters were truly the last thing to be taken for granted in our time. The many curious notes that have been struck in the course of these disputes seem particularly revealing. Thus, some American literati have professed their naïve belief that temptation and coercion are really the same thing, that no one can be asked to resist temptation. (If someone puts a pistol to your heart and orders you to shoot your best friend, then you simply *must* shoot him. Or, as it was argued—some years ago in connection with the quiz program scandal in which a university teacher had hoaxed the public—when so much money is at stake, who could possibly resist?) The argument that we cannot judge if we were not present and involved ourselves seems to convince everyone everywhere, although it seems obvious that if it were true, neither the administration of justice nor the writing of history would ever be possible. In contrast to these confusions, the reproach of self-righteousness raised against those who do judge is age-old; but that does not make it any the more valid. Even the judge who condemns a murderer can still say when he goes home: "And there, but for the grace of God, go I." All German Jews unanimously have condemned the wave of coordination which passed over the German people in 1933 and from one day to the next turned the Jews into pariahs. Is it conceivable that none of them ever asked himself how many of his own group would have done just the same if only they had been allowed to? But is their condemnation today any the less correct for that reason?

The reflection that you yourself might have done wrong under the same circumstances may kindle a spirit of forgiveness, but those who today refer to Christian charity seem strangely confused on this issue too. Thus we can read in the postwar statement of the *Evangelische Kirche in Deutschland,* the Protestant church, as follows: "We aver that before the God of Mercy we share in the guilt for the outrage committed against the Jews by our own people through omission and silence."* It seems to me that a Christian is guilty before the God of *Mercy* if he repays evil with evil, hence that the churches would have sinned against mercy if millions of Jews had been killed as punishment for some evil they committed. But if the churches shared in the guilt for an outrage pure and simple, as they themselves attest, then the matter must still be considered to fall within the purview of the God of *Justice.*

This slip of the tongue, as it were, is no accident. Justice, but not mercy, is a matter of judgment, and about nothing does public opinion everywhere seem to be in happier agreement than that no one has the right to judge somebody else. What public opinion permits us to judge and even to condemn are trends, or whole groups of people—the larger the better—in short, something so general that distinctions can no longer be made, names no longer be named. Needless to add, this taboo applies doubly when the deeds or words of famous people or men in high position are being questioned. This is currently expressed in high-flown assertions that it is "superficial" to insist on details and to mention individuals, whereas it is the sign of sophistication to speak in generalities according to which all cats are gray and we are all equally guilty. Thus the charge Hochhuth has raised against a single Pope—one man, easily identifiable, with a name of his own—was immediately countered with an indictment of all Christianity. The charge against Christianity in general, with its two thousand years of history, cannot be proved, and if it could be proved, it would be horrible. No one seems to mind this so long as no *person* is involved, and it is quite safe to go one step further

---

* Quoted from the minister Aurel v. Jüchen in an anthology of critical reviews of Hochhuth's play—*Summa Iniuria,* Rowohl Verlag, p. 195.

and to maintain: "Undoubtedly there is reason for grave accusations, but the defendant is *mankind* as a whole." (Thus Robert Weltsch in *Summa Iniuria,* quoted above, italics added.)

Another such escape from the area of ascertainable facts and personal responsibility are the countless theories, based on non-specific, abstract, hypothetical assumptions—from the *Zeitgeist* down to the Oedipus complex—which are so general that they explain and justify every event and every deed: no alternative to what actually happened is even considered and no person could have acted differently from the way he did act. Among the constructs that "explain" everything by obscuring all details, we find such notions as a "ghetto mentality" among European Jews; or the collective guilt of the German people, derived from an *ad hoc* interpretation of their history; or the equally absurd assertion of a kind of collective innocence of the Jewish people. All these clichés have in common that they make judgment superfluous and that to utter them is devoid of all risk. And although we can understand the reluctance of those immediately affected by the disaster—Germans and Jews—to examine too closely the conduct of groups and persons that seemed to be or should have been unimpaired by the totality of the moral collapse—that is, the conduct of the Christian churches, the Jewish leadership, the men of the anti-Hitler conspiracy of July 20, 1944—this understandable disinclination is insufficient to explain the reluctance evident everywhere to make judgments in terms of individual moral responsibility.

Many people today would agree that there is no such thing as collective guilt or, for that matter, collective innocence, and that if there were, no one person could ever be guilty or innocent. This, of course, is not to deny that there is such a thing as *political* responsibility which, however, exists quite apart from what the individual member of the group has done and therefore can neither be judged in moral terms nor be brought before a criminal court. Every government assumes political responsibility for the deeds and misdeeds of its predecessor and every nation for the deeds and misdeeds of the past. When Napoleon, seizing power in France after the Revolution, said: I shall assume the responsibility for everything France ever did from Saint Louis to the Committee of Public Safety, he was only stating somewhat emphatically one of the basic facts of all political life. It means hardly more, generally speaking, than that every generation, by virtue of being born into a historical continuum, is burdened by the sins of the fathers as it is blessed with the deeds of the ancestors. But this kind of responsibility is not what we are talking about here; it is not personal, and only in a metaphorical sense can one say he *feels* guilty for what not he but his father or his people have done. (Morally speaking, it is hardly less wrong to feel guilty without having done something specific than it is to feel free of all guilt if one is actually guilty of something.) It is quite conceivable that certain political responsibilities among nations might some day be adjudicated in an international court; what is inconceivable is that such a court would be a criminal tribunal which pronounces on the guilt or innocence of individuals.

And the question of individual guilt or innocence, the act of meting out justice to both the defendant and the victim, are the only things at stake in a criminal court. The Eichmann trial was no exception, even though the court here was confronted with a crime it could not find in the lawbooks and with a criminal whose like was unknown in any court, at least prior to the Nuremberg Trials. The present report deals with nothing but the extent to which the court in Jerusalem succeeded in fulfilling the demands of justice.

Gershom Scholem

ON EICHMANN

EICHMANN

Eichmann has been executed. In its public and historical aspects the Eichmann case is at an end. All the lessons that might possibly be learned from the great trial which terminated in Eichmann's death sentence can already be studied in full. Now the time has come to embark on the soul-searching the affair demands, and there is no end to thoughts and questions, most of which are without answer.

Those who approved of Eichmann's being put before the bar of justice, those who upheld the trial itself as well as the form chosen for it by the authorities, those who saw in the trial a tremendous moral achievement in educating the nation toward a major historical reckoning—a task as necessary to undertake as it must necessarily fail—in short, all those who are primarily concerned with the public, moral, and historical aspects of the trial rather than with its legal side—they are the ones who are bound to ask themselves whether the execution of Eichmann was indeed the appropriate finish to this enormous issue. I am certain that many thousands and hundreds of thousands of the people of this land are still preoccupied with this question, and I propose to answer it as best I can.

There is no question but that Eichmann deserved the death penalty. I have no doubt he did. I have not come forth to find any merit in him, or, indeed, to discuss any aspect of his deeds and responsibility that pertains to the legal aspects of the trial. I assume that from the legal point of view nothing remains to be said and that he deserved to die a thousand deaths each day. I come to plead on our own behalf, that is to say on behalf of Eichmann's potential (if not actual) victims.

The laws of human society are at a loss as to adequate punishment for Eichmann's crimes. On this point there is general agreement. There can be no possible proportion between this crime and its punishment.

Neither could his execution serve to teach a lesson to other murderers of our people. The application of the death penalty for the murder of millions is not a "deterrent" and will not deter any potential murderer likely to arise against us in the days to come. It is not the deterrent power of the hanging of one inhuman wretch that will prevent catastrophes of this kind in the future. A different education of men and nations, a new human awareness—these will prevent it. To achieve such a human awareness was the purpose of the Eichmann trial.

Eichmann was an excellent example of the systematic destruction of the image of God in man, the "dehumanization" the Nazi movement preached by all possible means and practiced as far as possible. The significance of this trial consisted of revealing to the whole world the meaning of such dehumanization; its effects and the price paid by a whole nation which falls victim to this process. For one can very well say that in the strict sense two nations, not one, were the victims: the Jewish people, whose millions were murdered, and the German people, who became a nation of murderers when it allowed the Nazi doctrine to gain power over it. If we are "to do justice," to deter or avenge the bloodshed of our people, then it must be done to tens and hundreds of thousands whose hands are soiled with blood.

Which brings me to the main point: the application of the death penalty to Eichmann constituted *an inappropriate ending.* It falsified the historical significance of the trial by creating the illusion that it is possible to conclude something of this affair by the hanging of one human or inhuman creature. Such an illusion is most dangerous because it may engender the feeling that something has been done to atone for the unatonable. One man, who is only the corrupt product of the corrupt system which made his existence and activity possible, is to be hanged, and many millions, especially in Germany, will see it as an end to the whole business of the murder of our people. It will be said that the Israelis have captured the chief organizer of the murder; let them hang him and be done with it.

As Jews and as human beings we have no interest in such a phony "finis." It was an easy, slight ending in two senses: it was slight both as to significance and judgment. This hanging was an anticlimax, the satyr play after a tragedy such as had not been seen before. One fears that instead of opening up a reckoning and leaving it open for the next generation, we have foreclosed it. What superficially seems severity of judgment is in reality its mitigation, a mitigation in no way to our interest. It is to our interest that the great historical and moral question, the question probing the depths which this trial has forced all to face—How could this happen?—that this question should retain all its weight, all its

stark nakedness, all its horror. The hangman who had to execute Eichmann's sentence added nothing to the situation, but he took away a
great deal. As I have said before, he introduced the misplaced suggestion that this marked "the end of the story." It would have been better if
we did not have the hangman stand between us and our great question,
between us and the soul-searching account we have to settle with the
world. Having gone through this trial we should ask ourselves: where do
we stand now with this accounting? What do we really want to prove to
the world? If we wanted to prove that justice is being done and that a
great historical reckoning is being effected, then a living Eichmann—
whether imprisoned by us or put into the hands of the Germans (who
had good reasons for not wanting him)—was not likely to stand in the
way of such a reckoning. But it is to be feared that an Eichmann who has
been hanged will indeed stand in the way—very much in the way.

LETTER TO HANNAH ARENDT

Jerusalem, June 23, 1963

Dear Hannah,

Six weeks have passed since I received your book on the Eichmann
trial; and, if I write belatedly, it is because only now do I have the leisure
to devote myself to a proper study of it. I have not, let me say, gone into
the question of the factual and historical authenticity of the various
statements you make. To judge by your treatment of those aspects of the
problem with which I happen to be familiar, however, I fear that your
book is not free of error and distortion. Still, I have no doubt that the
question of the book's factual authenticity will be taken up by other
critics—of whom there will be many—and it is not in any case central to
the critique I wish to offer here.

Your book moves between two poles: the Jews and their bearing in
the days of catastrophe, and the responsibility of Adolf Eichmann. I
have devoted, as you know, a good part of my time to a consideration of
the case of the Jews, and I have studied a not insignificant volume of
material on the subject. I am well aware, in common with every other
spectator of the events, how complex and serious, how little reducible or
transparent, the whole problem is. I am aware that there are aspects of
Jewish history (and for more than forty years I have concerned myself
with little else) which are beyond our comprehension; on the one hand, a
devotion to the things of this world that is near-demonic; on the other, a
fundamental uncertainty of orientation in this world—an uncertainty
which must be contrasted with that certainty of the believer concerning

which, alas, your book has so little to report. There has been weakness, too, though weakness so entwined with heroism that it is not easily unraveled; wretchedness and power-lust are also to be found there. But these things have always existed, and it would be remarkable indeed if, in the days of catastrophe, they were not to make their appearance once again. Thus it was in the year 1391, at the beginning of that generation of catastrophe; and so it has been in our own time. The discussion of these matters is, I believe, both legitimate and unavoidable—although I do not believe that our generation is in a position to pass any kind of historical judgment. We lack the necessary perspective, which alone makes some sort of objectivity possible—and we cannot but lack it.

Nevertheless, we cannot put these questions aside. There is the question thrown at us by the new youth of Israel: why did they allow themselves to be slaughtered? As a question, it seems to me to have a profound justification; and I see no readily formulated answer to it. At each decisive juncture, however, your book speaks only of the *weakness* of the Jewish stance in the world. I am ready enough to admit that weakness; but you put such emphasis upon it that, in my view, your account ceases to be objective and acquires overtones of malice. The problem, I have admitted, is real enough. Why, then, should your book leave one with so strong a sensation of bitterness and shame—not for the compilation, but for the compiler? How is it that your version of the events so often seems to come between us and the events—events which you rightly urge upon our attention? Insofar as I have an answer, it is one which, precisely out of my deep respect for you, I dare not suppress; and it is an answer that goes to the root of our disagreement. It is that heartless, frequently almost sneering and malicious tone with which these matters, touching the very quick of our life, are treated in your book to which I take exception.

In the Jewish tradition there is a concept, hard to define and yet concrete enough, which we know as *Ahavat Yisrael:* "Love of the Jewish people. . . ." In you, dear Hannah, as in so many intellectuals who came from the German Left, I find little trace of this. A discussion such as is attempted in your book would seem to me to require—you will forgive my mode of expression—the most old-fashioned, the most circumspect, the most exacting treatment possible—precisely because of the feelings aroused by this matter, this matter of the destruction of one-third of our people—and I regard you wholly as a daughter of our people, and as nothing else. Thus I have little sympathy with that tone—well expressed by the English word *flippancy*—which you employ so often in the course of your book. To the matter of which you speak it is unimaginably inappropriate. In circumstances such as these, would there not have been a place for what I can only describe with that modest German word—*Herzenstakt?* You may laugh at the word; although I hope you do not, for I mean it seriously. Of the many examples I came upon in your book—and came upon not without pain—none expresses better what I mean than your quotation (taken over without comment from a Nazi source!) about the traffic with the armbands with the Star of David in the Warsaw ghetto, or the sentence about Leo Baeck "who in the eyes of both Jews and Gentiles was the 'Jewish *Führer.*' . . ." The use of the Nazi term in this context is sufficiently revealing. You do not speak, say, of the "Jewish leader," which would have been both apt and free of the German word's horrific connotation—you say precisely the thing that is most false and most insulting. For nobody of whom I have heard or read was Leo Baeck—whom we both knew—ever a *"Führer"* in the sense which you here insinuate to the reader. I too have read Adler's book about Theresienstadt. It is a book about which a great many things could be said. But it was not my impression that the author—who speaks of some people, of whom I have heard quite different accounts, with considerable harshness—it was not my impression that Adler ever spoke of Baeck in this fashion, either directly or indirectly. Certainly, the record of our people's suffering is burdened with a number of questionable figures who deserve, or have received, their just punishment: how could it have been otherwise in a tragedy on so terrible a scale? To speak of all this, however, in so wholly inappropriate a tone—to the benefit of those Germans in condemning whom your book rises to greater eloquence than in mourning the fate of your own people—this is not the way to approach the scene of that tragedy.

In your treatment of the problem of how the Jews reacted to these extreme circumstances—to which neither of us was exposed—I detect, often enough, in place of balanced judgment, a kind of demagogic will-to-overstatement. Which of us can say today what decisions the elders of the Jews—or whatever we choose to call them—ought to have arrived at in the circumstances? I have not read less than you have about these matters, and I am still not certain; but your analysis does not give me confidence that your certainty is better founded than my uncertainty. There were the *Judenräte,* for example; some among them were swine, others were saints. I have read a great deal about both varieties. There were among them also many people in no way different from ourselves, who were compelled to make terrible decisions in circumstances that we cannot even begin to reproduce or reconstruct. I do not know whether they were right or wrong. Nor do I presume to judge. I was not there.

Certainly, there were people in Theresienstadt—as every former inmate can confirm—whose conduct is deserving of the severest judgment. But in case after case we find that the individual verdict varies. Why was Paul Eppstein, one of these "questionable figures," shot by the Nazis, for example? You give no reason. Yet the reason is clear enough: he had done precisely that which according to you he could afford to do without serious danger—he told people in Theresienstadt what awaited them at Auschwitz. Yet he was shot twenty-four hours later.

Nevertheless, your thesis that these machinations of the Nazis served in some way to blur the distinction between torturer and victim —a thesis which you employ to belabor the prosecution in the Eichmann trial—seems to me wholly false and tendentious. In the camps, human beings were systematically degraded; they were, as you say, compelled to participate in their own extermination, and to assist in the execution of fellow prisoners. Is the distinction between torturer and victim thereby blurred? What perversity! We are asked, it appears, to confess that the Jews too had their "share" in these acts of genocide. That is a typical *quaternio terminorum.*

Recently, I have been reading about a book, written during the days of catastrophe in full consciousness of what lay ahead, by Rabbi Moses Chaim Lau of Piotrkov. This Rabbi attempted to define as precisely as possible what was the duty of the Jew in such extremities. Much that I read on this moving and terrible book—and it does not stand alone—is congruent with your general thesis (though not with your tone). But nowhere in your book do you make plain how many Jews there were who acted as they did in full consciousness of what awaited them. The Rabbi in question went with his flock to Treblinka—although he had previously called on them to run away, and his flock had called on him to do likewise. The heroism of the Jews was not always the heroism of the warrior; nor have we always been ashamed of that fact. I cannot refute those who say that the Jews deserved their fate because they did not earlier take steps to defend themselves, because they were cowardly, etc. I came across this argument only recently in a book by that honest Jewish anti-Semite, Kurt Tucholsky. I cannot express myself, of course, with Kurt Tucholsky's eloquence, but I cannot deny that he was right: if all the Jews had run away—in particular, to Palestine—more Jews would have remained alive. Whether, in view of the special circumstances of Jewish history and Jewish life, that would have been possible, and whether it implies a historical share of guilt in Hitler's crime, is another question.

I shall say nothing concerning that other central question of your book: the guilt, or the degree of guilt, of Adolf Eichmann. I have read both the text of the judgment delivered by the Court, and the version you substituted for it in your book. I find that of the Court rather more convincing. Your judgment appears to me to be based on a prodigious *non sequitur*. Your argument would apply equally to those hundreds of thousands, perhaps millions, of human beings, to whom your final sentence is relevant. It is the final sentence that contains the reason why Eichmann ought to be hanged, for in the remainder of the text you argue in detail your view—which I do not share—that the prosecution did not succeed in proving what it had set out to prove. As far as that goes, I may mention that, in addition to putting my name to a letter to the President of Israel pleading for the execution not to be carried out, I set out in a Hebrew essay why I held the execution of the sentence— which Eichmann had in every sense, including that of the prosecution, deserved—to be historically wrong, precisely because of our historical relationship with the German people. I shall not argue the case again here. I wish to say only that your description of Eichmann as a "convert to Zionism" could come only from somebody who had a profound dislike of everything to do with Zionism. These passages in your book I find quite impossible to take seriously. They amount to a mockery of Zionism; and I am forced to the conclusion that this was, indeed, your intention. Let us not pursue the point.

After reading your book, I remain unconvinced by your thesis concerning the "banality of evil"—a thesis which, if your subtitle is to be believed, underlies your entire argument. This new thesis strikes me as a catchword: it does not impress me, certainly, as the product of profound analysis—an analysis such as you gave us so convincingly, in the service of a quite different, indeed contradictory thesis, in your book on totalitarianism. At that time you had not yet made your discovery, apparently, that evil is banal. Of that "radical evil," to which your then analysis bore such eloquent and erudite witness, nothing remains but this slogan—to be more than that it would have to be investigated, at a serious level, as a relevant concept in moral philosophy or political ethics. I am sorry— and I say this, I think, in candor and in no spirit of enmity—that I am unable to take the thesis of your book more seriously. With your earlier book in mind, I had expected something different.

A. Zvi Bar-On

MEASURING RESPONSIBILITY

"Collective guilt" is a nasty phrase. We recoil instinctively from the concept expressed by it. Collective indictment appears, at least *prima facie*, synonymous with injustice, vindictiveness, blurring of distinctions.

For all that, history has recorded quite a few cases of communities and even whole nations being condemned collectively. In recent years, moreover, we witnessed (in Vatican pronouncements) a significant act in the opposite direction: a people was acquitted of the collective guilt of deicide, of which it was accused nearly 2,000 years ago, this accusation having brought in its wake senseless hatred between nations and innumerable crimes against the people on whose forehead the mark of Cain had been set for no good reason. Were this the only case throughout history in which collective guilt had been imposed on innocent people, it would be sufficient to make its concept repugnant to us. All the more so, as it is one case among many. Did the Nazis not make collective indictment into a method, a constant component in their refined technique of oppression and destruction?

It is thus obvious that when dealing with the problem of guilt for the enormous crime of the Final Solution, we must be extremely cautious. And yet, the question has to be formulated in terms of collective guilt: is the whole German people guilty, and if so, what is the nature of that guilt? If not, who is to blame for the murder of six million European Jews during the period between 1939 (or perhaps 1933) and 1945? Who is to blame for converting an entire state into a well-oiled machine for executing this murder? A machine which was supposed to go on with the job until the last Jew in the world had been killed. Who then is guilty and what is the nature of the guilt? Trying to answer this question, I have no illusions; it is very complex and I may hope to contribute only partially to its solution. My approach will be to present the responses of three Germans to this problem, to analyze these responses critically and draw some conclusions. The three are Adolf Eichmann, Günter Grass, and Karl Jaspers.

COULD KANT SAVE EICHMANN?

I chose to analyze Eichmann's stand on the question of guilt for two reasons. *First,* this is the response of a man who had the top function in implementing the Final Solution. Few are the cases in which responsibility for the genocide of the Jewish people is as clear and unequivocal. *Second,* he was, as far as I know, the only Nazi who, when brought to judgment, attempted to determine the measure of his guilt by general criteria, invoking one of the most influential systems of ethics of our time. This exceptionally bold attempt deserves our utmost attention.

As it happened, there was a considerable difference between Eichmann's claims on this issue at the police interrogation and what he said in the courtroom. The investigator had heard from him a straightforward declaration that *all his life he was trying to follow Kant's philosophy and in particular the Categorical Imperative.* But at the cross-examination in court it became clear that there were two qualifications to this claim: (1) his interpretation of Kant's Categorical Imperative underwent changes in the course of years; (2) with the passage of time changes also occurred in the circumstances of his life which limited, as he came to think, the extent to which he was able to put into action Kant's requirement (as he understood it).

The main change in his interpretation of the Kantian principles was apparently the result of his studying Kant's *Critique of Practical Reason.* Strangely enough, this study took place only when Eichmann was already engaged in implementing the Final Solution. Until then, so he claimed, the Categorical Imperative was known to him merely in its simplified commonsense form. To quote from the proceeding of his trial (Session 105; July 20, 1961):

> *Question:* Is this when you learned for the first time the concept of the Categorical Imperative?
>
> *Answer:* No, I had known the Categorical Imperative earlier, but it was in a nutshell, in a summarized form. I suppose it could be summarized as, "Be loyal to the laws, be a disciplined person, live an orderly life, do not come into conflict with laws"—that more or less

was the whole essence of that law for the use of the little man.

This was Eichmann's "earlier version" of the Kantian principle. At the same cross-examination Eichmann also spelled out his later version of it:

Question: What did you understand by Kantian principles?
Answer: I meant by this that at any time and at any moment my way of life should set an example within the framework of the legislation of the laws . . . That is exactly what Kant said.[1]

As Hannah Arendt pointed out, his later version is "an approximately correct definition of the Categorical Imperative" (according to which my action can be considered moral only if "I can also will that my maxim should become a universal law"), while his earlier version is obviously incompatible with it.[2] We cannot be sure from his reported statements whether Eichmann himself so understood the relation between his two versions. But when he spoke of the circumstances that debarred him from living according to the Categorical Imperative, he had certainly in mind his later interpretation of this principle.

Now, what were these circumstances and what was in them to prevent Eichmann from fulfilling the requirements of Kant's ethics? He gave several answers to this question and they were not wholly compatible with one another. The most adequate answer was presumably the one which had connected the "turning point" of his life with the Wannsee conference in January 1942. Let us recall that this was the conference of the representatives of the top Nazi authorities, at which Heydrich read out the instructions for starting the implementation of the Final Solution. This was evidently the latest occasion on which Eichmann could have fully realized the function that he was to perform (if he did not know it earlier).

He was asked at the trial (Session 79) by his defense counsel, Servatius: "It appears from your remarks in reference to your memoirs as recorded by Sassen and from what you have said now, that you were gratified by this conference. Could you comment on this?" To which Eichmann replied: "Yes, but my satisfaction was of a kind different from that of Heydrich . . . after all the efforts [to find other solutions] I could, thanks to the Wannsee Conference, say to myself, declare myself, that [it is being done] against my will and not according to my plans, that I am not to blame, that like Pontius Pilate who had washed his hands I am innocent. For at that conference hard and fast rules were laid by the elite, the leadership, by the Popes of the Kingdom. And myself? I only had to obey."

Let us compare this assertion with Eichmann's answer to Judge Raveh during his examination of Eichmann's approach to the Kantian philosophy (Session 105):

> *Question:* In other words, you contend that your activities in connection with the deportation of Jews correspond to the imperative premises of Kantian philosophy.
>
> *Answer:* No, of course not—because what I referred to was not my life under constraint and compulsion. . . . After all, what I did was thrust upon me. What I meant was the situation where I could be my own master, where I could follow my own will and the dictates of my conscience.

The picture drawn by Eichmann in the courtroom is thus as follows. The Wannsee Conference, which sounded the bell for the implementation of the Final Solution, made Eichmann realize that the powerful political and military machine of Germany was embarking upon criminal activity on a vast scale. The plan was not agreeable to him. Admittedly, he believed firmly, just as did his comrades of the National Socialist Party, that the Jewish problem required a drastic solution, *i.e.,* that the German State had to be purged of Jews. Relentless means ought to have been used for that purpose, like terror, persecution, concentration in labor camps, and finally forced deportation (indeed, he had played a leading role in all these activities). But not mass killing! Of that he did not think, that he did not justify.

Were it to be decided by him—so he implied—the Germans would never have used such radical means. However, the *Führer* had decided and given orders—and he had to obey. As a good citizen, and true to the oath he had given to the *Führer* and the SS, he had to obey. It was at this stage that he concluded that he was no longer able to live according to Kant's Categorical Imperative; there were two reasons for this. *First,* the very content of the Final Solution was incompatible with the principle. As he put it in the courtroom (Session 105): "It could not be within the framework of the Categorical Imperative to kill people by force of arms. . . ." *Second,* the Final Solution was different from his own program, from the course of action which he had adopted out of his free will, and no one acting against his will and intentions could in any sense be considered a "lawgiver" and thus live according to Kant's Categorical Imperative.

It would follow that Eichmann's actions could no longer be considered moral, Kant's principle being taken as the criterion of morality. Yet, whoever had followed Eichmann's reasoning so far was now in for a big surprise: these circumstances, he nonetheless thought, were *not sufficient to incriminate him*. He was convinced that at least one of the two reasons which had obstructed his fulfilling Kant's requirements could at the same time serve as an excuse for his actions contrary to these same requirements. Since he had performed them against his will, but according to orders, it was not he who was responsible for them, but his superiors, and ultimately—the *Führer* alone. Thus, after all his efforts to find a helping hand in Kant's philosophy, Eichmann had to fall back upon the argument used *ad nauseam* by Nazi leaders and commanders of the German armies: the guilt for the crimes of the Germans against Jews, against other peoples, against the whole of mankind, does not taint the German nation, nor the Nazi party, nor even its leadership, but one man alone.

That was Eichmann's tale in Jerusalem. It is open to criticism on several counts. First of all, prior to the Wannsee Conference, did he really act according to his later version of the Categorical Imperative, which we have accepted as its approximately correct interpretation? Of course not. It would be simply ludicrous to describe his Nazi activity up to 1942 as compatible with Categorical Imperative, in particular if we recall one of Kant's alternative formulations of it, according to which a moral person must relate to his fellow-man, be he Christian or Jew, Gypsy or Negro, man or woman, not merely as to a means for his own plans and ambitions, but as to an end in itself. There is hardly any action of Eichmann's party, even before gaining power, there is no law it had initiated, no order its leaders had issued, which does not contradict directly the Kantian conception of ethics in its letter and spirit. It is also beyond doubt that while working out methods and policies for the implementation of the discriminatory laws and orders of the Nazi government, Eichmann showed wholehearted identification with their contents and spirit. He could therefore maintain that he was acting them out as if he were their legislator. But that, on its own, is far from being a sufficient condition for an action to accord with Kant's moral law. Moreover, there is in Kant's philosophy no trace of support for the contention that a man is allowed to forego the Categorical Imperative when pressed to do something against his will and sense of justice. Quite the contrary. Consider, for instance, the parable told in the *Kritik der praktischen Vernunft* (2nd ed., p. 54), where a vassal is ordered by his prince under the threat of death to bear false witness against an honest man whom the prince wishes to destroy. The moral of it is that a man's duty is to refuse to do anything which would harm his fellow man, even if he thereby endangers his future and his life. That, according to Kant, is the measure of a man's true freedom.

Until now we have assumed that Eichmann told the truth in the courtroom. However, the facts established at the trial contradict this assumption. It is clear that Eichmann's activity in the framework of the Final Solution was not against his will, as shown by his enthusiasm, initiative and diligence in carrying out his functions. The strongest evidence is provided by his behavior during the second half of 1944, when it was obvious that the fate of Germany had been sealed, yet Eichmann was feverishly continuing the deportations. Were the whole program contrary to his will, he would certainly have taken advantage of the tendency then prevailing among the leaders of the SS (apparently endorsed by Himmler) to stop the bloodbath, and have thereby returned to a state of "harmony" between himself and the Categorical Imperative. Instead, he continued his Final Solution activities; only that now *he defied the orders of his superiors.*

We are left with the following conclusions. There is no reason to assume that, throughout his Nazi career, Eichmann was at any time acting against his will and convictions. His identification with the Nazi ideology was complete throughout and his actions followed directly from it. There is also no argument to show that these actions were at any time compatible with the principles of Kantian ethics.

There was not and there could not be anything in his "Kantian argumentation" to strengthen his main line of defense, which sought, as we saw, to transmit all the guilt up the ladder of command to its very top, to Hitler alone, or at most to him and the group of his closest associates. This response, which in effect clears the whole German people of guilt, except for one or a few individuals, is not unique to Eichmann. It has been offered by many Germans and non-Germans; but a legion of arguers will not add a whit of validity to the argument.

GRASS'S ARGUMENT IN JERUSALEM

In the fascinating lecture which Günter Grass gave in Jerusalem, a few years after the Eichmann trial, there was a world of difference from the responses of Eichmann. The address, like all Günter Grass's writings, contained no trace of an intention to whitewash his compatriots or to transfer the guilt from the whole nation onto one man or a small group of men:

> We, the good-natured Germans, the dreamers and the shrewd fellows, the German eccentrics, inventive and industrious— when the order fell "sing together," "join in, everybody," we got up from our revels all over Swabia, Silesia, the Rhineland, and other provinces, and begot a political crime that exceeded all the provincial standards. And as soon as our Reich, which we had called "the third," was defeated, we came back without hesitation, everybody who had lived longer than our destructive arrogance came back to the idylls which were half-ruined, but we were able to repair them. As peasants who in the autumn bury their *mangel-wurzels* in heaps, so did the decent Germans try to bury their past. But the *mangel-wurzel* heaps are scattered about the ground in spring, and then the stench spreads all over the country and no idyll remains safe from the sour vapor. What freezes on the lips is altogether one sentence: the Germans, those who did it and those who let it be done, killed six million human beings. . . . Was it easy to burden the industrious and virtuous citizens with the elaborate program of the Final Solution, which needed participants in knowledge, participants in action, and silent witnesses? The process was dreadfully simple: it was announced in print, prepared according to laws and performed methodically.[3]

A few comments are appropriate to this passionate testimony. First, we may react uneasily to his speaking of the "order" to unleash the Holocaust, since we saw how Eichmann used this concept to transfer the guilt to one man only, who headed the chain of command. Yet, it is clear, both from the above passage and from the rest of the lecture, that it is not an excuse that is sought here, but an *explanation* (in the same lecture Grass condemned the conception "order compels," quoted from Globke, who had taught the Holocaust perpetrators the way to clear their names of guilt). Günter Grass describes colorfully the human landscape of Germany, where a number of traits are mixed together producing provincial creatures "hospitable and harmless, quarrelsome over trifles, always ready to forget themselves in singing, and often inviting the silent stranger to join in the glee." Despite the many differences between the inhabitants of various German provinces, practically all of them have a scale of values headed by the same few virtues: diligence, efficiency, thoroughness, and attention to detail in the performance of duties. This is how Grass explains why, when the "order" came, there were no questions about its sense and justice, but the Germans rose and performed the crime.

Even merely as an explanation of how the genocide came about, however, this appears to simplify matters. The number of Germans who volunteered to do the dirty work and then did it with conviction and overwhelming enthusiasm (as in Eichmann's case) was far too large for what Günter Grass suggests. We cannot ignore the need to search for deeper causes of the behavior of millions of Germans during the Holocaust.

Secondly, we may consider Grass's attitude to the meaning of the crime and the guilt for it. On this he is unhesitatingly outspoken: "the Germans . . . killed six million human beings." This is an unequivocal language of admission. Grass clearly holds that the responsibility for the crime affects *all* Germans, at least all those who were living in Germany at the time. But in what way does it affect them? Certainly not all of them equally. Had Günter Grass meant that all Germans are guilty to the same extent, it would practically not be far from the contention that none (or only one, now dead) was guilty. As a matter of fact Günter Grass *does* indicate distinctions between degrees of responsibility, or measures of guilt, but not so much explicitly and directly as by using expressions like "those who did it and those who let it be done," or "participants in knowledge, participants in action, and silent witnesses." This issue undoubtedly requires a more extensive and detailed analysis, such as will be found in the third response below.

Lastly, there is Grass's remark that the Final Solution was "prepared according to laws." We must again be careful not to imagine analogies with Eichmann's position. The reference to laws was made by Grass to provide a basis not for justification or forgiveness, but for defining the *nature* of the crime; its enormity was increased and not mitigated by its "legalization." Only that here too, Grass is not sufficiently precise and univocal. This is especially noticeable in another part of the paper, actually its central part, where he tries to point out the lessons that the new generation should learn from the Holocaust:

> The history of mankind, however hard we try to polish its lights, is also a history of crimes and genocide. Let us keep within the bounds of the European chapter and consider "The Short Description of the Destruction of the West Indies." With a belated shock we read the tale told by the Spanish bishop Bartholomeo de las Casas about the atrocities of his compatriots in Jamaica, Cuba, Haiti, Mexico, Guatemala and Vene-

zuela. Without going into details he tells of 500,000 Indians killed on one island, 200,000 on another, of two to three million Indians killed in Mexico. Who will take to heart these matters today? We got used to thinking of this chapter of European history as a gripping and horrifying subject in the school curriculum. There is practically no European nation which did not at one time or another make crime its political ally.[4]

True, at this point Grass warned his audience of a possible misunderstanding: in juxtaposing the Final Solution against numerous crimes from history he did not mean to obscure its enormity. His aim was to combat our getting used to crimes of any kind, and particularly crimes committed against entire nations. Yet, despite this disclaimer, one has the impression that the uniqueness of the Holocaust became lost in Günter Grass's presentation. In this respect too, the third response is much more adequate. It will show that an accurate determination of the character, dimensions, and meaning of the crime is indispensable for delimiting the guilt correctly.

FOUR KINDS OF GUILT

Now to the last position to be examined here, that of Karl Jaspers. He was one of those infrequent philosophers who do not feel exempted from the task of dealing with current problems and seeking answers to questions and challenges presented by living reality. Incidentally, Jaspers stayed in Germany throughout the Nazi period, but dissociated himself from the regime. He was dismissed from his post of professor at Heidelberg University in 1937, but remained in that town, together with his Jewish wife, till the disintegration of the Third Reich.

My analysis of his approach is based on three sources. The first is his book *Die Schuldfrage* (Heidelberg, 1946), a personal and also a national confession, a parallel to which can hardly be found in world literature. The second source is an interview given by Jaspers to the German weekly *Der Spiegel* in 1965, on the eve of the Bundestag debate on the Statute of Limitations in respect of Nazi crimes. The last source is a short address which he sent to the symposium on "The Unsolved Problem," held in Brussels in 1966 with the participation of Jewish and German scholars.

The interviewer from *Der Spiegel* argued that if merely German war crimes were excluded from falling under the twenty-year Statute of Limitations, there would be non-Germans who went scot-free after committing crimes similar to those for which the Germans were still to be punished. This was countered by Jaspers:

> This argument would not have been unwelcome if it were correct. But it ignores the radical difference between war crimes and crimes against mankind. War crimes are against humanity (*die Menschlichkeit*). . . . The pretension to decide which communities and nations are allowed to live on this Earth and which are not, and to materialize this decision by extermination is a crime against mankind (*die Menschheit*). . . . Such actions were done to Jews, Gypsies, the mentally ill.[5]

Jaspers continued:

> . . . The realization that what is involved here is a crime of a new type, is the precondition for judging the question of limitations. This question then finds its evident answer when one is clear about four closely related questions. First question: what kind of crime? Mass murder by the authorities, a new crime unprecedented in history. This crime presupposes a state of a new type—the state of criminals. Second question: by what law is [this crime] to be judged? By the law which unites all men, the Law of Nations. Third question: where is the legitimate tribunal to apply this law? So long as there is no institutionalized Tribunal of Mankind, which is the proper place for it, the tribunals are the law courts of those states which declare that the Law of Nations is normative for their own legal system. Fourth question: what punishment? To this unique crime against mankind there corresponds the death penalty, restored after its abolition, as an exceptional punishment for this exception.[6]

Of particular interest in our context is Jasper's answer to the first of his four questions, his definition of the crime. It should be noted that this stand concerning the crime committed against the Jews and other ethnic groups (which was to be continued, as Rosenberg's plan envisaged, by bringing "order" into Eastern Europe after the final victory of the Nazis) does not agree with the position taken by the jurists who formulated the Convention on Prevention and Punishment of the Crime of Genocide. They held (like Günter Grass) that the history of mankind has known precedents to this crime, while Jaspers maintains forcefully that the Nazi crime was new in its essence, perhaps mainly because it involved the transformation of an entire state into a state of criminals.

My impression is that the philosopher went deeper than the jurists into the specific circumstances of the planning and committing of the crime, that he noticed how the engineers of this crime succeeded in converting a modern state with all its components, such as the military, the economic, the juridical and even the cultural, which included science, into an instrument for criminal acts. Moreover, using his conception of the Nazi crime Jaspers transcended the juridical aspect of judgment and punishment. He used it to determine the measure of *the guilt of his people*. It becomes clear from his analysis that this guilt cannot be contained within the juridical framework of crime, guilt, and punishment.

Jaspers distinguishes between four kinds of guilt, all of which are relevant to the appraisal of the German's responsibility for the Nazi crimes. They are criminal guilt, political guilt, moral guilt, and metaphysical guilt.

Judgment and punishment in courts of justice relate only to *criminal guilt*. Not all Germans can be charged with it, only those who were directly involved in the planning, preparation, or enactment of genocide. It is peculiar to this modern crime of genocide that the guilt for it is attributable to tens or perhaps hundreds of thousands of people. Only if *all* the offenders are fittingly punished for this crime, will the German people be free of the past in which it constituted a state of criminals. As we saw, Jaspers demanded reintroduction of capital punishment just for that purpose, whereas otherwise he hailed its abolition in Germany and in other countries.

Political guilt applies in Jaspers' view to all the citizens of Germany. Every citizen of a modern state is responsible for the actions of its government and administration, unless he speaks and acts openly against them. But, as Jaspers stresses, there was no effective resistance to the regime until 1943. Where is the authority to judge the citizen and punish him for his political guilt? For Jaspers it is in the hands of the victors, *i.e.*, the Allies who defeated the Germans and dictated to them the conditions of their subsequent existence in the political, economic, and cultural fields. Occupation, reparations to be paid, conditions for reconstruction of the economy and culture, poverty and misery—all these are retributions for the political guilt. All the citizens of the state are somehow affected by these measures, and none has the right to complain of their injustice. The guilt is collective and so is the punishment. How long should these measures last and how extensive should they be? No one but the victor can answer this, and he will act as his interests suggest. The division of the state into two Germanies, the annexation of entire provinces by other countries—these are the effects of the collective political guilt.

The sources of *moral guilt* are all those actions and defaults of the German citizen which implied his support of the criminal regime, whatever the reasons, sincerity, and effectiveness of his support. There is no authority to judge this guilt, except in the conscience of every individual. The individual weighs and measures the extent of his guilt and decides himself what will absolve him, how he has to change and what he has to do in order to atone. But man is a social creature and his spiritual life does not proceed in isolation. Communication with his fellow man, and in this case first of all with his compatriots, is a part of his life. It would therefore be natural if mutual persuasion and influence made the processes of soul-searching, repentance, and spiritual renewal interlace and grow into a communal and finally a nationwide experience.

In this connection Jaspers asks whether every German was morally obliged to protect the victims of his country's regime, and in particular to protect the martyrs of the Final Solution. He gives a qualified answer to this question: the obligation existed and its non-fulfillment is a source of moral guilt, yet no man is morally obliged to give his life for his fellow man. In particular, no one is duty-bound to act in defense of his fellow man if it is obvious that the persecuted will not be saved, while the defender will be victimized as well. The mere fact that his Jewish friends were being deported and killed did not bring about moral guilt. The guilt it did generate is of a different kind, it is the *metaphysical* guilt, which Jaspers defines as follows:

There exists a solidarity among men as human beings that makes each corresponsible for every wrong and every injustice in the world, especially for crimes committed in his presence or with his knowledge. If I fail to do whatever I can to prevent them, I too am guilty. If I was present at the murder of others without risking my life to prevent it, I feel guilty in a way not adequately conceivable either legally, politically or morally. That I live after such a thing has happened weighs upon me as indelible guilt. As human beings, unless good fortune spares us such situations, we come to a point where we must choose: either to risk our lives unconditionally, without chance of success and therefore to no purpose—or to prefer staying alive, because success is impossible. That somewhere among men the unconditioned prevails—the capacity to live only together or not at all, if crimes are committed against the one or the other,

or if physical living requirements have to be shared—therein
consists the substance of their being. But that this does not
extend to the solidarity of all men, nor to that of fellow-citizens
or even of smaller groups, but remains confined to the closest
human ties—therein lies the guilt of us all. Jurisdiction rests
with God alone.[7]

As early as in 1945, in his first public address after the war, Jaspers
confessed movingly and dramatically to the metaphysical guilt of himself
and of all Germans:

We, the survivors, did not seek death. When our Jewish friends
were taken away, we did not go into the streets and shout until
we had been exterminated as well. We preferred to stay alive
for a weak though correct reason that our death cannot possibly help. That we are alive is our guilt.[8]

CONCLUSIONS

So far we have considered the positions of three Germans with
respect to the responsibility for the crime of the Final Solution. How will
this contribute to our attempt to answer our original question?

To the question: "Is it justified to apply in this case the notion of
collective guilt?", we should give a qualified affirmative answer. It must
be qualified because we do not wish to have the very notion of collective
guilt whitewashed from its pejorative meaning, whether in the law, in
morality, or in the political realm. We plead for an exceptional application in our case because of the entirely exceptional character of the
crime, which can be brought under the two headings: (a) the initiation,
planning, and execution of the genocide of the Jewish people within the
context of the Rosenberg style "biological reshuffle" of the population
of Europe (and later, presumably, of the whole world); (b) the transformation, for the sake of (a), of the German state, all its economic, juridical, and technical resources included, into a criminal state.

The crime is exceptional, entirely new, without precedent in the
history of mankind, and this fact justifies the use of the concept of
collective guilt when trying to measure the responsibility for the crime.
The application is however qualified. We use for this purpose two
cross-distinctions, one between the direct and the indirect, the other
between the personal and impersonal responsibility. The first of Karl
Jaspers' *kinds* of guilt—the "criminal guilt"—is both personal and di-

rect; the second, the "political guilt," is indirect and impersonal; while the remaining two—the "moral" and the "metaphysical" (whether they should be separated will be subsequently questioned)—are personal but indirect.

The clearest case is obviously the first one, that of the criminal guilt. It should be imputed—as Jaspers rightly urges—to every German (indeed, to every human being) who had participated in the initiation, planning, and execution of the Final Solution. The determination of the exact dimension of this kind of guilt, and of the punishment for it, is in the hands of the judiciary authority. Jaspers thinks, we remember, that for punishing this kind of crime—and only for it—the death penalty should be reintroduced (if it was revoked previously). I prefer to leave this question open. I consider proper the maximal penalty allowed by the state, but "death penalty or not"—is a very difficult question which deserves a separate analysis. Anyhow, the responsibility here is personal and direct, the heaviest known in the history of the law, I presume.

At the other end of the spectrum I would place the "political guilt" which is, as mentioned above, impersonal and indirect. But it is very real because of the fact that a whole state was transformed into an instrument of crime. Jaspers says: "Every citizen of a modern state is responsible for the actions of its government and administration, unless he speaks and acts openly against them." He says "modern state," not just "state." What he probably has in mind is that unlike previous times, in the modern state the relationship of a citizen with the state is such that he *nolens volens* has his share in keeping this state alive, even if he is not involved in what is commonly called "political life," does not belong to any political party, does not even bother to leave his house on the general elections day. Even such a person is responsible for the body politic. There is however no good reason available for considering this responsibility a personal one. And since the guilt is not personal, neither is the punishment. The state as a whole is punished and its citizens are affected only so far as their well-being depends upon the state.

We may accept Jaspers' view that in accordance with the nature of political reality the factor which was supposed to punish the guilty in this case was the victor, *i.e.,* the Allied Powers. But Jaspers also ruled that the victorious powers were justified in treating occupied Germany as they liked, in accordance with their own political interests; the Germans had no basis for complaints of injustice. If this means that the policy of the Allied Powers could have been completely arbitrary and not subject to any general criteria of evaluation and criticism, then this stand cannot be accepted. Such a conception would offend the sense of justice of us all, and not only of the Germans. I would therefore modify Jaspers' formula to the effect that the Allies should have acted in accordance with the interests of the whole mankind, or of the family of nations.

This implies that the occupation authorities should have done everything possible to eradicate from Germany—from its institutional and cultural structures—all that could reasonably be identified with roots of totalitarianism, and this includes the simplified "earlier" Eichmannian conception of the Categorical Imperative. Was this accomplished in postwar Germany? In West Germany, denazification proceeded to quite a considerable extent, while in East Germany it seems not to have materialized at all. The new regime there remained totalitarian. This totalitarianism may be different from that of the Nazi regime; it seems, however, to be in several respects more dangerous than the Soviet variety.[9]

Problems of a different nature are bound to arise in connection with the other two kinds of guilt. As Jaspers presents the moral guilt of the Germans, a certain incompatibility is revealed within the very concept of moral duty. The line of reasoning runs as follows: the source of the moral guilt of the Germans is any action or forbearance of action, that implied support, in any form, of the Nazi regime. Specifically, this guilt meant responsibility for the lot of the victims of that regime, including of course the victims of the Final Solution. But, asks Jaspers, did this responsibility impose on every German the moral duty of endangering his own life in an effort to save those victims? This question is answered with an unqualified "no." Such an answer is, we should say, not self evident. It requires reasons, justification. That is to say, the limit that Jaspers puts to the moral responsibility of the Germans is theory-dependent. And what theory will justify Jaspers' stand?

This question brings us back to the same ethical theory which Eichmann tried to use for his defense: the Kantian doctrine. According to it one has the moral duty to respect his fellow man, to refrain from offending him, never to treat him only as a means to further one's goals or ambitions. Thus, as we have seen, this theory could not possibly help Eichmann in the hour of his predicament. But alas, this same theory does not make everyone duty-bound to endanger one's own life in order to save one's fellow man from destruction.

Kant's ethical theory can be criticized on this account. It could even be argued that in the conditions of the Nazi terror such an ethical thesis must have played into the hands of the Nazis, providing an ethical excuse for the indifference to the fate of the victims. However, a person who had adopted the Kantian ethics before the Nazis seized power, could have felt it difficult to depart from it when with the change of regime it became inadequate. Should this person have proposed *ad hoc* an altogether new ethics?

This might have been Jaspers' dilemma which he attempted to solve by means of the distinction between the "moral" and the "metaphysical" guilt. If the guilt imputed to every German who did not do his utmost to save his fellow man from destruction did not follow from his moral duty, there is an alternative way of proving it real—by making it follow from the metaphysical fact of human solidarity. Nevertheless, the overall result of Jaspers' argument is unequivocal: every German who lived in Germany during the Nazi rule and did not actively oppose the regime, bears responsibility for the lot of the victims of that regime.

I think that Jaspers' dilemma would be avoided if we did not interpret the moral duty of man in terms of Kantian ethics which leaves outside of morality the (metaphysical) fact of basic human solidarity and co-responsibility. It seems to me more reasonable to combine moral duty with human co-responsibility from the outset and to interpret the one in terms of the other. Still, whichever way we treat these basic assumptions, Jaspers' final conclusion appears to be inevitable.[10]

NOTES

1. From the duplicated minutes of the Jerusalem District Court, Criminal Case 40/61 (The Attorney General of the Government of Israel v. Adolf, the son of Adolf Karl Eichmann, Jerusalem, 1961).

2. H. Arendt, *Eichmann in Jerusalem: A Report on the Banality of Evil* (New York: 1963), p. 121. My subsequent analysis of Eichmann's position, however, diverges from that of Arendt.

3. The Israeli newspaper *Ha-aretz*, March 24, 1967.

4. *Ibid.*

5. *Der Spiegel*, March 10, 1965, p. 57.

6. *Ibid.*

7. K. Jaspers, *The Question of German Guilt* (New York: 1947), p. 32.

8. From *Deutsche und Juden, Beiträge von Nahum Goldmann, Gershom Scholem, Golo Mann, Salo W. Baron, Eugen Gerstenmaier und Karl Jaspers* (Frankfurt: 1967), p. 110. There is a striking similarity in Stephen Spender's view expressed during his visit to Israel (*Jerusalem Post*, January 31, 1975): "If Israel were destroyed, it would be a devastating thing for all of us—not physically as bad as for the Israelis, but spiritually quite as bad. If Israel were allowed to go under, we would be in the

position of the Germans who allowed the Nazis to slaughter the Jews, we would all be guilty."

9. See in particular Zbigniew Brzezinski, "The Soviet Past and Future", *Encounter,* March, 1970, pp. 3–16, where it is argued that in contrast to Soviet difficulties in absorbing modern scientific techniques, "the combination of Prussian discipline, German scientific efficiency, and Leninist-Stalinist ideology has made German communism again a model for its Eastern neighbors." (p. 15)

10. I am indebted to the editors of this volume for their critical remarks which have enabled me to improve my exposition and enforce my argument. An earlier short version of this paper was submitted to the Conference "The Holocaust—A Generation After", held in New York in 1975. A Hebrew rendering of that version was included in the third volume of *Dapim Lkheker Tkufat Hashoah,* Hakibbutz Hameuchad Publishing House, Tel Aviv, 1984.

Hersh Smoliar, Raul Hilberg, Morris Schappes, and Yuri Suhl

JEWS, TRADITION, AND RESISTANCE

"THE LAMBS WERE LEGEND— THE WOLVES WERE REAL"

by Hersh Smoliar

I can remember it clearly: it was that wonderfully good person and great writer, *Der Nister* [The Hidden One, pen-name of the great Soviet Yiddish novelist, Isser Kahanovich] who had urged me a number of times:

"Tell it to everyone. . . . Tell *them* the truth. . . ."

They were practically all my old Moscow friends and acquaintances who, meeting me right after my return from the forests, put the self-same question: "How was it possible? How could it have happened that tens and hundreds of thousands of Jews were led like lambs to the slaughter?"

At first, this question seemed to me to be exceedingly wild. I asked myself wonderingly, "Why did it never occur to you, during all those years in the ghetto, to pose that riddle to yourself? Here are people who were *not* in the ghetto, who know it all second-hand, and yet know more than you do!"

Later, I developed a quiet resentment toward the absolute certainty with which these people (among them my old teacher and friend Prof. Yitzhok Nussinov [Yiddish literary critic], who was already then engaged in scientific research on the question) flatly averred that *the most characteristic feature of the period of total Jewish extermination was absolute Jewish passivity.* And then came the answer, after a long chat with *Der Nister:*

"It's a lie!"

When I asked the members of the Presidium of the Jewish Anti-Fascist Committee their reaction to *Der Nister's* proposal that we make an open declaration in Moscow against this lamb-legend, Prof. Solomon Mikhoels [director of the Moscow Yiddish State Theater and chairman of the Jewish Anti-Fascist Committee] gazed at me with tragic, pitying eyes in which one could read the query: how can you prove it?

That spring evening in 1945, the main auditorium of the Jewish Anti-Fascist Committee on Kropotkin Street in Moscow was jammed with people. I can't remember all I said that night. One thing I do remember is that I went a bit overboard in trying to prove that *there were no lambs at all among the Jews,* that every one in his own way tried to resist the bestiality of the Hitlerites.

At the time I was barely aware of the overall picture of scores and hundreds of ghettos in Poland, Byelorussia, Lithuania, the Ukraine. I knew only of "my own" ghetto and the miracle that was even then being revealed: thousands upon thousands of Minsk Jews, thanks to our organized program of arranging escapes to the partisan detachments in the surrounding forests, were able to survive and to return home after the liberation, bringing with them a record of years of armed struggle against our people's enemy. And all of them were certainly a living refutation of the legend that Jews were led to the slaughter like lambs.

But were they the only ones?

We in the ghetto had seen the most varied expressions of Jewish resistance day after day. *The armed battles were the pinnacle of a whole system of Jewish resistance, which came to life through truly Jewish initiative in the ghetto itself.*

Jews who returned each night from forced labor in the various German enterprises would uniformly repeat the same complaints of their overseers: "You *Ostjuden* (Eastern Jews) are unworthy, dishonorable folk. Now, your 'coreligionists' in Germany and Austria—they behaved with honor; they committed suicide in droves. But you . . . ?"

In "my own" ghetto, among some 85,000 Jews, there were only two known cases of suicide in all those awful years. This was, to our way of thinking, opposition to the Hitlerite desire to see the Jews as a will-bereft mass, among whom there could not develop any resistance whatsoever. Jewish armed resistance organizations, wherever they arose, had as their *fundamental base* this general climate of psychological-moral Jewish resistance. Whoever ignores this *basic factor* must consider the various forms of Jewish armed struggle either as acts of desperation or as accidental episodes—isolated occurrences which had no connection with the state of morale of the overwhelming majority of the ghetto Jews.

The whole system of hiding places—a subject that itself deserves a research project by specialists—of underground passages leading to the "Aryan side," of breakthroughs in the ghetto fences, represent fearfully extensive efforts which are, in every regular army, the task of entire specially-trained corps of engineers and technicians. In the ghetto, this work was done by practically every family, each in its own way. A world of initiative—and all carried out in the strictest secrecy, in an atmosphere of conspiracy which even those most well trained in "the trade" might well envy. These "burrowers" were a large segment of those resisting Hitler's sentence of total extermination. One cannot complete the reckoning without including this mass escape through hiding—which plays an acknowledgedly important part in every war—unless one wishes deliberately to obscure a significant, integral part of specifically *Jewish resistance*.

The tremendously complicated stratagems by which the ghetto defeated the Hitlerite plans for its starvation were the work of masses of ordinary Jewish people. Even the youngest were involved. Based on the nazis' food allocations, hundreds of thousands of Jews should have starved to death in the first six months after the ghettos had been closed off. And while hunger actually claimed tens of thousands of victims (principally among the poorest sections of the population and those without trades) there can be no doubt that if the Nazis had relied on hunger as their sole weapon against the Jews, millions would have survived. Whoever will undertake a full-scale survey of the Jewish anti-Hitler struggle for food would see revealed in its clearest light the collective, superhuman effort of millions in thwarting all the devilish regulations aimed at "taking" the ghetto by hunger. Was this an element of resistance? Suppose we posed this question to experts in military logistics: "By what means could regular army units, completely surrounded by the enemy, manage not to be overcome by hunger?" There could be only one answer: "Such a feat would require truly militant heroism!"

It is true that the mass base of Jewish resistance grew narrower as we proceeded up the scale toward the forms of direct, armed battle and the formation, in the ghetto, of armed groups sent to join the partisan detachments. This does not stem from any lack of sympathy among the Jews toward these particular forms of struggle. Far from it! The records of almost all the ghettos have demonstrated that, completely apart from the *organized* centers of resistance, there were everywhere small groups who secured their own arms, set out alone in search of contact with the partisans and conducted their own military operations.

But facts are facts: the special caution necessary under conditions in which the Gestapo had its agents throughout the ghetto, forced the organizers of armed resistance into special conspiratorial measures. Yet here, too, we dare not lose sight of the great numbers of Jews who directly aided the armed groups through gifts of money, food and medicines. In the partisan movement as a whole (in the Soviet Union, Poland, Yugoslavia, France) those who *aided* the active resisters were considered members of the resistance movement. Why, then, were we so inclined to eliminate these masses of Jews from the reckoning?

If it were possible to sum up the participation of Jews in all the varied forms of resistance (and we have listed only a few) we would obtain the full picture of Jewish determination, of Jewish energy, of Jewish opposition by every possible means to the destroyers of our people.

What then remains of the legend of the lambs?

There remains the horror-picture of millions of Jews, in all the extermination camps, being driven to the slaughter without any mass resistance *at that moment*. (We say this, while remembering that it was particularly Jews who staged uprisings in the death camps of Sobibor and Helmno!) I must confess that whenever this particular argument arose to buttress the lamb-legend, I became almost speechless. I would see in my mind's eye not the Jewish women with babes in arms, nor the old people (for they were the first victims in every raid) who were driven by shooting and beating through drunken hordes of S.S.-men and Ukrainian, Lithuanian and Latvian fascists. I saw, instead, the familiar picture of those times: huge, many-thousands-strong columns of war prisoners, "led" by handsful of armed Germans who kept up a steady fire, killing all stragglers and leaving a trail of blood all along the road.

Why did none of us feel resentment toward these men—former military men—who put up no resistance, who made no attempt to escape singly or to stage a mass escape?

One must know the psychological condition of people disarmed, robbed of the most elementary rights, often beyond the capacity for thought or perception, before directing any accusations at them. These millions of prisoners—whose behavior under such conditions was in no way differentiated by national group—cannot possibly serve to substantiate the lamb legend. It is not their tragic dying, but their living, which *as a rule* was the result of the most varied methods of resistance to the Hitlerite beasts, that is the determining factor in evaluating the period of total genocide, of complete Jewish extermination.

Those were my thoughts at the time of my first meeting with people who had seen what had happened from far behind the front lines, purely on the basis of others' reports.

This is still my view of the matter today, after having studied the more general picture of scores upon scores of different ghettos.

One thing I neglected to mention that spring evening in Moscow was—*the wolves!*

This was probably the result of two facts: first, in "my own" ghetto the *Judenrat* (Jewish Council) was most intimately bound up with the resistance movement; secondly, at that time we had only the meagerest reports of the behavior of the *Judenrats* in Warsaw, Bialystok, Vilna and many other cities.

Today we know for a certainty: just as there was a multi-faceted system of Jewish resistance, so too in many ghettos there was the influence of a many-sided Jewish anti-resistance, starting from psychological and physical demoralization, to keeping the people in the grip of illusions, to all sorts of manipulations in selecting the victims of the death camps and those to be granted temporary mercy, ending with the most shameful, direct participation in the apprehension and murder of fellow-Jews. (This refers to the Jewish ghetto police and especially to the operative groups who were in direct communication with the Gestapo; they were called GENS in the ghettos around Vilna.)

There was no mention of all this that evening in Moscow. Now we know that in the years of our most terrible destruction a situation developed which is to be found during hard times in all of our thousands of years of history. Always and everywhere we find expressions—to a lesser or greater degree—of two basic lines in our history: *the line of resistance* to the enemy, of opposing evil with every possible means, and *the line of accommodation*, of resignation, of surrender to the bloody foe to the point of serving his satanic plans for the Jewish people.

And if, in this most horrible period of our past—the reign of Hitler—there had been just the one single chapter of the *uprising in the Warsaw Ghetto*, that alone would have sufficed for us to say with the fullest certainty: *it was the line of Jewish resistance which emerged victorious!*

April, 1959

"JEWS, TRADITION AND RESISTANCE—2"

by Raul Hilberg

In courtesy to Dr. S.D. Kaplan and in response to your invitation, I should like to restate a few conclusions which seem to me compelling in the light of current evidence about the behavior of European Jewry under the Nazi assault.

Jews of all regions and all classes failed to resist in significant measure throughout the destruction process. Much as we would want to have it otherwise, we cannot increase the skirmishing to battle proportions without losing sight of reality. Morris U. Schappes, along with many other pained observers of the apocalyptic scene, would redefine "resistance" to include food smuggling, escapes and even elemental struggle for life under starvation conditions. To me, these evasion and alleviation reactions are not resistance. These activities did not stem the Nazi advance. They did not even divert or delay the assailants in any measurable degree.

I do not wish to minimize that which under trying circumstances was actually done. Therefore, I have taken all the care to record every incidence of true resistance that I was able to find. In my index, there are 15 references to such resistance activities. Allow me to add, with particular reference to the eastern sector, that I have probably seen more documents on the partisan war than any man in this country. What that documentation discloses is no spiritual impetus and no central movement, only half-armed desperate people in the woods avoiding combat so far as possible. Again, let us not cast blame. Let us, however, recognize the facts.

Just as we cannot create facts by wishing they were there, we cannot reconstruct "traditions" which did not emerge in crisis. Ideals did not motivate the millions of Jews under the Nazi regime. Self-preservation alone was decisive, but the old and tried methods which had worked before brought the victims death at the hands of an uncompromising foe.

"COMMENT"

by Morris U. Schappes

I regret that, having re-examined Dr. Hilberg's evidence as offered in his book, *The Destruction of the European Jews,* I find his restatement of his conclusions in his letter no more convincing than his original statement.

While Dr. Hilberg's documentation on the theme of the destruction of the Jews is indeed impressive and may well be exhaustive, his documentation of the subject of the Jewish resistance not only shows gaps but is at best spotty. Dr. Hilberg assures us he has recorded "every instance of true resistance" he was able to find, according to his narrow definition of resistance as armed fighting, and cites the 15 references to such resistance in his index. I have studied these references in their full context, with particular attention to the sources cited for his information. I must conclude that Dr. Hilberg has not systematically explored the subject of Jewish resistance either in his own or any definition of resistance.

Let me cite random examples of this serious deficiency, which of course affects his findings and conclusions. Of the resistance in Kaunas, Lithuania, for instance, Dr. Hilberg has less than one sentence, and the source he cites is an article in *Jewish Social Studies* in 1949 by a survivor. Dr. Hilberg seems unaware of the Yiddish volume (162 pages) published in Moscow in 1948, *Partizaner fun Kaunaser Ghetto,* by M. Yellin and D. Gelpern (M. Yellin is the brother of Haim Yellin, leader of the Kaunas resistance movement). In general, it seems that the extensive literature about Jewish resistance that has been published in Yiddish has not been investigated by Dr. Hilberg. But the Yellin-Gelpern book completely contradicts Dr. Hilberg's findings.

Dr. Hilberg's two sentences on the uprising in the Bialystok ghetto do injustice to the source he cites and to other material of which he seems unaware. "There was scattered fighting for about 24 hours," Dr. Hilberg remarks, citing Dr. Joseph Tenenbaum's *Underground;* but Dr. Tenenbaum had reported that on one street alone the Jews killed some 30 Germans, which, with similar omissions by Dr. Hilberg, renders completely unacceptable his conclusion (p. 663) that "it is doubtful that the Germans and their collaborators lost more than a few hundred, dead and wounded," at the hands of all Jewish fighters in all of European resistance movements. In Bialystok, by the way, in Aug. 1948, a street was named after and a monument raised to Yitzhok Malamud, the hero of the Bialystok ghetto resistance, who had with vitriol burned out the eyes of a group of SS men.

Of Bulgarian Jewish resistance, Dr. Hilberg has not a word, although a book on the subject was published in Sofia in 1958, *Jews Who Perished in the Struggle against Fascism,* in Bulgarian, 376 pages. One of these heroes, Leon Tager Ben-David, in 1942 set fire to a gasoline depot of the Nazi army, destroying over 266,000 gallons of gasoline. The Nazis hanged him. The Bulgarian government in mid-Jan., 1962, on the 20th anniversary of his execution, named the Rousse oil refineries after him.

Or let me conclude this section by noting that Dr. Hilberg, in his two sentences on the uprising in the Sobibor concentration camp, remarks that the Germans merely "lost an *Untersturmfuehrer* in the fighting." But from another source, not used by Dr. Hilberg, we learn that "the insurrectionists killed 16 of their jailers" and then attacked the sentries, among whom there were more than 50 casualties. (*The Black Book:* The Nazi Crime Against the Jewish People, compiled by the Jewish Black Book Committee—World Jewish Congress, Jewish anti-Fascist Committee in Moscow, Jewish National Council of Palestine, American

Committee of Jewish Writers, Artists and Scientists. Duell Sloan and Pearce, N.Y., 1946, pp. 376–77; article in the *Morning Freiheit*, Dec. 8, 1958, by a survivor, S.G.).

These and many other instances I could cite without attempting to be exhaustive lead me to conclude that the resistance theme was marginal to Dr. Hilberg's central subject of the destruction of the Jews and was not extensively explored by him.

Secondly, there is the matter of Dr. Hilberg's definition of resistance as armed fighting, and his explicit exclusion from the concept of resistance of what he derogatorily calls "alleviation" (petition, ransom, bribery, rescue) and "evasion" (escape, flight, hiding). Dr. Hilberg's definition seems to me wilful and not in keeping with the common usage of the term resistance both by the resisters themselves and by the organizations, such as Yad Vashem, the Jewish Historical Commission of Poland, the YIVO Institute for Jewish Research and others engaged in studying the subject. Thus the section, "Resistance," in the aforementioned *Black Book*, contains not merely many more examples of *armed* resistance than Dr. Hilberg's book but recognizes as honorable and effective resistance the many other forms that Dr. Hilberg has decided to exclude. Dr. Hilberg seems to fail to grasp the essential fact that resistance is a stance and a process that includes a great variety of acts and refusal to act, of which armed fighting is, for those physically able to resort to it, the most damaging to the enemy.

Finally, there is Dr. Hilberg's historically unsubstantiated view that the "Jewish tradition" of 2,000 years in the "Diaspora" had been a uniform tradition of non-resistance to and compliance with oppression. Judging by his cited sources, I should say his historical survey is inadequate. Dr. Hilberg has cited (and in part misrepresented) an article in *Jewish Life*, April, 1951 by the Polish Jewish writer, M. Edin. The following quotations from that very article will suffice for the time being: "Some naive researchers and publicists discovered the Jews for the first time in the ghetto barricades. These writers say that the Jews had not fought since Maccabean times, but that only in the presence of death in the ghetto did the Jew take to arms. This is not true. We shall not discuss here the fighting traditions of the Jewish masses of the 19th century, beginning with exploits of Berek Yoselevich's division [in the Polish uprising, 1832]. But only a superficial acquaintance with the participation of the Jewish workers and the Jewish intelligentsia in the labor movement of Poland and Russia from its inception down to the Nazi attack is enough to refute this view. For the Jews manifested heroism not only in cases of individuals like Shulman, Hirsh Leckert, Naftali Botwin and Engel, but, even more important, on the part of the Jewish working masses as a whole. From this working class tradition and from the intellectual and moral training and ideology of the working class movement did men and women like Joseph Levartovsky, Andjei Schmidt and a legion of Jewish resistance heroes, known and unknown, draw strength in this most tragic period. . . ."

Such criticisms of Dr. Hilberg's views on resistance and tradition, however, do not lessen the high quality of his thorough description of the process and methods used in the destruction of the 6,000,000 Jews by the Nazis.

April, 1962

"JEWS, TRADITION AND RESISTANCE"

by Yuri Suhl

On the occasion of the 18th anniversary of the Warsaw Ghetto Uprising, Prof. Ber Mark, director of the Jewish Historical Institute of Warsaw, wrote (*Yiddishe Shriften*, No. 4, Warsaw, April, 1961), "The 19th of April is the personification of all the aspects of Jewish struggle against Hitlerism, racism and genocide. Because the Jewish participation in this struggle is tremendous. If we were to mark, annually, every important act of resistance which the Jews have carried out in the years 1941–44 in all the countries of occupied and *gleichschaltet* Europe, our press would daily have to print articles dedicated to these anniversary dates.

"It is a pity that to date a calendar of Jewish resistance has not yet been prepared. Before our eyes would arise a grand image of Jewish heroism. From the shores of the Adriatic to the Vistula, Bug, Nieman and Dnieper; from the hills of Kavkaz to Marseilles; from Buchenwald and Auschwitz to the mountains of Slovakia; from Berlin to Sofia and from Belgrade to Amsterdam and Paris—everywhere Jews, individually and as national groups, have fought in the ghetto, in the camps, in partisan bands, in the undergrounds in cities among the Jewish masses and on the Aryan side. Jewish men and women fought with weapon in hand, served as couriers and agitators, as ordinary fighters and as resistance leaders of high rank. . . . Yes, we too have our Unknown Soldier and his name, to paraphrase Mickiewicz, is Million!"

This is a far cry from the Jew portrayed by Dr. Raul Hilberg, whose resistance, he claims, was both insignificant and inconsequential. Prof.

Mark, one of the foremost authorities on the martyrology and resistance of the Jews of Poland in the last war, is strangely absent from the Index in Dr. Hilberg's book. Nor will you find any reference to Hersh Smoliar, well known resistance leader of the Ghetto of Minsk, whose book, *Yiden On Geleh Lahtes* (Jews Without Yellow Patches), tells the story of fighting Jews who do not fit into Dr. Hilberg's theory of 2,000 years of submissiveness. So strong was the resistance movement in the Ghetto of Minsk that even the *Judenrat* (Jewish Council appointed by the Nazis) was compelled to take orders from its leaders.

"Measured in German casualties," writes Dr. Hilberg, "Jewish armed opposition shrinks into insignificance." And what if the same yardstick were applied to Polish, or Czech or French armed opposition? We are not speaking here of battle-trained, mechanized armies but of individual and group resistance from civilian populations.

The Poles, too, had a taste of German barbarism. Hundreds of thousands of Poles were sent to Auschwitz and other concentration camps; they were grabbed in street round-ups and taken to Germany for slave labor; the shooting and hanging of Poles in Warsaw and other cities was a daily occurrence. Yet, taking into account the relative freedom of movement enjoyed by the Polish population as compared to the Jews, who were imprisoned in ghettos and extermination camps, and considering the difference in the size of the two populations, was the number of German casualties suffered at the hands of the Poles really so significant?

On a battlefield where numerical superiority may spell the difference between victory and defeat, the number of casualties inflicted on an adversary takes on a decisive importance. But in civilian resistance, where individual heroism takes the place of mechanized strength, it is the act itself, however limited, that is significant, because it is symbolic and expressive of the moral force of a people.

"It is doubtful," says Dr. Hilberg, "that the Germans and their collaborators lost more than a few hundred men dead and wounded in the course of the destruction process." This ridiculously small estimate includes also the German losses in the Warsaw Ghetto Uprising, which Dr. Hilberg gives in precise figures of 16 dead and 85 wounded. A hasty check with our own files on the subject reveals an entirely different picture:

Glos Warszawy, organ of the People's Guard, which actively supported the Warsaw Ghetto Fighters, reporting on the uprising in its April 28, 1943 issue, wrote, "the German casualties during the first week of the struggle were about 360 dead and over 1,000 wounded."

(*Documents and Materials* about the Warsaw Ghetto Uprising, compiled and with foreword and comments by Ber Mark, published by *Yiddish Buch*, Warsaw, 1953, on the 10th anniversary of the Warsaw Ghetto Uprising, p. 185.)

In all of his 16 references to Treblinka, where Dr. Hilberg also touches on the revolt and the breakout in this extermination camp, he fails to mention the German losses in this heroic act of Jewish resistance. This omission becomes even more reprehensible when one discovers that in Hilberg's own cited sources for the Treblinka revolt (see Hilberg's page 119, footnote 67) the number of Germans killed is given as "over 20."

Or take Sobibor. The revolt that took place in that extermination camp on Oct. 14, 1943, is one of the unique and most dramatic acts in the annals of Jewish resistance and by and large, it was successful in its objective. For the student of Jewish resistance this revolt provides some revealing insight into the role of leadership. In a matter of three weeks an underground movement sprang up where none had existed before. And when the time came to strike the blow, practically the entire German *kommandatur* of the camp was wiped out in less than two hours. Dr. Hilberg has very little to say about the Sobibor revolt and what he does say is, in the main, at variance with the facts. He writes, "The German lost an *Untersturmfuehrer* in the fighting."

Is that all they lost? In addition to the facts cited by Morris U. Schappes (page 323 above) one again finds Dr. Hilberg contradicted by his own cited source: Tenenbaum, *Underground*, pages 261–64. But Tenenbaum wrote, "All in all 13 Germans were killed by the blows of hatchets." (According to a more recent account, 10 SS were killed and one wounded, and 38 Ukrainian guards were either killed or wounded.) But even more serious than Dr. Hilberg's omission of the number of Germans killed by the rebels is his failure to comprehend the significance of the Sobibor revolt, one of the most dramatic in the annals of Jewish resistance to Nazism. (See further, Yuri Suhl, "Is This Responsible Scholarship, Dr. Hilberg?" in JEWISH CURRENT:, June, 1964.)

One more example. On a May night in 1942, two young Jews sneaked out of the Ghetto of Vilna. One is identified as Yitzhok and the other as Vitke Kempner (now living in Israel and the wife of Aba Kovner, who testified at the Eichmann trial). At an appointed spot they met a third Jew from the Ghetto and together they mined the rails of a railroad line in anticipation of an oncoming German troop and supply train. The train was blown into bits.

The next morning, when the peasants were called out to gather the dead and remove the wreckage, they counted 200 German dead. The wounded were too numerous to count. The peasants stole whatever weapons and ammunition they could lay their hands on and hid them. Later when some Jewish resistance fighters broke out of the ghetto to fight in the woods they went to those peasants and got the weapons, with which they killed more Germans. The blowing up of the train by Jewish fighters was one of the first acts of sabotage of this kind in the entire area of Vilna. (*Vilner Ghetto,* by A. Sutzkever, IKUF, Buenos Aires, 1947, pp. 171–3.)

For a man who attaches so much importance to the number of German casualties, Dr. Hilberg displays a curious lack of zeal in tracking them down. Did he expect the German reports on Jewish resistance, on which he relies so trustingly, to have recorded faithfully this act of sabotage? Sutzkever did. But then again, Sutzkever's book is not part of Dr. Hilberg's bibliography.

Dr. Hilberg's massive documentation of the destruction of the European Jews is impressive and constitutes a major contribution to the ever-growing body of holocaust literature. But his picture of Jewish resistance and the conclusions he draws from it should be challenged, and challenged vigorously.

July–August, 1962

Roger S. Gottlieb

THE CONCEPT OF RESISTANCE: JEWISH RESISTANCE DURING THE HOLOCAUST

Social and political philosophers have provided extensive discussions of many of our relations to state power. They have analyzed its origin, extent and legitimacy—as well as our right to rebel against it. Likewise, there exist countless discussions of the concepts of liberty, equality, political rights, and civil disobedience. Yet little or no attention has been given to the concept of resistance, for example, in such a manner as to help to distinguish acts of resistance from those of passivity, compliance or collaboration. By focusing on the particular example of Jewish resistance during the Holocaust, this essay begins a philosophical account of that concept.

1. CONTRADICTORY USES

On April 19, 1943 the Jewish Fighting Organization (J.F.O.) of the Warsaw Ghetto began armed actions against the continued deportation of Jews to Treblinka concentration camp. In a leaflet accompanying its actions the J.F.O. stated its goals: vengeance, freedom, dignity, social and national honor, and the desire to "punish the enemy for his crimes."[1]

By contrast, consider two Jewish teenagers, Ludz and Fill, who served the Nazi S.S. in Dachau. Ludz and Fill flattered and imitated the S.S. guards. They achieved a limited power in their barracks and exercised that power at the expense of their fellow Jews, whom they abused, threatened, and referred to as "filthy Jews." From the description of them, it is clear that Ludz and Fill had fully internalized the values of the Nazis and were contributing to the Nazi enterprise of the destruction of the Jews.[2]

Chroniclers of the Holocaust have no difficulty in seeing the first of these two examples as resistance and the second as complicity or collaboration. Yet when confronted by less clear-cut examples, they use the term "resistance" in such different ways as to suggest fundamental disagreements about its meaning. Raul Hilberg, author of the influential Holocaust history *The Destruction of the European Jews*, defines resistance as "opposition to the perpetrator" and claims that "The Jews were not oriented to resistance. . . ."[3] By contrast, Holocaust scholar M. Dworzecki states that:

> Resistance of the anonymous masses must be affirmed in terms of how they held on to their humanity, of their manifestations of solidarity, mutual help, self-sacrifice and that whole constellation of manifestations subsumed under the simple heading of 'good deeds.'[4]

The disagreement here is not over obviously "factual" issues, for example, how many Jews formed underground organizations or engaged in armed struggle. Rather, it concerns the criteria for the application of the term, that is, what type of actions actually count as resistance.

Leni Yahil claims that both of the following are examples of resistance:

> In the one instance the rabbi holds a sermon on the meaning of 'Kiddush Hashem' [sanctification of the name, the Orthodox Jewish practice of dying as a martyr in such a way as to glorify God and His commandments] while he and his congregation stand at the edge of the pit which will soon be their grave. He completes his sermon and then turns to the German commander, who had been prodding him to finish, and says: "I am done; you may now begin." In the second case, a butcher leaps from the pit into which the dead and dying were thrown, sinks his teeth into the German commander's throat and kills him.[5]

Hilberg, by contrast, would classify only the second action as resistance. He would see the first as "automatic compliance," an example of the type of action which the Jews were required to carry out as part of the process of their own destruction. The rabbi's response, for Hilberg, does not resist the Nazis, but aids them. Hilberg indicates his criteria for resistance in the following reply to his critics:

> . . . many pained observers of the apocalyptic scene would redefine 'resistance' to include food smuggling, escapes and even

elemental struggle for life under starvation conditions. To me, these evasion and alleviation reactions are not resistance. These activities did not stem the Nazi advance. They did not even divert or delay the assailants in any measurable degree.[6]

2. THE "BRUTENESS" OF RESISTANCE

In offering an analysis of the concept of resistance, this essay will explain disagreements of the kind just described. What is at stake, it should be noted, is more than a simple semantic alternative between competing definitions. G.E.M. Anscombe has argued that descriptions exist in a conceptual hierarchy such that a particular description will be "brute" to (basic, essential for) establishing a more complicated, higher-order description.[7] The concept of resistance is significant partly because it is brute to descriptions which have highly important normative implications. For instance, "that a group resisted" may be brute to "the group had courage" or "the group is worthy of respect." One has a very different attitude towards, to put it bluntly, a Jewish community which "was not oriented towards resistance" than to one of which "the resistance of the anonymous masses must be affirmed."

The "bruteness" of resistance also figures in sociological and historical analysis. If the Jews "were not oriented towards resistance," then it makes sense to ask (as Hilberg and others have done) what was it about Jewish religion, culture, and social structure that induced passivity in the face of destruction. If we adopt Dworzecki's usage, on the other hand, we might investigate how Jewish religion, culture, and social structure helped the Jews to respond with strength and courage.

Finally, our use of the concept of resistance has implications for our account of social life as a whole. Resistance is a relational concept. To understand a particular set of actions as "resistance" is to understand something about those against whom resistance is carried out as well as something about those who are resisting. If we find resistance where we did not find it before we will, in all probability, find other things as well. To change the application of this one concept will be to change the applications of those other concepts with which it is logically connected; and this will alter a significant part of our description of social life as a whole.

In what follows I will describe what I take to be the essential features of resistance (3.); show how these features account for some crucial disagreements over the use of the term (4.); and describe some other difficulties in its application (5.).

3. RESISTANCE

We may define oppression as a relation in which one group exercises—on the basis of superior power, for its own benefit, and without
justification—control over another group. The first thing to note about
an act of resistance is that it exists within a context of oppression. Thus
resistance is typically the act of an already conquered or defeated people: We speak of the French Resistance in World War II only after the
regular French Army surrendered. But we do not speak of resistance
when we see no oppression: While blacks in South Africa may resist
white supremacy there, a murderer barricaded in an apartment does not
resist the police. Therefore, to characterize an act as one of resistance is
already to commit oneself to a moral evaluation of a particular set of
power relations and thus to a partisan position in respect to a social
conflict. There can be no "neutral" use of the term, since its use presupposes that the user already sides with one group rather than another.

Acts of resistance are, secondly, acts motivated by the intention to
thwart, limit, or end the exercise of power of the oppressor group over
the oppressed. Such an intention is distinct from an attempt to simply
transfer oppression away from oneself to another member of the oppressed group. Since relations of oppression exist between individuals
partly insofar as they are members of social groups, the goal of resistance must be to lessen the total quantity of oppression, not just to shift
it around. Otherwise one is not resisting, but simply trying to avoid
personal suffering.

Finally, in order to have the *intention* to thwart, limit, or end oppression, resistors must hold at least two sorts of *beliefs*. They must hold
certain beliefs about their identity. These are beliefs about what are the
crucial features of the individual's or group's existence. These beliefs
are essential to the oppressed recognizing that a part of themselves can
be threatened, dominated or destroyed in the relationship of oppression. Resistors must also have beliefs concerning the manner in which
the oppressor group is exercising its domination, about how the assault
on their identity is being conducted. These two types of beliefs, in turn,
give the resistor the capacity to identify a range of acts, some of which
are resistance and some of which are passivity or collaboration. Resistance is thus a *free* act in the sense that to resist is also to recognize the
possibility of engaging in alternative acts which are not resistance.

There already exists an enormous philosophical literature concerning the justified exercise of power. Therefore, while differences over
concepts or norms of justice may be central to disagreements over the
use of resistance, I will not discuss that issue here.

Similarly, crucial differences between the concepts of resistance and civil disobedience allow me to limit my discussion to the former. The central moral, political, and theoretical issues which cluster around resistance include the degree of courage manifested by an oppressed group, the capacity of a group to act rather than remain passive, and the ability of persons to resist the natural temptation to comply with superior and unjust powers. In general, the concept of resistance refers to a struggle by an oppressed person or group against the power of an oppressor. Civil disobedience, by contrast, may involve oppression and may not. Its focus is on the right to break a law, the nature and effect of social violence, and the conflict between belonging to a community and needing to change it. Civil disobedience is not primarily an action directed *against* a person or group. Rather, it reflects a belief in the commonality between those who engage in civil disobedience and the rest of the community. This commonality may be a "shared humanity" or it may be the fact that both groups face a potential universal calamity such as nuclear war. Going along with this belief in a commonality between demonstrators and non-demonstrators is a concern with one's own moral development.[8] In assessing acts which purport to be civil disobedience, therefore, we are typically concerned with whether or not the group in question actually is appealing to the society at large, whether they freely allow themselves to be "punished" (for example, by jail sentences) if their appeal fails, and whether their actions actually reflect deeply held moral convictions. When we seek to know whether or not Jews resisted the Nazis, such questions do not arise.

The remainder of this essay will therefore focus on two other themes. In 4. I will show how different beliefs about the identity of the oppressed and the nature of the assault can lead to differences in beliefs about what is resistance. In 5. I will examine the difficulty of knowing whether or not beliefs and intentions expressed in acts of resistance are consciously held by the resistors themselves.

4. IDENTITY AND THE ASSAULT

The Identity of the Oppressed. What aspect of Jewish identity was under attack by the Nazis? This appears to be a rather straightforward and easy question to answer. In a passage cited above, Hilberg asserts that Jewish resistance can be measured by the degree to which Jewish action stemmed, diverted, or delayed the Nazi advance. We face a difficulty, however, in that we cannot assess to what degree this "diversion," and so forth has occurred until we know precisely what the Nazis were advancing against, that is, what was in danger from the Nazi advance.[9] Hilberg obviously believes that what was in danger was the physical existence of the Jews and that therefore thwarting the Nazis could only be a thwarting of their threat to that existence. This belief, however, is much more problematic than Hilberg supposes.

Let us imagine a case in which a person did not believe that what was principally or only at stake in the Holocaust was the physical existence of a group of human beings. Suppose, rather, that one saw the conflict between Nazis and Jews as also one between metaphysical principles or powers. For example, one might believe that the two groups represented eternal principles of good and evil, or, more anthropomorphically, God and the Devil. On such a view, the identity of the oppressed and therefore both what was being attacked and the best mode of resisting that attack are very different than they are for Hilberg.

The view just described was, more or less, the one held by people who responded to the Nazis by Kiddush Hashem. For such people, the most important aspect of the Nazi attack was that it threatened their religious identity, their "souls," their connection to God, and perhaps God Himself. Therefore, for them, the causally efficacious response would not be one which sought to physically obstruct the oppressor. What was crucial, rather, was to respond in such a way as to defend and preserve their attachment to the principles of holiness, religiosity, and faith. The most dangerous threat was not physical annihilation by the Nazis, but their own betrayal of these principles. Such a betrayal might have been an abandonment or a weakening of their faith in the Power to which they had devoted themselves. In any case, it would have been a self-betrayal of that aspect of themselves which they had—in less extreme and trying times—valued the most highly.[10]

Disagreement over whether or not an act is one of resistance, then, will sometimes be the result of differences in what might be termed one's "social ontology," that is, one's beliefs about what are the types of existents which are involved in the social relations of oppression and domination. The believer in Kiddush Hashem sees different types of entities, entering into different types of causal relations, than does the secularist.

Two people may seek to cure a condition the symptoms of which enable them to identify it as the "same" disease. Yet if they have radically different views as to what is causing the disease, or what parts or organs of the body the disease is attacking, they will "resist" the disease in very different ways. We respond to germs differently than we do to unconscious fears, and to evil spirits differently than to both of those. In each case we are defending something quite different. Similarly, people who hold different social ontologies will resist their oppression in different ways.

Social ontologies need not be as different as those of traditional religion and modern secularism. As the following example indicates, crucial disagreement can also exist among those who agree on a fundamentally secular perspective: Over a year before the actual formation of the J.F.O. a group of young people in the Warsaw Ghetto began secretly organizing for physical resistance against the Nazis. They lacked weapons, military training, and numbers. When asked by an older member of the Jewish Council why they were planning militant struggle when they had no hope of inflicting real harm on their enemy, they replied:

> What will posterity say about us if we go to our death without any attempt at resistance? The Jews of the world, the succeeding generations, will be ashamed of us; they will believe that we . . . were meek, devoid of any sense of honor, and this will depress them. We want to act in a manner which will serve then as an example and testament of valour.[11]

These potential resistors did not accept the social ontology expressed in Kiddush Hashem. Yet they did not believe that Jewish identity, the object of the Nazi assault, was limited to the physical existence of the Jews of Europe. Rather, they saw the assault as directed against the Jews *as a people*. As a *people*, Jews are defined neither by possession of a particular territory nor by racial characteristics. The Jewish people, rather, are sustained by collective participation in a religious-cultural tradition. For this participation to continue, Jews must believe in the value and importance of being Jewish. This belief will be expressed in what might be called "internalized reciprocity"—the willing identification of each member of the group with the group as a whole. Because of the national minority and territory-less condition of the Jews, internalized reciprocity is a necessary condition for Jewish survival.

The weaponless militants of the Warsaw Ghetto were responding to threats against Jewish group pride and self-valuation, essential aspects of internalized reciprocity. Their resistance was constituted by the attempt to leave to posterity a memory of Jewish heroism, rather than by the goal of diverting or delaying the Nazi advance. For them, the object of the Nazi assault was not limited to the physical existence of the Jews. It included, rather, the collectively held ideals which kept the Jews as a people alive in history. Therefore resistance, for them, necessarily included the defense of those ideals. Their conception of Jewish identity —and that of resistance which it entailed—reflected a fairly commonplace (but often unrecognized)[12] fact about personal identity: that much of that identity is constituted by one's participation in the norms, practices and institutions of groups. This can be at least as important for one's self-identity as what might be termed more "individual" aspects of oneself, for example, one's physical body, sensations, or desires. In certain cases, therefore, resistance will take the form of a defense of our collective, rather than our merely individual, identity.

The Nature of the Assault. We have just focused our attention on the way differences in the concept of resistance may be a result of differences concerning what constitutes the identity of the oppressed group. Here we focus on how the same result may be produced by different answers to the question: what is the nature of the assault of the oppressor on the oppressed?

Life in the Nazi concentration camps often turned people into what the inmates themselves called "musselmen." These were people who had become like "living corpses." They barely had the strength or will to move, work, eat, or clean themselves. They had no physical or emotional energy to undertake the variety of manipulations, rule infractions, contacts with others, and general group interactions which were necessary for day-to-day survival. While performing such actions in no way guaranteed survival, failure to perform them meant imminent death.[13]

Nearly one-third of the six million Jews murdered by the Nazis died of starvation or disease. Resistance to starvation or disease, however, especially in the concentration camp context of military powerlessness, sometimes called for different forms than those undertaken by the J.F.O. Here resistance meant, in part, resistance against the forces leading one to become a musselman. Such resistance included maintaining the active mentality which would allow one to steal or smuggle food, cooperate with other inmates, offer and receive help in time of special weakness, and so forth. Maintaining such a consciousness—which might be defined as the will to live—helped one avoid the almost certain death which befell musselmen.

> Oppression as violent as that under which we lived automatically provoked resistance. Our entire existence in the camp was marked by it. When labourers at the spinning mills dared to slacken their working pace . . . when we . . . passed letters from one camp to another . . . when we endeavoured . . . to unite members of the same family . . . it was resistance.[14]

It might be asked, at this point: "Isn't there a distinction between resistance and simply trying to stay alive?" What our analysis has revealed, however, is that this distinction is not valid in all contexts. It would be valid, say, in an account of the French resistance in World War II, for the Nazis did not seek the death of every French person. This was, however, their goal as far as the Jews were concerned. The concentration camp was a fundamentally different type of context than the occupied country. A fundamentally different type of assault against the oppressed took place there, one which sometimes called for a fundamentally different type of resistance.

As an analogy, we may consider the plight of someone who is being subject to a variety of techniques of brainwashing—hypnosis, physical torture, psychological assaults of various kinds—the goal of which is to get him to commit suicide. In a context of physical powerlessness, such a person would resist by a simple refusal to kill himself. Such was, in one sense, the plight of the inmates of Nazi concentration camps. These inmates were not, as were the citizens of occupied France, subject to a regime the goal of which was the maintenance of political power and economic benefit. Rather, they faced genocide: an assault on all the physical, psychological, and collective conditions of their existence.

The query, "Isn't there a difference between resistance and just staying alive" is, however, an important one. It reminds us that one of the tasks of an account of resistance is to enable us to distinguish acts of resistance from passivity, compliance, and collaboration. If we take too broad a view of resistance, we will not be able to make this distinction. However, that difficulty can be surmounted here. Just as the Jews who sought to accomplish Kiddush Hashem could have, alternatively, lost their faith in the final moments, and just as the last Jews of Warsaw could have gone passively to Treblinka, so the Jews in concentration camps could *all* have become musselmen. The conditions they were under certainly were forcing them in that direction. In an environment dedicated to getting them to accept their death, a choice of life was itself an act of resistance.

Effectiveness and Intent. On the definition developed in section 3, the necessary and sufficient conditions for the existence of an act of resistance are the existence of a relation of oppression and the attempt by the oppressed to limit, thwart, or end that oppression. It might be asked, however, why I define resistance by the *intention* to thwart, limit, or end oppression rather than by the *actual* thwarting, limiting, or ending of it. Why make resistors' intentions concerning their acts more essential than the objective effects of those actions? Would not it make just as much sense to say "He tried to resist but failed" as "He resisted, but very ineffectively"—or, "He thought he was resisting but he was wrong"? This point is relevant here because questions about the effectiveness of resistance can lead to questions about the existence of resistance in precisely the kinds of cases we have just been considering. A person's resistance efforts may be judged wholly inappropriate, the result of a more-or-less total miscomprehension of the social situation, and not just the product of a tactical or technical error. Such a judgment could well have been passed on each other by militant secularists and pious believers. And such a judgment might include the claim that the other person simply was not resisting, since actual resistance requires that a person actually produce certain effects, that is, some limitation of the oppressor's power. On the definition of resistance offered so far, it might be argued, a person could be said to be resisting even though he or she in no way interferes with what the oppressor seeks to do and even though the oppressor can in no way recognize that he or she is encountering resistance. A very religious person might maintain a completely passive attitude of prayer while being beaten to death. This, it might well be suggested, is hardly resistance.

In response to this criticism, I would say, first, and most generally, that a focus on intention is essential to the concept of resistance. It matches the moral, political, and theoretical concerns of which the concept is the center. As we saw in section 2, when we inquire about the courage of an oppressed group, we want to know if they sought to resist, not whether they did so effectively. Likewise, when we analyze the culture of an oppressed group to see if it created a propensity to resist or comply, it is the will to resist and not the success of the resistance with which we are concerned.

This emphasis on intention does not mean that resistance exists whenever someone simply declares "I am resisting." To seek to resist oppression means to seek to thwart, limit, or end the actions of the oppressor. This attempt necessarily confronts the superior power of the oppressor. The existence and application of this power entails that resistors choose among acts, some of which are resistance and some of which are passivity or collaboration. The distinction is made in terms of the resistor's intention to accept, cooperate with, or obstruct the power of the oppressor. To obstruct that power is to place oneself in jeopardy: to face torture instead of "mere" incarceration; to risk death instead of torture, or a painful death instead of a quick and easy one; and to overcome, rather than be overcome by, one's own terror, shock, and despair. When we describe acts of Kiddush Hashem as resistance we do so partly because we see resistors facing these kinds of choices. The Rabbi who delivered the sermon mentioned in section 1 might have been tortured. Those Jews who observed religious commandments in the concentration camps did so against the explicit orders of camp authorities.

Second, we must note that a relation of oppression is typically based in certain norms. These include both ideologies of legitimacy which mask oppression and self-conceptions of the oppressed whereby they think of themselves as capable or incapable of resistance. Acts of resistance to sexism or racism in the contemporary United States thus typically involve resistance to the norms which legitimate those forms of oppression. For the Jews of Nazi-controlled Europe, acts manifesting pride and dignity were forms of resistance to the Nazi attempt to impose a sense of personal degradation and worthlessness on Jews. Such acts did not stop machine gun bullets or gas chambers. Nor were they intended to. But relations of oppression are rarely limited solely to physical aggression. The Rabbi's sermon, to return to our most problematic example, was directed against the attempt to destroy the capacity of the Jews to act as Jews in any way whatsoever. And it was thus directed against a significant aspect of the oppressor's power—a power based partly on the belief by the oppressed that they were incapable of action.

Third, we may observe that an oppressed group is usually being controlled or assaulted in many different ways. Life, property, religion, family, self-respect, culture, community—all these things may be under attack. Consequently, one may resist some of one's oppression but not all of it. One may defend one's family and abandon one's religion, or hold on to community and abandon property. In the problematic case we have been discussing, we could say that followers of Kiddush Hashem such as the Rabbi were manifesting resistance in defense of their religious identity, while passively accepting oppression of other aspects of their lives.

Finally, keying a concept of resistance to effect rather than intention, besides not meeting the interests traditionally associated with the concept, is not without its own potentially anomolous effects. We need only think of a member of an oppressed group who seeks to collaborate in the hope of receiving some special favors, but who mistakenly performs an act which injures the oppressors. Would we wish to call this an act of resistance?

Despite these reflections, it must be pointed out that on the concept of resistance being developed here a use of the concept commits us to an interest in the effectiveness of acts of resistance. That is why it is difficult to view a wholly ineffective act of resistance as an act of resistance. This peculiar feature of the term derives from the fact, noted in my initial definition of resistance in section 3., that to speak of resistance is to take sides in a social conflict. The existence of acts of resistance entails the existence of oppression. Our recognition of oppression, in turn, commits us to an interest in, partisanship or support for, the overcoming of oppression. We cannot be neutral about the success or failure of the intentions expressed in acts of resistance, though of course we may be too frightened, weak, or lazy to actually come to the aid of the resistors. Thus it is essential to the concept of resistance that we be able to speak of the "effectiveness" of such an act. Being able to characterize the effectiveness of resistance acts is (at least potentially) part of the practical project of making such acts as effective as possible. Our interest in this project is, however, for the reasons just indicated, entailed by the use of the term itself.[15]

My replacement of "He thought he was resisting but was not" by "He was resisting very ineffectively" does not mean that there are no contexts in which "He thought he was resisting but wasn't" could be used. There are, in fact (at least), two. The first is one in which the person believes that he is oppressed but he is not. In such a case we might say, "He thinks he is resisting, but is really a criminal (undisciplined, a petit-bourgeois individualist, a dirty red)." The second case is much more complicated. An examination of it will reveal that an oppressed person can be mistaken not just about the *effectiveness* of his or her resistance but about its *existence*—and therefore its nonexistence—as well.

5. PROBLEMS OF INTENTIONALITY

The preceding section focused mainly on differences in the beliefs which are expressed in acts of resistance and on how such differences can lead to judgments that certain acts are or are not acts of resistance or that certain acts of resistance are or are not effective. It is now necessary to confront the problems which arise from the fact that the beliefs and intentions which are expressed in acts of resistance may be held in various ways and in various degrees, and from the fact that it may be difficult to know whether or not they are held at all.

Tacit Resistance. The intentions and beliefs which are expressed in resistance can exist on a spectrum. At one end of this spectrum we find a fully articulated political and moral critique of oppression combined with a long-term commitment to overcoming it. At the other, there is what I will call much more "tacit" resistance: an inchoate, inarticulate and temporary antagonism to a power figure. One may have a strategy for overthrowing what one believes to be an entire system of domination. On the other hand, one may simply refuse to obey a particular order, feeling a combination of hatred and guilt rather than a conviction of being in the right. Spontaneous black ghetto rebellions seem to be motivated by a sense of oppression; but they lack an overall plan and are preceded and followed by long periods of passive acceptance of a racist society. A usually docile wife may one day burst into an uncontrollable rage at her domineering husband, only to lapse back into docility the next day. Factory workers may intentionally slow the brutal pace of a speeded-up assembly line, while still respecting the basic principles of a capitalist economy.

When a person's beliefs and intentions become too tacit, we might want to say, a particular refusal or rebelliousness simply fails to qualify as an act of resistance. Overly inarticulate and inconstant beliefs and intentions render the act one which can no longer be described as intentionally directed against oppression. Similarly, we can say that actions can be acts of resistance to varying degrees. Other things being equal, an act is more fully an act of resistance the more fully the agent understands it as such.

Unconscious or Self-Deceptive Nonresistance. There is a fundamental difficulty which must be faced by the kind of account of resistance which I have given, that is, one in which the existence of beliefs and intentions is logically primary to the application of a term which refers to a type of action. This difficulty stems from the fact that an agent's beliefs and intentions cannot always be immediately or unproblematically identified.

When the Nazis invaded Poland, they forced Jews into constricted ghettos in a small number of large cities. In each ghetto, they appointed a Judenrat, a council of (usually) influential Jews who became responsible for the day-to-day administration of the ghetto. In most cases the Judenrat administered deportations to the death camps; and members of the Judenrat often opposed, sometimes even betrayed, militant resistance groups. Yet members of the Judenrat usually expressed the belief that they were engaged in an intelligent and effective strategy of resistance, that their surface cooperation was part of a larger strategy of saving as many Jewish lives as possible. Their arguments took the following form:

> Our people is being denied all human rights. . . . From now on our right to exist in this world is based on our ability to do manual work . . . our existence will depend on whether we succeed in organizing matters so that the Germans can derive maximum profit from our work. . . . If we do not arrange it, the Germans will. . . . They will . . . achieve their aim anyway, but the suffering of our community will be incomparably greater than if we do it ourselves.[16]

Despite their claims to the contrary, however, it is clear that in some instances members of the Judenrat were not telling the truth about their intentions. Sometimes they sought self-protection at the expense of fellow Jews, not the collective safety of their people. They were not engaged in a resistance effort which was shaped by different beliefs than those possessed by the militants. Rather, they were not resisting at all.[17]

Now while such a self-serving deception will in some cases be obvious, in many others it will not. Thus defining acts of resistance partly on the basis of an agent's beliefs and intentions leaves us open to the problem that in some situations we can only identify those beliefs and intentions by appealing to a description of the person's behavior. But this behavior, as in the case of the Judenrat, may itself be ambiguous. Its real nature may be known only by reference to the agent's explanation. This explanation, in turn, may be rendered questionable by the ambiguous nature of the behavior. In such cases, beliefs and intentions do not serve as unproblematic criteria for the existence of a type of act. Rather, behavior, intentions, and beliefs form a logically interdependent and obscure circle.

Our suspicion that the agent is asserting untruths about himself may be aroused by the degree to which we see the agent's purported resistance as ineffective or misconceived. That this is an appropriate response is indicated by the following analogy.[18] If we encountered entities which seemed to be speaking but whose sentences translated into beliefs too much at variance with our own, we might well revise our initial belief that the behavior of the entities was linguistic. We would choose to believe that these entities simply did not have beliefs at all rather than that they had such strange ones. Similarly, if a person's purported beliefs about how to resist in a given situation are sufficiently different from our own, or if his or her behavior is so different from what we think resistance should be, we may simply refuse to believe that the person intends to resist. If a Judenrat chairman betrays the militants, saves his own family at the expense of other Jews, uses his power to enrich himself, and so on, it will be very hard to accept his claim that he was resisting. We would have a similar response if someone claimed that their form of resistance required total identification with the Nazi's beliefs. Such people, we would think, are either trying to fool us or succeeding in fooling themselves. What the agent claims is conscious resistance we might describe as unconscious complicity.

Unconscious Resistance. Let us now consider the reverse of the situation just described. An oppressed person claims to be obeying her oppressor. She denies all intention to resist and projects an attitude of fear, helplessness, or willing obedience. Yet when her actions are examined, a pattern emerges. Her behavior actually thwarts the oppressive acts and the intentions of her oppressor. Yet in each case she claims her behavior is caused by mistake, weakness, or accident. The emerging pattern, however, makes these pleas suspect. We begin to think that this person is resisting without admitting that she is, or, more importantly, that we are witnessing a form of resistance of which the agent *herself* is unaware.

Let us call the pattern just described "unconscious resistance." Such resistance has received attention by writers concerned with the behavior of oppressed groups. Feminist writers, for instance, have claimed that certain forms of female behavior usually defined as "neurotic" are in fact unconscious forms of resistance to male domination. Some examples they take are the "frigid" woman whose "frigidity" makes her husband doubt himself sexually, the depressed woman whose emotional paralysis reduces both her husband and her (male) psychiatrist to helplessness, the neurasthenic woman who is simply "too tired" to do housework any more. In each example the woman seems, on the surface, simply to be weak or sick. And insofar as the behavior is viewed as a "syndrome" it may reinforce her inferior social position. Yet, it is argued, the behavior *also* reflects an unconscious aim to resist the superior power of the oppressor. In certain ways, the result of the behavior is that the oppressor can no longer get the oppressed to fulfill her subservient role. Sex, housework, and cheerfulness are no longer obtainable on demand.[19]

It is clear that there are significant differences between unconscious and actual resistance. To resist unconsciously is to resist ambivalently. The recognition of and desire to overthrow oppression is combined, in some way or other, with fear or acceptance of the oppressor. This leads unconscious resistance to often be expressed in a way which may be more damaging to the oppressed than it is to the oppressor. In the cases cited, the man does not get what he wants, but the woman exacts a high price from herself in order to make good her refusal to give it to him. Unconscious resistance necessarily expresses itself in behavior which will be characterized as weakness, illness, incompetence, or inadequacy. Thus the ambivalence of the motivations expressed by the unconscious resistor confers a contradictory character on the effects of unconscious resistance, one which perpetuates the condition of oppression. The public meaning of unconscious resistance is thus of a very different character than that of conscious resistance. (We may note, in passing, that the same is true of unconscious complicity. The public meaning of the acts of the Judenrat—insofar as they represented themselves as still part of the Jewish people and not as having gone over to the Nazis—is very different from that of people, such as Ludz and Fill, who publicly renounced their membership in the oppressed group in favor of some tie to the oppressors.)

Given these differences between unconscious resistance and resistance as such, we might want to deny that the former is a species of resistance at all. Even if we do so, however, there are two reasons to maintain a close conceptual connection between unconscious resistance and actual resistance. First, to describe behavior as unconscious resistance is to identify the existence of motives—however unconsciously or ambivalently held—to resist domination. This identification can be integrated into what has traditionally been called a "dialectical" analysis of society, one which seeks to understand the possibilities for change inherent in the present form of society so as to take advantage of those possibilities for a given end.[20] The concept of unconscious resistance provides direction to political organizing, the goal of which is to turn unconscious resistance into open rebellion. Use of the concept makes it possible to see prospects for the success of such organizing where before, without it, none may have existed at all.

Second, if there is unconscious resistance, there is actual oppression. Seeing resistance—where before we saw weakness or neurosis—makes possible a moral critique of social relations that might previously have been impossible. The concept of unconscious resistance has implications not only for a redescription of behavior or for political organizing directed towards an oppressed group, but for our account of social life as a whole.

The preceding analysis of the concept of resistance may have raised as many questions as it has answered. Yet this final point helps reveal the significance of the concept for social theory and political action, and thus the importance of continuing efforts to understand it.[21]

NOTES

1. "Appeal of the Jewish Fighting Organization," April 23, 1943, in *Anthology of Holocaust Literature,* ed. J. Glastein, I. Knox *et al.* (N.Y.: Atheneum, 1977), p. 328.

2. Israel Kaplan, "In the Sick Hut," Ibid., pp. 264–71.

3. Raul Hilberg, *The Destruction of the European Jews,* (N.Y.: Harper & Row, 1979), pp. 662–65.

4. Meir Dworzecki, "The Day to Day Stand of the Jews," in *Jewish Resistance During the Holocaust* (Jerusalem: Yad Vashem, 1971), p. 174.

5. Leni Yahil, "Jewish Resistance—An Examination of Active and Passive Forms of Jewish Survival in the Holocaust Period," in ibid., p. 44.

6. Raul Hilberg, Letter to the Editor, in *Jewish Currents Reader,* ed. Morris Shappes, (N.Y.: Jewish Current, 1966), p. 135.

7. G.E.M. Anscombe, "On Brute Facts," *Analysis,* 18 (1958): 69–72.

8. For statements reflecting concern with a "shared humanity," a "universal calamity" or the moral self-development of those engaging in civil disobedience, see the essays by James Farmer, Bertrand Russell and Mahatma Gandhi (respectively), *Instead of Violence,* ed. Arthur and Lila Weinberg (Boston: Beacon Press, 1963).

9. The same problem attends many definitions of resistance. See, for example, that of Yehuda Bauer, *The Jewish Emergence from Powerlessness* (Toronto-Buffalo: University of Toronto Press, 1979), p. 27: "[resistance is] any group action consciously taken in opposition to known or surmised laws, actions or intentions directed against the Jews by the Germans." Such a definition leaves unanswered the question: what is it about the Jews that the laws, and so on, of the Germans are directed against?

10. For a development of this theme see Yosef Gottfarstein, "Kiddush Hashem over the Ages and its Uniqueness in the Holocaust Period," in *Jewish Resistance During the Holocaust.*

11. Nathan Eck, "The Place of Jewish Political Parties in the Countries under Nazi Rule," in ibid., pp. 136–37.

12. See, for example, a criticism of such individualism in Rawls' conception of what are social goods: Milton Fisk, "History and Reason in

Rawls' Moral Theory," in N. Daniels, ed. *Reading Rawls* (N.Y.: Basic Books, nd.).

13. See Terence Des Pres, *The Survivor* (N.Y.: Pocket Books, 1977).

14. Ibid., p. 125.

15. I realize that this is a rather complicated claim. It rests on at least three assumptions which I do not have the space to defend here: (i) that part of the meaning of the first person (sincere) use of moral terms is motivational; (ii) that therefore while someone may have an interest in seeing the immoral occur, to the extent that he or she sincerely (and not, say, ironically) uses moral terms, he or she *also* has an interest in the success of the moral; (iii) that therefore, it makes no sense for someone to say "I believe that x is morally wrong and I unambivalently want it to happen."

16. Zvi A. Bar-On, "Jewish Leadership—Policy and Responsibility," in *Jewish Resistance During the Holocaust,* pp. 229–30.

17. Ibid., as well as the classic study, *Judenrat,* by Isiah Trunk (N.Y.: MacMillan, 1972).

18. See Richard Rorty, "The World Well Lost," *Journal of Philosophy,* 69 (1972): 652–53.

19. The application of the point of women's psychological "symptoms" is made by Miriam Greenspan, *A New Approach to Women and Therapy* (N.Y.: McGraw-Hill, 1983) and Phyllis Chesler, *Women and Madness* (N.Y.: Doubleday, 1972). For similar treatment of behavior by black slaves, see Eugene Genovese, *Roll, Jordan, Roll* (N.Y.: Pantheon, 1974).

20. It should be clear that this discussion of "unconscious resistance" owes much to Marx's distinction between a class "in-itself" and a class "for-itself." For a discussion of what I have termed "dialectical analysis," see George Lukacs, *History and Class Consciousness* (Cambridge: M.I.T., 1968).

21. The author wishes to thank Richard Schmitt, Joan Ringelheim, Miriam Greenspan, and Peter Dalton for helpful criticisms of earlier drafts of this essay.

Part V
PRESENT AND FUTURE QUESTIONS: HOPE, SURVIVORS, AND MEMORY

We conclude with reflections that continue to challenge our sense of what the Holocaust can mean for our existence as moral agents. George Kren and Leon Rappaport discuss ways in which the event alters our sense of the human condition. Bruno Bettelheim and Miriam Greenspan directly focus on the meanings the event may have for us today, both for survivors and for those whose experience of the event is indirect. Primo Levi, Jerry Samet, and I reflect on the experience and value of memory, and the way obeying the frequently repeated injunction to "never forget" may be part of our painful but essential attempt to heal the savage wounds the Holocaust has left in us all.

George Kren and Leon Rappaport

THE HOLOCAUST AND THE HUMAN CONDITION

When a universe of accepted meanings begins to go seriously out of joint, the result is fearful disorientation and paralysis of action. Human reactions to the unthinkable are invariably primitive and visceral: the hair rises on the back of the neck prior to a rational certainty that something is wrong. More concretely, people tend to perceive the onset of unthinkable events as a child perceives the transformation of humans into monsters in a horror film—with nervous, smiling disbelief and a rising fear that it may actually be true.

Just as an individual life crisis will be accompanied by feelings of chaos and fear that seem to accumulate without volition in the depths of the nervous system, so it is with major historical crises, and so it most certainly was for those caught up in the Holocaust. Nothing in the Nazi extermination program contributed more to its effectiveness than its shocking unbelievability. And apart from the testimony of survivors, nothing is so revealing of this truth as the way Holocaust material penetrates the ordinary psychosocial adjustment mechanisms supporting scholarly detachment. None of those who engage in serious study of these extraordinary happenings, including trained scholars, can escape without experiencing a deep personal crisis. In this sense, the enduring meaning of the Holocaust is profoundly rooted in the feelings it evokes.[1]

This is not a matter directly concerned with conventional standards of academic objectivity, for the emotional impact first occurs far back in the rear areas of awareness. This impact has no immediate connection with bias or distorted perception of facts, but operates instead in those dim reaches of the mind sheltering taken-for-granted beliefs about human nature and the basic requirements for all forms of social living.

Among serious scholars, the accumulated horrors of the Holocaust ultimately force recognition that these events defy both cognitive and emotional assimilation because they are off the scale of established human knowledge. There are, to be sure, intense feelings of disgust,

347

rage, and frustration. It could hardly be otherwise, particularly during the early exploratory phase of study. But for those who persist, and it should be noted that there are many who cannot, these early or "preliminary" emotions eventually recede because they are too superficial; too variable, passionate, and "normal" for the material in hand. Rage and disgust can serve for a time to satisfy the transitory ego-defensive needs of tourists and dilettantes; such feelings are melted away from minds that are held in the fires of the Holocaust for prolonged periods.

What remains is a central, deadening sense of despair over the human species. Where can one find an affirmative meaning in life if human beings can do such things? Along with this despair there may also come a desperate new feeling of vulnerability attached to the fact that one *is* human. If one keeps at the Holocaust long enough, then sooner or later the ultimate personal truth begins to reveal itself: one knows, finally, that one might either do it, or be done to. If it could happen on such a massive scale elsewhere, then it can happen anywhere; it is all within the range of human possibility, and like it or not, Auschwitz expands the universe of consciousness no less than landings on the moon.

The tourists of the Holocaust, people with only casual or relatively stereotyped knowledge of the events, do not understand this. They see the SS as monsters, not representative human beings; and they see the Jews as martyred innocents, flawed only by their failure to fight back against the primitive forces of destruction. Here, for example, is how a prominent literary critic has attempted to use the Holocaust to explicate the idea of tragedy: "The Holocaust is, among a thousand things, one immense story revealing precisely the major theme of traditional Tragedy: *the fragility of human culture before the state of nature.*"[2] Innocent and well-meaning as this statement may be, it is, nevertheless, a terribly offensive falsification because most serious students of the Holocaust know that what it reveals is the *fragility of nature* in the face of human agents operating with the technical and conceptual tools of "advanced" culture. As others have already noted: "There is more than a wholly fortuitous connection between the applied technology of the mass production line, with its vision of universal material abundance, and the applied technology of the concentration camp, with its vision of a profusion of death. We may wish to deny the connection, but Buchenwald was of our West as much as Detroit's River Rouge—we cannot deny Buchenwald as a casual aberration of a Western world essentially sane."[3]

In such matters, however, those deeply engaged in Holocaust studies usually find themselves alone, and they tend to work out their despairs in odd ways. The appropriate model here is the myth of Medusa:

like the ancient Greeks who were turned to stone if they looked upon the serpent-crowned head, those who gaze deeply into the Holocaust may also find themselves, if not turned to stone, then at least profoundly changed.

This personal impact of the Holocaust upon people who have experienced it indirectly, through their efforts at historical reconstruction, is particularly noteworthy because it emphasizes a fundamental quality of all historical crises. That is, although they involve events that can be described in linear sequence, understood in terms of individual or group psychological processes, and even placed in some plausible context of historical development, their larger meaning nevertheless remains threatening and ambiguous, a subject of doubt and controversy as succeeding generations struggle for interpretations relevant to their immediate and remote historical circumstances. At the level of personal knowledge, therefore, historical crises are crises of knowing, knowing about events of such magnitude that their ultimate meaning appears unknowable.

The superficial illogic of this state of affairs does not preclude inquisitive discussion. Not only may one think about the unthinkable, but perhaps even more important, one may think about how people think about the unthinkable. And since it stands as the primary unthinkable crisis of our century, the Holocaust has inspired an abundance of relevant material. In this connection, the efforts of scholars may be temporarily set aside. Their special contribution as cultural sensor instruments "designed" for detection and recording of historical earth tremors has already been indicated. What remains of critical importance, however, is the thinking of survivors about their own experience.

This presents itself initially as chaotic and as diverse as the experiences and viewpoints that have inspired it. Yet the cutting edge of the question of knowing eventually reveals a simple truth: people who have experienced the Holocaust crisis tend to think of it mainly in accord with their dominant existential concerns.

Thus, for Jewish survivors and others primarily concerned with politics and matters of community, the Holocaust has come to serve as both the political and the moral foundation for the state of Israel. Having suffered unprecedented slaughter and persecution, Jews are not only entitled to their own place in the world, but must also maintain it at all costs lest they again become vulnerable to destruction. More generally, almost any form of political activity can now be justified by appealing to the Holocaust.

At the opposite extreme from the politically oriented, however, are those who understand their experience in metaphysical or quasi-religious terms. Survivor writings of this type emphasize a search for meanings that transcend all politics and practical affairs. The victimized Jews are seen here as instruments of a supernatural force guiding the destiny of humanity, and to the extent that their suffering in the Holocaust seems beyond human comprehension, this only strengthens the inclination toward a supernatural interpretation.

Lying between the two extremes are a wide variety of highly personal, individualized survivor accounts. What these works have in common is their projective-defensive quality: writers tend to project their own basic needs or tensions into their testimony. Thus, whereas some accounts constantly emphasize small acts of resistance as a saving factor, others note that any act of resistance was tantamount to suicide. And again, whereas some survivors rather proudly describe their ability to "organize" extra food or good work assignments, others describe such activities as contemptible. Occasionally, differences between personal views of the Holocaust surface with brutal clarity, as in this excerpt from Primo Levi's description of an incident immediately following an SS "selection" for the Auschwitz gas chambers: "Silence slowly prevails and then, from my bunk on the top row, I see and hear old Kuhn praying aloud, with his beret on his head, swaying backwards and forwards violently. Kuhn is thanking God because he has not been chosen. . . . If I was God, I would spit at Kuhn's prayer."[4]

This is not to say that survivor accounts are factually untrustworthy or that easy moral or psychiatric judgments can be made about them. It is, rather, to stress the general psychological principle that the more threatening and ambiguous any situation is, the more likely individuals are to react to it in accord with their own habitual pattern of social-emotional adjustment mechanisms. Prisoners in the unreal world of the Nazi camps could only construe their experience by looking inward to the ideas and values they had brought with them. Indeed, many have said that they only survived by retreating into an inwardly focused and self-centered shell which permitted them to ignore much of the surrounding horror.[5]

In the face of these limitations, it should be plain that no definitive understanding of the Holocaust can be drawn directly from the survivor literature. This literature may be the best source of the facts, but the facts do not interpret themselves. Where the viewpoints of survivors are not determined by doctrinaire secular or metaphysical considerations, they frequently reflect the relatively narrow personal concerns of individual authors.

Consequently, the general questions of meaning that are provoked by the Holocaust are no more likely to be resolved by survivors bearing witness through their direct experience than by scholars with indirect experience. It is arguable that the former have been so close to the events that they cannot put them into a broader historical or psychological context, and that the latter work upon the events from a distance that only allows them either to assimilate the Holocaust into conventional history by ignoring its uniqueness, or to languish in numb despair at this spectacle of human degradation.

In part, it is this very impenetrability of the Holocaust, its persistent resistance to any straightforward analysis, that requires it to be recognized as an historical crisis. Those who search deeply into the events of the Holocaust probing for meanings find themselves overcome by the dark enigmas that accompany historical crisis. Nor should this be surprising, for historical crises break the preexisting social consensus and shared values. In more formal terms, historical crises involve events that shatter the credibility of preexisting epistemologies. In *The Structure of Scientific Revolutions,* T.S. Kuhn suggests that this occurs in science when a dominant paradigm for theory and research is overturned by new ways of thinking about scientific phenomena. It is being suggested here that an analogous process occurs in history when real events outstrip the conceptual structures of historians, philosophers, and laymen alike.

Yet the Holocaust may be hard to grasp as a historical crisis because the breakdowns of consensus and culturally defined meanings consequent to it are not easily perceived. There were no great changes in ideas concerning government and political power, for example, because the Holocaust was not a revolution. Economic systems and practices were not influenced, for it was not a financial or economic collapse. Furthermore, the Holocaust itself led to no startling changes in national boundaries; it did not generate any sweeping new religious forms or views of human nature; and it had no discernible impact on modern science.

In fact, if there is any approximate analogy to be found between the effects of the Holocaust and other historical crisis events, it is to the Black Plague, which also left in its wake uncountable millions of dead bodies. Yet even this analogy is very unsatisfactory, because the plague was an unselective, natural phenomenon that profoundly disrupted the major communities of Europe. The Holocaust, by contrast, for the most part stripped only the Jews from communities, which were otherwise intact and able to conduct business as usual. The enduring psychosocial effects of the Holocaust, therefore, are not easily perceived, and may conveniently be denied or ignored, because once the bodies are out of the way nothing remains of it except mental images. Yet these images persist and grow and have steadily spread out into the moral foundations of Western society.[6] Morality, of course, is also invisible, intangi-

ble. And, as we do with other intangibles supporting our human existence, most of us ignore morality until something happens to compel
attention.

Because it lies deeply within the fabric of society, morality, including all standards of ethics and value judgments, only becomes conspicuous when it dramatically fails, as in the case of senseless crimes or other
sharp violations of accepted social practices. Furthermore, when questions of morality do surface, they are typically engaged by legal or
religious institutions. The former provides approved technical procedures for handling transgressions, and the latter provides metaphysical
discussions and rationales aimed at giving everyday meaning to the
events at issue. Supported in practice by the efforts of culture agents
such as parents and teachers, the primary institutions of law and religion
maintain the historical norms in matters of justice, equity, and the sun-
dries of everyday conduct.

The Holocaust stands as a crucial moral crisis because within the
Nazi state, and in most of the territory it eventually came to control,
neither traditional law or religion could prevent or comprehend the
massive killings. Moreover, those nations allied against the Nazis in the
name of law and religion not only failed to act effectively against the
Holocaust, but tried for a time to maintain an official unawareness that
it existed.

The explanations ordinarily given for this state of affairs emphasize
the difficulties of resisting Nazi power and the inability of both peoples
and governments to realize that such crimes were possible. Such explanations may be true enough, but they also disguise a more fundamental
and threatening truth: that the legal and religious structures of morality
were simply inadequate to confront an unprecedented form of organized evil supported by the authority of a modern state.

In Germany and the occupied countries, most of the major social
institutions made no special effort to oppose the Holocaust, and those
persons who attempted to do so acting as individuals or in small groups
were easily brushed aside and eliminated. If anything, the drastic punishments meted out to such people served to further intimidate others
who might have followed their example. It is also a fact that the fate of
the Jews under German control was not an important concern of any of
the allied governments fighting Germany. It has been well established,
furthermore, that the Christian churches generally did not take a firm
institutional stand against Nazism and the Holocaust despite persistent
efforts toward this end by some individual members of the clergy. There
is even material available suggesting that the leaders of various Jewish

communities in Europe, America, and Palestine did not use all the resources at their disposal to act against the Holocaust.[7]

Given these facts, the conclusion seems inescapable that the existing moral structures failed. The basic explanation for this failure is, at least in principle, not hard to discover. Insofar as Western concepts of morality have evolved in connection with the rise of secular nation-states, these concepts and practices have gradually come to derive their authority from the state rather than any higher force. Both the institutional actions and the traditional values of law and religion are for all practical purposes only allowed to operate in whatever framework is made available to them by the state. By one means or another, the salient interests of the state must be served by law and religion. If these interests are not served, then legal and religious institutions will be threatened or intimidated until they either conform to state policies, or state policies change. Frequently, however, the state will ally itself with one of these institutions in order to isolate and intimidate the other, which usually then retreats to a compromise position allowing its continued existence.

There is nothing particularly new about the foregoing analysis, but when taken in conjunction with the Holocaust, it leads to stark conclusions: within certain limits set by political and military power considerations, the modern state may do anything it wishes to those under its control. There is no moral-ethical limit which the state cannot transcend if it wishes to do so, because there is no moral-ethical power higher than the state. Moreover, it seems apparent that no modern state will ever seriously interfere with the internal activities of another solely for moral-ethical reasons. Consequently, in matters of ethics and morality, the situation of the individual in the modern state is in principle roughly equivalent to the situation of the prisoner in Auschwitz: either act in accord with the prevailing standards of conduct enforced by those in authority, or risk whatever consequences they may wish to impose. Just as there was no higher moral authority outside Auschwitz to which the prisoner could appeal, there is no such authority available to citizens of the modern state. If they are critical of the dominant ethos, they can only express this criticism within the limits permitted by the state.

Exceptional persons, such as Solzhenitsyn and Sakharov in the Soviet Union, and the Berrigan brothers in the United States, may test the limits for moral-ethical criticism, in effect pitting their personal will to meaning against the power of the state. People with such heroic qualities are rare, however, and when they act in accord with their moral convictions it is usually necessary for them to go beyond the established boundaries of law and religion. But the survival of such persons is always uncertain, and the practical effect of their heroic action always remains questionable. Like the occasional heroism shown by prisoners in Auschwitz, such actions seem to provide moments of moral inspiration precisely because they are so far beyond the capacity of most people. Put otherwise, it may be said that whereas many can be inspired by the life of Jesus, there are few indeed who can be carried by their inspiration to the point of risking crucifixion. The fact that certain exceptional people may set themselves against injustice, therefore, does not materially alter our view of the Holocaust as a historical crisis revealing that the conventional moral structures of law and religion have little or no meaning when set against the authority of the state.

This conclusion may seem obvious or even trivial when it is given in the language of sociology and confined to implications about the credibility of social institutions. Indeed, as George Steiner, Thomas Szasz, and other thinkers have argued, the language of social science can hardly do anything but trivialize human experience by turning it into an alien and mystifying subject matter.[8]

Psychologically, however, the profound impact of the Holocaust is that it leaves the individual stripped of moral authority and moral security. If millions of innocents could be systematically murdered at the very center of modern European civilization, then that civilization can provide no firm sense of moral security to its inhabitants. Prior to the Holocaust, Western ethics and moral values that had gradually been accumulated and codified in the institutions of law and religion were generally thought to be virtually immutable—a basic element in the makeup of Western humanity. Centered in cultural ideals represented by such figures as Goethe, Newton, Tolstoy, and Beethoven, the modern European might have acknowledged the presence of exploitation and injustice, but direct, extensive human slaughter was simply unthinkable except as it might occur among relatively uncivilized peoples such as "the Turks."

The strength of this belief was indicated by the reactions of those caught up in the Holocaust as victims, perpetrators, or spectators. Yet this question of "how such things are possible," which springs so spontaneously from the revealed impotence of the moral-ethical values that had been taken for granted in the modern West contains within it the ultimate psychological demonstration supporting our conclusion. That is, since the Holocaust *was* possible, prior cultural values supposed to make it impossible were manifestly false, and a moral crisis is imposed upon the whole fabric of the culture.

What the Holocaust forces upon us, therefore, is recognition of nothing less than a moral equivalent of the Copernican revolution. Western European culture is not an orderly, ethical center for our social universe, and the historical development of its moral instrumentalities —law and religion—was a failure ending in Auschwitz. But to accept this conclusion as a justifiable psychohistorical or philosophical statement is only to make a small step toward understanding the sociocultural significance of the Holocaust. Without careful consideration of how the process for killing millions could work, the crisis posed by the Holocaust will remain as hardly more than a basis for the proliferation of questionable alternative moral value systems.

Those who see no further origins for the Holocaust other than simple failures of the legal and religious institutions that should have prevented it reveal the limits of their understanding by arguing for reform or extension of these institutions. Exponents of Western law, for example, look toward development of an enforceable international system of jurisprudence, a world court that can override the authority of any nation state. Implicitly, at least, such views are in agreement with the premise that no national legal system can prevail against the power system of which it is a part. Yet insofar as there seems little possibility for the development of supranational law—if anything, the steadily declining status of the United Nations makes this prospect look dimmer than ever—the credibility of law as a primary vehicle for Western morality is no greater today or in the forseeable future than it was in 1942. Actually, a good case could be made for the argument that the moral credibility and potential of law has been steadily shrinking as the power of modern nation-states has expanded.[9]

Religion seems to be an equally empty alternative, and for much the same reason, namely, that no Western religious institution has been able to stand successfully in clear opposition to the power of the modern state. Thus, despite calls for morality in government and appeals to a higher moral law against killing, torture, and all of the other forms of political repression that have become so familiar in this century, there is no evidence to suggest that religious institutions have any greater capacity to influence national policies today than they had in Hitler's Germany. Dissident clergy today may still be routinely arrested, harassed, or otherwise discredited wherever they attempt forceful opposition to secular authorities.

The Holocaust has made it clear that the two traditional pillars of Western morality, law and religion, are inadequate to the task of protecting human beings. However well these institutions may have served in the past to prevent masses of people from thinking or doing the unthinkable, they have been rendered impotent by modern political power systems and the bureaucratic structures these systems have created. Traditional Western religions are hard put to confront problems of "authorized" mass murder or lesser wrongdoings, because they have in practice identified sin or evil with motives of either passion or profit. The idea that it might indeed be fundamentally sinful to carry out orders issued by established state institutions weighs little in the balance against centuries of church teachings to the contrary.

As the only new Western moral-philosophical movement to have emerged strongly during the second half of this century, existentialism undoubtedly became popular because it addressed the moral emptiness revealed by the Holocaust. Existentialism rests on the assumption that human beings are alone. The existential view follows from realization that neither law, religion, nor science can provide compelling satisfactory answers to the questions, "Why not commit murder? Why not commit suicide?" And in the face of the Holocaust, the existentialist response has been to explore these questions with the suggestion that morality can only be understood as an act of will. That is, if one does not commit suicide or murder it is because one chooses not to do so, rather than because of any fear that retribution will eventually follow. Alone, therefore, persons hold their lives in their own hands and existence itself is hardly more than a construct of consciousness. It cannot be derived from any exterior metaphysical or scientific principle, nor even from culturally determined aspects of consciousness, for if the culture can be recognized as being flawed or fraudulent, then culturally dictated aspects of mind cannot be accepted as a foundation for morality.

In this connection, the popularity of existentialism in all the diverse forms it has assumed over the past thirty-odd years may be attributed as much to the institutional failure of science as to religion or law. The science and technology which had been increasingly celebrated for almost a century as the bastion of Western rationality and had become synonymous with liberal-progressive thought turned out to be a major factor contributing to the feasibility of the Holocaust.

THE FAILURE OF SCIENCE

It is not particularly difficult to grasp the arguments for the failure of law and religion; both are primarily institutions oriented to matters of morality and the maintenance of civilized behavior, and the fact that the Holocaust could happen is prima facie evidence for their failure. It is much more difficult to grasp arguments pointing toward the failure of science, because science is still generally thought to be amoral, a value-free enterprise devoted solely to the accumulation of knowledge. Furthermore, although it is clear that applied science provided the technology that made the mass killing possible, it is also true that applied science provided means to fight against the killing. In short, the prevalent view is that science is neutral, a method of gaining knowledge leading to control over the physical and social environment, and evil only insofar as evil people may use it badly.

Our view is different. In a number of ways, the evidence surrounding the Holocaust suggests emphatically that from its dim origins in the concentration camps and the euthanasia program to its final large-scale industrial actualization in Auschwitz, the scientific mode of thought and the methodology attached to it were intrinsic to the mass killings. Quite apart from the technology, the mentality of modern science is what made the Holocaust possible.

At a fairly superficial level, it is quite obvious that the rational-abstract forms of conceptual thought required and promulgated by science provided the basis for systematic and efficient identification of people by race, transportation of large numbers to concentration points, killing, and body disposal. But the more central role of science as a mentality was in providing the inspiration and justification for these technical activities. The abstract, categorical thinking encouraged by the culture of science paves the way for acceptance of categorical racist ideas.

In present-day American psychology, for example, the argument is all too widely made and all too frequently accepted that scientific studies of intelligence test scores reveal intelligence to be about 80 percent genetically determined and that because of their genetic structure black Americans are on the average well behind whites in their intellectual achievements. Once it is accepted that such abstractions as genes distributed in populations are, so to speak, "real facts" instead of theoretical constructs, the way is opened toward instituting and justifying social policies based on these "facts."

The point at issue here has nothing to do with whether or not there can be some merit or utility in the accumulation of evidence leading to scientific generalizations about people; it is that in a scientifically oriented culture, people will accept generalities produced by science as fact, particularly when the generalities fit other culturally determined predispositions or biases. Thus, a detailed study of the history of European racism shows that with the rise of science during the Enlightenment, preexisting mythic racist traditions were not truly repudiated but simply assimilated into the new context of "reason." Instead of justifying racism by appealing to interpretations of the Bible, for example, reasonable people began to justify it by appealing to morphological data and the specimens of native humanity encountered in Africa and the Americas.[10]

It was Hitler's political genius and an intrinsic aspect of his psychopathology as well, to shape his racist ideas in such a way as to meld both the scientific mentality allowing theories to be reified into concrete thought patterns and the more primitive emotional feelings which have traditionally energized racist beliefs.[11]

The scientific orientation in Western civilization also encourages and even forces people to detach their emotions from the rational intellect. Education is virtually synonymous with the ability to be dispassionate and detached. This is not to say that ignorant, brutish people with no education and no ability to detach emotions from intellect are not capable of performing horrible actions. The camps had a full share of brutal guards recruited from the Ukrainian peasantry, in addition to some sadistic Kapos (inmate "trusties") and SS men. Moreover, it could hardly matter to victims whether they were killed by a blow from an excited brute or a calm and detached SS officer with a master's degree in biology. But there is a difference in the scale of the killing. Ferociously anti-Semitic peasants might organize vicious attacks on Jews, and might even kill a sizable number during a rampage, but they are not capable of killing millions by designing an efficient system of death camps. The latter is only possible as a manifestation of detached technical expertise grounded on a scientific rationale or *logos,* and only in a relatively small degree supported by emotionality or passion.

Recent studies suggest that Hitler's inspiration in exterminating the Jews had diverse sources in traditional Austrian anti-Semitism, the social Darwinism promulgated through Haeckel's Monist League, and assorted mystical-political ideas—all of which became an integral part of his psychosocial adjustment following his experience as a soldier in World War I. What is most striking, however, is his success in attaining power by playing his own special pathology in harmony with the deep psychic traumas of defeated German society. Yet the genocide program succeeded only because the middle- and low-ranking organization men directing its day-to-day operation could reduce massive killings to a routinely efficient industrial operation.

Insofar as SS leaders realized that emotional reactions might interfere with efficient operation of the death camps, they took rational precautions. Men who objected to death or concentration camp assignments (there were not many) were either transferred or coerced into participation. Special training was given to members of the branch of the SS charged with running the camps, the *Totenkopf,* under the direction of Theodore Eicke. The attempt, which seemed to be successful enough, was to teach men to keep emotional interference down to the minimum by encouraging practices that tended to define Jews as inferior organisms, not really human beings. The splitting process involved is roughly analogous to the way some animal research scientists come to view their rats or monkeys without any trace of empathy. (Undergraduates, who—perhaps with good reason—often show spontaneous feelings of empathy with caged laboratory animals are traditionally seen as poor lab assistants because of their inability to maintain a proper scientific detachment.)

It should be clear that the mental splitting which separates emotionality from rationality is deliberately inculcated by science-oriented Western culture in order that people may repress or suspend reflexive emotions that might block achievement of abstract, distant goals. The ability to categorize objects, to then perform mental (imaginary) operations upon these objects, and thus transform the meaning of the objects into something other than what one started with is fundamental to all science. Indeed, it is precisely this ability that has come to be accepted as our definition of intelligence in accord with the cognitive development theory of Jean Piaget and the empirical efforts of intelligence testers. Yet this capacity for scientific-intellectual functioning in Western culture is what can make extraordinary horrors possible. By exercising this capacity, we can make judgments that some people are better than others, and, ultimately, that some people are not even people at all. So it is that the scientific mode of thinking—the mode of thinking required and promulgated by science—allows us to perform promethean acts that transform the world.[12]

Philosophers and historians of science who have studied the underpinnings of scientific activities typically point out that the issues here involve the language of science. That is, the abstract and abstracting thought patterns associated with science are distinct from more reflexive forms of thinking, and cannot be attained without the use of special language systems. These systems may be entirely symbolic and empty of all content, as in the various algebras and geometries, or they may involve ordinary words used only according to certain agreed-upon rules of meaning.

Analysis of the general implications of the special language system essential to scientific thinking became the life work of Ludwig Wittgenstein. He recognized the dangers inherent in the amoral language of science and based his work on the tradition of moral philosophy established by Schopenhauer and Kierkegaard. The former had argued against Kant's idea of equating morality with rationality based on the assumption of a "categorical imperative" moral law. For both Schopenhauer and Kierkegaard, morality was clearly independent of rationality or intellect. They argued that the ultimate source of moral thoughts, feelings, and actions could not be rationality. Instead, the immediate transfer or communication of emotions between people must be recognized as the touchstone for all genuine passion, moral or otherwise. We all experience this in limited ways as adults, and more generally as children, when the sight of another child being punished evokes immediate fear and sadness, or when seeing another person hit their thumb with a hammer makes us cringe at the vicarious experience of pain. Just where this reflexive, empathic aspect of human nature comes from and how it is to be explained remains an open question, but the fact that it exists, and that it has nothing whatever to do with intellect or rational calculation, is indisputable.

Wittgenstein's contribution begins here. Unlike Kierkegaard and Schopenhauer, he was very much a man of the twentieth century, raised in upper-class fin de siècle Viennese society, decorated for bravery under fire in World War I, and for almost ten years a professor at Cambridge prior to his death in 1951. As it was for so many philosophers and intellectuals of his generation, the great challenge to Wittgenstein concerned the meaning of science, its theories, methods, and implications.

He saw this problem in terms of the special language of science, and his early work elaborating upon the denotative validity of scientific language was interpreted as a powerful justification for the view that scientists should eliminate all speculative, ambiguous, and evaluative elements from their language—from the substance of their work. The closing line of his famous first book, *Tractatus Logico-Philosophicus,* was "Whereof one cannot speak, thereof one must be silent." It was generally understood to mean that speculative, discursive language had no place in science, or in any other disciplined human enterprise; language could only be useful when its terms were tied down to empirical evidence or operations. In any other case, one had best be silent. But this was not what Wittgenstein meant at all. Instead, as his students and biographers later pointed out, he wanted to suggest that precise scientific language did not allow one to speak of the really important matters in life, matters of morality and values. One could use precise language in a positivistic fashion to "do" the sciences well enough, but that was all. As his friend Paul Englemann explained: "Positivism holds—and this is its essence—that what we can speak about is all that matters in life. Whereas Wittgenstein passionately believes that all that really matters in human life is precisely what, in his view, we must be silent about."[13]

Later on, Wittgenstein's work changed, and he began to see that language was not only the means by which people could create certain realities (as in science) and assert certain values (as in religion), but that it is more generally the means by which all human affairs are connected to physical or social realities. This change in Wittgenstein's ideas has been epitomized by H. Stuart Hughes: "[Earlier] he had maintained that language proceeded from reality—that the structure of the real world determined the structure of speech. Now he had come to believe that the reverse was the case: language, as the vehicle for understanding reality determined the way in which people saw it."[14]

From this standpoint, science and the special use of language allowing the conduct of science is irrelevant to questions of morality or value, which stand at the center of the human condition. Science appears, consequently, as hardly more than a wonderfully complex and plastic plaything of the intellect, a toy that can be shaped in whatever forms clever intellects wish to shape it. It follows that science is totally amoral and terribly dangerous because its potent effects are ungoverned by any intrinsic human limits. We see it ever more clearly these days, of course: the weapons, nuclear plants, food additives, pollutants, etc., that cumulatively, as the result of science, threaten the future existence of our species and determine the conditions under which we exist.

Where then was morality to be found? Having "seen through" science via analysis of language, toward the end of his career Wittgenstein began to echo, somewhat, the ideas of earlier humanist philosophers, and some of his ideas also had a Nietzschean tone: "It is the will, rather than the reason, that introduces value into the world: I call 'will' first and foremost the bearer of good and evil."[15] He argued rather concretely that the real purpose of philosophical analysis was to protect human reason from being "bewitched" by human language. Toward the end of his career, as recorded in the essays titled *Philosophical Investigations,* Wittgenstein's efforts were chiefly devoted to showing just how easily reason may be distorted or manipulated by language.

It should be plain enough, at this point, why the Wittgensteinian perspective on the connections between language, science, and morality is basic to any serious discussion of the Holocaust and the human condition. As the most powerful creation of Western civilization, science too stands revealed as completely ineffective and indifferent when it comes to preventing humanity from inflicting extraordinary horrors upon itself. More specifically, Wittgenstein's analysis of the language of science indicates that it is not only amoral, but that to an even greater extent than religion or law, science may be bent to any purpose—no matter how extreme or "unthinkable"—for it contains no internal

mechanism to serve as a limiting factor. Instead, like any common weapon, science, and reason itself, may be picked up and used for whatever
purposes can be justified by clever rhetoric.

The Holocaust provides such an overwhelming burden of evidence
to this effect that perhaps people refuse to recognize it lest they be
forced to acknowledge their own participation in horrors akin to those
perpetrated by the Nazis. In connection with planning and implementation of the genocide program, for example, the capacity to think and act
according to euphemistic language became a widespread and apparently
effective form of individual psychological adjustment. Euphemisms such
as "final solution," "relocation," and "shower bath" seemed to work
nicely for the SS as a means of imposing a rationalized, business-as-usual
emotional framework upon activities too atrocious to be contemplated
in the raw. It was precisely in this same vein of word-magic-via-euphe-
mism that the American forces in Vietnam conducted programs of
"forced urbanization" (herding people into concentration camps) and
"defoliation" (poisoning the natural ecology).

But in these and many other obvious examples of how euphemistic
language facilitates the reification of atrocious activities into acceptable
and routine "operations" that may then be implemented without a
qualm by the corporate technicians of modern applied science, what one
sees revealed is merely the tip of an iceberg. The deeper implications
flowing from the falsification of language produced by political interests, on the one hand, and technical-scientific interests, on the other,
ultimately involve the gradual disappearance of all authentic human
experience. That is, fundamental elements of culture and civilization are
slowly sinking out of sight in a mire of bureaucratic structures functioning in the name of humanity, against humanity. As Horkheimer and
Adorno have noted: "There is no longer any available form of linguistic
expression which has not tended toward accommodation to dominant
currents of thought; *and what a devalued language does not do automatically is proficiently executed by societal mechanisms.*"[16]

If this discussion of language and the Holocaust seems excessive, it
should be recalled that the history of this century is, manifestly, a record
of the manipulation of reason by rhetoric. Not for nothing has this era
been called the "age of ideology." It is entirely clear, furthermore, that
the most massive human killings and horrors are closely associated with
those societies in which ideologies have been most highly developed and
pervasive in everyday life. People themselves are probably no more
ferocious by nature in one place than in another. But ideologies, which
blend linguistic rationalizations with political imperatives to the dracon-
ian actions made possible by modern science, have yielded such extraor-

dinary horrors as the Holocaust. It is particularly noteworthy, in this connection, that American liberalism only became readily visible as an ideology in the 1960s, when it was perceived that the horrors of racism and the Vietnam war could be conveniently rationalized in the language of liberalism and carried out with the instruments of that same rigorously "objective" science that was, according to the values of liberalism, the foundation of human progress.

It is difficult to grasp the institutional significance of science in relation to ideology. Compared with science, for example, religion and law seem hardly more than primitive word structures. These institutions have no hardware or technology other than whatever crumbs may fall to them from the table of science. Religion and law have been effective governors of human action only where majorities of people have accepted the arbitrary assumptions these institutions are based upon: ideals of imminent justice, equity, retribution, life after death, revelation, and so on. None of these assumptions exists or can be demonstrated to exist in nature, except insofar as people impose them by collective acts of will. One can, for example, interpret the frenzied killing actions of a wolf or shark as either a terrifying judgment of God or a benign demonstration of ecological balancing processes. If one is persuaded of the value of ecological balance achieved in this fashion—a view which has become relatively popular only during the 1970s because of arguments created by biological science experts—well and good. But the key issue to see here is that one's view follows not from the phenomenon itself, but from a verbal interpretation of the phenomenon which may or may not satisfy prevailing criteria for the revealed word of God or the revealed facts of science.

This path of analysis is particularly difficult to follow because scientific thought has for more than three centuries been steadily discrediting and eroding the unverifiable assumptions underlying religion and law, substituting in their place the apparently verifiable, disinterested principles of reason, rationality, and empirical inquiry. The apparent disinterest of scientific thinking has, until recently, seemed to be a clearly superior value when compared with the vested interests built into the assumptions of law and religion. Yet as Wittgenstein saw, and as an increasing number of contemporary philosophers and scientists are beginning to see, placing trust in the rationalized assumptions and empirical methods of science is, fundamentally, just as much an arbitrary act of faith or "will" as trust in religion, or law, or voodoo witchcraft.[17]

Auschwitz and Hiroshima were as much enterprises of applied science (rationality armed with technology) as the Albigensian slaughter and the Inquisition were enterprises of applied religion (mystique armed with secular power). The chief difference between these two categories is only that the former destroyed more people in a far more impersonal but no less horrible way than the latter.

If anything, the Holocaust and other major horrors of this century must be laid more directly upon the doorstep of science than upon the doorstep of either religion or law. This is partly because science has been responsible for reducing the inhibitory "power" of religion and law. Thus, social science and biology have effectively wiped out most of the inhibitions prescribed by religion, whereas political science and sociology have revealed the arbitrary qualities of secular law. Science is far more deceptive than either religion or law, because the words describing the essence of science—reason, enlightenment, and so on—are taken to indicate the core of civilization as opposed to barbarism.

Nevertheless, events of this century show such definitions of science to be an extraordinary semantic trick. One assumes, and is everywhere assured, that scientific thinking is antithetical to the ferocious passions that can unleash barbarism. Even to question this proposition seems "irrational." However, the fact is that our twentieth-century age of science is also, at least from 1914 onward, the age of both unparalleled mass human destruction and individualized human torture. How can the proposition that science is opposed to barbarism be reconciled to these plain facts? The proposition must in some way be wrong or misleading. The inescapable conclusion, it seems, is that whereas scientific thought is indeed antithetical to the wild passions of barbarism, it is not at all antithetical to efficient, dispassionate destruction, slaughter, and torture. The equation that fits the historical data is this: As the quality of thinking grows more rational, the quantity of destruction increases. In our time, for example, terrorism and torture are no longer primarily instruments of passion; they have become instruments of political rationality. Governments adopt them dispassionately, as policies aimed at discouraging revolution; revolutionaries adopt them dispassionately, as methods to intimidate governments and the apolitical masses. Furthermore, the empirical rationality of terrorism and torture has become so apparent that to question their use is to risk the accusation of irrationality.

Viewed against the fallacies and failures of law, religion, and science, it appears that those supposedly sadistic monsters of the Nazi SS, "Gestapo" Müller, "Hangman" Heydrich, "Papa" Eicke, "Reichsheinie" Himmler himself, and the many middle-management administrators of the death camps were perhaps no more insane than anyone else who has ever thought they were performing heroic actions for the sake of future generations. As noted earlier, there is little evidence to show that either the directors or the majority of the functionaries who participated in making the Holocaust took great pleasure in their work, although most took a certain pride in their ability to handle such a difficult assignment. On the contrary, there is considerable evidence showing that the majority of the killers found the substance of their work somewhat depressing and sometimes quite sickening. On the whole, it is in most instances true that they were "just following orders." What can this mean?

At the immediate individual level, for the killers themselves, it meant that their atrocious activities lost their "normal" meaning as atrocities. Authorized and encouraged by the state, organized to a high degree of industrial efficiency in accord with scientific technology, justified by the "political" imperatives of ideology, and verbalized in the abstract, euphemistic language of science, the routinized genocide program in our judgment influenced the mentality of the killers in much the same way as other repetitive, rationalized forms of industrial work influences the ordinary worker. That is, the activity becomes relatively meaningless and quite detached from the actor's sense of self. On an assembly-line job, one daydreams about vacations, plans how to get a new car, and is more concerned with how long it will be to the next break than with the quality of what one is doing. Moreover, the industrial worker does not identify himself as maker of automobiles or creator of refrigerators, but rather as an installer of radiators, a freezer-coil welder, a steam fitter, or some such. This is a definitive characteristic of alienated labor as Marx understood it: "the product of his labor confronts the worker as an alien (meaningless) object."

It become possible, finally, to comprehend those SS men who freely admitted mass killings when they were on trial, but indignantly refused to accept the idea that they could be called murderers. Their argument has logic. Would workers in the chemical plants that produced napalm accept responsibility for burned babies? Would such workers even be aware that others might reasonably think they were responsible? The analogy to alienated labor is far from perfect, of course, but it suggests why so many of the SS leaders and rank and file could not fully recognize their activity as murder. Caught up in the totally organized environment of the Holocaust, their general behavior seems directly in line with the idea that routinization and fractionization can reduce anything (violence, sex, torture, or whatever) to the status of alienated labor.

At the sociocultural level, the rationality of the Holocaust reveals that religion and law have no independent capacity to inhibit atrocious behavior because both institutions are subordinate to the state. The moral principles codified in these institutions can only be enforced at the discretion of secular political leaders. Moreover, these principles have steadily lost their intrinsic force under the impact of Enlightenment philosophy and science.

The idea of evil is a relevant case in point. All the major traditions of morality in our civilization have specified that evil actions are primarily those that serve selfish interests. Evil has traditionally been identified and defined by the emotional or material satisfactions it brings: wrongdoing has occurred when an emotional thrill, sensory pleasure, or material profit is gained. The whole structure of Western morality conveyed by the institutions of religion and law is based on this premise, and the Judeo-Christian tradition of wrongdoing is utterly clear on this point: sin is unauthorized pleasure. It is also very clear that hardly anywhere in this tradition is there any story or statement to the effect that "thou shalt not obey legal orders from superiors if they seem atrocious to you." Abraham, who was prepared to obey the directive to murder his son Isaac as a demonstration of his faith in the superior being of Jaweh, is not condemned for his blind obedience, but rather held up as exemplary. The Protestant tradition of individualism and the direct confrontation of the individual to God has emphasized that individual conscience applies almost exclusively to *private* rather than *public* acts. Luther's own position on war and the peasant revolts is significant in the origins of this tradition. By traditional religious standards, therefore, it is difficult to identify the Holocaust as evil because of its rationality as a program implemented in obedience to higher orders, and without any substantial motives toward achieving pleasures of the flesh or the pocketbook.

The intrinsic irrelevance of the Western legal tradition of morality can be epitomized easily enough by the various contingencies it provides for killing people. If you kill people by accident, it is not murder; it is manslaughter. If you kill people in order to protect your person or property against serious transgression, it is not manslaughter, it is justifiable homicide or self-defense. If you wear a uniform and kill people named as enemies of the state that gave you the uniform, in accord with legal orders, it is not self-defense, it is patriotic duty. As Wittgenstein might have argued, depending on how killing is categorized in language, religion may condemn you or bless you, and you will be either punished or honored by lawmakers. Once the moral essence of the Holocaust is seen to lie in obedience to constituted authority, then the failure and irrelevance of religion and law become apparent, for insofar as both institutions have construed obedience to constituted authority to be the cornerstone of morality, they are impotent before situations in which that authority has been corrupted.

Added to this state of affairs is the unique contribution of science, which, apart from devaluing the premises of religion and law for their unverifiability, also makes possible the organization and control of massive human enterprises to such an extent that horrors may be perpetrated as a form of alienated labor. Taking all these considerations together, it may be suggested finally what the Holocaust reveals about the human condition: none of the chief achievements of our civilization offer protection against infernal horrors. By virtue of the Holocaust it is clear that religion and law, and science in particular, not only have failed to ennoble humanity or prevent inhumanity, but have contributed to its degradation. Much of what has been taken for granted as defining the "ascent of man," may be seen as equally defining a descent toward self-destruction.[18]

Apart from its substantive horrors, the terrible fascination exerted by the Holocaust resides in its bloodless rationality, and in what this rationality shows us about ourselves and our culture. Nothing we have created in the way of religion, law, or science can be taken at the face value our language provides. In proportion as these creations furnish the good things of modern life, they also make possible the horrors. The prevailing rationality functions to celebrate the former and conceal the latter. In the Holocaust, however, one may see what lies beneath the mask called civilization. There is no morality per se, because there is no immutable religious or legal standard for human behavior. Insofar as morality exists, even as a concept, it does so as an act of an all-too-fallible human will.

There is no scientific progress in the naive sense of the phrase, there is only an ever-increasing supply of technology, virtually all of which has as much potential for destroying life as for enhancing it. There is, indeed, no normality, for the madness or amorality of one generation or one culture may be the required norm for another. And there is, finally, no special sacredness, purpose, or minimal dignity to human life—except insofar as these values can be created and sustained against all the forces that tend to traduce them.

The ultimate fact staring all of us in the face is that starting with nothing except personal determination, Hitler could mobilize enough of the elements of modern civilization subsumed under the headings religion, law, and science to create a human inferno, a hell on earth. Since the institutions supposed to prevent this sort of thing could not do so, and since these institutions are today, with the possible exception of science, no stronger than they were in Hitler's day, the truth of our human condition is that existence now is more and more recognizably in accord with the principles that governed life and death in Auschwitz.

Like the prisoners who struggled to survive by banding together in little fraternities of desperation, people today appear everywhere clinging together in groups devoted to their special interests. Living immersed in an atmosphere of power and bluff, of the frequent threat and occasional reality of violence; distrusting others and often ourselves, we yet realize that the tensions and struggles for life security, if not prosperity, are taking their steady toll. In Auschwitz, the prisoner population was culled by SS physicians who seemed virtually a force in nature; in contemporary society, we are culled by forces in nature (heart disease, cancer) which seem as inevitable as SS physicians. And, in the ground and under the seas, there are the instant mobile crematoria: nuclear missiles carefully crafted by master scientists to be always ready to burn us en masse if some unknown person should make a mistaken calculation or decide, perhaps rationally, that life on earth requires drastic alteration.

Of course, the world is not literally an Auschwitz, and we merely live under the shadow of nuclear holocaust. But the Nazi Holocaust did happen; and now the only visions of the world that can be taken seriously are those that come through the irrevocably ash-darkened prisms of post-Holocaust sense and sensibility.

NOTES

1. George Steiner expresses the personal dynamics of serious feeling-reactions to the Holocaust by nonparticipants in an essay describing his fears for his children, "A Sort of Survivor," in *Language and Silence: Essays on Language, Literature, and the Inhuman* (New York: Atheneum, 1967); in a very different vein, Amos Elon has described the ambivalent feelings of Israeli youth toward their Holocaust heritage in *The Israelis: Founders and Sons* (New York: Bantam Books, 1972); the most extensive and valuable discussion of this general point, however, appears in Lawrence Langer's *The Holocaust and the Literary Imagination* (New Haven and London: Yale University Press, 1975).

Some personal eccentricities known to us are also noteworthy. One young scholar at an East Coast university occasionally gets drunk on brandy and pounds the floor in time to recordings of SS marching songs. Another older professor who fought in Germany as a young American soldier keeps a captured Luger in his desk for use when toying with the idea of suicide. A third writes anonymous accusatory poems; yet another has become a fanatic partisan of the state of Israel who claims to feel disgust at the mere sight of a Volkswagen.

2. Samuel Hux, "The Holocaust and the Survival of Tragedy," *Worldview*, 20, no. 10 (Oct. 1977), 4–10. (Italics added.)

3. Edmund Stillman and William Pfaff, *The Politics of Hysteria* (New York and Evanston: Harper & Row, 1964), pp. 30–31. Richard Rubenstein reached a similar conclusion: "We are more likely to understand the Holocaust if we regard it as the expression of some of the most profound tendencies of Western civilization in the twentieth century." *The Cunning of History: The Holocaust and the American Future* (New York: Harper & Row, 1975), p. 21. Herbert Marcuse wrote: "It may even be justifiable, logically as well as historically, to define Reason in terms which include slavery, the Inquisition, child labor, concentration camps, gas chambers, and nuclear preparedness. These may well have been integral parts of that rationality which has governed the recorded history of mankind." Herbert Marcuse, "A Note on Dialectic," in Andrew Arato and Eike Gebhardt, *The Essential Frankfurt School Reader* (New York: Urizen Books, 1978), p. 450.

4. Primo Levi, *Survival in Auschwitz* (London: Collier-Macmillan, 1969), p. 118.

5. There is an extensive clinical literature on the psychological effects of Nazi camp experience. See for example, A. Russell, "Late Psychosocial Consequences in Concentration Camp Survivor Families," *American Journal of Orthopsychiatry*, 44, no. 4 (July 1974), 611–619, and P. Matussek, *Internment in Concentration Camps and Its Consequences* (New York: Springer-Verlag, 1975).

6. See Stanislov Grof, "Perinatal Roots of Wars, Totalitarianism and Revolutions; Observations from LSD Research," *Journal of Psychohistory* 4, no. 3 (1977), 269–308.

7. See Amos Elon, *The Israelis:* "There is today no doubt that the resources of the Jewish community of Palestine, meager as they were . . . were not exhausted in efforts to ward off the greatest disaster in the history of the Jewish people. Some Israelis argued in 1945 that, in deference to British sensitivities, these independent resources were hardly used. The question has haunted Israeli politicians ever since. Its moral dimensions are monstrous" (p. 276). Dr. Nachum Goldmann, former president of the World Jewish Congress, has publicly admitted that "we are all guilty of not having gone to all lengths. . . . We were too impressed with the argument that the [allied] generals should be left in peace to fight the war" (pp. 276–277).

8. "Much of present sociology is illiterate. . . . It is conceived in a jargon of vehement obscurity." George Steiner, *Language and Silence*, p. 19. Thomas Szasz has made similar arguments about psychiatry, most concisely in the preface to his book *The Second Sin* (New York: Double-

day, 1973). Language is considered in more specific detail later in this chapter.

9. In his authoritative *Political Theory* (Princeton: Princeton University Press, 1959) Arnold Brecht stipulates that toward the end of the nineteenth century the moral force of law had begun to decline drastically under the impact of analyses by G. Simmel and H. Rickert (pp. 136–211). These philosophers demonstrated that value judgments distinguishing between what is and what ought to be were simply arbitrary. And Simmel's fundamental argument was that "The logical inference from what is to what ought to be, is false in every case" (Brecht, p. 211). By 1914, moreover, according to Brecht, the philosopher of law G. Radbruch could argue that all concepts of law and justice were essentially matters of politics: "Philosophy of law is necessarily political philosophy, and vice versa. So perfect is this ultimate identity that we are justified in speaking of 'political and legal philosophy' in the singular form" (p. 138). A more contemporary formulation of these ideas appears in the work of Hans Kelsen, most notably in *The Pure Theory of Law* (translated by Max Knight; Berkeley: University of California Press, 1967). The notion of justice must be eliminated from "positive law," according to Kelsen, because it is a value not a scientific concept open to empirical investigation or determination. "Legal science" cannot be concerned with matters of ethics and politics because these matters are irrelevant to "pure knowledge." See H. Kelsen, "What Is Justice?" *Law Quarterly Review*, 51 (1957).

10. Robert Pois, who discusses implications of the Poliakov work in connection with the rise of German romanticism in his unpublished article "Historicity versus History: Some Reflections on the Philosophical Implications of the Holocaust" (available from the author at the University of Colorado). Daniel Gasman's *The Scientific Origins of National Socialism* posits that Haeckel and his science-oriented colleagues of the Monist League were specifically concerned with correcting or eliminating the Jewish racial characteristics they had "objectively" identified as sources of corruption in German society. Haeckel himself never called for actual physical destruction of the Jews but the idea of using physical force against them appears in the writings of at least one Monist League author, Heinrich Pudor.

11. A number of psychohistorians have attempted to locate the psychological sources of Hitler's anti-Semitism in his childhood and adolescence.

12. Michael Polanyi provides a very general discussion of this issue in his book *Personal Knowledge: Towards a Postcritical Philosophy* (Chicago: University of Chicago Press, 1958). After noting that a dehumanized

"objective" science can allow humans to dominate nature, he concludes: "Then man dominates a world in which he himself does not exist. For with his obligation (to nature) he has lost his voice and his hope, and been left behind meaningless to himself" (p. 380). Similar views are expressed by the philosopher of science Ian Mitroff in the conclusion of his work *The Subjective Side of Science* (New York: American Elsevíer, 1974), p. 271: "We have developed the kind of science (Apollonism) that knows how to reach 'the starry heavens above.' We have yet to learn how to develop the kind of science (Dionysiar) that knows how to reach 'the moral law within.' " See also Floyd Matson, *The Broken Image* (New York: Anchor Books, 1966). The theme recognized in various ways by an increasing number of writers is essentially this: human affairs conducted according to a dehumanized science must ultimately reduce people to objects. Thus "the acceptance of living beings as machines, the domination of the modern world by technology, and the mechanization of mankind are but the extension and practical application of the mechanistic conception of physics" (Ludwig von Bertalanffy, *Problems of Life*, New York: Harper Torchbooks, 1960, p. 202).

13. Quoted in A. Janik, and S. Toulmin, *Wittgenstein's Vienna* (New York: Simon and Schuster, 1973), p. 191.

14. H.S. Hughes, *The Sea Change: The Migration of Social Thought 1930–1965* (New York: Harper & Row, 1975), p. 53.

15. Quoted in Janik and Toulmin, *Wittgenstein's Vienna*, p. 195.

16. Max Horkheimer and Theodore Adorno, *Dialectic of Enlightenment* (New York: Seabury Press, 1969), p. xii. Italics added.

17. Probably the most radical exponent of this general viewpoint today is the philosopher of science Paul Feyerabend. In *Against Method* (London: NLB, 1975), he argues that all progress can only be understood as an expansion of human consciousness, and this being the case, any idea can only be evaluated by contrasting it with other, different ideas. One example he provides it that there is no "reason" for modern medical experts to ignore voodoo witchcraft as a means to medical knowledge. To the extent that studying voodoo is ruled out by established medical research methodology and the institutional norms of science in general, the exclusion is arbitrary and tends to impose conformity to the status quo while having nothing whatever to do with "the science" of medicine. Feyerabend's general view of scientific knowledge is as follows: "Knowledge so conceived is not a series of self-consistent theories that converges towards an ideal view; it is not a gradual approach to the truth. It is rather an ever increasing *ocean of mutually incompatible (and perhaps even incommensurable) alternatives,* each single theory, each fairy tale, each myth that is part of the collection forcing

the others into greater articulation and all of them contributing, via this process of competition, to the development of our consciousness. Nothing is ever settled." (p. 30). Less dramatic but similar statements relevant to the view of science presented in this chapter may be found in Everett Mendelsohn, "The Social Construction of Scientific Knowledge," in E. Mendelsohn, P. Weingart, and R. Whitley, eds., *The Social Production of Scientific Knowledge* (Dordrecht, Holland: D. Reidel & Co., 1977), pp. 3–26; J.R. Ravetz, *Scientific Knowledge and Its Social Problems* (Oxford: Clarendon Press, 1971), especially the concluding section, "Critical Science: Politics and Morality," pp. 423–436.

18. Richard Rubenstein, *The Cunning of History*, reached a very similar conclusion: "Thus, the Holocaust bears witness to *the advance of civilization*, I repeat, to the advance of civilization, to the point at which large scale massacre is no longer a crime and the state's sovereign powers are such that millions can be stripped of their rights and condemned to the world of the living dead" (p. 91). In a more general context of culture critique, Arianna Stassinopoulos has said: "It should have been obvious by now, even to the most fanatical believers in the 'locomotive of history,' that something has gone badly astray and the suspicion that the engineer is a homicidal maniac can no longer be ruled out. Instead, the belief persists that the locomotive is somehow chugging on in the direction of progress" (*After Reason*, New York: Stein and Day, 1978, p. 12). It may be presumed that these perspectives, and others like them, are what led Hannah Arendt to conclude: "In other words, I have clearly joined the ranks of those who for some time now have been attempting to dismantle metaphysics, and philosophy with all its categories, as we have known them from their beginning in Greece until today. Such dismantling is possible only on the assumption that the thread of tradition is broken and that we shall not be able to renew it." *The Life of the Mind, I: Thinking* (New York: Harcourt Brace Jovanovich, 1978), p. 212.

Bruno Bettelheim

THE HOLOCAUST—
ONE GENERATION AFTER

My business is not with the dead, but with the living. The events of the Nazi holocaust are by now an appropriate subject for historians; my concern is with its significance for the present generation. This generation should not distort the meaning the holocaust carries, not just because of the terrible things done by average people to average persons one short generation ago, but because of the warning it holds for man today.

It is understandable that we wish to avoid coping with the deeply disturbing perspectives on man which the holocaust opens up; man as a wanton destroyer, and as a victim shorn of all defenses. The appalling nature of that which we ought to understand and build into our view of the world as a terrible warning induces us to avoid facing the true nature of the problem by denying some of its most upsetting aspects, and by distorting others.

All this is hardly new; from the very beginning of the long series of events which we now call the Nazi holocaust, the psychological mechanisms used to deal with it have not been recognition of the facts, correct assessments and interpretations of their implications, and mastery of the event on this basis. Instead we have used various distancing devices, false analogies, and forms of outright denial, so as not to have to come to grips with a grim reality.

Denial is the earliest, most primitive, most inappropriate and ineffective of all psychological defenses used by man. When the event is potentially destructive, it is the most pernicious psychological defense, because it does not permit taking appropriate action which might safeguard against the real dangers. Denial therefore leaves the individual most vulnerable to the very perils against which he has tried to defend himself.

One Jewish survivor of the concentration camps reported recently on the TV news that she did not know about the camps at the time she was transported there from her native Hungary. This is dubious, because from the very beginning of Naziism in 1933, Hitler and all Nazis declared most publicly, innumerable times, that they would make Germany *Judenrein*—that they would clear all Jews out of Germany and all the other countries to fall under their power. The Nazis further declared that if there was a war, at its end no Jew would remain alive in Europe.

Actual abuse and vilification of the Jews existed from the moment the Nazis came into power, and even before. The Nazis propagandized the concentration camps, using them deliberately as a threat to intimidate and subdue their opponents, and even their followers, when these showed any sign of independent opinion. This was so much the case that an often-quoted saying sprang up: *Lieber Gott, mach mich stumm, dass ich nicht nach Dachau kumm* ("Dear Lord, please make me mute, so that I won't be sent to Dachau").

When after the war, therefore, some Germans claimed that they had not had any knowledge of the concentration camps—about which they had read so often in their daily papers as a warning not to transgress Nazi rules—this was either an outright lie, or due to their wish not to have known what they could easily have known, but which they (unconsciously) chose not to know. In this context it must be remembered that denial, even when it begins as a conscious process, soon becomes an unconscious one; otherwise it could never work so well, and so completely.

While the concentration camps were public knowledge, the extermination camps were treated more like a poorly kept secret. Poorly kept, because it had been publicly announced that no Jew would be left in Europe after the war. Poorly kept, because anybody who wanted to find out about the extermination camps could do so—too many people were involved, and no news was ever received from or about those who were sent there. Neutral embassies, the Vatican, the American and the other Allied governments, and many other official bodies were well informed about them. Thus knowledge about the extermination of the Jews could be gained, and many efforts were made to spread this knowledge among Jews. Still, officially the extermination camps were treated as something to be kept secret, and there is an interesting reason for this.

Actually, the systematic extermination of the Jews began after U.S. entrance into the war, when it became likely that Germany would be defeated. The Nazis then decided that the very widespread but until then somewhat haphazard killing of Jews would not eliminate them all before the war ended. Had Germany won the war, the extermination would probably have proceeded more slowly, since a program of sterilizing all Jewish men or women or both was very seriously considered, and it included letting those already alive die out slowly through natural death, while taking advantage of them as slave laborers until then. This, too, would have achieved the purpose of making Europe free of Jews. But with German defeat now a serious prospect, the final solution of the Jewish problem was sharply accelerated.

The first use of the gas chambers was not for the elimination of Jews, but in the so-called euthanasia program, the elimination of those the Nazis considered misfits—mental defectives and inmates of psychiatric hospitals. This was the first group to be systematically killed off, quite a few of them in the first mobile gas chambers. Although this program of extermination was camouflaged—initially, it was claimed that some new, potentially dangerous treatment would be tried out on these people, which had some chance of success although it entailed serious risk of death, etc.—it soon became known what was really going on. There was such a strong reaction against this slaughter of mental patients among religious leaders and the common people that despite massive propaganda and much against their desire, the Nazis had to discontinue this important part of their official eugenics program. This demonstrates that when unpleasant facts are not dealt with by means of denial but are faced squarely, even the most ruthless totalitarian regime can be forced to back down by determined public action.

No such public, widespread objection, however, made itself heard about the persecution of the Jews, or about the random killing of large masses of Jews, or even the extermination of all of them; quite the contrary. If anything, the German people seemed in their overwhelming majority either to applaud the persecution of the Jews, or to condone it by a sin of omission, a very few isolated voices raised against it notwithstanding.[1] These few voices could easily be suppressed and disregarded by the government, since they found no following.

To some extent the absence of opposition was due to the massive anti-Semitic propaganda, and to the fact that the screws cutting off Jewish breathing space were at first tightened slowly. It would be tedious to retrace here the steps by which the Jews first were made second-class citizens, then robbed of all their citizens' rights, prevented from practicing their professions, then prevented from earning anything, banned from public gatherings, their children excluded from school; how Jews were first publicly ridiculed, then beaten up, jailed, and finally put into the camps.

For a time, these measures were differentially applied; for example, those who had served in the First World War were exempted from some of them, etc. At each step, the Jews could delude themselves with the thought that as terrible as the hardships imposed on them were getting, they could somehow live with them. With each regulation they could fool themselves into believing that this was the last step in putting them down. While at first they had thought that the threats were mere propaganda to gain new followers for the Nazi party and satisfy old ones, soon this proved incorrect. As the hardships became more severe, the greater the Jews' need to take protective action became. But unfortunately for many, the protective action they took consisted of engaging in denial, in order not to give up, fall into despair, or commit suicide. With each new and harsher treatment—abuse, beatings, deportations—the Jews were pushed into two opposite groups.

Those who did not engage in denial but could see things for what they were became ever more convinced that their only safety resided in escape. While up to a point in their mistreatment they had been willing to suffer rather than give up all they possessed, they came to realize that giving up almost everything dear to them, including all material things, was a small and necessary price to pay for mere survival. Most of them managed to escape, although some were later overtaken by the German occupation of the countries to which they had fled.

By contrast, those who engaged in denial tried to tell themselves that things couldn't, or wouldn't, get any worse; that the bark of the Nazis, bad as it was, was worse than their bite; that while some other Jews were taken to the camps, they themselves would for some reason or other be saved from such a fate. With each new hardship, denial had to be increased and extended over wider areas in order to be kept up. That is why, in the end, these Jews did not know what they could easily have known, had they not blinded themselves to make the insufferable seem sufferable.

For example, some Jews managed to escape and make their way back to Warsaw; they warned others that in the camps Jews were being killed. They were berated for spreading such rumors and told to remain quiet, because what the Jews needed was to be comforted, not additionally worried. The reason for not listening to the warning voices, for disregarding the writing on the wall which was there for all to read, was the wish to continue with the denial of what was taking place.

If such behavior seems strange, consider the well-known fact that terminal cancer patients typically meet their fate with one of two opposite states of mind. Those who face what is in store for them with clarity soon also gain considerable equanimity of mind; they do everything that can and needs to be done, realizing how little time they have left to do so. But the majority, the closer they come to their end, deny ever more insistently that this is so. They claim that they are getting better, making ambitiously large and unrealistic, even delusional plans and arrangements for their future.

If a terminal cancer patient engages in massive denial, this does not change what is going to happen to him, although it makes it easier for him to live through his ordeal, which is his unconscious purpose. But for Jews under Hitler who engaged in denial for the same basic reason—to make their ordeal more bearable—this denial kept them from doing what they might in fact have done, and so cut them off from such possibilities as actually existed to save themselves. Their denial prevented them from trying to arrange for an escape; or going underground; or preparing to fight back, by joining partisan groups, for example.

Such denial was not restricted to the Jews of Europe, who at least had the excuse of terrible straits for using such a desperate and ineffective psychological defense; it was also the characteristic attitude of the West, very much including the U.S. Most nations which engaged in such denial did so mainly out of self-interest. From 1933 until the beginning of the war—for over six years—the Nazis were more than ready to let the Jews go; as a matter of fact, they tried everything to get rid of the Jews, provided they left all their belongings behind. But no country, not excepting the U.S., let more than an entirely insignificant trickle immigrate to it. The justification was again based on denial: things were not all that bad for the Jews; the Nazis did not really mean what they said, etc.

Later, after the extermination policy was in full swing, and after the American government knew about it, the Nazis offered to American Jewish groups a clandestine deal: they would let the Jews go, if they received in payment for them a number of trucks. (First they had asked for war materiel, but accepting that this could not be done, had reduced their request to trucks.) When American negotiators raised the question of how they could trust Germany to keep its promise, the Nazis offered a down payment. Without it being suggested or requested by the Americans, the Nazis delivered, free of charge, a trainload of Jews into Switzerland to prove that Jews were of no value to them, that all they wanted was to get rid of them. After that, when it was obvious that the Nazis meant business, the negotiations were broken off because the American government would not permit the deal.[2]

It could be argued that the trucks would have helped the Nazi war effort. But even before the war started, a shipload of German Jews had arrived at the American coast, but had not been permitted to land. They were ultimately returned to Europe, where most of them later perished, being again caught by the Nazis in the countries where they had found refuge. In 1939 a bill was introduced in Congress whose aim was to save at least some German Jewish children by permitting 10,000 of them to immigrate in 1939/40 under a special quota.[3] They would not have created a glut on the labor market since they would all have been under fourteen years of age, and would have been taken in by American Jewish families of means who were ready to raise them like their own children, guaranteeing that they would not become an economic liability to anybody. President Roosevelt, however, refused to endorse the bill, despite repeated urging to do so on the part of the American Jewish community. Because of his and Congress's lack of interest the bill died in the judiciary committees. These refusals to save the doomed Jews were greatly facilitated by a widespread denial of what fate had in store for them, although the Nazis had made their intentions amply clear.

The reason for all this is that it is easier to deny reality when facing it would require taking unpleasant, difficult, or expensive actions. Not to take such actions out of self-interest would evoke guilt-feelings. So that one need not feel guilty for not acting, one denies the facts. Thus denial makes life easier, at least for the moment and if one does not care what the consequences of such denial are for oneself or for others.

Denial, as mentioned before, is the most primitive of all psychological defensive mechanisms. The small child, confronted with some unpleasant fact, will insist that it is not so. Usually as we get older, we no longer use this primitive defense when confronted with incontrovertible facts. But when anxiety becomes overwhelming, even normal adults tend to regress to using it. That is why Jews under Nazi domination, in the face of obvious facts but in mortal anxiety, engaged in denial so massive that under other circumstances it would have been considered delusional.

Americans denied the reality of the extermination camps as the simplest way to avoid facing an unpleasant truth. When they could no longer blind themselves to what thousands had seen with their own eyes, Americans began to apply more subtle and devious defensive mechanisms to avoid facing what the holocaust had been like. Imagining it would have meant experiencing it to some measure. Better to declare it unimaginable, unspeakable, because only then could one avoid facing the full horror of what had happened in its details, which would be extremely upsetting, guilt-provoking, and anxiety-creating. These more subtle psychological defensive mechanisms still dominate many Americans' present approach to the true significance of the holocaust.

To begin with, it was not the hapless victims of the Nazis who named their incomprehensible and totally unmasterable fate the "holocaust." It was the Americans who applied this artificial and highly technical term to the Nazi extermination of the European Jews. But while the event when named as mass murder most foul evokes the most immediate, most powerful revulsion, when it is designated by a rare technical term, we must first in our minds translate it back into emotionally meaningful language. Using technical or specially created terms instead of words from our common vocabulary is one of the best-known and most widely used distancing devices, separating the intellectual from the emotional experience. Talking about "the holocaust" permits us to manage it intellectually where the raw facts, when given their ordinary names, would overwhelm us emotionally—because it was catastrophe beyond comprehension, beyond the limits of our imagination, unless we force ourselves against our desire to extend it to encompass these terrible events.

This linguistic circumlocution began while it all was only in the planning stage. Even the Nazis—usually given to grossness in language and action—shied away from facing openly what they were up to and called this vile mass murder "the final solution of the Jewish problem." After all, solving a problem can be made to appear like an honorable enterprise, as long as we are not forced to recognize that the solution we are about to embark on consists of the completely unprovoked, vicious murder of millions of helpless men, women, and children. The Nuremberg judges of these Nazi criminals followed their example of circumlocution by coining a neologism out of one Greek and one Latin root: genocide. These artificially created technical terms fail to connect with our strongest feelings. The horror of murder is part of our most common human heritage. From earliest infancy on, it arouses violent abhorrence in us. Therefore in whatever form it appears we should give such an act its true designation and not hide it behind polite, erudite terms created out of classical words.

To call this vile mass murder "the holocaust" is not to give it a special name emphasizing its uniqueness which would permit, over time, the word becoming invested with feelings germane to the event it refers to. The correct definition of "holocaust" is "burnt offering." As such, it is part of the language of the psalmist, a meaningful word to all who have some acquaintance with the Bible, full of the richest emotional connotations. By using the term "holocaust," entirely false associations are established through conscious and unconscious connotations between the most vicious of mass murders and ancient rituals of a deeply religious nature.

Using a word with such strong unconscious religious connotations when speaking of the murder of millions of Jews robs the victims of this abominable mass murder of the only thing left to them: their uniqueness. Calling the most callous, most brutal, most horrid, most heinous mass murder a burnt offering is a sacrilege, a profanation of God and man.

Martyrdom is part of our religious heritage. A martyr, burned at the stake, is a burnt offering to his god. And it is true that after the Jews were asphyxiated, the victims' corpses were burned. But I believe we fool ourselves if we think we are honoring the victims of systematic murder by using this term, which has the highest moral connotations. By doing so, we connect for our own psychological reasons what happened in the extermination camps with historical events we deeply regret, but also greatly admire. We do so because this makes it easier for us to cope; only in doing so we cope with our distorted image of what happened, not with the events the way they did happen.

By calling the victims of the Nazis "martyrs," we falsify their fate. The true meaning of "martyr" is: "one who voluntarily undergoes the penalty of death for refusing to renounce his faith" (*Oxford English Dictionary*). The Nazis made sure that nobody could mistakenly think that their victims were murdered for their religious beliefs. Renouncing their faith would have saved none of them. Those who had converted to Christianity were gassed, as were those who were atheists, and those who were deeply religious Jews. They did not die for any conviction, and certainly not out of choice.

Millions of Jews were systematically slaughtered, as were untold other "undesirables," not for any convictions of theirs, but only because they stood in the way of the realization of an illusion. They neither died for their convictions, nor were they slaughtered because of their convictions, but only in consequence of the Nazis' delusional belief about what was required to protect the purity of their assumed superior racial endowment, and what they thought necessary to guarantee them the living space they believed they needed and were entitled to. Thus while these millions were slaughtered for an idea, they did not die for one.

Millions—men, women, and children—were processed after they had been utterly brutalized, their humanity destroyed, their clothes torn from their bodies. Naked, they were sorted into those who were destined to be murdered immediately, and those others who had a short-term usefulness as slave labor. But after a brief interval they, too, were to be herded into the same gas chambers into which the others were immediately piled, there to be asphyxiated so that, in their last moments, they could not prevent themselves from fighting each other in vain for a last breath of air.

To call these most wretched victims of a murderous delusion, of destructive drives run rampant, martyrs or a burnt offering is a distortion invented for our comfort, small as it may be. It pretends that this most vicious of mass murders had some deeper meaning; that in some fashion the victims either offered themselves or at least became sacrifices to a higher cause. It robs them of the last recognition which could be theirs, denies them the last dignity we could accord them: to face and accept what their death was all about, not embellishing it for the small psychological relief this may give us.

We could feel so much better if the victims had acted out of choice. For our emotional relief, therefore, we dwell on the tiny minority who did exercise some choice: the resistance fighters of the Warsaw ghetto, for example, and others like them. We are ready to overlook the fact that these people fought back only at a time when everything was lost, when the overwhelming majority of those who had been forced into the ghettos had already been exterminated without resisting. Certainly those few who finally fought for their survival and their convictions, risking and losing their lives in doing so, deserve our admiration; their deeds give us a moral lift. But the more we dwell on these few, the more unfair are we to the memory of the millions who were slaughtered—who gave in, did not fight back—because we deny them the only thing which up to the very end remained uniquely their own: their fate.

There are books and other publications which try to present the facts, so that we may know what has happened. There are other writings which search for the meaning of these terrible events; and they have been given poetic form. Others express the guilt of the survivors, the mourning for the deceased. Unfortunately with the passing of time all these receive less and less attention. By now the interest seems to have shifted to books and movies which exploit the fate of these hapless victims. The more serious of them attempt to provide us with some psychological relief. Such efforts take essentially one of three forms: in the first, these most unfortunate victims are elevated into heroes; in another, their fate is reduced to the everyday level; in the last, what happened to them is made to appear insignificant by drawing attention away from them and concentrating it only on the survivors, who also are made into something they were not, and are not now.

There are other, much more obnoxious ways the camps are used in the media. Among these are novels and films which use the corpses of the death camps to arouse and satisfy a morbid curiosity, or as a background for cheap comedy. There are also efforts to deny validity to the extermination camps by claiming that it never happened, or by directing our attention away from the victims to their murderers, who are made to appear in a favorable light as "interesting" characters.

The most serious and prevalent psychological device used today to distract us from the death camps is to view what happened to the victims as an event deserving of most severe criticism but commonplace nevertheless. This device takes the form of equating Auschwitz with Hiroshima or My Lai, or talking of genocide when referring to government-sponsored sterilization or birth-control programs. Equating My Lai and the death camps denies the crucial difference between isolated homicidal outbreaks in war—the consequence of anxiety, exasperation, or a temporary breakdown of controls which, inexcusable and criminal though it may be, nevertheless remains within the human dimension—and the careful planning and precise, deliberate execution of "the final solution." The essential differences are the premeditation which went into the one, compared with the breakdown of rationality and taking-over by primitive emotions characteristic of the other; and the application of all the machinery and power of the state in one case, compared to the breakdown of controls in individual persons of which the state severely disapproves in the other.

Equating what the Nazis did with the American bombing of Hiroshima seems on the surface a more appropriate comparison, since in both instances governmental preplanning was responsible for what happened. But it is actually an even more vicious distortion, because it implicitly accepts one of the biggest Nazi lies as truth—namely, that the Jews were an enemy waging aggressive war against Germany. In reality, as is well known, the Jews were Germany's most peaceful and most tragically obedient subjects. These comparisons consciously or unconsciously take the side of the Nazis against that of the Jews, and this subtle siding with the Nazis is one of the most pernicious aspects of the attitudes of all too many American intellectuals toward the extermination of European Jews. It is but the other side of the coin when the same intellectuals applaud books and films which use the death camps as background to titillate or excite, and in this way make them appear as just an ordinary part of life.

Quite opposite from that psychological defense are efforts to make the survivors appear as unusual, most superior persons because of their experiences in the extermination camps. This was attempted most effectively in Terence Des Pres's 1976 book *The Survivor*, which has found much acclaim in intellectual circles. The book draws our attention away from the millions who were murdered, and concentrates only on the all too few who survived, and survived only because the Allied armies rescued them at the last moment. It makes heroes out of these chance survivors. By stressing how the death camps produced such superior beings as the survivors, all our interest is focused on the survival of the few, at the cost of neglecting the millions who got slaughtered.

Survivors feel exasperated and helpless when others who have not the slightest idea what their experiences were like hold forth about what these experiences were all about, and what their real meaning is. Elie Wiesel expresses well survivors' reactions to the psychological defenses presently used to avoid facing the upsetting reality of what the extermination of the Jews was all about. Speaking of those who write about the survivors, he says:

> Those who have not lived through the experience will never know; those who have will never tell; not really, not completely. The past belongs to the dead, and the survivor does not recognize himself in the images and ideas which presumably depict him. Auschwitz means death, total absolute death—of man and of all people, of language and imagination, of time and spirit. . . . The survivor knows. He and no one else. And so he is obsessed by guilt and helplessness. . . . At first the testimony of survivors inspired awe and humility. At first, the question was treated with a sort of sacred reverence. It was considered taboo, reserved exclusively for the initiated. . . .
>
> But popularization and exploitation soon followed. And then, with the passing of time, it all began to deteriorate. As the subject became popularized, so it ceased to be sacrosanct, or rather was stripped of its mystery. People lost their awe. The Holocaust became a literary "free for all," the no-man's land of modern writing. Now everyone got into the act. Novelists made free use of it in their work, scholars used it to prove their theories. In so doing they cheapened the Holocaust; they drained it of its substance.
>
> To ward off survivors' criticism, the exclusive right to that title was taken away from them. Suddenly, everyone began calling himself a survivor. Having compared Harlem to the Warsaw ghetto and Vietnam to Auschwitz, a further step has now been taken: some who had spent the war on a Kibbutz or in a fancy apartment in Manhattan, now claim that they too have survived the Holocaust, probably by proxy. One consequence is that an international symposium [on the Holocaust]

was held recently in New York without the participation of any Holocaust survivors. The survivors don't count; they never did. They are best forgotten. Don't you see? They are an embarrassment. If only they weren't there, it would be so much easier.

The survivors will soon be unwelcome intruders. Their assassins are now in the limelight. They are shown in films, they are scrutinized, they are humanized. They are studied at first with objectivity, then with sympathy. One movie tells of the loves of a Jewish woman and a former SS. Gone are the days when the dead had their special place, and gone the days when their lives commanded respect. People are more interested in their killers: so handsome and attractive, such pleasure to watch. This attitude exists among Jewish and non-Jewish intellectuals alike.[4] . . .

We cannot fully grasp the nature and the implications of the death camps if we shy away from facing the destructive tendencies in man.

The aggressive part of our animal inheritance which in man has assumed its specifically human and peculiarly destructive form was called the death drive by Freud, and by Konrad Lorenz, "the so-called evil."[5] Freud believed that in man the life and the death (destructive) drives wage continuous battle, and that we can truly accept ourselves, and relate positively to the other, only when the life drives are in ascendancy—when they succeed in dominating our life as they manage to neutralize the death drive and its derivatives.

I think we cannot understand the Hitler phenomenon—and there were other monsters like him in history, although fortunately they very rarely reached similar dominance—unless we recognize by Hitler's actions and those of his henchmen that the death drive had completely overpowered the life drives. Hitler's belief that his cherished man of pure Aryan blood could flourish only when the lower races were completely exterminated created a death mania which, while it began with the Jews, did not end with them. Many others were also to be exterminated—the Gypsies, the mentally or physically deficient—while the Poles, Russians, blacks, and members of other "inferior" races were to be radically reduced in numbers under Hitler's thousand-year Reich.

Had Hitler not been so obsessed by the conviction that other races had to die for the Germans to live, he might well have won the war, and with it much of the world. Not only German Jews, but vast numbers of Polish, Ukrainian, and even Russian soldiers would have joined the German army and might have brought it victory, had Hitler's wish to exterminate some and to enslave the others not prevented him from integrating them into his army.

So it happened as it must: those beholden to the death drive destroy also themselves. In the end, Hitler wished—and even tried—to exterminate the Germans who had served him so well. His insistence that his army at Stalingrad had to let itself be killed, rather than try to save itself, is one example. Another is Hitler's carrying the war on long after it had been lost, trying to have every German fight until death rather than make peace.

However, the behavior of the Jews who, without offering resistance, permitted themselves to be walked to the gas chambers, cannot be comprehended either without reference to the death tendencies that exist in all of us. After the horrible transport into the death camps, when confronted with the gas chambers and crematoria the life drives in the Jews, who were deprived of everything that had given them security, robbed of all hope for themselves and, worst of all, deserted by the entire world, were no longer able to keep their death drive in bounds. But in their case, the death tendencies were not directed outside, against others, but turned inward, against the self.

That is why they should be memorialized at the places where they were collected for transportation—because there, although their life drives had been terribly weakened by their preceding experiences, they had not yet been extinguished. They were still wishing and trying to live, not yet entirely incapacitated by their own death drive. During the terrible transportation into the death camps, the horror of which was unimaginable, the power of their life drives must have slowly drained away. Having been on two of these transports,[6] I know that the horrors one was subjected to made one wish for death as a relief; that is, as the life drives recede, the door is opened for the death drive to overpower the individual. That is why the victims could be herded to the gas chambers without resisting: the transport had turned many of them into walking corpses. In those who were selected for slave labor, slowly the life drives returned, weak though they remained, and they tried their very best to survive.

And here, finally, I come to the American contribution to the holocaust—a sin of omission. The euthanasia program mentioned before had to be stopped, dear as it was to Hitler, because too much opposition was aroused by it. Had there been as much concern abroad about the extermination of the Jews as there had been about the killing of the mentally defective and the insane, then the Nazis would probably have had to stop their extermination of the Jews also. But the world remained silent; the Pope, the world's clergy—all who had raised their voices for the mentally defective—remained silent when Jews were murdered.

This same lack of world concern, as it weakened life drives, reinforced the death tendencies in the Jews, because they felt completely abandoned, felt that nobody else cared, that nobody but they themselves thought they had a right to live. Unfortunately, one's own belief in one's right to live is not enough to keep the death tendencies within controllable boundaries. Most suicidal persons think they have a right to live; they try to commit suicide either because they are convinced that nobody else cares whether they live or die, or to find out whether this is so. They give up their suicidal ideas as soon as they come to feel that there is someone else who is deeply concerned that they live, and who is willing to go to great lengths to help them live.

The SS knew instinctively all there is to be known about the death drive; for good reason did the "death's-head units" of the SS run the camps and wear skulls on their uniforms. It was their systematic aim to destroy the strength of the life drives in prisoners.

Long before Jews permitted themselves to be transported into the death camps, long before they allowed themselves to be herded to the gas chambers, the Nazis had systematically destroyed their self-respect, robbed them of the belief that they could be masters of their fate. What happened to them impressed on them that nobody cared whether they lived or died, and that the rest of the world, including foreign countries, had no concern for their fate. One cannot meet catastrophic events and survive when deprived of the feeling that somebody cares.

The worst damage to our life drives does not come from the hateful and destructive actions of our enemies. While we may be unable to resist them physically, we can cope with them psychologically as long as our friends, those who we think ought to be our rescuers, live up to the trust we put into them.

Had the Jews felt that important voices in the rest of the world were raised in their behalf, that people in the free world cared and truly wanted them to live, they would not have needed to engage in the defense of massive denial, but could have realized what was going on, and reacted differently to it. They could then have coped better with the fact that the Nazis wanted them to perish and had planned for their destruction, although nobody can cope really well with this. But many people have enemies who wish them evil; it was the indifference of all those others who should have come to their rescue which was so finally destructive to Jewish hopes.

The Nazis murdered the Jews of Europe. That nobody but the Jews cared, that the world, the United States, did not care, was why Jewish life drives lost the battle against death tendencies.[7] This was why the camp inmates had already relinquished life as they dug their own graves, and why, as the poet put it, "there was earth in them." The most extreme agony is to feel that one has been utterly forsaken.

Murderers can only kill; they do not have the power to rob us of the wish to live nor of the ability to fight for life. Degradation, exhaustion, and utter debilitation through starvation, sickness, and mistreatment— all these seriously weaken our will to live, undermine our life drives, and with this open the way for the death drive. But when such conditions— in which the Jews found themselves because of Nazi persecution and degradation—are worsened by the feeling that the rest of the world has forsaken us, then we are totally deprived of the strength needed to fight off the murderer, to refuse to dig our own grave.

This level of despair is given words towards the end of Celan's poem by the desperate cry "Oh someone," and then there is the final giving-up, when one realizes that there is "no one." We ought to have been their someone, but we were their no one. This is our burden. Just because we cannot atone for it, it is wrong to deny or obfuscate it.

As if from beyond their grave—which was of course never allotted to these victims—the poet speaks to us with their voice: "oh you:/Where did it go, if nowhere it went." Only if we stop denying—for our comfort, and to our lasting detriment—what the holocaust was all about, will it stop going nowhere; will we know where it went.

Our obligation—not to those who are dead, but to ourselves, and to those around us who are still alive—is to strengthen the life drives, so that never again—if we can help it—will these be so totally destroyed in so many, least of all by the power of a state. A true understanding of the holocaust ought to imbue us with the determination that we shall never again permit that men, overcome by their desperation and enslaved by their death drive, should walk to their death as their murderers wish.

With the poet's help, finally, I can be more specific about what is needed:

> Oh you dig and I dig, and I dig myself towards you,
> and on our finger the ring awakes us.

If, with empathy and compassion, we dig towards those who have so completely given up all hope that "there is earth in them," this will bind us together (as the ring does in a betrothal) and we both will awaken: they from their living death; we from apathy to their suffering.

That we ought to care for the other, that with our concern we ought to counteract the death-like and death-provoking desperation that there is nobody who cares for one, has been taught since the beginning of time. But in each generation, one event more than any other makes this lesson especially pertinent, giving it a character specific to that age. For this century I believe this event is the extermination of the European Jews in the gas chambers, because the way it happened was possible only in a totalitarian, technological mass society, obsessed by a pseudo-scientific delusion. (In the case of the Nazi state the particular pseudo-scientific delusion was its eugenic mission to improve the genetic inheritance of man.) Nothing will give us a more acute and pervasive understanding of the evils of such totalitarianism than when, in our minds, we dig toward the millions who have been so cruelly, so senselessly, so wantonly exterminated. It is the best we can do to forge a bond between them and us. While it will not awaken them, it may well awaken us to a more meaningful life.

NOTES

1. Today, after all these years, it is easily forgotten how many Germans—by no means only Nazis—derived tangible advantages from the persecution of the Jews. The vast majority of Jews either owned business enterprises or held lucrative positions; nearly all owned nice homes. They were deprived of these, which were handed over to Germans. During the last year before the war, when Jews emigrated they could take none of their possessions with them, and the same was true during the war when they were sent first to the ghettos in Poland and later into the camps. Rather than see the Nazis acquire all their possessions, on being forced to leave most Jews preferred to give their art objects, jewelry, valuable furniture and clothing, and whatnot to gentile acquaintances, either as presents or for safekeeping. The end results were nearly always the same: the Jews died in the camps, and nobody was left to claim what was left in safe-keeping.

With a Jewish family's enterprise or position going to one gentile German family, their home to another, and their possessions to three or four others, easily five or more German families profited greatly from the persecution of a single Jewish family. Enough reason—if not to be happy with—at least not to object to a policy which greatly enriched them without any effort on their part.

2. For details of these negotiations as well as for the ship of refugees who were not permitted to land in the U.S., see, for example, Arthur D. Morse, *While Six Million Died: A Chronicle of American Apathy* (New York: Random House, 1967).

3. It was the Wagner-Rogers Child Refugee Bill.

4. Elie Wiesel, "For Some Measure of Humility," *Sh'ma, A Journal of Jewish Responsibility* 5 (October 31, 1975), pp. 314–16.

5. Konrad Lorenz, *On Aggression* (New York: Harcourt, Brace & World, 1966). The English title fails to do justice to the original title Lorenz gave his book, which is *Das sogenannte Böse.*

6. First from Vienna to Dachau, the second time from Dachau to Buchenwald. Still, these transports cannot be compared to what went on years later on the transports to the death camps.

7. One of the last messages received by the outside world from the Warsaw ghetto said, "The world is silent; the world *knows* (it is inconceivable that it should not) and stays silent; God's vicar in the Vatican is silent; there is silence in London and Washington; the American Jews are silent. This silence is incomprehensible and horrifying." (George Steiner, *Language and Silence* [New York: Atheneum, 1967].) But it was not only silence which met the destruction of the Jews. German newsreels show what those in the ghetto must also have observed: the frequent laughter and applause of Polish spectators as they watched houses being blown up and Jews perishing in the flames.

Miriam Greenspan

RESPONSES TO THE HOLOCAUST

I have had, since childhood, a recurring dream that I must pack my bags and flee. I must get to a train on time, before something horrible happens. The compelling terror of this nightmare is the urgent sense of time running out before the inevitable catastrophe arrives—sometimes an invading force, sometimes an unnamed horror. I am always totally alone in this dream, without family. Or, sometimes, I am trying to "save" a member of my family, unsuccessfully.

It occurred to me one day that, in a sense, this was my mother's dream. Or, rather, that it was my mother's life that I was dreaming! What I dreamed, she lived—in fleeing her hometown of Lodz, Poland, when the Nazis invaded in Sept., 1939, and leaving her family behind. The panicky sense of Deadline in the dream was literal in my mother's life: she had to leave or be dead. She was, at the war's end, the sole survivor of her family. Most of those who did not pack and leave as she did died in the ghetto or in concentration camps.

Being a child of survivors, born just after the Holocaust in a German Displaced Person's Camp, I have always felt that I imbibed the Holocaust experience with my mother's milk. My parents' lives during the Holocaust is the substance of my dreams. What they experienced directly and consciously, I have experienced in indirect, attenuated form. Not only direct survivors of the Holocaust like my parents, nor just children of survivors like myself, but every Jew alive has internalized the Holocaust. We all live in a post-Holocaust world, a world in which the mass industrialized death of the Jews as a people is not an unimaginable nightmare but an accomplished fact. We carry this fact within us—some consciously, in our waking thoughts and actions; others more subliminally, in waking and sleeping images too obscene and frightening to allow ourselves to see clearly. Some Jews try, consciously and/or unconsciously, to obliterate all traces of the Holocaust from their minds, with varying degrees of success. But this denial of reality is also a result of the Holocaust. No one escapes its effects.

In this essay, I will describe four basic ways that the Holocaust has been internalized by survivors and children of survivors, as well as by Jews in general. My goal is to help clarify some common themes in our responses to the Holocaust, as well as to highlight some of the strengths and drawbacks of each response. I am not judging these responses on a scale of any kind. Nor do I believe that they exist in isolation from one another. We are all likely to have at least traces of all four responses in combination.

The first response is *Total Obsession with the Holocaust*—the sense that nothing ever happened *but* the Holocaust, or that the Holocaust is the only world event of any significance. It is as though time froze with the Holocaust and, with it, all possibility of sustained hope or joy. There is a profound sense of despair about the victimization of the Jews, and a generalized "paranoia" about anti-Semitism, a fear that behind every bush, or, rather within every Gentile breast, lurks the heart of a bona fide anti-Semite.

It has been said, however, that "paranoia" is a word for *heightened awareness*. For the Holocaust survivor, "paranoia" is an ironic word, for no fear could be as dreadful as what, in truth, happened. I have read accounts of survivors of the concentration camps which describe the experience of dreaming in the camps. The inmates would, of course, have nightmares. But when they awoke and saw where they were, they prayed to return to their dreams. Consider the word "paranoia" in the context of just a few facts about the Holocaust:

- The rigid quota systems in almost every country which prevented Jews who might have escaped the Holocaust from doing so.
- That the Swiss government suggested that the Nazis identify the passports of Jews with the letter "J" and sent such passport-holders back to Germany to die.
- That the Jewish underground was the only underground in Europe that could not count on the support of the Allied High Command for weapons. Or that, despite the fact that there was a highly organized Jewish Fighting Organization in the Warsaw Ghetto, it received little aid from the "progressive" Polish underground.
- That the Pope could never bring himself to utter a word on behalf of the Jews, even when such a word might have helped to mitigate the extent of the genocide.

- That no attempt was made by any of the Allied Forces to destroy the extermination installations at Auschwitz and other camps, even when their exact locations were known.

- That the U.S. government not only knew about the Final Solution plan and did nothing to help the plight of the Jews until nearly the end, but in fact *obstructed* the rescue of Jews by discouraging protests of Hitlerism among American Jews; by insisting that early reports about the Final Solution not be made public; by denying a Swedish plan to rescue 20,000 Jewish children on the grounds that this would antagonize the Germans; by not even coming close to filling the meager immigration quotas allotted to Jews between 1933 and 1943. (Hitler knew about and used this last fact to further his war against the Jews, saying that the U.S. did not want the Jews either.)

Not surprisingly, Jewish "paranoia" exists. It sometimes takes the form of huddling together and believing that the Jews are the only people who ever *really* suffered, that all other oppressed peoples are just not significant because they never had it as bad as the Jews. Along with this, there is usually the attitude that we must take care of our own people because no one else will and that "the whole world hates us—let them take care of themselves."

Given the aforementioned facts, i.e., the complicity of much of the world in the nearly successful genocide of Europe's Jews, this response becomes understandable. While it may not be "rational" to suspect that every non-Jew you meet is a Jew-killer, paranoia and isolation among Jews are a distortion of a basic truth about Jewish oppression: that is, that not only during the Holocaust, but throughout our history, we have been persecuted by Gentiles.

We must not blame Holocaust survivors or Jews in general for their "paranoia" or ghettoization. ("Clannishness," which Jews are so often accused of, is, among other things, an anti-Semitic word for Jewish solidarity.) Rather, we must see the historical basis for such behavior in a world in which Jews have been systematically hated and scape-goated. The "nobody ever suffered but the Jews" attitude, though a distortion, expresses the justified bitterness and suppressed rage of Jewish people towards the Gentile world. It also expresses, again in distorted form, a great caring for the Jewish people.

We must recognize that *there is a social/historical basis for fear and hatred of Gentiles among Jews,* just as there is a social basis for class hatred in working people and man-hating in women. It is often difficult for Jews to acknowledge our rage at Gentiles. Like all oppressed people, many of us tend to turn it inwards at ourselves. Some become fanatic over-achievers and perfectionists in the attempt to be "good" Jews, hating ourselves if we make the slightest mistake, hating other ("bad") Jews, hating our Jewishness. Or some become compulsive assimilationists, trying to kill themselves off as Jews.

We must learn to see that Jewish rage is no less righteous than the rage of any oppressed people. I am not advocating anger as a program. I am saying that we must allow ourselves to experience and to validate our rage at Gentiles. Anger can help wash us free of our fear, can help us to come "out of the closet" as Jews.

A second form that Total Obsession with the Holocaust takes is the view of the *Holocaust as Sacred Event*. The danger of this response is that it de-politicizes the Holocaust by taking an essentially religious attitude towards it: "Six million martyrs died and we must never forget. NEVER AGAIN!" But never to forget what? That the Jews died at the hands of Nazi butchers?

The problem with this approach is that there is more to remember about the Holocaust than this. We must remember not only *that* the Jews died, but *why* and *how* they died, so that we can avert any future holocausts—so that "Never Again" has a *real*, not merely symbolic, meaning. And in order to do so, we need to know the answers to questions like: Who were the Nazis and how do we account for their rise to power? How can we understand the Holocaust in concrete, historical terms, not as some supernatural, demonic aberration carried out by a few deranged Germans, but as a historical event planned and executed by real men, fascist forces in Germany who were backed up by right-wing (and even "democratic") forces in the world?

What did the Holocaust have to do with the rise of the German monopoly capitalist class and its desire to destroy the socialist, communist and labor movements in Germany? How did anti-Semitism and anti-communism work together? How can we understand the world-historical forces of anti-Semitism in terms other than the inadequate and limiting categories of either religious or materialist dogma?

The view of the Holocaust as Sacred Event mystifies the answers to these questions and goes along with a decided ignorance of the forces of fascism and anti-Semitism, not only as they existed in World War II Europe, but as they exist in the world today. The Holocaust becomes a holy object for individual contemplation rather than something which happened in history and which must inspire continued resistance today. "Never Again" too often comes to mean honoring the dead through the individual act of remembrance itself—as in saying *Kaddish*—rather than through collective action to assure that anti-Semitism never again triumphs in the world.

Sometimes this response goes so far as to speak of the "chosenness" of the Jews for extermination, that God chose us for a special agony and a special mission that we, as mortals, cannot fathom. This attitude is the converse of the Nazi ideology that the Jews are a satanic race "chosen" to be destroyed. It is one of the most extreme versions of the Chosen People idea of Judaism, which, whatever its origins, often functions today as a kind of counter-myth of the oppressed.

The belief that we are God's special people often camouflages a radical terror of being Jewish. If the victimization of our people was, somehow, "chosen" by God, then it seems less insufferable. Behind this response is the attempt to come to terms with unbearable atrocity.

The second response is the reverse of Total Obsession—*Total or Partial Denial of the Holocaust.* This may take the personal form of simply never thinking about it, or of thinking of the Holocaust as something that is over and done with: "It happened There and not Here." In this light, the Holocaust appears not to be relevant to how we see ourselves or how we act in the world. Usually, this attitude goes along with total or partial assimilationism—the cultural denial of ourselves as Jews.

The attempt to eradicate all traces of "Jewishness" from our minds, our hearts, our actions and our bodies—I call this "gentile identification." We develop impeccable Gentile table manners, never read anything that has a Jewish theme, get nose jobs, hate our bodies for not looking WASP enough. Or we feel contempt when we hear Yiddish spoken or whenever anyone acts conspicuously, identifiably "Jewish." Or we lavishly celebrate Christmas, but not Passover. These are all internalizations of the anti-Semite's message that Jews are not worthy to live. We die culturally.

In the death camps, the walking dead—called "Musulmen"—tried to survive by killing themselves off psychically, doing the work of their persecutors for them. Musulmen were often the first to die—theirs was not a tenable strategy for survival. In denying the Holocaust, the "goy-identified" Jew, like the Musulman, chooses to kill himself off spiritually and culturally. His life is the living death of Jewish identity.

The denial of the Holocaust is both an internalization of, and a buttress for, the anti-Semite's recent attack: that the Holocaust never happened, that the Holocaust is a Jewish hoax. (Sixty-five books have been published to date making this case; Wiesel calls this "killing the

Jews a second time.") Thinking of the Holocaust, if at all, as something which happened There and not Here, a closed event which can no longer hurt us, is also a way of denying the fact that the forces of anti-Semitism and fascism which brought Hitler to power are still alive (in their original and in neo-Nazi forms) in Europe, South America, Iran, the U.S., etc. Anti-Semitism has always moved in waves—periods of lull followed by periods of renewed persecution. After the 30-year lull due to the world's shock and guilt about the Holocaust, we can now see a resurgence in the U.S. neo-Nazi parties, the Ku Klux Klan, still appealing to the same old brand of virulent anti-Semitism, telling us that Hitler never finished the job.

The Jewish denial of the Holocaust and "gentile-identification" weakens us as a people. But it must be understood with some compassion. "Musulman Jews" must be reached. During the Holocaust, the visible Star of David was the mark of death. In a post-Holocaust world, the fear of being noticeably Jewish is sometimes overwhelming, whether conscious or not. Jews know that total extermination is a real possibility. We live with a deep-seated fear of annihilation. But there is the possibility of Jewish rebirth in even the most "gentile-identified" Jew.

The third response to the Holocaust is a sense of *shame and/or contempt for those who survived,* or for the Jewish people as a whole. My mother tells me that of her friends who are survivors of concentration camps, there are those who never stop talking about the Holocaust and those who never talk about it at all. The latter are ashamed. Many of them feel, "Why did the others die and I survive?", as though their survival were an abandonment and betrayal of those who died, as though being alive after the Holocaust was a "sin" against those who were "martyred." This is more than simply a matter of what is called "survivor guilt." Both direct survivors of the Holocaust and the rest of us often may feel a generalized shame about being Jewish, a shame that somehow, in some profound way, the Jews themselves are to blame for the Holocaust.

I felt these kinds of feelings from a very young age. I was so ashamed of Yiddish that I quickly obliterated my ability to speak it and insisted that my parents speak English. I also remember feeling that Jews who survived the Holocaust should somehow be "sanctified" above the rest of humanity. Instead, I found many of them crass, materialistic, petty, morally weak and cowardly. Their survival itself seemed to render them "suspect" in my eyes.

I had internalized the anti-Semite's appraisal of the Jews as blameworthy. I had also inherited the myth that the Jews "went like sheep to the slaughter." Widely accepted since the Holocaust, this myth is in fact one of the worst examples of blame-the-victim ideology of all time. (Many scholars who write on this theme have as their historical sources none other than photographs and records kept by the Nazis. It is more than ridiculous to expect that the Nazis, who had gone to unprecedented lengths to dehumanize Jews, would keep an accurate record of Jewish heroism!)

Most Jews know something about the Warsaw Ghetto uprising. But few know that in practically every ghetto and in almost every labor camp and concentration camp, there existed a Jewish underground that not only kept up Jewish morale and reduced the physical suffering of the Jews as much as possible, but committed acts of sabotage, organized escapes and, against incredible odds, amassed arms and planned and executed revolts. Rosa Robota, a young girl who saw her family marched to the gas chambers, led a group of 20 women in helping to explode and put out of commission one of the four crematoriums of Auschwitz. Sobibor and Treblinka, two of the most notorious death camps, were put out of operation by the inmates.

A document from the Vilna Ghetto tells us about the kinds of decisions Jews were forced to make in order to fight the Nazis. Knowing from the news of other ghettos that the Nazis intended to liquidate all the ghettos and kill all remaining Jews in concentration camps, the men and women of the resistance organization of the Vilna Ghetto had to decide whether to try to escape to the forests to join the partisan units there, or to stay in the ghetto to help Jews who could not escape to fight the Nazis. The document shows clearly that these Jews knew that either road meant death and that they were only choosing *how* to die.

In the end, they chose to do everything possible to help those who could fight to escape to the woods and join the partisans. But they would stay to help those remaining to make a last stand against the Nazis. In the ghettos that were not able to smuggle in arms, Jews fought the Nazis with knives, clubs and bare hands. In the Warsaw Ghetto, it took the combined forces of tanks, ground troops, bomber planes and incendiary bombs to destroy the ghetto. Each enclave of resistance was an inferno. To destroy the Warsaw Ghetto, Hitler had to destroy it brick by brick.

But these are only some of the most dramatic stories and the ones that are most accurately documented. There are literally thousands of stories of Jewish courage and resistance that we do not know about, largely because the survivors themselves are often humble people and do not think their stories something to rave about. Or because they are not writers or historians. Or because there is no one who will listen to them.

It is important to remember that all acts of Jewish resistance took place against a background of incredible psychological as well as physical warfare waged by the Nazis against the Jews. From the beginning, transportation to the death camps was called "resettlement" and included elaborate deceptions like train fares and schedules. The murder at the end of the line was called "special treatment"; the gas chambers "showers," and so on. From the moment someone entered a death camp, it was not simply the knowledge that each day her brothers and sisters were going to their deaths that the inmate had to contend with, or the hard labor and starvation. It was also the systematic brutalization of the human image.

People's heads were shaven. They were not allowed to wash. They were made to stand and lie and sleep in their own shit. So that when a concentration camp inmate looked at another Jew, what she or he saw was someone who looked sub-human: a starved, shrunken, shit-covered beast. This made it easier for the Nazis to do their distasteful job of not only gassing people but burning their bodies. (In Treblinka, 15,000 Jewish bodies were burned every day.) It is easier to gas and burn something that looks like a beast than a human being.

Despite this, for the most part, Jews did not treat each other like beasts. They retained their humanity in the midst of an environment totally geared to its destruction. They were not simply *victims*. They were *subjects* and *agents* insofar as this was possible in a situation completely dedicated to their dehumanization.

They carried on, as much as possible, with customary ways of life. They made birthday cakes from crumbs. They stole from the Nazis and traded with one another (this was called "organizing"). They sang songs and told jokes. Against the monstrous inhumanity of the camps in which everything around them authorized despair, they kept the thread of Jewish human life going. To do so was to wage an act of extraordinary defiance against the Nazis' entire purpose. In this sense, every Jew who survived the Holocaust without betraying a Jewish brother or sister is a hero.

The fourth type of response to the Holocaust is a deep conviction that somehow *joylessness and suffering are the only possible justifications for living after the Holocaust*. This is one of the most noticeable responses of direct Holocaust survivors, whose lives are often a succession of smaller or larger ailments—both physical and emotional—called *tsouris*. I have inherited this sense that to be alive without pain is a disgrace. I think this is a way to do penance for surviving after the Holocaust, and of trying to "keep up" with the terrible anguish, not only of those who perished but also of those who suffered more than me.

To feel unmitigated pleasure after the Holocaust is often experienced as a betrayal of those who died. Suffering becomes a kind of cement that glues survivors to the ordeals of those they left behind. At bottom, there is a conviction, held not only by survivors but by many Jews, that "I don't deserve to live." This was, of course, the entire message of the Nazis, and their legacy to us. There is also a concomitant feeling that only suffering and unremitting hard work make life justifiable, make us worthy to be alive.

A psychiatrist once said of children of survivors that "a life that is not a given but an unexpected gift may become not a life but a mission." I have felt this sense of mission all my life: everything I did, all of my achievements, were somehow victories against Hitler. I am bound by a very burdensome sense of what I owe, not only to my parents, but to the Six Million.

I also see this sense of mission in Jews who are, for example, disproportionately represented in all "progressive" causes—for Blacks, for women, for working-class people, for Eritreans, for Palestinians, for everyone—and very often, for everyone except the Jews. There are a lot of us running around trying to save the world. This comes not only from the urgent need to make the world safe for Jews—often without actually taking the risk of "coming out" as a Jew—but also from an often unconsciously held idea that we don't really deserve to live unless we're doing something good (whether it's saving the world, being brilliant, having children, becoming a helping professional, or doing any of the things at which Jews excel).

From all of these internalized responses and often overwhelming feelings about the Holocaust—the guilt, the shame, the rage, the terror, the despair—*it is possible to emerge with a radical pride and, yes, even joy about being Jewish.* I will end with a few ideas about what we can and need to do to help ourselves and others make this journey. We need, first of all, to understand our responses to the Holocaust, both personally and politically. To do this, we must look inside to our feelings, sometimes long buried and very painful, about what the Nazis did to us. We need to start with whatever feelings of terror, guilt and despair are there, and to allow ourselves also to experience our anger and our pride, power, joy and solidarity with other Jews. Together, we need to do consciousness-raising about internalized effects of the Holocaust.

But this look *inside* must also be accompanied by a look *outside*. That is, we must read and learn more about what the Holocaust was. We need to understand more about the Holocaust as a world event, rather than as a circumscribed German-Jewish phenomenon. We need also to gain a balanced picture of Jews, not merely as victims but also as fighters, resisters, actors. We also need to understand the relation of the Holocaust to the creation of the Jewish state.

We need, finally, to respect the knowledge of survivors—not to see them as merely victims of their experience but as people who have areas of knowledge which they see more clearly than we do, being closer to the source. We must also identify where their extraordinary suffering may lead to some distortions of knowledge. We need to respect their wisdom and their strengths, neither to honor them blindly and romantically, nor to be ashamed of them. We need to be able to talk to them and to hear their stories.

Recently I spent several hours staring at pictures of the Holocaust in a book called *The Yellow Star*. I'd seen these pictures before, when I was a child. At that time, I'd seen only the unspeakable horror, the despair, the total abasement and destruction of the Jewish people. This time I saw also the looks of pride and dignity and defiance on the faces of many of the Jews, even as they went to their deaths. These were all, of course, photos taken by the Nazis, so I imagined how many more such photos could have been taken of Jewish strength, solidarity and courage which the Nazis never took.

I felt a renewal of one of the most profound lessons of the Holocaust, which I'd learned in the past by reading accounts of life in the death camps: that is, the absolute value of life itself. Against all hope and reason, against everything around them which shrieked "Die!", the Jews of Europe chose to live, to survive. I was reminded that I did not owe it to my family, murdered in Treblinka and Auschwitz, to suffer. If anything, I owed it to them to live with joy.

To live with joy is to say No to the Nazis, who thrived on death. To treat my life as a blessing, not as something of which I am not worthy, is also to say No to the Nazis. To fight with all of my strength the continued spectre of fascism and anti-Semitism, as well as other forms of oppression, still alive in the world, is to say No to the Nazis. To be a Jew, with the courage, dignity and pride I saw pictured in the faces of Jews on their way to die, is to say No to the Nazis. To be a Jew with compassion and love for other Jews is to say No to the Nazis.

Primo Levi
THE MEMORY OF THE OFFENSE

Human memory is a marvelous but fallacious instrument. This is a threadbare truth known not only to psychologists but also to anyone who has paid attention to the behavior of those who surround him, or even to his own behavior. The memories which lie within us are not carved in stone; not only do they tend to become erased as the years go by, but often they change, or even grow, by incorporating extraneous features. Judges know this very well: almost never do two eyewitnesses of the same event describe it in the same way and with the same words, even if the event is recent and if neither of them has a personal interest in distorting it. This scant reliability of our memories will be satisfactorily explained only when we know in what language, in what alphabet they are written, on what surface, and with what pen: to this day we are still far from this goal. Some mechanisms are known which falsify memory under particular conditions: traumas, not only cerebral ones; interference from other "competitive" memories; abnormal conditions of consciousness; repressions; blockages. Nevertheless, even under normal conditions a slow degradation is at work, an obfuscation of outlines, a so to speak physiological oblivion, which few memories resist. Doubtless one may discern here one of the great powers of nature, the same that degrades order into disorder, youth into old age, and extinguishes life in death. Certainly practice (in this case, frequent re-evocation) keeps memories fresh and alive in the same manner in which a muscle often used remains efficient, but it is also true that a memory evoked too often, and expressed in the form of a story, tends to become fixed in a stereotype, in a form tested by experience, crystallized, perfected, adorned, installing itself in the place of the raw memory and growing at its expense.

I intend to examine here the memories of extreme experiences, of injuries suffered or inflicted. In this case, all or almost all the factors that can obliterate or deform the mnemonic record are at work: the memory of a trauma suffered or inflicted is itself traumatic because recalling it is painful or at least disturbing. A person who has been wounded tends to block out the memory so as not to renew the pain; the person who has inflicted the wound pushes the memory deep down, to be rid of it, to alleviate the feeling of guilt.

Here, as with other phenomena, we are dealing with a paradoxical analogy between victim and oppressor, and we are anxious to be clear: both are in the same trap, but it is the oppressor, and he alone, who has prepared it and activated it, and if he suffers from this, it is right that he should suffer; and it is iniquitous that the victim should suffer from it, as he does indeed suffer from it, even at a distance of decades. Once again it must be observed, mournfully, that the injury cannot be healed: it extends through time, and the Furies, in whose existence we are forced to believe, not only rack the tormentor (if they do rack him, assisted or not by human punishment), but perpetuate the tormentor's work by denying peace to the tormented. It is not without horror that we read the words left us by Jean Améry, the Austrian philosopher tortured by the Gestapo because he was active in the Belgian resistance and then deported to Auschwitz because he was Jewish:

> Anyone who has been tortured remains tortured. . . . Anyone who has suffered torture never again will be able to be at ease in the world, the abomination of the annihilation is never extinguished. Faith in humanity, already cracked by the first slap in the face, then demolished by torture, is never acquired again.

Torture was for him an interminable death: Améry, about whom I will speak again in Chapter 6, killed himself in 1978.

We do not wish to abet confusions, small-change Freudianism, morbidities, or indulgences. The oppressor remains what he is, and so does the victim. They are not interchangeable. The former is to be punished and execrated (but, if possible, understood), the latter is to be pitied and helped; but both, faced by the indecency of the irrevocable act, need refuge and protection, and instinctively search for them. Not all, but most—and often for their entire lives.

By now we are in possession of numerous confessions, depositions, and admissions on the part of the oppressors (I speak not only of the German National Socialists but of all those who commit horrendous and multiple crimes in obedience to a discipline): some given in court, others during interviews, others still contained in books or memoirs. In my opinion, these are documents of the utmost importance. In general, the

descriptions of the things seen and the acts committed are of little
interest: they amply coincide with what victims have recounted; very
rarely are they contested; judgments have been handed down and they
are by now part of history. Often they are regarded as well known. Much
more important are the motivations and justifications: Why did you do
this? Were you aware that you were committing a crime?

The answers to these two questions, or to others which are analogous, are very similar to each other, independently of the personality of
the interrogated person, be he an ambitious and intelligent professional
like Speer or a gelid fanatic like Eichmann, a short-sighted functionary
like Stangl in Treblinka or Höss in Auschwitz, or an obtuse brute like
Boger and Kaduk, the inventors of torture. Expressed in different formulations and with greater or lesser arrogance, depending on the
speaker's mental and cultural level, in the end they substantially all say
the same things: I did it because I was ordered to; others (my superiors)
have committed acts worse than mine; in view of the upbringing I received, and the environment in which I lived, I could not have acted
differently; had I not done it, another would have done it even more
harshly in my place. For anyone who reads these justifications the first
reaction is revulsion: they lie, they cannot believe they will be believed,
they cannot not see the imbalance between their excuses and the enormity of pain and death they have caused. They lie knowing that they are
lying: they are in bad faith.

Now, anyone who has sufficient experience of human affairs knows
that the distinction (the opposition, a linguist would say) good faith/bad
faith is optimistic and smacks of the Enlightenment, and is all the more
so, and for much greater reason, when applied to men such as those just
mentioned. It presupposes a mental clarity which few have and which
even these few immediately lose when, for whatever reason, past or
present reality arouses anxiety or discomfort in them. Under such conditions there are, it is true, those who lie consciously, coldly falsifying
reality itself, but more numerous are those who weigh anchor, move off,
momentarily or forever, from genuine memories, and fabricate for
themselves a convenient reality. The past is a burden to them; they feel
repugnance for things done or suffered and tend to replace them with
others. The substitution may begin in full awareness, with an invented
scenario, mendacious, restored, but less painful than the real one; they
repeat the description to others but also to themselves, and the distinction between true and false progressively loses its contours, and man
ends by fully believing the story he has told so many times and continues
to tell, polishing and retouching here and there the details which are
least credible or incongruous or incompatible with the acquired picture

of historically accepted events: initial bad faith has become good faith. The silent transition from falsehood to self-deception is useful: anyone who lies in good faith is better off. He recites his part better, is more easily believed by the judge, the historian, the reader, his wife, and his children.

The further events fade into the past, the more the construction of convenient truth grows and is perfected. I believe that only by this mental mechanism is it possible to interpret, for instance, the statements made in 1978 to *L'Express* by Louis Darquier de Pellepoix, former commissioner of Jewish affairs in the Vichy government around 1942, and as such personally responsible for the deportation of seventy thousand Jews. Darquier denies everything: the photographs of piles of corpses are montages; the statistics of millions of dead were fabricated by the Jews, always greedy for publicity, commiseration, and indemnities: there may perhaps have been deportations (he would have found it difficult to dispute them: his signature appears at the foot of too many letters giving orders for these very deportations, even of children), but he did not know where to or with what results; there were, it is true, gas chambers in Auschwitz, but only to kill lice, and anyway (note the coherence!) they were built for propaganda purposes after the end of the war. It is not my intention to justify this cowardly and foolish man, and it offends me to know that he lived for a long time undisturbed in Spain, but I think I can recognize in him the typical case of someone who, accustomed to lying in public, ends by lying in private, too, to himself as well, and building for himself a comforting truth which allows him to live in peace. To keep good and bad faith distinct costs a lot: it requires a decent sincerity or truthfulness with oneself; it demands a continuous intellectual and moral effort. How can such an effort be expected from men like Darquier?

Reading the statements made by Eichmann during the Jerusalem trial, and those of Rudolph Höss (the penultimate commander of Auschwitz, the inventor of the hydrocyanic acid chambers) in his autobiography, one can see in them a process of re-elaboration of the past, more subtle than Darquier's. In substance, these two defended themselves in the classical manner of the Nazi militia, or, better yet, of all militiamen: we have been educated in absolute obedience, hierarchy, nationalism; we have been imbued with slogans, intoxicated with ceremonies and demonstrations; we have been taught that the only justice was that which was to the advantage of our people and that the only truth was the words of the Leader. What do you want from us? How can you even think to expect from us, after the fact, a behavior different from ours and that of all those who were like us? We were the diligent executors, and for our diligence we were praised and promoted. The decisions were not ours because the regime in which we grew up did not permit autonomous decisions: others have decided for us, and that was the only way it could have happened because our ability to decide had been amputated. Therefore we are not responsible and cannot be punished.

Even projected against the background of the Birkenau smokestacks, this reasoning cannot be considered purely the fruit of impudence. The pressure that a modern totalitarian state can exercise over the individual is frightful. Its weapons are substantially three: direct propaganda or propaganda camouflaged as upbringing, instruction, and popular culture; the barrier erected against pluralism of information; and terror. Nevertheless, it is not permissible to admit that this pressure is irresistible, especially in the brief twelve-year term of the Third Reich. In the affirmations and exculpations of men responsible for such serious crimes as were Höss and Eichmann, the exaggeration and, to an even greater degree, the manipulation of memory is obvious. Both were born and raised long before the Reich became truly "totalitarian," and their joining the Nazi party was a choice dictated more by opportunism than enthusiasm. The re-elaboration of their past was a later work, slow and (probably) not methodical. To ask oneself whether it was done in good or bad faith is naive. They too, so strong in the face of others' suffering, when fate put them before judges, before the death they deserved, built a convenient past for themselves and ended by believing in it, especially Höss, who was not a subtle man. As he appears in his writings, he was in fact a person so little inclined to self-control and introspection that he does not realize he is confirming his coarse anti-Semitism by the very act in which he abjures and denies it, nor does he realize how slimy his self-portrait as a good functionary, father, and husband actually is.

As a comment on these reconstructions of the past (but not only on these: it is an observation that holds for all memories) one must note that the distortion of fact is often limited by the objectivity of the facts themselves, around which there exists the testimonies of third parties, documents, *corpora delicti*, historically accepted contexts. It is generally difficult to deny having committed a given act, or that such an act was committed; it is, on the contrary, very easy to alter the motivations which led us to an act and the passions within us which accompanied the act itself. This is an extremely fluid matter, subject to distortion even under very weak pressure; to the questions Why did you do this? or What were you thinking as you did it? no reliable answers exist, because states of mind are by nature labile and even more labile is the memory of them.

An extreme case of the distortion of the memory of a committed guilty act is found in its suppression. Here, too, the borderline between good and bad faith can be vague; behind the "I don't know" and the "I do not remember" that one hears in courtrooms there is sometimes the precise intent to lie, but at other times it is a fossilized lie, rigidified in a formula. The rememberer has decided not to remember and has succeeded: by dint of denying its existence, he has expelled the harmful memory as one expels an excretion or a parasite. Lawyers for the defense know very well that the memory gap, or the putative truth, which they suggest to their clients, tends to become forgetfulness and the actual truth. It is not necessary to trespass in the field of mental pathology to find human examples whose declarations perplex us: they are most certainly false, but we are unable to detect whether the subject does or does not know he is lying. Supposing, absurdly, that the liar should for one instant become truthful, he himself would not know how to answer the dilemma; in the act of lying he is an actor totally fused with his part, no longer distinguishable from it. A glaring example of this during the days in which I am writing is the behavior in court of the Turk Ali Agca, the would-be assassin of Pope John-Paul II.

The best way to defend oneself against the invasion of burdensome memories is to impede their entry, to extend a *cordon sanitaire*. It is easier to deny entry to a memory than to free oneself from it after it has been recorded. This, in substance, was the purpose of many of the artifices thought up by the Nazi commanders in order to protect the consciences of those assigned to do the dirty work and to ensure their services, disagreeable even for the most hardened cutthroats. The *Einsatzkommandos,* who behind the front lines in Russia machine-gunned civilians beside common graves which the victims themselves had been forced to dig, were given all the liquor they wanted so that the massacre would be blurred by drunkenness. The well-known euphemisms ("final solution," "special treatment," the very term *Einsatzkommando,* literally, "prompt-employment unit," disguised a frightful reality) were not only used to deceive the victims and prevent defensive reactions on their part: they were also meant, within the limits of the possible, to prevent public opinion, and those sections of the army not directly involved, from finding out what was happening in all the territories occupied by the Third Reich.

At any rate, the entire history of the brief "millennial Reich" can be reread as a war against memory, an Orwellian falsification of memory, falsification of reality, negation of reality. All of Hitler's biographies, while disagreeing on the interpretation to be given to the life of this man so difficult to classify, agree on the flight from reality which marked his last years, especially beginning with the first Russian winter. He had forbidden and denied his subjects any access to truth, contaminating their morality and their memory; but, to a degree which gradually increased and attained complete paranoia in the Bunker, he barred the path of truth to himself as well. Like all gamblers, he erected around himself a stage set woven of superstitious lies and in which he ended by believing with the same fanatical faith that he demanded from every German. His collapse was not only a salvation for mankind but also a demonstration of the price to be paid when one dismembers the truth.

Jerry Samet

THE HOLOCAUST AND THE IMPERATIVE TO REMEMBER

> The need to tell our story to "the rest", to make "the rest" participate in it, had taken on for us, before our liberation and after, the character of an immediate and violent impulse, to the point of competing with our other elementary needs.
>
> Is it necessary or good to retain any memory of this exceptional human state?
>
> PRIMO LEVI
Survival in Auschwitz

I. INTRODUCTION: THE IMPERATIVE TO REMEMBER[1]

The need that Primo Levi and his fellow inmates felt is nearly universal among Holocaust survivors. Two generations later, that need is still with "the rest" of us in some form; the present volume is an expression of that need. But although everyone agrees that we need to remember the Holocaust, we are rarely told *why* we should. Why does the mere suggestion that we put this tragedy behind us and forget about it strike us all as bizarre and horrible? As if such forgetting would compound the tragedy? The impulse to remember is strong, but it is only dimly understood. Let me give a few examples of the sorts of questions that remain unanswered. First of all, what is it exactly that needs to be told? And who exactly has to do the telling? There are also important questions about how this testimony ought to be received. Who precisely has to listen? Is it the guilty, the future generations of survivors, all of western civilization? Perhaps the world at large? And how must we remember? Levi's second rhetorical question raises a further perplexity about the status of this deeply felt need. Is it simply a psychological compulsion of those who have experienced the atrocities of the Holocaust, or does the impulse to

407

give testimony and the correlated demand that it be heard and remembered have a broader moral standing? Is there an ethical imperative on
all of us to remember?

In this essay, I hope to lay bare the anatomy of this need. As is the
case with anatomical studies, a large part of the process is demarcating
areas that need to be explored and articulated more fully. We will find
that there are many more questions than answers, and that the answers
themselves are not unequivocal.

In commenting on the opening quote from Primo Levi I posed a
number of questions that we might pursue to help us clarify the special
"call to memory." We can sort these questions into four groups. The
first group deals with the object of memory, with *what* it is precisely that
must be remembered. The second addresses the question of the subject
of memory: *Who* specifically is supposed to remember. A third asks
about the experience of memory itself: *How* exactly are we to remember?
The last takes up the over-riding question of reasons—that is, *why* we
must remember.

II. WHAT MUST WE REMEMBER?

A. *The Suffering of the Victims*

If we let the survivors be our guides, the answer is clear: we must
remember what the Nazis did to their victims. And to whatever extent
possible, we must see these atrocities from the victim's perspective. The
individual testimonies that make such remembering possible—both
first- and second-hand—are what Primo Levi calls the "things that imperiously demand to be told."

Still, one might ask: Are the victims' and survivors' accounts really
central after all? Perhaps survivors respond to this "imperious demand"
by focusing on their individual histories because that is what they know
best; that is what they, and no one else, are able to contribute. Perhaps
we should not understand the need to "remember the Holocaust" as
having *any* central element. The alternative would be to see it as multi-
dimensional, as a quilt made up of many diverse pieces. The survivors'
testimonies would contribute a distinctive experiential sense of the
atrocities committed, but would be fitted together with the analyses and
insights of historians, sociologists, theologians, novelists, philosophers,
anthropologists, political scientists, and so on.

It would be hard to find anything objectionable in this picture of
how a culture comes to understand itself and its past. It does describe

the cultural facts of remembrance as they indeed are; "Holocaust Studies" rightly includes all these contributions. From this perspective, the survivor is one contributor among many. He or she may be an especially *important* contributor—an eyewitness—and as such is a unique source of evidence and corroboration. But other sources might provide their own unique perspectives as well.

I want to point out, however, that acknowledging this multi-dimensionality does not fully answer our original question. We want to understand the special status that remembrance seems to have vis-à-vis the Holocaust. Much of the intellectual attention paid to the Holocaust— we can take as an example the careful analysis of the structure of the Hitlerjügend ("Hitler Youth")—is part of our cultural record, but not a distinctively motivated part. Whatever the historian's original motivation may be, the contribution is generally offered qua historian. The survivor, on the other hand, has an internal log of "things that imperiously demand to be told." Does the hierarchical structure of command in the Hitlerjügend make this sort of demand on anyone? Even on the historian?

Perhaps it does. But if it does, it does so derivatively. It may be that there *is* something deep and illuminating about the Nazi mentality that manifests itself in the organizational structure of the Hitlerjügend. But I would argue that the special importance of this sort of discovery is dependent on its ultimate connection to the Nazi treatment of Holocaust victims. It is because this organizational structure foreshadows or reflects the genocide that it too might "demand to be told." And why does the suffering of the victims stand apart? This is a question we will pass through again and again, but I will mention one crucial component: only the experiential memories of the individual suffering and brutalization—the stories, the pictures, the testimony—make the appropriate moral response possible.

In the same way that we must be careful not to conflate the distinctive need to remember with the *broader* set of normal historical and intellectual interests, we must also not confuse it with a *narrower* motivation—i.e. the desire to keep the memory of one's family and forebears alive. This psychological need expresses itself in many ways—e.g. in our tendency to save pictures and mementos, to write histories, to work up family trees, and so on. Because of Judaism's special conception of its own history Jews are especially drawn to this sort of memorialization.[2] Indeed, remembering the Holocaust is often, as a matter of fact, remembering one's departed family members; to this extent, the two needs converge and are mutually supportive. But even though they do dovetail in this way, they are different.

One can see this is by the difference in effect. The attempt to collect the names of *all* the Holocaust victims at Yad Vashem in Israel, and the various archival centers that have sprung up in the last decades, signify a special need. It is not simply a matter of creating an archive of the past. Those who died natural deaths are not included in this effort. It is a *special* past that we try to record. It is hard to lay bare the underlying psychology of this sense of specialness, but I want to suggest the following way of looking at it. Our forebears lived and died, and their lives are, to varying degrees, psychologically entwined with ours. Their histories are, in an extended sense, *our* past. But in the normal course of generations, we look back at them; they do not call ahead to us. We actively choose to look back and select what we will memorialize. The Holocaust is different. Our response to it—and one can see this vividly in the pervasive metaphors and images of victims crying out to us—is a response to something that *demands* our attention. We think of ourselves not merely as observers of self-contained past lives. We are, in a strange sense, the intended *audience* of those who suffered. The victims, those who lived and those who perished, demanded witnesses, demanded that someone else see what was happening to them and empathize with their plight. But the actual witnesses were, on the one side, the perpetrators who *would* not see, and, on the other, their fellow sufferers, who for the most part *could* not allow themselves to see fully. In remembering the Holocaust, our remembering is a response to this *call* to witness.

B. The Humanity of the Victims

Alongside the suffering of the victims, and perhaps as important an object of memory, is the humanity of the victims. This has two dimensions. First, we must remember the victims as they were before their great tragedy—as active, productive human beings with communities, friends, and families, hopes and dreams. The more we can grasp the victim as a person, the more we can identify with him or her. And the stronger the identification, the more fully we can empathize with his or her suffering. In a recent television documentary, a fifteen-year-old visiting Auschwitz reports that the horror "hit her" most deeply when she saw a photo display of a victim having dinner at home with his wife and baby.

There is also another element to this aspect of memory. There is a felt need to commemorate the brave humanity of many of the victims *in their very conditions of extremity,* in the face of the severe attempts to dehumanize them. Nearly every chronicle of the Holocaust experience pays special attention to moral behavior in an amoral world of camp inmates, of passion and pity and bravery in an environment in which such emotions and traits presented mortal danger, of the endurance of hope in many when rationality could provide no basis for such hope, and even of the rare humanity of the oppressors, wherever it could be found.

C. The Perpetrators

It goes without saying that one cannot remember the victims without at the same time remembering their oppressors, and we have touched on this briefly in considering the contributions of the social scientist, psychologist, etc. and the analysis of Nazi Germany. You can't describe the experience of the victims in the Warsaw Ghetto without talking about what the Nazis did and planned. The analysis of the structure of the Nazi machine, the range of involvement of the population and institutions, the individual psychology of those at various levels in the pecking order, have all been pursued assiduously. At the same time, we are also pulled in the opposite direction. First, to the extent that memory enables the perpetrators to "live on" past their demise, we are reluctant to accord them this immortality. We would prefer that they be nameless and faceless; we want their grandchildren to be embarrassed by them. They are simply faceless soldiers in the service of evil. Second, to the extent that we reconstruct their psychology, make them the subject of biographical and psychological research, begin to understand them, and inevitably humanize them and rationalize them, we are fearful that we will find a way to forgive them, or at least mitigate their responsibility. This reflects a broader dilemma about our attitudes toward evil: the more monstrous the crime, the more like a monster the criminal seems to become. But the more monstrous the criminal, the less human; and the less human, the less we can ascribe moral responsibility for his or her actions. The antiquity and the generality of this problem does not make its solution any easier. In fact, the dilemma is more poignant in the case of the Holocaust perpetrators, because we fear a betrayal of the victim in understanding the perpetrator.

D. Remembering and Forgetting

In considering *what* we must remember, there is one especially perplexing question: Are there things we *need* not remember, perhaps even things that we *should* not remember?

The answer to the first question seems to be: yes. Events, by their very nature, always involve peripheral details. So while we should not forget that Jews were transported to the gas chambers in cattle cars, we need not remember what color the cars were on the outside. But to abstract from the details in this way can be dangerous, because it disregards the nature of human memory and the associativity that defines it. We do not remember only by directing attention to stored representations of past events. Our memories work busily without such conscious direction. As we all know, one thing *reminds* us of another—without our willing it to—and things "pop into our heads," often without our being able to discern the connections that trigger them. Although the color of the cattle cars is not a "thing which imperiously demands to be told," it too serves its purpose. Details, although sometimes irrelevant to the broader phenomena, often have a perceptual salience that enables them to release important memories that might otherwise be repressed. Equally important: "irrelevant" details often hold the key to releasing repressed *emotions*. This is a common element that runs through survivors' accounts—i.e. the emotional power of a stray visual image, a barked order in Polish, the sound of a wooden shoe, a melody hummed by a child. So there is a sense in which we should remember even what we need not remember. We cannot write off any element as without value.

The deeper question, however, is whether there are things we *ought* not to remember. But what, we may ask, could this be? What would be a valid reason for the suppression of memory? One possibility that is mentioned often is that there are things that are too *painful* to remember, either for the survivor or for the "rest" of us. The pain of memory is an undeniable fact, but it would be a deep misunderstanding to construe this as having anything to do with the *suppression* of memory. There are things which, *for particular victims,* are too painful to bring to memory again, and therefore too painful for them to recount. We must respect this. The same might hold true *for particular listeners.* For example, a young child in our culture might pick up hints of the Holocaust by osmosis, but we might legitimately decide that the personal devastation of learning the details would be too great, *too* painful. This is not to say that we must wait till the memory is *not* painful. The painfulness of memory is not only unavoidable, it is part and parcel of the imperative: we are compelled to remember so that we may experience this pain and sorrow. Memory without pain might be worse than no memory at all.

But this in itself is not to say that there are things that *of their very nature*—as opposed to the state of mind of a particular potential witness—should not be remembered. There is a difference between not being able to dredge up certain memories, and wanting certain facts and experiences to be suppressed. The latter involves the desire that *no one* recall them, and this is an attitude we rarely find in the testimony of survivors.

Where we do find a commitment to the systematic suppression of memory, of course, is with the Nazis themselves. The survivors' need to remember parallels the Nazis' intention to suppress. Although they were obsessive about keeping records, numbering their victims, and so on, the Nazis were at the same time determined to obliterate the memory of their final solution. Mass graves of executed victims were regularly dug up, even years later, and the corpses were incinerated and the bones pulverized. In the Nazi case, this was simply the criminal impulse to conceal a crime, or, in their eyes, to conceal a necessary but unpleasant duty. As a reaction to the Nazis, remembering can be viewed as a belated victory—i.e. we remember *because* they wanted the world to forget.

But independent of the operative intentions in the case of the Nazis, we need to recognize that the *idea* of the suppression of cultural and historical memory—the determination that certain aspects of the past must be passed over in silence and allowed to fade—can be the product of more complex motivations than simply the desire to do away with incriminating evidence. It is deeply ironic and troubling that the idea of such suppression manifests itself in the Old Testament, where we have something like a principle of the selectivity of moral memory—i.e. the essential imperative to remember is paired with an imperative to repress.

What I have in mind is the biblical account of the confrontation between the Hebrews, who were in transit from Egypt to Canaan, and the Amalekites, who attacked them as they passed through their territory. The story is told in three installments. In the first installment, we get a brief recounting of the main events of the battle, which features a miraculous victory for the Hebrews, and the injunction that Moses should record this miraculous victory (and transmit it to the next generation of leadership) because God intends to destroy the memory of the Amalekites (Exodus 17). In the second installment, the Hebrews are enjoined, first, to remember the attack of the Amalekites, and, second, not to forget to ". . . eradicate the memory of Amalek" (Numbers 24).[3] In the final chapter, which tells of events occurring generations later, God reminds Samuel that He has not forgotten the sin of the Amalekites, and enjoins king Saul to attack them. Saul does attack, but fails to carry out the total annihilation that is commanded, and is punished (1 Samuel 15).

The original incident and its aftermath are obviously rich in theological import, and they have been variously interpreted by millennia of commentators. The aftermath of the attack and the simultaneous themes of remembering and forgetting are especially troubling when placed side by side with the Holocaust. But it is not my intention to discuss these questions here. What I want to highlight is, first, the obvious point, that the imperative to suppress memory can be something quite distinct from the attempt to cover up any misdeed. God's command, Saul's attack, and the subsequent details are not glossed over; they are all made very explicit. And, second, there is an almost paradoxical attitude about remembrance. Plainly, if one wants to destroy the memory of Amalek, it is counterproductive to record the encounter and commemorate it. The command to "never forget" is in direct tension with the command to "eradicate the memory." We might therefore conjecture that there was something about Amalek—about their ethos or about their action that makes their crime against the Hebrews especially heinous. And this is the important point: the text never fully specifies what that something is. All we *are* told is that they deviously attacked them in transit and tried to sabotage them. Although not praiseworthy, such actions are certainly not monstrous. In fact, the Canaanite opponents whom the Hebrews subsequently conquered are explicitly portrayed as far more venal, but there is no corresponding play of these themes of forgetting and remembrance. If the Amalekite actions did have a monstrous element, the text is silent about it; this *has* been effectively eradicated. What we have left of them is not a reflection of how they were and what they did, but simply that they were defeated through a miracle. This opens the door for speculation about their transgression, but perhaps it is just such sleuthing and revelations that the text seems to prohibit. The attempt to "rediscover" the Amalekites seems to directly contravene the injunction to eradicate their memory.

We have taken this digression into biblical scholarship to raise a point about the imperative to remember. That point is that there is at least one normative tradition—one that is central to our culture, and also uniquely relevant to the Holocaust—that does *not* invariably pair national tragedy with full memory. The Bible records that there was a heinous crime, committed by the Amalekites against the Hebrews, whose nature cannot be revealed *by the victim*. But at the same time, there seems to be a moral and/or religious duty to remember that there was such a so-terrible-it-cannot-be-recalled crime. If the Amalakites were guilty of some terrible offense in their attack on the nomadic Hebrews, the text is not intent on articulating it for future generations of Hebrew readers; it is only vaguely specified. From the biblical perspective, these atrocities are, in some unfathomable way, the polar opposites of Levi's memories. These are things that imperiously demand *not* to be told.[4]

III. WHO MUST REMEMBER?

"We must remember," we are told. But who are "we"? There is no single right answer, but it is worthwhile to reflect on different possibilities and the issues they raise. I want to consider four such groups: the survivors, the circle of care around the victims and survivors, the perpetrators, and the world at large.

A. *Survivors*

The survivors are plainly in a unique position vis-à-vis the responsibilities of memory, because of their experiential awareness of what it was like. This unique position is directly linked to the special need of survivors to *testify* as witnesses in their own behalf. It is their testimony that can make the experience real for us, and in that way allow us to remember. But there is a crucial difference between testimony and remembrance. Testimony is an act that begins and ends; it is a recounting of what one has experienced or witnessed. It may recur, in that one may tell the story over and over again, but it is a discrete episode. Remembering, on the other hand, suggests an open-ended continuous state of the person. The reason this distinction is important is because it is reflected in the psyches of many survivors. Levi points out that the survivors he knows react in two very different ways to their concentration camp experiences. Some cannot help but remember their brutalization and are forever haunted by it. Others find a way to keep it out of their minds and lives; if it is not forgotten, then at least it is compartmentalized and held at bay.

So we need to ask: If there is a responsibility on the survivor to tell his or her story, when is this responsibility fulfilled? In a recent documentary a survivor says this: "I did my part; I went to Jerusalem to testify against Eichmann. I thank God that I can forget." Testimony, ironically, can sometimes lessen the weight of haunting memories. Those of us who grew up surrounded by survivors knew of many who could not bring themselves to confront their memories of the Holocaust and certainly were not able to recount their experiences to the next generation. The acknowledgment of the importance of memory was there; these were not people who thought attention to the Holocaust and to the suffering of its victims was inappropriate. But the fear of confronting the past, of having their children's sense of themselves and their parents be colored by the memories, was too great. Some might criticize this course of action from a clinical perspective, but can there be any grounds for thinking that survivors fail to do their duty? that they can be compelled to testify and remember? I think not. As I claimed earlier, although "the world" should not be allowed to forget, the survivor himself or herself may be treated deferentially. The pain of re-experiencing, for some, is too great. Just as there may be some things we ought not to remember, there may also be some whom we ought not to call to testify.

B. The Circles of Care

We can move from consideration of the survivors themselves to the question of the imperative as it relates to the "circles of care" that surround them. For instance, is there a differential responsibility on the children of survivors and victims to keep alive the memory of what their parents went through? The same question can be asked about the larger circles of care and concern: friends, lovers, extended families, co-religionists, fellow citizens, members of western civilization, and so on. Do gypsies have a special responsibility to remember the fate of the gypsies in Auschwitz? Do homosexuals have a special calling to remember the fate of homosexuals simply because of shared sexual orientation?

One's answer to such questions will depend on how one understands these circles of concern. Are they a matter of voluntary commitments and identifications? If so, then remembering and commemorating will be a conditional imperative—e.g. if you think of yourself as a Jew, you must not ignore the Holocaust. On the other hand, if we think of these circles or ties as existing and creating responsibilities whether we want them or not, then they cannot be simply repudiated.[5] The complexities of this question are also often reflected in the chronicles of survivors. We are often given descriptions of a concentration camp world in which personal ties of friendship and love were almost totally forsworn. They were first of all dangerous, and the routine depersonalization of inmates made them almost impossible psychologically. Despite this numbness, which I will argue is central to understanding the imperative to remember, the experience of suffering together created a bond—a circle of care—which, though it was not fully experienced emotionally at the time, calls the survivors to "witness" for each other. Levi tells the story of the brief life and death of a strange three-year-old boy, and comments: "Nothing remains of him: he bears witness through these words of mine."

C. The Perpetrators

We come now to the other side of the experiential perspective: the perpetrators. One reaction is that the perpetrators must be confronted and forced to remember; that justice demands that we not allow them to escape the feelings of guilt. But we know—and the survivors knew—that this reaction, though normal, misjudges the entire situation. As the Nuremberg trials showed, those most directly responsible for the Holocaust could not be made to experience guilt for their deeds. Levi speaks eloquently of coming to this painful awareness while passing through Germany on the way back to his home after his liberation from Auschwitz:

> We felt we had something to say, enormous things to say, to every single German, and we felt that every German should have something to say to us; we felt an urgent need to settle our accounts, to ask, explain, and comment, like chess players at the end of a game. Did "they" know about Auschwitz, about the silent daily massacre, a step away from their doors? If they did, how could they walk about, return home and look at their children, cross the threshold of a church? If they did not, they ought, as a sacred duty, to listen, to learn everything, immediately, from us, from me; I felt the tattooed number on my arm burning like a sore.
> . . . I felt I was moving among throngs of insolvent debtors, as if everybody owed me something, and refused to pay. . . . I felt that everybody should interrogate us, read in our faces who we were, and listen to our tale in humility. But no one looked us in the eyes, no one accepted the challenge; they were deaf, blind, and dumb. . . .
> . . . I found myself searching among them, among that anonymous crowd of sealed faces, for other faces, clearly stamped in my memory, many bearing a name: the name of someone who could not but know, remember, reply; who had commanded and obeyed, killed, humiliated, and corrupted. A vain and foolish search; because not they, but others, the few just ones, would reply for them. (370-1)

The most guilty would selectively remember something quite alien from what we feel "needs to be told." One might pursue the question of responsibility nonetheless—i.e. whether they will or they won't, whether the perpetrators have a *duty* to remember their role and to testify. To the

extent that they can acknowledge their roles and recognize such a responsibility, they have it. For those who cannot, what can we say?

We are left in a perplexing position. The most guilty, generally
speaking, remained rooted in the "normative" order of Nazism; they
can be morally judged but cannot take up the burden of moral response.
The "few just ones" Levi searches for presumably have little to remember and to testify to. What then becomes of the perpetrator's perspective? Is it to be lost forever? Is it a perspective well-lost? The temptation is to settle on those who *do* experience guilt, who *are* capable of
sincere regret. Such individuals might be found among the accomplices
and collaborators: all those who might not have pulled the triggers or
turned on the gas, but without whose active compliance the Holocaust
would not have been possible. Such individuals might indeed recognize a
need to testify and a duty to do so. But this group, and it includes the
bulk of the population of the Third Reich, raises a further issue: Is their
testimony enough? Is there some obligation to *not* let them put their
experience behind them, to not let them expiate their guilt and resume
their lives? We are really asking if the crimes committed call on us to
respond differently to these perpetrators than we would respond to
murderers, rapists, and the like. In both cases, those in the victim's inner
circle of care might experience a vengeful desire to punish the perpetrator forever. But does this response have a different moral standing
with regard to Holocaust criminals? Even though the severity of the
accomplices' crimes pales when compared to the worst evil of those in
charge of planning and carrying out the Holocaust, is it still so large that
they are guilty of a maximal wrong? Are we dealing with the differences
between orders of infinity?

D. The World

Consider now the broadest scope we can apply to the imperative to
remember: where the "we" in "We must remember" is the world at
large.[6] Can we literally feel that *everyone* must remember the Holocaust?
That there is something of import achieved in recounting the whole
story to, say, primitive tribesmen in New Guinea? Such a view seems
deeply counterintuitive. We, certainly, feel no moral compulsion to
learn about *their* tribal tragedies. There may indeed be a compulsion to
tell, but there does not seem to be a need to listen. If we are to be guided
by the responses of those we ordinarily take to be normal moral agents,
we find that the response to national tragedy is quite limited. The outcry
against pre- and post-Nazi holocausts against Armenians, Cambodians,
Biafrans, and others has always been the work of a very small minority.

To many, grouping the Holocaust with these "holocausts" has been seen as expressing a residual anti-semitism, an unwillingness to acknowledge the special crime against the Jews. The Holocaust, it has been argued, is unique mainly because of the ideology and intent that drove it. This may well be true, but it is not relevant to this point. Philosophers, historians, psychoanalysts, jurists, etc. may be able to establish the uniqueness claim. But even if the Cambodian tragedy of a decade ago *were* presented as the counterpart of the Nazi's ideologically-motivated destruction of the Jews, there is little reason to think that ordinary moral agents, geographically and culturally remote from the devastation, would be drawn into the national tragedy of the Cambodians. Many would and did offer some degree of support, but there is little sense, at least in the West, of a cultural imperative to remember.

The depressing fact is that it is not simply the geographical divide that matters. In Claude Lanzmann's documentary film *Shoa,* a Polish farmer whose field abutted the train tracks entering Auschwitz is asked whether he was afraid for the Jews he saw arriving on the trains. He already knew that they were doomed. The translator summarizes his reply: "Well," he says, "it's this way: if I cut my finger, it doesn't hurt him." This farmer certainly does not strike the viewer as a person of deep moral sympathies, but the sad fact is that this is more-or-less the normal reaction. Survivors were gripped by the feeling that if the world only knew the details of the atrocities they underwent, the world would be shaken out of its complacency. But they were wrong: most people were simply shocked, and got over it. What is more pertinent is that the survivors' *need* to give testimony, to remember, has not been seriously weakened by the depressing knowledge that few really want to listen.

Is there a midpoint between the immediate circle of concern and the world at large? One possibility is that the duty to remember rests on the civilization that gave rise to the Nazi phenomenon. Indeed, those of us in the West are continuing members of this civilization. We will return to this issue shortly.

IV. HOW SHOULD WE REMEMBER?

I have so far been talking about memory and remembrance loosely, as if there were a single uniform mental operation involved. But this is a gross oversimplification. There are many different sorts of activities that fall under the concept of remembering, and consequently much to be said about the *how* of memory—about what we are called upon to do.

Here I want to provide the gross anatomy of this issue; I will only be able to skim the surface of this question.

The concept of *remembrance* that is relevant to the Holocaust is much broader than the cognitive psychologist's notion of *remembering*. Remembrance encompasses various sorts of social activities and cultural institutions; the psychologist's notion of memory is narrower and has as its sole focus the mind of a single subject. Nevertheless, there are important distinctions to be made even if we confine ourselves to the psychologist's domain.

First, we can draw a familiar distinction between remembering as a *capacity* to recover some particular memory information, and remembering as a conscious *activity* of calling memories to mind and re-experiencing them. We remarked earlier that even those who choose not to remember in the second sense normally still remember in the first.

A more important set of distinctions can be made within the category of conscious remembering. We can recall something in a number of different ways; here are a few.[7]

(i) We might have access to it simply as a piece of information. It is part of a *narrative* with which I am familiar. I might know, for instance, that many of the Jews of Chelmno were executed by the Germans only two days before the Russians reached the town. This is an historical fact, and as such is available to anyone. Once I've stored this fact, you can potentially remember it.

(ii) Those present in Chelmno at the execution might also remember the fact, and might call it to mind, but as more richly detailed and more personally relevant. They might see the whole scene in their mind's eye—the victims lined up in the cold, the soldiers aiming their rifles, and so on. This is not the perspective of the narrator, but of the *observer*. We should note that this sort of memory is not limited to those who have had the actual experience. It may be constructable by a vivid imagination, spliced together from film clips and so on.

(iii) I described the last sort of memory as perceptual, as a case of seeing the scene in one's mind's eye, but the perceiver's perspective is from a distance—it is the whole scene that is laid out, in the way that a landscape painter might visualize it. But there is still a more personal level of remembering. That is the scene as it appeared from the perspective of the *participant*. In this sort of remembering, I am not at a distant point watching the action, but actually in the midst of the action. This sort of remembering has an element of re-experiencing in that it recreates the participant's perceptual perspective.

(iv) There is another form of experiential memory, however, that takes the perspectivism one step further. In this case, the memory is enriched so that it includes not just the perceptual perspective of the participant, but the full gamut of emotional and physical responses that the participant felt—i.e. the memory of the fear, the nausea of seeing bodies drop, and so on. Here it is not just enriched by the *knowledge* that certain specific feelings and emotions were felt; instead, the actual emotions and feelings are *re-experienced*. Such memory is the stuff of nightmares.

These four categories of personal memory simply highlight some of the major differences between our ways of responding to the past. We could easily articulate further types of remembering that fall on the lines between these four categories. One especially important case is the role that empathetic identification can play in allowing us to reconstruct the emotions—and perhaps actually come to experience them at some level —of participants other than ourselves.

V. WHY SHOULD WE REMEMBER?

The desire not to forget the Holocaust strikes many of us as so appropriate and so natural that we fail to notice how singular it is. We suffer individual tragedies, but often don't want to talk about them at all. If we *do* want to talk about a particular one, we often simply want to get it off our chests so that we can forget about it and go on. Those who suffered through the Holocaust underwent immeasurable personal tragedy, and as such they often experienced the same needs—"the liberating joy of recounting . . ." is how Levi puts it. But the need we've been anatomizing in this essay is something beyond this, something very different. It is the sort of burning need that—unbelievably—can give one a will to survive.[8] This is not the normal response to normal trage- dies, no matter how personally painful. We must therefore seek a deeper understanding of its force and power: why should we remember?

A. Prevention

To many this seems to be the one question that *does* have a clear answer: so that it may never happen again. But this answer only tells one part of the story—and possibly a small part at that. The idea that we must remember in order to prevent a recurrence no doubt motivates many. As such, this need is simply an expression of the general moral imperative to prevent atrocities in any way we can. But I want to urge that the duty to remember runs deeper; the value of testimony and remembrance is independent of its effectiveness in prevention.

We can begin to see this by noticing the simple fact that remembrance, in this domain at least, has never been an effective means of prevention. Ironically, no one knew this better than the Jewish people. From the perspective of Jewish history, the Holocaust carried to the limit patterns of racist behavior and policies that were ever-recurrent in European history. Inquisitions, pogroms, expulsions, and disenfranchisements were not forgotten, but the collective memory of such anti-semitism did very little to prevent the Holocaust. In fact, Jewish thinkers have always had to respond to the opposite argument—i.e. that memory is counterproductive, that if the history of victimization, which led to a self-image of the Jew as victim, had been forgotten, the Jews of Europe would have been better off. This might be a deep mistake, but the fact that the argument could surface should alert us to the fact that the link between remembrance and prevention is far from guaranteed. By the same token, the Gentile memory of centuries of anti-semitism never served as a preventive. On the contrary, it established such anti-semitism as part of the European cultural inheritance.

In actual fact, the testimony offered by those fortunate enough to escape in the very midst of the Holocaust was *not* effective in preventing the devastation. A generous interpretation of this is that the story these escapees carried out of Poland and the camps was simply too incredible to believe. It *was* too incredible to believe, but one must still ask: Why didn't the collective memory of anti-semitism *prevent* such pervasive incredulity and denial? If memory was not a preventive for the victims, can we be confident it will prove generally effective?

One moral to draw is that memory can only help prevent a recurrence if there is a system of shared values. It is how one reacts to the knowledge that is crucial, and the reactions are not guaranteed merely by remembering. Indeed, it was part of the Nazi post-war plan to establish a museum of extinct races that would feature the Jew.

To probe our intuitions about remembrance and prevention a bit further, imagine that it was established to our satisfaction that remembering the Holocaust had more deleterious effects than benefits. What if telling the next generation was found to lead inexorably to an irreversible pessimism and nihilism in a certain percentage of the population? Or more grotesquely but more plausibly: What if it were found that it contributed more to the possibility of the revival of Nazism than it did to prevention? That the allure of the Aryan superiority tended to overcome the guilt of genocide? How would we respond? These are difficult questions, but my own sense is that the need to testify would continue. It might perhaps go underground; it might be exercised more selectively. But such a prospect would *not* give rise to a need to suppress and forget, which is what we might expect if the grounds for remembering were purely utilitarian and preventive.

Preventing another holocaust is of supreme importance, but it is not the purpose of our commitment to remember. Even if attempts to gain publicity, to establish foundations, to erect memorials, to hold conferences, and the like are aimed at prevention, the survivor's compelling need to remember and the need of the many who are called to listen has little to do with utilitarian conceptions of the effectiveness of such remembrance.

B. Deathbed Wish

Another suggestion that one finds in the writings and testimony of survivors is that remembrance is a debt owed to the dead.[9] This is sometimes expressed in terms of the fulfillment of a deathbed request. The idea is that the victims had an overriding desire to have their plight remembered, and the living survivors remember as payment of this debt. Let me comment briefly on some of the interesting ramifications of this view for our earlier discussions.

One is what it suggests about our earlier question regarding *who* must remember. If the obligation has its basis in a promise, then those who tacitly or explicitly made such a promise have the immediate responsibility. We might then think of the obligation as being passed on, although how we should describe the mechanism of inheritance here is not very clear. To take one salient case: Judaism, as we mentioned earlier, is a tradition that sees its identity as inextricably tied to history. Jewish history is not simply the record of what has happened to the Jews; it is seen as an expression of its national essence, of its destiny. Given this fact, the obligation to remember might be tied to the individual's identification with this history. The mechanism of inheritance of the responsibility would then be group-identification. By the same token, though, if it *is* viewed as a promise, it is unlikely that it could be thought universal.

It also gives us some direction about *what* we ought to remember: the victims, their humanity, their suffering. In remembering all of this, we keep our promise. But much of the rest of what has been kept alive about the Holocaust might be outside the scope of this particular imperative, so construed. The rest may be important for other reasons—perhaps preventive—but would not be part of this moral imperative.

Finally, if the source of the obligation is promising, then the considerations of utility and prevention we brought up earlier must be seen in a different light. Generally speaking, we cannot break a promise simply because we determine that breaking it leads to an overall preferable result. Even if it is unrelievedly painful to tell my son about what happened to his grandparents and their parents, I may be under some obligation to do so. And even if I decide that in the long run it will do him more harm than good, that it may shatter his innocent conception of a safe world, I may be obligated nonetheless.

So the notion of remembrance as promising is interesting. Nevertheless, it seems to delay the main question rather than answer it. Let me explain. We are trying to understand the deeply felt "need to tell the story" that we started with. But the analysis in terms of promising amounts to this: we need to tell it because we promised *others* who needed to tell it that we would. The problem should be obvious: What about the need of those who exacted the promise? It is this basic impulse that we are out to understand, and it is this impulse that was felt by survivor and victim alike.

We can see this if we keep in mind two further points. First, not every deathbed request automatically creates an obligation to fulfill it. The request, and the need that prompts it, must be in some way be seen as reasonable or right. The second point is that having such a powerful desire is itself part of what needs to be explained. Every day people die horrible deaths—some of these by disease, but some by criminality and brutality. But neither survivor nor victim typically feels compelled to have the precise details recorded for posterity. Quite the opposite. Often the desire is to be remembered "as we were," to remember the good times. The Holocaust brought out completely different sentiments from those who faced death. In remembering we certainly *are* keeping a promise to the unfortunate victims, but to take this as the basis for the need to testify stops short of the real point.

C. Integration and Redemption

We have already touched on the "liberating joy" that survivors experienced—and continue to experience—in telling their stories. Joy might be unexpected in this context, and much of the telling and remembering is just the opposite of joyous. Nevertheless, the ease of mind that comes with sharing a psychological burden is a real feature of survivors' testimonies. What is more, there is not only pain and horror in these stories, but humor and exhilaration as well. But the power of the need to remember is *not* simply an effect of the exceptional weight of the burden of memory the survivor carries. This view of testimony as "getting it off your chest"—like a child with a secret too big to keep in—fails to comprehend the extremity of the situation that the survivors and victims experienced. The key to understanding the need to remember lies in understanding this extremity, in understanding how one responds and copes at the time, and, finally, in understanding how such a term of existence may be integrated into a life.

I want to focus here on the concentration camp experience, which I take as the ultimate distinctive expression of Nazism, and as the paradigmatic horror of the Holocaust. This experience was designed to throw inmates into shock, and it almost invariably succeeded. This is not the place to recount in detail the humiliation, torture, and degradation the inmates experienced; there are many invaluable accounts of this. Nor will we discuss the important psychological analyses of the sorts of individual responses that were common.[10] For our purposes it will be enough if we keep in mind that the Nazis wanted much more than the simple destruction of the Jews. In the camps, there was a concerted effort to turn those who were not immediately exterminated into the Nazi caricature of the Jew: degraded, filthy, diseased vermin. What is it like to be in such a situation? Two passages from Levi's account of Auschwitz communicate something about this psychological extremis very well:

Nothing belongs to us anymore; they have taken away even our clothes, our shoes, even our hair; if we speak, they will not listen to us, and if they listen they will not understand. They will even take away our name: and if we want to keep it, we will have to find ourselves the strength to do so, to manage somehow so that behind the name something of us, of us as we were, still remains.

Already for many months I had no longer felt any pain, joy, or fear, except in that detached and distant manner characteristic of the Lager [concentration camp], which might be described as a conditional: if I still had my former sensitivities, I thought, this would be an extremely moving moment.

These are reports of attempted and successful dehumanization. Their emotional responsiveness was stripped away, their normal attitude toward life and death was altered, their cognitive responses were radically changed, their moral responsiveness was severely diminished, their bodies' normal needs of food, sleep, privacy, sex, and on and on were all mutilated or obliterated. In short, every attempt was made to get them to stop living as human beings, and to stop thinking of themselves as human beings. They were driven to see themselves only as the Nazis saw them, to confirm the image of them that supposedly motivated their treatment.

But there is more here than dehumanization. There is also depersonalization. The sense of individuality, of one's identity as a person with a past and a future, was also violated. The most salient aspect of this is the tattooed numbers that served as new "names" for the Auschwitz inmates. But shaving heads, refusing to accommodate in any degree to the native language of the inmates, and the often random reassignments to barracks are instances of the same assault on individuality.

How does the human psyche react to such circumstances? Resignation and a quick death were common responses, and so was depersonalization. That is, depersonalization was not only a condition inflicted upon the inmates; it was also a psychological defense—a survival mechanism—against the pain and debasement. It is in this sense that Levi's remark about "detachment" is relevant. When one cannot afford to feel, to reflect, to experience, one somehow closes off the channels and normal triggers for these operations. One looks for advantage without concern for fairness, one sees suffering without an empathetic response, and so on. There is a break between the self as remembered, and the shadowy existence in the Lager. The discontinuity and lack of integration was so great that most survivors report a constantly recurring state of disbelief: Is this really happening to me? Am I dreaming? And it is important to realize that this psychological displacement was felt as much *after* liberation as within the walls of the Lager.

It is in the context of this personal extremis that we should understand the need to remember. An important piece of the puzzle is conveyed in Levi's remark above about the state of numb detachment. Although he doesn't stress this point, it is clear that he is not talking about a state in which the emotional side of the psyche has stopped operating. Without *some* emotional system, it would be impossible to appreciate even the *conditional* nature of the situation. So although Levi speaks as if he had lost all his emotional sensitivities, the fact that he could recognize the situation as moving at all tells us otherwise. The *experiential* appreciation and *emotional* response of a tender moment might have been closed off, but the classification of moments into these categories—tender, sad, important, profound, loving, etc.—must have continued in Levi, and in many other survivors as well. The Nazis robbed them of the capacity to fully experience them.

What happens to these stolen moments? To this world of emotional and cognitive responses postponed and stored? I want to suggest that they are given their due in testimony and memory. Through memory and testimony they are redeemed.

Related to this is the important fact that the need to testify and have the world remember was an impulse making itself felt not only on liberation but throughout their captivity. Levi speaks of the strength of this impulse and compares it to the elementary physical needs, but others have even spoken of it as their main motivation for survival. I want to suggest that this desire served as a lifeline to the humanity and sense of individuality that the Nazis tried to strip away. The desire to remember is a projection of the self into the future, to a time in which the painful present is in the past, and one can look back, repersonalized, and re-experience the suffering from a regained personal perspective—out of shock, no longer numbed, perhaps reunited with family and friends. This is a tremendously courageous vision, in that it typically had to co-exist with the awareness that one's own death was imminent. The desire is a lifeline in that only a person with a sense of his or her own life—with a past, present, and future—can entertain such a hope. The victims knew that the world within which they came into personhood and within which they defined themselves was gone. They saw their families led off to the gas chambers; they lost virtually every link with their past. Those who were able to survive this assault on personhood found a link to the future that would drive them. This is the desire to tell the story.

The desire to remember and to testify is in this sense the moral and emotional counterpart of Descartes' epistemic "cogito ergo sum." Descartes showed convincingly that even if I am in epistemic extremis, where everything I take as true is wrong and I am being fooled at every turn by some supreme force out to deceive me, I still can know that I think and therefore that I exist as a thinking thing. The moral is that one cannot find oneself epistemically "stripped bare." It is always possible to secure at least one truth, and to use that truth as a basis for the reconstruction of a system of true knowledge. The point about remembrance is strikingly similar. Even in the extreme condition in which an attempt is made to deprive one of every human emotional and moral resource, one can still generate a distinctively human emotional response, a straw to grasp—the desire to remember—and in this way retain a lifeline to personhood. And this lifeline serves as the foundation for the reconstruction of the person as a full emotional and cognitive being.

For the survivors, the time in the Lager represented a discontinuity; a gap in their personal lives. In re-experiencing this period with the help of memory, the past is repersonalized; it is experienced from the perspective of the individual, not by the dehumanized, depersonalized, shell of a man or woman. If my view is right, it sheds some new light on various nuances of this need.

First, it helps explain the common experiences of survivors that memory must wait "till one is ready." Readiness, in this sense, requires a reservoir of emotional strength, but what that emotional strength is *for* should now be clearer. Just as the full emotional experience of tender moments was postponed, so too was the full emotional response to the ongoing horror. Even if horror was *identified* as horror, it wasn't always fully experienced as such. One cannot dig up corpses all day in a constant state of horror—one *must* become numbed. In remembering, paradoxically, the survivor must do more than simply go through the whole thing twice; he or she must emotionally go through much for the first time. Many survivors seemed to be intuitively aware of the enormity of this impending task, of the costs of "making themselves whole." But there is still a further dimension of readiness: one must reopen the channels that have been closed off; one must be repersonalized; one must first find oneself to a sufficient degree, so that the personal perspective so critical for memory is present. Levi, who was especially driven by the need to tell his story, would dream of recounting his existence in the Lager *to his family.* Those survivors who had no stable family setting to slip back into had to wait longer to find personal stability. They had to begin "new" lives; one's new life and new identity had to be established to some degree before the needs of memory could be met.

Second, it provides a deeper understanding of why the individual particular stories of the survivors are valued the way they are. These are more than attempts to provide specific evidence and understanding of general patterns. Rather, they are valuable in their particularity and specificity. Each individual's story represents the redemption and reconstitution of the self.

Finally, we need to reconsider our earlier question of memories that might be well-lost. Levi, in discussing the behavior of the inmates on their first night in Auschwitz, tells us: "Many things were then said and done among us; but of these it is better that there remain no memory." It would be utopian to expect that the human psyche could smoothly reintegrate and reanalyze everything. It cannot. The more the survivor re-experiences the camp events—catches up on postponed reactions and responses—the more difficult it may be to come to terms with his or her own actions. One important unresolved question related to this is: To what extent does the depersonalization and dehumanization we have been discussing imply that inmates have only diminished responsibility, or perhaps no responsibility at all, for their actions in those circumstances? To what extent is Primo Levi the same moral agent as Auschwitz prisoner #17451?

The Interpersonal Dimensions of Memory

I want to consider one last set of questions that all center around the interpersonal dimension of remembrance. Our treatment of reintegration as crucial to remembrance has focused on the survivor. It is the survivor who must create continuity in a personal memory that is discontinuous—who must find himself or herself in his or her past—and remembering is a necessary condition for this. But this still leaves us within the confines of the survivor's mind: Why isn't the private remembrance of the survivor and his or her private reintegration adequate? How does the *personal* need to remember become an *interpersonal* need to tell?

Part of the answer, I think, lies in understanding what is required for repersonalization. It is not enough to simply remember, and it is not enough to simply tell. The passive tape recorder which absorbs the memories in Beckett's *Krapp's Last Tape* will not suffice. The survivor requires a special sort of listener. We must keep in mind that the inmate's grasp of reality in the Lager was very tenuous. There was a backdrop of incredulity that I have already spoken of—"Is this really happening?"—and after the liberation, many survivors experienced terrifying recurrent fantasies and dreams of being back in the Lager. It has long been argued that our stable sense of the world around us—both physical and social—depends on the coherence of our experience with our expectations, and on the affirmation we draw from our knowledge that others experience the world as we do. These claims are not without their philosophical problems, but that does not impugn their standing as expressing important psychological truths. In the camps, both of these stabilizing influences were absent. First, the world into which the victims were thrown obviously did *not* cohere with the world they knew. Survivors also learned quickly that there was little internal coherence or stability possible in the camps. The thousands of anticipations of experience that ground the normal mind in a setting were useless there and even dangerous. Part and parcel of the inmate's cognitive shock came from having to give up these patterns of mental functioning. Second, the reactions to the extreme displacement were too widely varied—so there was little security in uniformity. The upshot of all this is that in hearing the testimony of survivors, we perform a vital service: the experiences "bounce off" us, and the survivor's perceptions and classifications can be socially validated and confirmed. Because we hear the voices of many survivors, because we believe what we hear, because we react emotionally as persons, the survivor's individual vision becomes entwined into a conception of a broader social reality. We re-establish that the victim's way of seeing the moral order is in fact the way the moral order is, that the Nazi world was an alien order. In this way, we can provide a kind of moral reality-testing.

The externally-directed need to tell, in its turn, gives rise to a correlative responsibility on us to listen. Remembrance thus becomes a interpersonal public imperative: we remember together. But it is crucial to see that *this* idea of remembrance as a public imperative, though right as far as it goes, does not go far enough. The role and responsibility of those who did not suffer directly involves *more* than simply providing affirmation for those who did. After all, what will happen when the generation of survivors have passed on? Surely this will not make the need to remember obsolete. The imperative to remember, as it addresses itself to us, cannot just be a matter of something we owe to the survivors. It concerns what we owe *ourselves*.

The reason is that the reintegration that the survivor must achieve has its counterpart in a reintegration that the rest of us must accomplish in the wake of the Holocaust. The victims and survivors certainly suffered the greatest devastation, but the Holocaust happened to all of us in the West. There is no neat and pungent encapsulation of Nazism, or of what the Nazis wrought in their brief period of power. But their existence and their actions are more than a dark period in Jewish history. They represent a blot on the history of Europe, on Christianity, and on Western culture and civilization as a whole. They brought our civilization, and the moral order that helped sustain it, to the edge of extinction. To the extent that our self-conception depends on the socio-historical reality within which we identify ourselves—as a Jew, as a Christian, as a participant in our Western culture, as a member of a family, etc.—the Holocaust is relevant to *our* wholeness and sense of individuality as well.

Perhaps a concrete example can convey this thought more easily. I was born in 1950—after the demise of the Nazis. But to the extent that I conceive of myself as the son of my parents, the Holocaust is part of me. To the extent that I consider myself a Jew, the Holocaust is part of me. To the extent that my intellectual life has its roots in European thought, the Holocaust is again inextricably entwined in my broader sense of who I am. One may never be aware of these ties, or may be unable to clearly see how they are knotted together. But without remembrance such awareness is totally impossible. In our culture, we all must situate and define ourselves partly in terms of the socio-historical reality that confronts us. We may see ourselves as sons and daughters, perhaps as Christians, as Jews, some perhaps only as members of our culture and civilization. But the shadow of Nazism has darkened the path of all of these frames of reference, and of virtually every affiliation that could prove significant for us as a basis for self-understanding. For an individual who situates himself or herself socio-historically—and I am suggesting that this includes us all—not to remember the Holocaust is to lack an important kind of self-knowledge.

In this way, our responsibility extends beyond the survivors; memory is something we owe ourselves. But now we can close the circle, and appreciate the reciprocity involved in telling and listening. I have spoken of how we can help the survivors in listening; now we can see that they give us something more important in the telling. The bare facts are easy for them to recall; our unfettered emotional responsiveness can help them recontextualize and re-experience these bare facts. Our approach is just the opposite: our emotions are intact but our cognitive acceptance and credibility is overwhelmed. One can immerse oneself in the Holocaust literature—personal, historical, etc.—and *still,* of a moment, find oneself saying: I can't believe it happened. In some sense it is like an anti-miracle, no more credible than Abraham's report of a divine command to sacrifice his son. But by a collaborative effort of speaker and hearer, the past can become real.

Out of this collaboration we can begin to become alert to the past as it exists in us. We can begin to grasp what it was like *as a Jew* to be singled out as vermin. We can begin to understand what it was like for one living within its relatively secure confines of our moral order to enter an alternative order: where praise and blame have nothing to do with what you do, where biology can reverse the moral polarity of actions and traits, and so on.

VI. CONCLUSION: MORALITY AND MEMORY

The survivors who bear witness do more than simply describe the horror. They have been in a moral place where few of us have traveled. As such they bring us a kind of moral news, not just in terms of what they have to say, but in their overriding desire to speak and to call us to listen. Each one of their stories is different; they have all seen the same horror, but from different angles. The one constant is their consuming desire to bear witness, and to insure that what they saw and experienced is not forgotten. This impulse to remember is a moral impulse. It is one important moral response to extremity. Emil Fackenheim has captured the state of mind of survivors on this question: ". . . not to tell the tale, when it might be told, was unthinkable."[11]

Raul Hilberg, the famous historian of the Holocaust, when asked why the Nazis did what they did, replied: "They did it because they wanted to do it."[12] Their immorality, and their responsibility, is stark and unmediated. Ironically, one is tempted to say the same about memory: we need to remember because we are called upon to. The difference is that while the Nazis wanted to destroy a human community and overturn our moral order, the desire to remember serves to redeem that humanity and extend that order.

We have been trying to understand, to anatomize, to analyze this call. But the call is louder and more important than the analysis. As with all matters moral, the force of the imperative cannot always rest on our fully understanding it. For me, and I hope for others as well, the call to memory is still compelling. This work is in essence a personal response to this call. Whether we understand it fully or not, we must hear it and try to answer.

NOTES

1. I would like to acknowledge Debbie Zaitchik's major contributions to this work, and Roger Gottlieb's valuable editorial advice. This essay is dedicated to my parents and to the memory of their families who perished in the Holocaust, with the hope that in remembrance resides the secret of redemption.

2. My primary focus here is the Jewish victimization and response, but I believe that what I have to say has broader implications.

3. In the traditional Orthodox Jewish liturgy, the incident is commemorated yearly as the "Sabbath of Remembrance," on which day the appropriate sections of the Torah are recited.

4. It is interesting that a reflection of this "imperative to forget" is also present in the parenthetical curse traditional Jews often affix to the names of national enemies: "may his name and the memory of him be obliterated."

5. I have simplified the statement of the alternatives, but philosophers have always grappled with these two ways of understanding the basis for interpersonal responsibilities. Are they based on voluntary *contractual* relationships or on *natural* connections between individuals?

6. We could go further and consider the set of all possible rational beings, but this would be fruitless.

7. Amelie Rorty pointed out some of these distinctions to me and set me thinking about this question.

8. "Perhaps I was helped too by my interest, which has never flagged, in the human spirit and by the will not only to survive (which

was common to many) but to survive with the precise purpose of re-counting the things we had witnessed and endured." (Primo Levi, *Survival in Auschwitz,* p. 397)

9. Eli Hirsch first suggested this possibility to me.

10. Terence Des Pres, *The Survivor* (Oxford University Press, 1976), is one such study; Bruno Bettleheim's *The Informed Heart* (The Free Press, 1960) is among the best-known (and most controversial) psy-choanalytic treatments.

11. Emil Fackenheim, "The Voice of Auschwitz," in Nahum N. Glatzer, ed., *Modern Jewish Thought,* New York, 1977, p. 189.

12. In conversation with Emil Fackenheim; quoted in the latter's "The Holocaust and Philosophy," *The Journal of Philosophy,* volume LXXXII, number 10, October 1985, p. 509.

Roger S. Gottlieb

REMEMBRANCE AND RESISTANCE

Let us begin by considering a photo, taken immediately after the defeat of the Nazis, of a group of Jewish partisans who had fought in the forests of Poland around the city of Vilna. Even if we can recall such events as the Warsaw ghetto uprising, this image of Jewish resistance fighters— men and women, armed and determined—is not a typical image of the Holocaust. The Holocaust is usually remembered as a time when the Nazis killed millions of Jews. Our dominant emotions are fear and grief for the Jews, hatred for the murderers. We do not see Jews with machine guns and army uniforms, but piles of dead bodies, naked victims, crying children, desolate women, defeated men. Our witnessing of these victims leads us to the resolve "Never forgive, never forget."

But what is it that we are supposed to remember? That they murdered us? Or, if you are not Jewish as I am, that they murdered Jews? Do the Jewish partisans have as rightful a place in our memory as the Auschwitz crematoriums? Suppose, in addition to fear and grief, the victims' shame and the survivors' guilt, we could feel, if only for a moment, pride and even joy at Jewish resistance? Suppose one of our dominant responses to the horrors of the Holocaust were to become wonder that the victims could live, love, create and struggle? Suppose delight were to take its place beside sorrow?

Also, what is the point of remembering? That it should never happen again, we insist. But what is the relation between our memories and the present? And how can we so confidently say "never again" when mass murders have happened, again and again, since the time when this photo was taken? And when every day it threatens to happen "again" for the last time, in a nuclear holocaust in which, as Elie Wiesel says, "the whole world will become Jewish."

These are the questions I will consider in the following, and which I invite you to think about along with me.

434

1. RESISTANCE

First, some facts, facts documented beyond the shadow of historical doubt but which are absent from popular consciousness about the Holocaust.[1]

The forced labor and death camps which annihilated nearly four million Jews were not only sites of the destruction of the Jews but sites of Jewish heroism. In almost every forced labor and concentration camp, undergrounds were organized which kept up the inmates' morale, committed acts of sabotage, organized escapes, collected arms, planned and in many cases carried out revolts. For example: a crematorium was destroyed at Auschwitz after tiny pieces of dynamite had been smuggled out of the munitions factory by forced laborers. In Starovitza, an inmate remembers, "we started a revolt against a company of Germans and Ukrainians with machine guns with one pistol." Treblinka, where the last of the Warsaw ghetto fighters were taken, was destroyed by inmates in an uprising.

Besides these acts of violent resistance performed by untrained, starved and tortured people, concentration camps saw everyday acts expressing the persistent choice of life against death. The Jews sang songs, wrote poems, dreamed of revenge and freedom and put forth the energy to share food, trade with one another, give support and love. Charlotte Delbo describes the struggle to simply keep standing at the daily roll call in Auschwitz, knowing that showing physical weakness would probably mean being selected for the gas chambers.

> It is roll call. All the blocks yield up their shadows. With her neck retracted into her shoulders, her chest pulled in, each woman puts her hands under the arms of the woman in front of her. In the first row they cannot do this, and they are rotated. Chest to back, we stand huddled together. And although we thus set up a common circulation for all, . . . we are all frozen. We must stand motionless for hours in the cold and in the wind. We do not speak. We stand motionless and the amazing thing is that we are still standing. Why? No one thinks 'What is the use' or else does not say it. With our last bit of strength we stand.

Jewish resistance in the ghettos is perhaps better known than that which occurred in the camps. But while the image of the ghetto fighters of Warsaw is available, few people realize that these fighters—untrained and armed with pathetically few outdated weapons—resisted the Germans longer than the sovereign nations of Czechoslovakia and Poland. Fewer still realize that there were armed resistance movements in Bialystock, Lackwa, Vilna, Minsk and dozens of other ghettos. Or that Jews fought back despite a lack of arms and training. And this despite the fact that they were largely abandoned and sometimes even murdered by the anti-semitic Polish underground compatriots in a fight against a common enemy. An army of smugglers, facing death if caught, helped the ghetto-dwellers survive the Nazis' attempt to starve them. Schools and publications flourished, poems and songs were written. Jewish identity was maintained, taking institutional and artistic forms which could be punished by imprisonment, deportation or execution.

The following song is called "Unter Deine Veisse Shtern," "Under Your Starry Skies." It was written in the Vilna Ghetto in 1943 and sung in the ghettos and the forests. The lyricist, Avraham Sutzkever, survived to live in Israel after the war. The composer, Abvraham Burdon, perished in a concentration camp. Though it speaks of sadness, the very beauty of the melody bespeaks a hidden joy. Its words:

> Here beneath the starry splendor
> give to me your gentle hand;
> Let me offer words as tender
> as my tears within your hand.
> See the darkness reigns unvanquished
> in the dungeon of my heart—
> and no radiance, only anguish
> in return, can I impart. And dear God, I have been yearning
> To entrust myself to you
> For in me a fire's burning
> And my days are burning too.
> Underground, the sunlight shunning
> Is the horror now laid bare
> Over rooftops I keep running
> And I search: where are you, where?
> Chasing onwards, so I blunder
> Up and down the steps of pain
> As a chord that's torn asunder
> Do I sing to you again.
> Here beneath the starry splendor
> Give to me your gentle hand
> Let me offer words as tender
> As my tears within your hand.

Jews also resisted by performing acts of sabotage in the forced labor camps. Max Bork, a survivor of several concentration camps, remembers how he and a small group of men stopped production of the V2 missile which the Nazis were secretly building in their forced labor camp.

> You can imagine the feelings if you see that missile, so big as the whole house, goes up and all of a sudden turns back around and goes down. Then you know you accomplished something. You know the feeling. You didn't care or you ate or you didn't ate or you . . . thirsty, whatever. You just knew you did something.

The Nazis murdered close to a million Jewish children. But like their parents, Jewish children fought back: as smugglers, couriers, guides, and with weapons. David and Banko, for instance, were inseparable thirteen year old friends. Together they led Jewish groups from the ghetto of Minsk, Russia, to join partisan units. Banko had agreed to this work only on the condition that David go with him. When Banko gathered his people and supplies, he addressed his gathering as a commander speaking to soldiers:

> In two hours we will be leaving . . . from that moment on you are partisans. If we should run into a German patrol there is no way back because it would endanger Jews in the ghetto. If the situation becomes critical we resist. Those who receive grenades will throw them . . . those who have pistols will open fire. . . . Anyone who creates a panic or refuses to obey my command will be shot. . . . I hope that all will go well and that in a few hours from now you will be free people without yellow badges.

In August, 1943, Germans surrounded the forest in which Banko and David fought as partisans. Twenty-two Jews were killed, Banko among them. His body was half burned, his arms pulled back and tied with barbed wire. David stood at Banko's open grave and cried bitterly. The entire detachment cried with him.

The proudest moment of the Jewish resistance was the struggle at the Warsaw ghetto. The Jewish fighters possessed a paltry arsenal of a few machine guns, some homemade or stolen grenades, molotov cocktails, iron bars, axes and clubs. They were outnumbered 10 to 1. It was like, a participant tells us, "a fly against an elephant." But the Nazis could not defeat this fly in combat. On the morning of April 19, 1943, an eyewitness recalls,

> German columns with tanks started marching into the ghetto. The Jewish fighters let the Germans enter deep into the ghetto. Suddenly our people attacked. Bullets, grenades and molotov cocktails were thrown from windows, doorways, from roofs. The Germans retreated, taken by surprise.

It took the Germans forty-four days to defeat Warsaw's Jews—and to do so they had to destroy the ghetto brick by brick.

The spirit of Warsaw inspired the Jews of Vilna to resist, and led to the creation of the most famous resistance song, "Zog Nit Kein Mol." It was written by Hirsch Glick, a Vilna Jew who himself died a hero's death fighting with partisans. His comrade and fellow poet S. Katcherginsky remembers:

> We suddenly saw clearly the flames of the Warsaw ghetto and the Jews fighting with arms for their dignity and self-respect. We armed ourselves. The news of the uprising lifted our spirits and made us proud. One day Hirske came to my room. 'Now listen carefully, I'll sing a new poem for you.' He began to sing it softly, but full of excitement. His eyes glowed with little sparks . . . Kumen vet noch undzer oysgebenkte sho—'the hour for which we yearned will come anew—" Where did he get his faith? His voice became firmer. He tapped out the rhythm with his foot, as if he were marching . . . Dos hot a folk tsevishn falindike vent, dos lid gezungen mit naganes in di hent—'A people midst the crashing fires of hell sang this song with guns in hand until they fell . . .' May, June, July, August . . . we lived with the spirit of April and the Warsaw ghetto uprising. . . .

The song in English:

> Never say that there is only death for you
> tho leaden skies have been concealing days of blue
> The time is coming
> yes, the time is very near
> Beneath our tread
> The earth shall tremble
> 'We are here.'

From land of palm tree to the far off land of snow
We shall be coming with our torment and our woe
And everywhere our blood has sunk into the earth
shall our bravery, our vigor blossom forth.

This song was written with our blood and not with lead
It's not a song that summer birds sing overhead
It was a people among toppling barricades
that sang this song of ours with pistols and grenades.

2. NEVER FORGET

What kind of memory do such heroes and victims of the Holocaust deserve? Let us begin by noting that their own greatness lies partly in the fact that memory could play little part in what they did. They faced a reality for which no training or expectation could prepare them. It took years before Europe's Jews could begin to understand what was happening to them: eyewitness reports of the death camps were dismissed as the ravings of the deranged. The resistors faced choices which would have been literally unthinkable a few years before—to stay in the ghetto or flee to the forest, to escape from camps in small groups or large, to save a sister or a wife, help an aging father and die with him or protect oneself for future revenge, to give one's child away to a Christian family or take the child to the cattle trains.

The Jews faced a reality, that is, which was wholly their own. In a peculiar way they were free, for the extremity of their situations kept them from imitating a life lived by anyone else.

What then is to be our memory of them? Can we bring them to our minds in a way which preserves their freedom while enhancing our own? Can our memory exalt ourselves as well as them?

Some ten years ago I began to immerse myself in the Holocaust. For a time that world of burning bodies and burning souls became— through imagination, empathy, and thought—my own. Seated on a subway car, my mind would superimpose images of boxcars rolling toward crematoriums. A police car's siren in the middle of the night could bring me instantly to the roundups of Jews in Amsterdam or Paris. I was not having a psychotic break—rather, I was obeying the injunction to remember.

Or, at least, so it seemed at the time. In retrospect, I now realize, I was escaping into the Holocaust. Perhaps a necessary stage in coming to terms with it, but in no way a model for memory. For in my absorption, I

was forgetting myself. I could enter that world—could remember 'completely'—only at the cost of avoiding who I was in reality. I was not a
hunted Jew in Warsaw or a ghetto fighter, but an American citizen,
living a comparatively privileged, safe, and easy life. My obsession was
inauthentic because it was an attempt to blot out the self who was the
subject—the agent—of the act of remembering. Any total obsession
with the past dissolves the reality of the present in acts of imagination by
which we seek to become the past. But we can never be our past. We can
only live a present which will be betrayed if it is sacrificed to memory.
The emotional excesses which immersion in the Holocaust may cause—
excesses of grief, despair, rage—exhaust our moral capacity in the present. Our own dangers, responsibilities and destinies pale in comparison
to "What they faced." Our own situations become wraithlike while memories are seen as the only truth. The act of memory becomes the only act,
as our own being is emptied out into the compelling power of the past.
In the end, we may fail ourselves, our families, our duties to the larger
world, because we have exhausted ourselves into a time for which our
actions can have no meaning.

Surely this cannot be an authentic way to remember. We must try to
avoid the mistake of becoming consumed by the hypnotic images of
Jewish triumphs, suffering and death. We cannot authentically honor
the resistors if we do not at the same time distance ourselves from them.
We cannot subjectively appropriate the experience of the Holocaust—
make it essential to our understanding of life, and to our actions in the
world—if we do not at some point break away from those images. Our
memory of them cannot be authentic if it is not at the same time a
forgetting.

Alternatively, we may forget the Holocaust in remembering it. We
may, that is, approach it with a predefined purpose consciously or unconsciously in mind. In such a use, the Holocaust is wrestled into the
present, its configurations altered to fit the contours of our particular
agendas. While it was the Jews who fought and died at the hands of the
Nazis, those past identities are super-imposed on some present conflict
or problem. Celebrating their resistance and death becomes a simple
pretext for a current argument: about whom to hate in the Middle East,
or the virtues of democracies, or the evils of monopoly capitalism. The
mind-numbing capacity of the Holocaust is so great that invoking it
tends to muffle dissent. If the PLO is Nazi-like, surely it must be opposed, no matter what the legitimate grievances of the Palestinian people. If the Soviets are totalitarian like the Nazis, there can be little hope
for arms control. If Hitler's regime served the interests of monopoly
capitalism the left need expend little effort in studying the particularity

of the Jewish experience of anti-semitism. We need only dissolve that particular experience in the generalities of class conflict and economic development.

These uses of the Holocaust are possible because they are partly true: much of Arab nationalism has been anti-semitic; Soviet communism is a brutal totalitarian society; we cannot understand the Nazi rise to power without understanding German capitalism. Yet it is a distortion of both the Holocaust and these contemporary realities to reduce either to the other. The Holocaust is degraded if it becomes a convenient peg for some contemporary purpose, as if the death of the six million took place only so that Israelis could hold onto the West Bank, Reagan utter pious nonsense about reconciliation with ex-Nazis or Soviet bureaucrats congratulate themselves for having been anti-fascist. Just as the present cannot masquerade as the servant of the past, so the past should not be the servant of the present. The men, women and children who destroyed tanks in the Warsaw ghetto or died escaping from Treblinka did so as agents of their own fate, compelled by a cruel fate to freedom from imitations of the past. While our fate may be less cruel, less dramatic and in some ways structured by more confusing moral imperatives, their lesson for us is that we also must have our own fate, our own choices. We may take them as exemplars, as heroes, we may vow never to forget them—and we never should—but their heroism and suffering cannot tell us what to do in the present, nor justify actions and policies. "Because the six million died . . ." is not a phrase that tells us what to do about anything. Nor does it allow us to do what we will to others. While we may derive some general *morals* from this event, it justifies no particular *policies*.

As the Holocaust should not be grist for partisan politics, neither should we expect it to be the source of a simple or uncomplicated spiritual message. The Holocaust does not prove either the essential goodness or badness of human beings. Witnessing Hitler's fall should not comfort us that good eventually triumphs over evil. Nor should we look on the Holocaust with confidence that human beings are learning from evil, and that the suffering of the six million will be redeemed by a future global enlightenment. It is one thing to believe in some spiritual vision of human experience and evolution. It is another to remember the Holocaust to use it as evidence for such a belief. Any attempt to spiritually appropriate the Holocaust is necessarily opportunistic. We look to *their* experience to prove something about *our* lives. The Holocaust becomes a problem to be solved rather than a persistent reality which can be encapsulated by theology only at the cost of denial. This denial supposes that human experience can be redeemed by theory—

that is, by an intellectual representation which anticipates life. But, as Kierkegaard observed: life may be understood backwards, but it is lived forward. We look back at the Holocaust while looking forward to our own choices. When we try to redeem the Holocaust we are really seeking to solve our own dilemma—how to live in a world of unjustified suffering—by focusing on someone else's: that of the six million. But we cannot authentically remember the Holocaust by retrospectively substituting our spiritual visions for their worldly hell. Future bliss does not compensate for their suffering; nor can their heroism be explained simply as some sort of example to others. To remember the Holocaust is not to dissolve its reality but to preserve it. The task, I believe, is to hold in our present imaginations what was *their* present—a present that did not include Hitler's fall, the creation of Israel, or the miraculous transformation of so many of the survivors into "normal" people with families, jobs, and daily lives. Their present did not know our future. If, then, we are to remember them, we must think ourselves into a time of terror and pain, of immense bravery and crushing fear—keeping always in mind that this time was an all-encompassing present which for them could not be redeemed by retrospection, could not be a painful moment in a benign eternity. Even if some of them viewed it as such, their spirituality was nevertheless accompanied by fear and trembling for the actions they had to take—how to get weapons, support friends, care for parents and children, face pain, starvation and torture.

3. THE FREEDOM TO BE

If there is a dominant theme in these reflections it is that we only authentically remember the Holocaust by simultaneously embracing and escaping it. To embrace that reality is to face the actual terrors of their situation: to teach ourselves the details of their daily existence, the crushing obstacles they faced, the choices over which they agonized, their immense defeats and short-lived victories. Yet as we immerse ourselves, we must not forget the differences between us and them. We who remember them must not forget that they could not live in memory, could not appropriate their own experience as an example of some political theory or spiritual vision. Their reality was not only terrible, it was unfinished.

It is precisely that unfinished quality which is often so difficult to preserve when we seek to remember them. Yet if our memory is to be authentic, if their lives are to be in some way an example for our own, our consciousness of their terrible freedom must be maintained at all costs. If we will imitate them, we can only do so by turning away, after a time, from their lives to our own. If we will do them honor, we must be honorable ourselves. And as they faced a life for which memory could not fully prepare them, so do we. Just because we honor them, we must turn from their present to ours. Unless we will do violence to the truth of their lives by encapsulating them in our concerns or forgetting our own lives to gape at theirs, we must keep our distance from their spell-binding fate.

4. AND YET

And yet . . . we are instructed during the observance of the holiday of Passover to recreate the Exodus from Egypt "as if it has happened to us personally." And yet . . . as Miriam Greenspan observes, what happened directly to every Holocaust survivor happens indirectly—in fantasy, imagination and dream—to their children. And yet, there is a sense in which every living Jew—no matter where she or he was born and has lived—is a survivor and a child of survivors.

If this is true, what then do we take from the Holocaust? We may indeed preserve our distance, refuse to bury ourselves in it, not turn a living experience into a confirmation of some dead theory. But these are all negativities. Is there no way to talk about what we *do* remember? to find some common idea or meaning from the event whose reality is perhaps the most potent and accurate symbol of the twentieth century? As Jews or gentiles, radicals or democrats, as human beings, are we to make nothing of their experience?

At the risk of committing the very errors which I have cautioned against, I will suggest some meanings of our memory of the Holocaust, especially that of Jewish resistance.

It is difficult for me to look at Jewish resistors to the Holocaust and not be overwhelmingly struck by the difference between their lives and mine, to compare their greatness to the basic ordinariness of my life, their enemies to my petty frustrations. Such comparison is an inevitable temptation, but one which should be avoided. For the most part, as far as we can tell, the heroes of the Holocaust were ordinary people—like me, like you—thrust into terrible situations. Had the Holocaust not occurred, the Davids and Bankos, the underground at Treblinka, would have gone through life as the rest of us do. In remembering them, therefore, we do not witness the acts of *special people,* but see people *made special* by their acts.[2]

Moreover, we must remember that these special acts were often undramatic: as we saw in Charlotte Delbo's memoirs of Auschwitz, resistance might simply mean staying on one's feet in the face of unspeakable exhaustion. Or it might mean sharing a piece of bread, facing death with dignity rather than fear, or quietly collecting documents to provide the outside world with a history of Jewish life and death under Hitler. Our first lesson from resistance, then, is that people who seem ordinary may become extraordinary, that hidden within many of us lies greatness.

Second, notice that this greatness is not defined by what the world typically thinks of as important. Those Jews who resisted the Nazis did not pursue institutional power or wealth. Their fame, such as it is, comes only after years of silence, and surely many of the bravest remain anonymous. Yet as their acts, writings, and artistic creations show, these people were not only great in our eyes, *they themselves* often achieved great happiness. They wept at death and rejoiced at victory, but above all they were conscious of the power of their acts to define their own reality. As Mordechai Aniliewicz, socialist-Zionist commander of the Warsaw Ghetto uprising, wrote shortly before he was killed:

> The last wish of my life has been fulfilled. Jewish self-defense has become a fact. I am happy to have been one of the first Jewish fighters in the ghetto.

Or listen to Samual Pecharsky, a Russian Jewish soldier who helped lead a mass escape from the death camp Sorbibor.

> 'Comrades, forward' I called out. Someone on my right picked up the words. The slogans reverberated like thunder in the death camp, and united Jews from Russia, Poland, Holland, France, Czechoslovakia, and Germany. Six hundred pain-racked, tormented people, surged forward with a wild hurrah to life and freedom.

The greatness of Jewish resistors, we see, lies not only in their courage, but in their capacity to call forth out of themselves that which is most holy: a love of life, and of other people, and the capacity to manifest that love in a way which is both gloriously selfish and selfless at the same time. In fighting for themselves, each other, and the future of the Jewish people, the resistors served others as they served themselves. Happiness, in the deepest sense of the word, and doing the right thing, went hand in hand. To resist was to recover one's humanity in the face of a Nazi machine bent on destroying it. No wonder that the memoirs of resistors, though laced with pain at Jewish death, and without any certainty of ultimate victory, shine with joy at being alive, being strong, and fighting back.

Our second lesson from these ordinary people turned extraordinary resistors is thus that personal fulfillment, joy in life and service to all that is best for humanity may coincide.

I personally began to learn this lesson during the birth, two month hospitalization and subsequent death of my first child—my son, Aaron, who was born with severe brain damage. During Aaron's life I faced physical, emotional and moral dilemmas which would have been unthinkable before. I had to function without sleep, had to face this everyday tragedy as it made a shambles of the hopes and dreams my wife and I had had. Together we made decisions about Aaron's care—to extend or limit it, to accept or reject the specialists' endless tests. We had to find some way to allow this baby, this mystery, to develop without interference . . . if he ever would. We had to think about what kind of life for him was worth living—and what was not.

I would not bring this matter up if—as Thoreau said—there was anyone else's life I knew so well. But the point of my "mini-holocaust" as I jokingly call it, is that I learned—or, better, got some inkling that I might someday fully learn—what I think the Jewish resistors of the Holocaust had always been trying to teach me. It is this: In our moments of extreme pain, anguish, fear, and hopelessness—if we can rise above, rise *through* these feelings to meet, to embrace, the realities which give rise to them, we can know the greatest happiness any human being can know. I did not have to face German tanks, but my son's seizures and choking; not the hatred of the Nazis but my own difficulties in loving Aaron. I did not confront my own death or the destruction of the Jewish community, but the death of hopes and dreams, and finally of Aaron, who breathed his last in my arms. And I learned that through all my pain—dim though that pain was compared to that suffered in the Holocaust, it was the greatest I had ever felt—that the only thing which could keep me going was love: for Aaron, for my wife, for parents of other kids on the ward, for life itself. And that love meant not just some feeling in my heart, but small acts of bravery and kindness to others— and to myself. It was through these acts—to whatever extent I managed to perform them—that the alchemy of love transformed tragedy and pain into joy, terrible loss into the greatest of treasures: the realization that active, transforming human love is the only sure source of happiness and goodness. It was this same alchemy—on an infinitely greater scale—that the resistors performed when they embraced their fate by struggling against it and helping each other.

We have returned to the question I raised at the beginning. What if, in looking back on Jewish resistance to the Holocaust, we think of the six million with joy as well as sadness? We may well do so, if the message of their lives reaches our own: to transform the sorrows we experience and the oppression we witness through acts of loving kindness and struggle. But this transformation requires first that we find our sorrow and confront oppression: of ourselves, of others near and far, of the earth. During a Holocaust or with a gravely ill child in a hospital, of course, we need not search. But most of our lives—including mine at the moment —are less dramatic. If we would remember the Holocaust, remember those who resisted, we must begin by searching our hearts and our world for the Holocausts and illnesses in our own lives. If the heroes of the Holocaust can help inspire us to this task, they will have won yet another victory over the forces of darkness as some of their bravery and joy illuminate our lives.[3]

NOTES

1. The historical material in the following pages originates in a large number of personal testimonies and historical works. These resources formed part of the basis of the multimedia presentation *They Fought Back: Jewish Resistance to the Nazis 1939–45* (performed in Boston 1981 and 1984, script available from the author) from which much of Part 1 is taken.

2. Of course not all people engaged in resistance will be examples of the virtues I am describing here. My picture here is of the "truth" of resistance, not necessarily of its "actuality" in every instance. For a more detailed account of what makes behavior an example of resistance, see my "The Concept of Resistance: Jewish Resistance During the Holocaust," *Social Theory and Practice* 9 (1983): 31–49.

3. This paper was read in April, 1987 as part of "Ethical Issues and the Holocaust," a lecture series given at Keene State College, Keene, NH, with funding from the New Hampshire Council for the Humanities. *Social Theory and Practice* would like to thank Professor Sander Lee of the Department of Philosophy at Keene State College for arranging for this paper to be submitted to us.